IN SEARCH OF COLUMBUS

IN SEARCH OF

COLUMBUS

THE SOURCES FOR THE FIRST VOYAGE

David Henige

THE UNIVERSITY OF ARIZONA PRESS

TUCSON

The University of Arizona Press
Copyright © 1991
The Arizona Board of Regents
All rights reserved

⊗ This book is printed on acid-free, archival-quality paper.
Manufactured in the United States of America
96 95 94 93 92 91   6 5 4 3 2 1

LIBRARY OF CONGRESS CATALOGING-IN-PUBLICATION DATA
Henige, David P.
 In search of Columbus : the sources for the first voyage / David Henige.
  p.   cm.
 Includes bibliographical references and index.
 ISBN 0-8165-1090-3 (acid free paper)
  1. Columbus, Christopher—Landfall.   2. Columbus, Christopher. Diario.
3. America—Discovery and exploration—Spanish—Historiography.   4. America—
Discovery and exploration—Spanish—Sources.   I. Title.
E112.H46   1991   90-20201
970.01'5—dc20   CIP
British Library Cataloguing in Publication data are available.

Publication of this book is made possible in part by a grant from
The Program for Cultural Cooperation Between Spain's Ministry of Culture
and United States Universities.

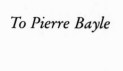

To Pierre Bayle

CONTENTS

PREFACE

My interest in the history and historiography of Columbus's first voyage was initially excited by the anthology *In the Wake of Columbus*, which detailed several past and present attempts to localize Guanahaní, the island where Columbus and America first met. In one essay John Parker, with what I was to discover was exceedingly rare objectivity, chronicled the progress of this study, which currently encompasses no fewer than eleven hypothesized landfalls and an even greater variety of overall itineraries through the Bahamas from Guanahaní to Cuba.

In another essay, a minor masterpiece of its type, Robert Fuson confronted the inevitable and intriguing question of how one text—the so-called diario of the voyage—could yield so much disagreement. Fuson addressed the unedifying pattern of carefully careless translation, transcription, and interpretation that has marked the modern study of the diario, as well as a relentless special pleading that seems almost unrivaled in its intensity and futility. To a historian especially interested in the use and abuse of sources, the temptation to explore the matter proved irresistible. The present study is the measure of just how irresistible it was.

In his superb distillation of the issues, Fuson has made my work, and I hope the work of others, much easier. Even so, it is hard to imagine that any truly critical student of the diario and its historiography would not be struck by the cavalier treatment accorded this text almost from the very beginning. It took more than a century and a half, for instance, to provide students with an edition that actually had as its goal the presentation of the diario as it is rather than as modern editors would have preferred it to be. Beyond the matter of presenting the text itself is that of interpreting its message, and here the record is extraordinarily provocative, even disquieting. Clearly, it became the habit of students of the voyage to accept or reject the evidence of the diario solely to satisfy their own predilections as to Columbus's activities and their loci. As a result, arguments on the matter have frequently been wrenched from the context of the diario and projected onto a new and unjustified habitat of modern predispositions.

At the same time, and rather paradoxically, it became routine to treat the diario as if it were almost entirely an undefiled version of the shipboard log that Columbus presumably kept. It is true that one-fifth of the diario's text purports to be in Columbus's own words. It is also true that by the time Las Casas, in whose hand the diario is written, came into possession of whatever text he copied and paraphrased, it had undergone an unknown number of transmissions, with all the corruption this necessarily entails. To treat the diario as the product of Columbus is simply to banish caution and substitute for it a species of credulity that can have little hope of withstanding serious scrutiny. Little enough seems certain about the diario, but one thing that should be beyond cavil is that its principal author is not Christopher Columbus but Bartolomé de las Casas, aided and abetted by Columbus and any number of intermediate scribes. It is this point of view and its consequences that underlie and sustain, indeed require, many of the subversive arguments that follow.

ACKNOWLEDGMENTS

When one approaches a new field of study for the first time, one must incur debts quickly if progress is to be made. As I have noted elsewhere, my first obligation was to Robert Fuson, whose discussion of the diario text and its interpretation irresistibly whetted my interest. Fuson is one of a fairly large group of students of the landfall, all of whom approach the question with unbridled earnestness and zeal and engage the text with unaccustomed but exemplary attention to detail. Their guiding principle is that no aspect of the diario's evidence is too negligible to bring into play.

I have benefited from this modus operandi and from the views of each of them, although particularly from those of James E. Kelley, Jr., and Oliver Dunn, who have taken particular trouble to disagree with me often enough to force me to attempt to sharpen my arguments more than I might otherwise have done. Under the circumstances, I regret that they and their colleagues are likely to regard the conclusions I reach as poor recompense, but I am no less certain that they will extend the colloquy profitably by responding to many of the points I raise.

Margarita Zamora took the trouble to read an earlier draft in its entirety. In doing so, she both provided advice on my understanding of certain passages and offered insights based on her own continuing study of the Columbian texts, which is derived from the academically distinct but closely kindred perspective of literary criticism.

Demetrio Ramos Pérez of the Academia Real de la Historia in Madrid, whose own work on the early historiography of the Discovery is so thought-provoking and exacting, kindly provided me with both information on the manuscript of Las Casas's *Historia de las Indias* owned by the Academia and encouragement in my encounter with these materials.

Once again, as so often over the past twenty years, I find myself in debt to the interlibrary loan department of Memorial Library at the University of Wisconsin—Madison. My desire to approach the study of the diario comparatively and historiographically inevitably led me to consult an unusually wide range of materials, a task I could not have completed without the services of Judy Tuohy and her staff. So again (and probably not for the last time), my thanks.

Along the way, others with an interest in the field that preceded my own have encouraged my work. I am thinking particularly of Helen Nader of Indiana University and Fredi Chiappelli of the Repertorium Columbianum at UCLA. I can only say that this encouragement was immensely welcome because it was immensely reassuring.

The maps included here were prepared by Barbara Whitehead. They are based on a map of the Bahamas by William N. Dunwoody and a map of Watlings Island by Claudine Vansina.

Two editors at the University of Arizona Press contributed mightily to the present work. In suggesting that I might have a book-length study in me (even though on a different subject), Gregory McNamee forced me to agree that he might be right. When the manuscript of the present book was completed, Alan Schroder subjected it to a searching scrutiny, and in a myriad of large and small ways made it much better than it had been. His craftsmanlike effort shows that those who think that serious copyediting has been sacrificed on the altar of camera-ready copy are wrong.

Although I resolutely sought not to let Columbus, Las Casas, and the others penetrate every aspect of my life, I am sure that they proved more than a little distracting and at times proved quite noisome. For her forbearance in this, I thank my wife, Jan Behn.

A few words need to be said about the dedication to Pierre Bayle that I have included with this book, as it may seem obscure. Pierre Bayle's time has either come and gone or never came at all. I can do no better in explanation than to quote the opinion of Voltaire, who was much influenced by Bayle's thought and who felt obliged on one occasion to resort to characteristic irony to express his admiration for him. In his *Entretien d'Ariste et d'Acrotal,* Voltaire used one of the interlocutors to indicate, while masking, Voltaire's own feelings. He wrote, "Has anyone ever seen a more abominable man? He strips things bare with such disgusting fidelity; he lays before one's eyes the pros and cons with such craven impartiality; he does this with a clarity so intolerable that he puts men blessed only with common sense into a state of weighing and even of doubting. It is more than one can stand and, as for me, I admit that I go into a state of holy anger whenever this man or those like him are mentioned."

IN SEARCH OF COLUMBUS

1. Apotheosis and the Historian

Columbus scholarship is a fertile ground for that peculiar academic blindness whereby an interesting but indefensible hypothesis is followed to its logically necessary but increasingly lunatic conclusions.   PETER HULME

In 1866 Karl Theodor von Piloty exhibited a painting in which he attempted to convey his view of Columbus.[1] The result was a portrait little resembling those renditions that historians believe represent Columbus most closely.[2] The earliest depictions showed Columbus as an average-looking beardless fellow. The demeanor and aspect of von Piloty's Columbus, on the other hand, suggests that he was raised in Nazareth rather than Genoa, that the deck beneath his feet might as well have been the waters of the Atlantic, if not the Sea of Galilee, and that the charts at hand were really baskets of loaves and fishes in disguise.[3]

While von Piloty's interpretation of Columbus may appear extreme, it was very much in tune with its time. At that very moment Columbus was being touted for sainthood—a process that no less a personage than Pius IX encouraged and that produced works hardly less hagiographic than their counterparts of a millennium earlier.[4] At the same time poets and biographers were writing of Columbus in equally perfervid terms.[5]

1. For von Piloty, see Benjamin 1877:4–7; Ludwig 1980:1394–97.
2. A copy of the portrait is in Martini 1986:opp. 360.
3. For a listing of 130 mostly nineteenth-century portraits of Columbus, see Real Academia de la Historia 1892:565–75.
4. For histories of the canonization campaign, see Roselly de Lorgues 1880; Barros Araña 1892; Vignaud 1909. For a modern fictional treatment, see Carpentier 1980.
5. Whitman 1874; Regazzoni 1987. For earlier views see Gárate Córdoba 1977; Salone Cartei 1979; Nagy 1988.

In fact, although the push toward the liturgical calendar has yet to suc-
ceed, Columbus became more or less another St. Christopher in the eyes
of many. Imperialism in its several guises was in full swing, and it owed a
lot to Christopher Columbus.

The twentieth century has taken a slightly less devotional approach to
Columbus's character and achievements, but not necessarily a more measured one. Some have merely transformed him from a saint into a paragon
whose indomitable spirit and unparalleled navigational instincts permitted him—and only him—to effect "the most important and epoch-
making voyage . . . in human history."[6] Others have professed to see in
his accomplishments the dim but perceptible beginnings of the modes of
thought that propelled the Renaissance into the scientific revolution and
ultimately the Enlightenment.[7] Others still limn a tincture of sanctity in
the man.[8]

In the process—which, if anything, is certain to be invigorated in the
next few years—attitudes toward the sources for Columbus have mirrored those toward the person himself. The greatest adventure of all time
must have sources worthy of it. Serrano y Sanz thought that despite their
"humble language" Columbus's writings constituted no less than an epic
poem of colossal grandeur.[9] In the same spirit, Wagner and Parish, so-
ber bibliographers of the writings of Columbus and his successors, pro-
claimed the journal of Columbus's first voyage to be "the most fabulous
document in the history of America," and they have been far from alone
in their enthusiasm.[10] These views have been reinforced by the natural
tendency to grant critical immunity to sources that provide unique access
to major historical occasions, and no source fills this bill better than the
journal of Columbus's maiden voyage to America. As a result, the mythi-
fication of the sources for Columbus's activities has been manifest from
the very beginning of the study of his journal nearly two centuries ago.

The purpose of the present study is to test the merit of these views. In
this sense it is above all a sustained exercise in devil's advocacy, premised

6. Morison 1939b:261; cf. Jos 1952:77–79.
7. Recently Taviani 1987a.
8. E.g., Taviani 1985. For similar cases see Weber 1988:31–32 and esp. Connelly
1977.
9. Serrano y Sanz 1905:xxvii.
10. Wagner and Parish 1967:198.

on a conviction that the more attractive and congenial a set of beliefs proves to be, the more necessary it is to question their bases.

I

If the journal (hereafter called the diario) is exceptionally important as a historical document, it is no less peculiar in provenance, content, and form. As we have it, the diario is a document of sixty-seven double-sided folios in the hand of Bartolomé de las Casas, noted historian and advocate of the Indians.[11] Beyond that we know virtually nothing, since the diario is bereft of all context. In form as well as in content the diario is a markedly hybrid text. About one-fifth of it is expressed as the *ipsissima verba* of Columbus, and Las Casas lent verisimilitude to this claim by using first-person, present tense verb forms, and direct speech. The remaining four-fifths of the diario seems to be a paraphrase to some degree, the precise degree being a matter of opinion. Many believe that Las Casas, particularly in the long descriptive passages, probably found it easiest to transcribe verbatim but did not bother to say so.[12] If true, then modern students of the text could comfortably rely on these passages to represent just what Columbus saw or said he saw. While not necessarily unreasonable, such a notion suffers from our inability to test it either in aggregate or in particular instances.

In both absolute and relative terms, the diario may be considered a primary source. Certainly in its verbatim passages it claims to represent the classic definition of the genre, while the remainder still constitutes the source nearest to any lost Ur-text, whatever it might have been. Even so, the fact that the diario is clearly not the same text that a shipboard log would have been has inevitably led to a host of hypotheses about its historical value. The best-case scenario—and the opinion most widely held—is that Columbus was an exceptionally astute observer, that the inconsistencies in the diario reflect his unwillingness to tamper with his

11. For a description of the physical characteristics of the diario manuscript (some of them unique among Las Casas's surviving writings), see Varela/Columbus 1989: 11–14.

12. This view was strongly expressed by Gould (1984:205), who, in commenting on the incident of the light discussed in chapter 10, thought it "probable that if we changed the third person to the first, we would have the manuscript by Columbus."

log by retouching entries even when he came to realize they were wrong or confusing, that he did not refurbish the log on the return trip or during his time in Spain before he surrendered it to the authorities, that the royal scribes and other transcribers worked unhampered by outside considerations and contrived to be models of punctiliousness in every instance, and finally that Las Casas, the last link in this long chain, was himself a slave to accuracy, whether in quoting or in paraphrasing.[13]

Here I will argue that, like most best-case scenarios, this version of matters impetuously sacrifices experience to hope, in this case by turning a blind eye to real-life situations that impinged on the odyssey of this text from shipboard to Las Casas's scriptorium. Moreover, it ignores telltale signs in the text of the diario itself that betoken its limitations. While it is certainly tempting to treat the diario and the log as virtually identical texts, doing so flies in the face of common sense and a rapidly growing body of text-critical studies.

II

The present study is divided into two slightly unequal parts. Part I deals with the effects of textual criticism both generally and on the diario itself. After briefly discussing the role of textual criticism and documentary editing in historical inquiry during recent years, I turn to the interrelationships among the major early sources for Columbus's first voyage—the diario, the *Historia de las Indias* of Las Casas, and the *Historie* attributed to Columbus's son Ferdinand. The focus here is on the differences in emphasis and expression among these sources and the likely reasons for them. One effect of studying such differences (perhaps they are discrepancies as well) is that it underscores the corrosive effects of transmitting written texts.

These effects continue to reveal themselves in modern editions of the diario. Despite their frequent claims to the contrary, only a few of its modern editors have come close to attaining the standards that documentary and textual editors have come to take for granted. It is extraordinary that nearly two centuries elapsed between the discovery of the diario and the first modern edition that attempted to present the diario's text as it is.

13. Or as one recent editor of the diario put it, it is possible to "recover even the very words of the archetype [the log]" (Varela/Columbus 1982:xix).

In this discussion I pay special attention to various physical aspects of the text and their interpretive significance, since modern students have all but ignored the matter.

The first section continues with chapters on the distances recorded in the diario and on some signs that the text evolved over a period that may have been as long as sixty years. A final chapter illustrates the wide scattering of "expert" opinion on both the text and the meaning of various passages in the diario, a scattering so wide that it seems to invite caricature.

In Part II, I turn to the matter of the landfall. In October 1988, amid much fanfare, "an urn of sand from the Columbus landfall" was presented to the Spanish ambassador to the Bahamas to be returned to Spain and deposited at the monastery of La Rábida, so intimately associated with Columbus.[14] This occasion, no doubt the precursor of more to follow, encapsulated the sustained interest and rhetorical certainty that characterizes one particular aspect of Columbus's voyage, the identity of Guanahaní, the island where he first set foot in the New World. The study of the evidence in the diario is crystallized with stunning effect by what might be called the Scramble for Guanahaní. Pinpointing Columbus's landing place has been big business for more than a century and a half, and while the matter may seem incredibly trivial to some, this work does have historiographical and methodological value. It serves as an unsurpassed example of the myriad ways in which a single text can be excavated time and again until such treatment can only be regarded as abuse.

During the two weeks that Columbus wandered around the Bahamas, he fell prey to his hopes, fears, and expectations, and perhaps most of all, to a belief that he had reached the Far East. Whether because of this or for other reasons, the testimony of the diario for this period is remarkably exiguous, marked by contradictions, lacunae, and insistently vague descriptions. The result has been predictable. Modern proponents of one island after another have seized upon this word or that passage in hopes of demonstrating beyond cavil their choice for Guanahaní. The result is that no fewer than eleven Bahamian islands currently vie for the honor, though hardly with equal force. By looking at the text of the diario for

14. Smith 1988.

five days, 11 to 15 October, I try to demonstrate that none of these contenders can claim anything like an airtight case.

III

Fredson Bowers, one of the most prominent modern textual critics, observed with some trace of optimism that "[s]ometime in the future . . . recognition will come that the study of texts is the most intimate and exact study of an author [and] that no other study has any demonstrable validity until study of the text is completed."[15] Overwrought? Perhaps, but throughout the present study I argue that it is not incorrect. My position concerning the centrality of the text qua text has been inspired by the work of literary critics, who have found time and time again that to write is to miswrite, to read is to misread, and to copy is to miscopy. Of course, in literary criticism the search for the "authoritative" text is usually seen as an end in itself, whereas in historical inquiry this activity is merely a prelude to other acts of interpretation. Perhaps this explains, if perversely, the indifference toward textual matters that characterizes so much historiography.

Recently there has arisen the so-called reader-centered criticism, which places the reader, rather than the text, at center stage. At its most extreme, this argument asserts that texts are so unstable that they mean what each reader cares to make of them. Consequently all texts are individuated and are characterized, as they must be, by indeterminacy. This point of view allows for a great deal of argument but no conclusions. The notion of a dissolution of the text by each reader might seem to be of little value to historians, but they would be remiss if they sought to exclude the reader entirely from their examination of texts. To carry this a step further, historians must give thought to the intended readership of the texts they study. In the case of the diario, the approach must be twofold. First, we must imagine the readers for whom Columbus wrote his log and the extent to which he shaped that document to suit them. Second, we must ask ourselves whether Las Casas had any readers in mind—other than himself—as he transcribed and paraphrased his source and created the diario. If he did this late in life, for instance, he may have doubted that he would have the opportunity to refashion it as part of the *Historia de las Indias*. In the event, he did live to incorporate it into the

15. Bowers 1967:36.

larger work—and to reconfigure it as he did so.[16] In imposing a moratorium of forty years on the publication of the *Historia*, Las Casas intimated his desire to present his work to a larger audience. Given his passionate avowal of the Indians' cause, he could hardly have done otherwise.[17]

Certainly the diario mirrors well Las Casas's expectations in this regard, for hardly anyone doubts that in it the Indians became far more central than they had been in previous recensions of the log.[18] The Indians and the first person march in lockstep through the diario, and there is scarcely an extended mention of the Indians in which Las Casas does not claim to be quoting. Clearly one of the principal reasons he both transcribed and paraphrased the text before him was to recruit the absent Columbus to the cause of restoring the Indians to center stage.

IV

To my knowledge, this is the first extended study devoted to Las Casas's transcription of the record of Columbus's first voyage that is concerned with the text itself without being an edition of the diario. It may seem odd, then, that I deal with so little of the text directly, but the analysis I offer in the second part of this study is intended simply as a case study of the arguments that precede it. Moreover, at a practical level the complete exegesis of the diario along the lines suggested here would require a volume of quite impractical size. As is often the case, a relatively short text can generate an immense amount of commentary.

In the first sentence above I was about to write "Columbus's diario"; after all, this has been the common parlance in the matter. The phrasing I adopted in its place has the advantage of begging no question. It emphasizes that the text we have is, by the transcriber's own admission, largely a paraphrase of another secondary text. By the same token, it does not presume that what Las Casas had before him was wholly—or even largely—written by Columbus.

A defect of such phrasing is the use of the term *diario*, which implies a

16. For some of Las Casas's lapses in this regard, see Henige n.d. and below, chapter 4.

17. For various views on the reasons for Las Casas's embargo, see Hanke 1952: 42–44; Martínez 1959:80–82; Cioranescu 1966.

18. E.g., Saint-Lu 1981:129–30; Zamora 1989.

text comprising a series of spontaneous observations made regularly and with no knowledge of the future. The complete text in these cases would be a composite of discrete parts, each characterized by immediacy—a rare commodity much in demand among historians. For better or worse, however, the term "diario" has become the routine designation of the text in Las Casas's hand that has come down to us, and I use it here to describe and define that particular text and nothing else. Conversely, I employ the term *log* to refer to whatever record Columbus kept during the voyage, as well as, with rather less justification, whatever document he turned over to the royal authorities about a month after his return to Spain. Of course, the contents of the log and the diario overlap, and part of the discussion that follows addresses the nature and degree of that overlap.

Since the author of the diario is Bartolomé de las Casas, it is necessary in many instances to distinguish between Columbus and Las Casas. For the sake of argument, I presume Columbus to have been the author of the quoted passages in the diario and hold Las Casas responsible for the balance, but to make this distinction constantly would be cumbersome. Just the same, readers should bear in mind that when I write "Columbus wrote," or words to that effect, I am taking much for granted.

A final point on usage must be made about the site where Columbus encountered the New World. He presumed to call it San Salvador but vouchsafed that the Indians called it Guanahaní. In deference to modern wisdom, Watlings Island in the Bahamas was formally rechristened San Salvador in 1926, which is as confusing as it is presumptuous.[19] Because of this, when referring to events of 1492, I avoid the name San Salvador entirely (except in quotations) in favor of Guanahaní.

In short, the point of the present series of essays is to proceed with but one methodological principle in mind: to take nothing for granted. In this I will not proceed from a belief that the diario is a hoax or a fraud; nor will I argue that it is inconceivable that it is one or the other. This posture seems to me indispensable in the analysis and interpretation of problematic texts, and the more valuable the text might be as a historical source, the more compelling is the need for this demeanor.

19. This island is variously spelled Watling, Watling's, and Watlings in both official and unofficial sources. It was denominated Watlings in the 1926 Act (Landfall 1926), and on these grounds this spelling is used here.

PART I

The Documents

2. Transmission, Transcription, and Translation

One man copies not what he reads but what he thinks he understands; another supposes that everything he does not understand to be corrupt, and changes the text as he thinks best following no guide but his own imagination; a third detects perhaps that the text is corrupt, but while trying to emend it with an unambitious conjecture he introduces two mistakes in place of one, and while trying to cure a slight wound inflicts one that is incurable.   ERASMUS

Las Casas's transcription of the diario stands outside any manuscript tradition, having no known predecessors and no other contemporaneous versions. Even so, we know from its own testimony that it had more than one textual ancestor and has had descendants in the form of various modern editions. Thus, although we cannot make direct comparisons, it is important to place the study of the diario as firmly as we can into a more general framework of textual transmission theory.[1]

A large body of evidence developed in the course of thousands of textual studies suggests that no author has been fully successful in conveying precisely what he meant to say. The failure results from authors' changing their minds from manuscript to first printed edition or from one edition to the next, or from lapses in the posthumous transmission of his or her work. Realizing this, textual editors strive first of all to recover and then to preserve "final authorial intent," thereby establishing a (or better yet, the) text. Authorial intent is a protean and controversial concept, and it is not unusual for there to be many variants of a given text, from which editors must choose and then defend their choice.[2]

In seeking to establish any text, editors are faced not only with deci-

---

1. A few such case studies are Hall 1913; Vinaver 1939; Andrieu 1950; Center for Editions of American Authors 1972; Zetzel 1981; McGann 1983; Henige 1987a; Kline 1987.

2. The tangled question of authorial intent is currently the center of a rancorous debate over the eclectic edition of the works of James Joyce (Joyce 1984); see Wilson 1985; Hammond 1986; Kidd 1988a, 1988b; O'Hanlon et al. 1988.

sions regarding words but also with what are known as the "accidentals"—punctuation, spelling, abbreviations, capitalization, word order and placement, and even ellipses. In short, no part of a written text is regarded as immune from an editor's scrutiny, and no text survives that scrutiny unscathed, so that the public face of an edited text is invariably different from any single version of the "same" text and from all other edited versions. The impulse to introduce changes is often justified by arguing that editors are the agents most familiar with the author's writing style. Moreover, according to this argument, presenting readers with an unaltered text would burden them with every interpretive responsibility.

In short, editors can transform texts in the very process of seeking to restore them to their authors, however perverse this may seem. In so modifying the texts—at least consciously—editors may follow three procedures. They may indicate in a preface that they will be making certain kinds of changes—for example, by modernizing spelling or punctuation or normalizing inconsistencies—and then proceed to make them without further comment. Or they may simply introduce such changes without troubling even to indicate that this is part of their modus operandi. Finally, they may introduce changes explicitly, visibly, and with justification in each instance, retaining the original version in the text and signaling the change in the annotation, or vice versa.

Most textual critics have come to recognize only the last of these practices as appropriate scholarly behavior, because it alone preserves the author's original text or texts for inspection. G. Thomas Tanselle puts this position most unequivocally in his assertion that "a scholarly edition of letters or journals should not contain a text which has editorially been corrected, made consistent or otherwise smoothed out. Errors and inconsistencies are part of the total texture of the document and are part of the evidence which the document preserves relating to the writer's habits, temperament, and mood."[3] Tanselle goes on to point out an awkward, if ineluctable, truth: "It is frequently difficult to avoid a modern bias in deciding what constitutes an error."[4] In short, Tanselle would argue, on several counts the editorial strategy of silent emendation is anathema.[5]

3. Tanselle 1978:48; cf. Tanselle 1989:27–28, 60–64.

4. Tanselle 1978:48. There have, of course, been arguments on the other side. For a dissenting opinion, at least with regard to historical texts, see Taylor 1981.

5. Other studies dealing with editorial strategies for changing text include Kenney 1974:21–74 and Warren 1985.

Yet there was a time not that long ago when silent emendation, even in documentary editing, was not only accepted but applauded as the triumph of literary style over mere slavish copying. Early editions of the writings of George Washington and other American notables illustrate this.[6] As Jared Sparks, the most prolific of these early modern editors and an open practitioner of the art of "improvement," put it: "It would be an act of unpardonable injustice to any author, after his death, to bring forth compositions, and particularly letters written with no design to their publication and commit them to the press without previously subjecting them to careful revision."[7] Sparks went on to proclaim: "I have of course considered it a duty, appertaining to the function of a faithful editor, to hazard such corrections as the construction of a sentence manifestly warranted, or a cool judgment dictated."[8] With the door to editorial license thus left ajar, Sparks stepped smartly through and proceeded to demonstrate his point of view thousands of times in his twelve-volume edition of the writings of Washington.[9]

The double form of emendation, in which readers are not apprised of the practice no matter how thoroughly they scour the editorial apparatus, is, of course, undoubtedly the cardinal sin of textual editing. Not only does it deprive the reader of possible insights into both the author and the editor but it also offends against propriety and against posterity. The editor who stealthily emends misconceives his role as a facilitating intermediary between author and reader as to the nature of the text.

Some editors have argued that their authors would have appreciated having "obvious" typographical or calligraphic "errors," apparently unwitting replications, or unseemly language corrected, that these were never a part of authorial intent and that retaining them only subverts that intent. Even the critics' critic, A. E. Housman, wrote that "if the sense requires it I am prepared to write *Constantinopolitanus* where the MSS have the monosyllabic *o*."[10] But the belief that all authors are inherently as rational as, say, editors, that they are aware that certain things are true

---

6. Cappon 1973; Callcott 1959.

7. Washington 1838–39, 2:xv; cf. Sheldon 1979.

8. Washington 1838–39, 2:xv; see also similar remarks at Washington 1838–39, 1:viii.

9. Knollenberg 1940:151–55.

10. Housman 1988:333.

(or not true), or that they invariably aspire to tell the truth is certainly unwarranted.

In fact, rather paradoxically, perhaps the worst reason to emend a text is to make it conform to historical fact as we know it. This is as true for historical sources as for imaginative literature. To take but a single instance, recent editors of *1 Henry IV* have replaced Shakespeare's Falstaff with "Sir John Oldcastle" because they believe that this is historically more accurate. Their argument is that Shakespeare knew this but was forced by political exigencies to omit Oldcastle's name.[11] Shakespeare's change alone is immensely helpful in understanding the constraints under which authors sometimes work, so "Falstaff" deserves to be kept on those grounds, as well as on the more straightforward principle that, whatever the circumstances, "Falstaff" is what Shakespeare wrote and what his actors spoke. In this case, however, modern editors not only have made the change but made it silently so that the interested reader must learn about it from the review literature—or not at all.[12]

No doubt the most popular method of changing a text is simply to omit passages that the editor considers redundant or irrelevant. A particularly alarming example of this was the habit of Renaissance editors of earlier chronicles of omitting "dicitur" (it is said) in their editions, thereby creating the impression that these chroniclers had accepted some statements as certain, whereas they had actually been trying to make it clear that they had their doubts![13] In like fashion, if with more visible diffidence, Muslim historians frequently interjected the phrase *allahu aʿlam* ("God knows best") when they wanted to advise their readers of conflicts and contradictions in their evidence and of their own doubts. They also prefaced certain passages with an *isnad,* or chain of authorities, which was the recognized validation for whatever followed.[14]

Textual changes, whether authorial or editorial, inevitably emanate from the times and circumstances in which they are made. During much

---

11. Bevington 1987:502–3, 509–10. For a defense of the practice, see Wells 1988: 71–75.

12. For the effects of meter and pronunciation on such decisions, see Schäfer 1988:71–75.

13. Tinsley 1987:389–90.

14. For *hadith* and *isnads* see, among others, Robson 1955–56; Juynboll 1983: 161–217; Hawting 1984. Rapoport-Albert 1988:128–29 discusses a more recent example of the same form of legitimation.

of the nineteenth and early twentieth centuries, social mores inhibited rendering texts accurately if they offended public morality. Editors of texts of all kinds were diligent in excising any word or phrase that might bring a blush to a maiden's cheek or, for that matter, which failed partisan purposes. In this way the perceived sensibilities of anticipated readers overrode the integrity of the text.[15]

Changing a text to suit the knowledge of an editor (which itself may be defective) presents readers with an inaccurate picture not only of the text itself but also possibly of the state of knowledge of its author and of his times.[16] Seventeenth- and eighteenth-century accounts of Africa are notoriously lacking in sound geographic and cartographic knowledge, but it has not often been the practice of Africanist historians to change these sources arbitrarily to conform to what we now know to be the case. On old maps, for instance, the Niger River is still allowed to flow westward into the Atlantic. Nor were errors committed solely by armchair travelers. James Phipps, who spent nearly twenty years on the Gold Coast, occasionally misplaced or misidentified an inland polity.[17] For historians, knowing this contributes to an understanding that the European presence in Africa in those days was very tenuous indeed.

Nor have only written texts been treated with disdain. In modern recordings, the intent of composers seems to be honored as much in the breach as in the observance. Conductors routinely employ instruments, tempos, and performing forces considerably different from those stipulated by the composer, to whom some of the instruments and much modern orchestral and choral theory were simply unknown. The argument for much of this is that the modern ear is not attuned to earlier musicianship, even though modern taste might very well be attuned to early compositions themselves if properly edited.[18]

Oral texts present special editing problems, as can be seen in the work

15. For examples, see Cappon 1973; Reid 1984; Aarsleff 1985; Dumville 1985; Grafton 1985; Burkhardt 1986; McCarter 1986; Burkhardt 1988; Machan 1989; Scott and Thesing 1989. For examples of emending on such grounds, see Jackson 1986, Crane 1988, and Clements 1990.

16. For an extended discussion of the relationship of known facts to textual analysis see Tanselle 1979 and sources cited there.

17. For Phipps, see Henige 1980a.

18. Arguments on both sides of the question are collected in Kenyon 1988. See also Maunder 1988, Helm 1989, and Rothstein 1990.

of historians of oral societies. Here it has been typical during the past twenty-five years to collect materials on tape, transcribe them, and use the transcriptions for research purposes. The tapes themselves (we might consider them the analog of Columbus's shipboard log) are almost never carefully or faithfully edited, if they are edited at all, and soon become lost or deteriorate. It may not be possible to edit such texts effectively because hesitations, inflections, pregnant silences, listener reactions, and the like can never be intelligibly transformed into written words that can evoke the "meaning" of the oral text, but this is all the more reason not to allow the primary source to disappear.[19]

It is widely held that there are, or should be, tactical and procedural differences between editing literary and historical texts. Historical texts, some argue, require more annotation and contextualization but less attention to the physical and verbal details of the text as text. To put it another way, literary textual editors should be more interested in establishing what a text is, and historical editors in what it means. By this line of reasoning, a literary text is sacred because of the very way in which it is expressed, and so-called accidentals are important largely because they affect rhyme, cadence, or style. Historical texts, on the other hand, are seen less as objects in their own right than as windows on larger matters. The textual variants of the United States Constitution as it evolved are of some value, to be sure, but the really important textual exegesis comes only after it became the guiding document of our political system. By this argument, its history began only after it was adopted; that which preceded is merely prehistory, whose interest is narrow and whose importance is fleeting.[20] Textual editors would argue that, on the contrary, historical documents are no less important as texts than are literary works, that understanding how they came to be is crucial for understanding what they seem to be.[21] Many editors favor a compromise that presents the

19. Henige 1980b; Galloway 1981; Henige 1982. Videotaping should help, but it is costly and cumbersome at best, impractical and impossible at worst. Nor is it foolproof; see *Illustrated London News* 1987 for the effects of digital imaging on authenticity. For an earlier example of iconographic emendation, see Newman 1985 : 109–11.

20. See Kaminski 1987, in disagreement.

21. Gilman 1971; Rutland 1976; Shaw 1976/77; Tanselle 1978; Teute 1980; Orth 1984; Tanselle 1986; Kline 1987. In particular see the good advice in Haggard 1941 : 109–22.

literal text but in some highly accessible fashion, something like a so-called "clear text," in which any emendations are placed either in footnotes or in appendices.[22] All things being equal, there is little harm in this, as long as the reader does not forget that the historian's ends are not a clear text but a clear idea of the thought processes of the authors of the texts.

Even though borrowed from literary textual critics, these are powerful arguments for historians because they insist on the centrality of the text without sacrificing any "larger" picture. In fact, in concentrating on the text itself, they come closest to replicating the circumstances of its creation by granting it a diachronic as well as a synchronic character. After all, if the study of history is held to be the study of change, then the study of historical sources should likewise concentrate on the changes the sources have undergone.[23] Conflating parts of various texts into a coherent (or sometimes incoherent) whole that aims to reproduce authorial intent produces an eclectic text that sometimes fails to satisfy anyone completely but at least captures and arrays the fluidity of texts for which we have multiple versions. As a preliminary step it is necessary and fruitful.

Even for texts that exist in only a single version, as with the diario, there is a need for early and accurate diplomatic transcriptions that seek to present, sometimes by symbols, the state of the manuscripts as they exist, including all corrected and uncorrected errors, all interpolations, all evidence of later tinkering, and so forth so that the transcription can serve as a more accessible surrogate for the manuscript itself. The problem with such editions is that they tend to be virtually unreadable without a great deal of commitment. When, because of a text's limited appeal or sheer size, it is feasible to produce only a single edition, the question is whether to serve the audience of scholars or the often only hypothetical general reader. Nevertheless, it is difficult to conjure arguments against producing at least one carefully crafted diplomatic edition of all major historical texts. Although a great deal more could be said about the principles and practices of literary and documentary editing, it is time to turn

22. E.g., Kline 1987:129–31, 148–50. An example both good and relevant is the edition of Washington Irving's life of Columbus (Irving 1981), in which more than 300 pages of emendations are detailed in appendices.

23. For evidence that the editors of such collected works are beginning to take a higher editorial road see Schultz 1988.

to considering very briefly the way in which editing the diario fits into this tradition.

I
_____

The diario was discovered in 1791 and was first published thirty-four years later. Since then countless editions and translations have appeared, but there was no attempt to produce a diplomatic edition until 1976. From the very first published edition until the present there has been virtually no evidence of any overriding concern for the text that might protect it from unacknowledged revisions, omissions, and sheer carelessness. Of course, it has not been possible to produce an eclectic edition of the diario because only a single manuscript exists. De Lollis made an effort along these lines by indicating analogous passages in Las Casas's *Historia de las Indias* and Ferdinand's *Historie,* but at the same time he declined to provide a diplomatic transcription and ignored most of the changes within the diario itself.[24] Still, until 1976 his remained the best available edition.

While a diplomatic transcription is, of course, no substitute for the original manuscript, it is frequently practicable to use a facsimile. The best facsimile so far available is that of Carlos Sanz, who complemented it with a transcription that conveniently marches in lockstep with the holograph, affording easy collation. Apparently, however, Sanz did not expect consultation and comparison, for he took no steps to make the transcription resemble the holograph except incidentally. In comparing only the 220 lines that cover the three days at Guanahaní, we find between 1,200 and 1,500 differences, depending on how one counts.[25] The majority are garden-variety changes: modernizations of spelling, accentuation, punctuation, and capitalization. These might not seem terribly important, but they reveal a problem that is rather more significant when it results in the loss of all interlineated and crossed-out matter. Moreover, Sanz both italicized and placed within quotation marks all those passages that Las Casas or he attributes to Columbus, an expedient that is conve-

_____

24. See chapter 6 for more on modern editorial practices.

25. Sanz/Columbus 1962:8v–11r. The exact number is a matter of interpretation; for example, is "Pinzón" for "pinçon" one change or three? Unfulfilled promises seem to characterize Spanish historical editing; another example is discussed in Geary 1983–84.

nient for readers but that is largely an interpretation rather than a presentation of the text.[26]

Sanz's transcription fails to meet modern standards in other ways as well, but since he is by no means alone in this, it is perhaps unfair to single out his editorial work, except that his juxtaposition of the original text and its massively deformed transcription graphically emphasizes the cavalier attitude that modern editors of the diario have taken, as if the source that they thought important enough to edit was not important enough to present as itself. The chapters that follow discuss numerous examples of the defects of modern editing; here the purpose is simply to contrast the editorial tradition of the diario with editorial philosophies that editors should have followed but have not.

II

Bereft of any antecedents for comparison and unedited until modern times, the diario is likewise without any context in its own time and place. The text begins *in medias res* with a prologue, continues until it reaches the end of the postscript, and abruptly ceases. Las Casas added numerous marginal notes but not a single word that could provide a clue as to the circumstances surrounding the creation of the diario's text. Naturally this question is of much concern to its modern students, many of whom have tried to detect in the diario hints as to the conditions under which Las Casas copied it and the date at which he did so.

Most agree that Las Casas would have copied the diario only to serve as an aide-mémoire as he toiled away at his leviathan *Historia,* a work he actually began to write in 1527 but for which he probably started collecting materials some time earlier.[27] It would clearly be of value to know when Las Casas transcribed the diario, for such knowledge would allow for more reasonable inferences about the state of both the text and Las Casas's mind at the time. The later it was transcribed, the more Las Casas's increasingly impassioned views on the Spanish treatment of the Indians would affect the character of the work, which is, after all, largely paraphrase.

26. For more on Sanz's edition, see chapter 5.

27. Studies of the history of the *Historia de las Indias* include Wagner 1945: 196–204, 290–92; Hanke 1951; Hanke 1952:13–31; Wagner and Parish 1967:195–204; Pérez Fernández 1981:206–10.

It has sometimes been thought that, despite its lack of explicit clues, the diario offers at least two textual hints about the date of its composition. On several occasions Las Casas wrote of "estas Indias" (these Indies), and he once referred to Hispaniola as "esta isla" in paraphrasing Columbus.[28] Not wholly without reason, this has been taken to indicate that Las Casas must have transcribed his source text sometime before he left the New World for good in 1547.[29] In isolation the point seems suggestive, if somewhat fragile, but more than thirty years ago Marcel Bataillon demonstrated how unwise it is to decontextualize this information when he reminded us that Las Casas used the same language in the prologue to the *Historia,* a prologue he did take the trouble to date, to 1552, long after he had returned to Spain.[30] Bataillon speculated that this anomaly reflected the fact that the New World remained Las Casas's spiritual home to such a degree that during the 1550s he had hopes of returning there and publishing the *Historia,* which, of course, actually remained unpublished for three centuries.[31]

Whether or not we fully accept Bataillon's explanation of Las Casas's motives, the latter's usage in the *Historia* by itself negates any argument that these words in the diario can provide a *terminus ante quem* for its composition. This has in no way impeded several authors from doing just that, however. Their conclusions vary widely, and although none of them can be shown to be correct, a few are certainly incorrect. A widespread if largely implicit view is that expressed most recently by Fuson, who asserts that "the epic *Historia de las Indias* was begun in 1527 and the *Diario de la bordo* had to be in Las Casas's hands at that time."[32] Indeed, Fuson even hints that Las Casas may have come into possession of the source for the diario even before he arrived in Hispaniola in 1502 as a young man of eighteen.[33]

28. Taking seriously this last phrase would presume a date before 1536, when Las Casas left Hispaniola; see Cioranescu 1960a:228–32; Cioranescu/Columbus 1961: 387n70.

29. E.g., Fuson 1987a:6, 12n; Varela/Columbus 1982:30n; Varela/Columbus 1989: 172n33; Taviani/Columbus 1988:21; Heers 1981:227; Arce Fernández 1974:58.

30. Las Casas 1951, 1:21.

31. Bataillon 1959. See now Vaquero 1987:12–14.

32. Fuson 1985:53.

33. Fuson 1985:53, as does Duviols 1985:335. On Las Casas's birth date (1484, not 1474) see Parish and Weidman 1976, and Pérez Fernández 1984:89–97.

Such an argument is without basis. Certainly Las Casas seems to have transcribed the diario largely as an adjunct to compiling the *Historia,* but we have no way of knowing the compositional history of that monumental work, other than that it was in process for over thirty years. It is just possible that it was written entirely in chronological sequence and in very much the form in which it survives. If so, Fuson would be correct, since the contents of the diario, heavily edited, occupy an early portion of the work. But it is considerably more likely that what was to become the *Historia de las Indias* grew fitfully as Las Casas came into possession of more and more data relevant to his purposes, which themselves no doubt changed over time. Nor is there the slightest reason to doubt that part or all of it was rewritten, perhaps many times, as new evidence came to hand or Las Casas's own attitudes changed.[34] After all, this is generally the way that any large composition evolves from a gleam in the eye to its final form.[35]

In fact, the two extant manuscripts of the *Historia* are synthetic and synchronic transcriptions of previous recensions, and among other things they show that Las Casas continued to tinker with one of the copies, perhaps until he died in 1566. In short, there is nothing to require a date earlier than the late 1550s for the transcription of the diario. For all we know, chapters 35 to 75 of Book 1 of the *Historia,* the account of Columbus's first voyage, were the very last to be written.

Some have supported an early date—and have even suggested that Las Casas was able to copy the original log itself—by wrongly imputing a personal relationship between Las Casas and Columbus.[36] The fact that Las Casas transcribed the diario rather than availing himself of scribal assistance could be seen as suggesting an earlier date, before he returned to Spain, where he had at his disposal the institutional support of his Dominican confreres. On the other hand, he must have regarded the copy of the log he chanced upon as the centerpiece of his projected work, and

34. As we know to be true for the work of Bernal Díaz del Castillo, for instance; Wagner 1945:155–90; Díaz del Castillo 1982:xxx–xli, 11–86; Barbón Rodríguez 1985.

35. Taviani/Columbus 1988:38. Varela wonders whether the text was edited as part of the Pleitos process, that is, between 1515 and the 1530s (Varela/Columbus 1989:38). For literature on the revising tendencies of authors see chapter 6. Brumble 1988:72–97 is relevant here, as is Las Casas 1989:16–25, 33–35.

36. Winsor 1892:49; Cronau 1921:8; Duff 1957:89.

he may have felt obliged to attend to its transcription—and its editing—himself.

Currently, the most widely favored date for this activity is 1552, when Las Casas spent some time in Seville at the inchoate Biblioteca Colombiana.[37] That year was an unusually prolific one for Las Casas, and one implication of such a dating is that Las Casas would probably have had to work hurriedly on his transcription. As we will see on numerous occasions, signs of haste festoon the text of the diario.

In sum, the date of the transcription of the diario remains uncertain; it may have been anywhere between about 1515 and the late 1550s. Arguments that attempt to pinpoint the date more closely founder on the lack of evidence and solid reasoning. It remains only to point out that a later date—say 1552, when Las Casas was in full rhetorical flight over the plight of the Indians—would encourage a wider range of arguments concerning the partisan uses to which he may have felt obliged to put the diario, beginning with its very transcription.

III

Although knowing when Las Casas composed the diario is clearly of interest, it would be more important to know how he went about the task. Unfortunately, we have no more information on this aspect of the textual history of the diario than on its date, and we are left to infer from the state of the manuscript as we have it. In the absence of the original log, the most crucial of all questions—to what extent Las Casas transcribed and paraphrased faithfully, or even intended to—is quite beyond answering, despite numerous claims to the contrary both for and against Las Casas's carefulness.[38]

We must not begin with Las Casas's last transcription, however, but with the first acknowledged copying of the log in 1493. We know that after Columbus surrendered his log, or a copy of it, to the royal authori-

37. Arranz/Columbus 1985:62; Ferro/Columbus 1985:9–10; Pérez Fernández 1981:611; Mahn-Lot 1982:182; Pérez Fernández 1984:835–36, 956; Martínez Hidalgo y Terán 1985:203. Giménez Fernández (Las Casas 1965:lvii–lxxxvii) dates the transcription to 1552.

38. High, if passing, praise for Las Casas's transcribing fidelity includes Leyva y Aguilera 1890:96n; Pérez de Tudela in Las Casas 1957, 1:liv; Laguardia Trias 1974:63; Parry 1974:231; Almodóvar Muñoz 1986:3–5; among many others.

ties, at least two scribes were set to work during the summer of 1493 to make at least one copy of it. As I discuss elsewhere, there is some evidence in the diario to suggest aspects of the scribal routine adopted during the process.[39] These indicate that the scribes probably worked alternately in creating the next recension. We can assume that their work was calligraphically superior both to Columbus's shipboard log and to the diario.[40] We can hardly go so far as to assume, however, that the judgments the scribes made as to the words before them were without their fair share of errors, since from all accounts Columbus was not available for consultation.[41]

As we will have numerous occasions to notice, modern scholarship has not been shy in attributing errors either to Columbus or to Las Casas, but we must also consider the influence of these intermediate scribes[42] and the possibility that Columbus copied his own handiwork before relinquishing the log, perhaps making a second copy for himself in case princely gratitude failed to materialize satisfactorily. There is much to suggest that, despite his dulcet words, he placed bounds on his trust in the royal goodwill.

Be that as it may, we now come to Las Casas, though without clearly knowing the trail we have followed. Las Casas's own complaints about the frequently difficult handwriting that confronted him, interjected as obiter dicta into the diario, indicate that, whatever he used, it was not the first copy made, which must at least have been presentable in its penmanship. Rumeu de Armas has argued energetically that Las Casas used a version that had already been summarized by someone else.[43] Such a view would be supported by asking why Las Casas bothered to paraphrase passages that probably could have been transcribed literatim more easily if it were just a matter of efficiency. But as we will see, Las Casas averaged many more transcriptional errors in the paraphrased portions of the diario, which can suggest only that he approached these differently—that is, summarized them and frequently changed his mind while doing so.

39. See below, chapter 6.

40. For normative scribal practices of the time, see Martín Postigo 1959

41. Pace McElroy 1941:210

42. On the tendency of medieval scribes to revise and "correct" as they went about their task, see Greenway 1986 and Tarrant 1987

43. Rumeu de Armas 1973b:173–76; Rumeu de Armas 1976. This view has since been adopted in Morales Padrón/Columbus 1984:7–8, 13

This does not, of course, preclude the possibility that he was dealing with a previously paraphrased text, but it does remove him from the status of "slavish copyist" into which Rumeu de Armas would place him.

At any rate, once Las Casas had decided to transcribe his source and paraphrase most of it at the same time, he must have set to work in some haste; the sheer magnitude of his published and unpublished corpus suggests that he invariably worked at speed. However, paraphrasing a text while retaining its flavor and detail is no easy matter.[44] The difficulty manifests itself in the more than one thousand scribal corrections and additions noted below in chapter 6. The average frequency of these, about seven per folio page, is by no means disproportionately high and suggests either great paraphrastic skills on the part of Las Casas, little interest in being precise or accurate, or a rewriting of an earlier transcription, perhaps his own. There is no way at the moment of knowing which is correct.

On the basis of the relatively small number of such cases in the diario, some have charged Las Casas with a lack of interest in, and ignorance of, nautical details, as well as a concomitant surfeit of interest in Indians. Of the latter there can be no doubt, but any deleting of miscellaneous nautical details may well have taken place at the very beginning of the transcriptional chain, given the hovering, prying Portuguese who were at the Spanish court to press their claims to the newly discovered lands.[45]

More to the point is any relationship between Las Casas's copying and the role he foresaw for the text of the diario. There is no reason to believe that he copied it with any other purpose than to insinuate it in some redigested state into his projected *Historia*, so his conception of that work would necessarily affect how he transcribed whatever he had in front of him. Bearing this in mind, it is not reasonable to ascribe the indiocentricity of the diario to anyone but Las Casas, whether by means of adding material or deleting it. As we will see, it is not possible, on the basis of comparing the diario with Ferdinand's *Historie*, to determine to what extent Las Casas himself was responsible for any abridgment of the text. It seems likely, though, that even with the best will in the world,

44. On the demanding art of paraphrasis, see Roberts 1985, Brambilla Ageno 1986, and Townsend 1988
45. But see below, chapter 6 on the Spanish monarchs' later request for more geographical detail from Columbus

Las Casas would inevitably stray from the text as he sought to paraphrase and to place the Indians even closer to center stage than Columbus had done. Presumably he would not have paraphrased at all unless doing so would considerably shorten the task ahead. Las Casas's failure to note several obvious errors in his text (see chapter 5) leads to the conclusion that he was able to commit only limited time to copying his source and that he gave priority to editing and paraphrasing.

Finally, it is necessary to place Las Casas's work in the framework of transcriptional theory, as outlined earlier in this chapter. Here it can simply be reiterated that the volume and significance of identified transcriptional error mounts with each passing year.[46] Works for which the possibility once seemed unthinkable are now being subjected with increasing rigor to the notion that they have been contaminated with careless, as well as careful, changes in the transcribing or printing stages, and often in both. Mounting evidence relegates the Faithful Copyist to a null set—such a paragon has never existed and perhaps never can. While this finding will not take us far along the path of imputing particular errors and incongruities to Las Casas, it helps show the need to take that road.

IV

In addition to discussing modern editions of the diario that are transcriptions of the holographic manuscript, we need to look at translations, since these are likely to have had a wider effect than editions in Spanish. Morison briefly evaluated several translations that had appeared by the late 1930s, but many others have appeared since then, including Morison's own.[47] This last I have discussed elsewhere,[48] and I would like now to comment on one of the most recent translations of the diario, one that is certain to become popular and influential.

46. In addition to those cited earlier, recent studies include Metzger 1968; Windeatt 1979; Malla 1985; Ramsey 1986; Bruford 1986; Elias 1987; Holmes 1987; Easson 1987; Kaiser 1987; MacBain 1987; Mattina 1987; Emerton 1987–88; Brodsky 1988; Burkhardt 1988; E. Crane 1988; Fahy 1988; Hay 1988; Neumann 1988; Tov 1988; Field 1989

47. Morison 1939; Morison/Columbus 1963. See chapter 5 and Henige 1988 for more on these translations.

48. Henige 1988.

Significantly, this translation is entitled *The Log of Christopher Columbus*. The translator is Robert Fuson, who characterizes his work as "unique, though no less accurate than other good translations."[49] It is the second half of Fuson's opinion that is at issue here. In a startling about-face to his earlier work, discussed above in the Preface, Fuson adopts three strategies that completely breach the etiquette of documentary translation. He incorporates many parts of Las Casas's *Historia* and Ferdinand's *Historie* that he believes were directly based on parts of the original log omitted by Las Casas or other transcribers. As if in expiation, he also eliminates "certain redundancies" from the diario as we have it. Finally, "the first person is restored where Las Casas and Ferdinand switch to the third person," or about 80 percent of the time.[50] These stunning departures from long-established editorial norms render Fuson's claim to accuracy risible, and about each of them something must be said.

It may well be that parts of both Las Casas's and Ferdinand's works were based directly on the log, although it is not easy to imagine just how Las Casas would have been able to include such matter in the *Historia* if it is not in the diario. Perhaps it came from Ferdinand's work in manuscript, or from other written sources, or even from free-floating oral tradition. If so, and even if not so, there is no good reason to treat these as once-integral parts of the diario and to "restore" them by enshrining them without indication in a new and expanded version of the diario, now called the "log," and thereby creating a hybrid that is without historical or textual justification.

The results of Fuson's practice are alarming. Many entries are much longer in his translation than in the diario. That of 23 September, for instance, is nearly twice as long.[51] Further, Fuson's account of Columbus's sojourn in the Canaries between 10 August and 5 September is little more than fiction and Ferdinand dressed up as Columbus's original log.[52] In Fuson's hands the diario's reticence about the crews' discontent disap-

49. Fuson 1987a:11.

50. Fuson 1987a:11.

51. Fuson 1987a:66; cf. Alvar/Columbus 1976, 2:34; and Dunn and Kelley/Columbus 1989:38–40.

52. Fuson 1987a:57–61; cf. Alvar/Columbus 1976, 2:25; and Dunn and Kelley/Columbus 1989:24–27.

pears in favor of long passages about them—an amalgam of Las Casas's *Historia,* Ferdinand's *Historie,* and who knows what else.

Omitting "redundancies" in a delicate balancing act may add to the populist tenor of this rendition, but it hardly contributes to scholarship, and it lacks even the exiguous justification for adding matter. Fuson apparently regards Columbus's most extended and intriguing comment on instituting the double distances as superfluous simply because two briefer comments appear earlier in the diario.[53] As I have suggested elsewhere, this very repetition is significant, yet Fuson omits it entirely.[54]

Most extreme, though, is Fuson's transformation of the diario's third-person past tenses into his translation's first-person present tenses. While this gives a tone of immediacy to the translation, it also gives the *Log of Christopher Columbus* a narrative tenor completely different from the text it purports to translate. This procedure leads Fuson to translate Columbus's enigmatic "yo creí y creo" in the entry for 11/12 October as simply, "I believe."[55] "Creí" is held to be redundant, and of course in a sense it is, but its very superfluity leads us to ask questions about it, questions that cannot arise on the basis of Fuson's idiosyncratic translation.[56]

The greatest impact of Fuson's procedure is to give his text the illusion of a double sense of immediacy that is largely lacking in the document he is translating. In the *Log,* Fuson is credited only with being the translator; in reality he is almost as much its author as Las Casas or Columbus.

If Fuson's effort reminds us that translation is an art before it is a science, other translations of the diario do much the same in lesser but no less profound ways. Let one example suffice here in hopes that it can make the point sufficiently by illustrating the ways in which translation is so often in thrall to other skills and attitudes.

On 7 October, after many days of sailing west, the fleet turned southwest. Had it not done so, America would have been discovered somewhere along the eastern coast of the United States, making this change of

---

53. Fuson 1987a:67; cf. Alvar/Columbus 1976, 2:36; and Dunn and Kelley/Columbus 1989:42.

54. Henige and Zamora 1989; see also chapter 7.

55. Fuson 1987a:77; cf. Alvar/Columbus 1976, 2:53, and Dunn and Kelley/Columbus 1989:66.

56. See chapter 6 for more details.

direction one of the more intriguing "what ifs" of history. At any rate, the fleet did change direction, and the diario describes the occasion as follows:

> Since by the afternoon they had not seen land, that which those on the caravel [the *Niña*] thought they had seen, and because a great multitude of birds passed from the north to the southwest, from which it was believed that they were going to sleep on land, or perhaps were fleeing from winter, which in the lands from which they came must be about to arrive [and] *because the Admiral knew that most of the islands that the Portuguese held they discovered by means of birds.* Because of all this Admiral *acordó dejar* the route of the west.[57]

For us the key phrase is "acordó dejar," or more precisely "acordó." In Spanish "acordar" can mean many things, but it most often means "to agree to or with"; that is, it defines a passive, reactive behavior. This common meaning actually seems to fit well here because Martín Alonso Pinzón had advocated such a change just the day before, but Columbus had replied that the mainland of Asia could best be reached by continuing to sail west.[58] The text suggests that Columbus decided, if belatedly, that Pinzón—and now the birds—were correct.

While this might be one's first instinct on encountering the word "acordó" in the text, rendering this as "agreed" has not found much favor among modern translators. Markham lived up to his reputation as a notoriously tendentious translator by translating "acordó" as a muscular "resolved."[59] Thacher also employed "resolved."[60] The word, after all, has a masterly ring about it and fits nicely with prevailing views of Columbus. In fact, "resolve" carries with it quite the opposite connotation of "agree," implying determination on a course of action despite odds or opposition. Jane, Morison, and Fuson, on the other hand, all concluded that "decided" is the best way to translate "acordó."[61] While

57. Alvar/Columbus 1976, 2:43 (with emphasis added); Dunn and Kelley/Columbus 1989:52–55 (with emphasis added). Las Casas (1951, 1:195) repeated "acordó dejar" in his *Historia*.

58. Alvar/Columbus 1976, 2:41–42; Dunn and Kelley/Columbus 1989:54. Cf. Las Casas 1951, 1:194. For a useful discussion from a non-Columbus perspective see *Pleitos Colombinos* 1989:xxxvi–xl.

59. Markham/Columbus 1893:33.

60. Thacher 1903–4, 1:528.

61. Jane/Columbus 1960:20; Morison/Columbus 1963:61; Fuson 1987a:71.

not as emphatic as "resolved," it keeps Columbus in charge, clearly the appropriate demeanor for the soon-to-be Admiral of the Ocean Sea.[62] Dunn and Kelley are virtually alone in treating the text with respect by translating "acordó" as "agreed."[63]

But "acordó" is not the strong verb to match the strong actions the other five translators attribute to Columbus, and the question remains: Who used this word—Columbus himself, followed by Las Casas, or only Las Casas? This is another unanswerable question, but note that Las Casas was seldom one to cast Columbus in anything less than the most favorable light, and if he had chosen the verb to use here, we can at least suspect that he would have selected "determinó" or "resolvió." Perhaps, then, it was Columbus himself who used the word "acorde" and Las Casas merely changed it to the third-person preterite form. The matter raises issues of transcription and paraphrase that I address elsewhere, but it seems slightly more likely that Columbus used the appropriate form of *acordar*, particularly if the shipboard log happened to be accessible to the other captains, including, of course, Martín Alonso Pinzón, the original advocate of a southwesterly course.[64]

This ambiguity emphasizes the quandary that the historian encounters as against the translator of works of imagination. Literary translation has its own problems, but those of historians are more refractory in the sense that any translation of a historical source must aim to elucidate what really happened, thereby reducing considerably the chance to be "right" without in the least concomitantly reducing the scope for error. In the

62. Earlier opinion conceded less to Columbus. Winsor 1892:206 and Adams 1891:85 use "yielded." Unusually, Charcot (1928:152) argued as well that Columbus acceded to the desires of Pinzón.

63. Dunn and Kelley/Columbus 1989:55.

64. This passage presents an additional problem worth mentioning here. The words from "because" to "birds," which are italicized above, are actually in the margin with, as Dunn and Kelley/Columbus (1989:55n) put it, "a line drawn to a plus sign above the full stop after *venir*." This, together with the fact that it is in the right margin (whereas Las Casas most often added his own comments in the left margin), has led some modern editors (but not Alvar [see Alvar/Columbus 1976, 1:82, 2:43]) to incorporate it within the text. On the other hand, it is very much the kind of extraneous justification that typifies so many of Las Casas's own interpolations in the diario. Perhaps the fact that the statement also appears in Ferdinand's *Historie* (Colón 1930, 1:156) would be conclusive if we could only be certain that the two sources were independently derived (see chapter 3).

discussion of the landfall controversy that comprises the second part of this work, I cite several examples of translations that do not stand up under scrutiny. As often as not, these emanate from a special desire to emulate Humpty Dumpty's boast: "When *I* use a word, it means just what I choose it to mean, neither more nor less." But even when a translator has no special agenda, or at least thinks he or she has none, accurate translation remains an elusive will-o'-the-wisp that forces the hunter to shed one layer of caution after another in hopes of becoming as protean as his elusive quarry.

3. Ferdinand Columbus vs. Las Casas

*And some of them were both on the same expedition
together and made there sojourns together, like those who
helped Alexander to subdue Asia; yet they frequently
contradict one another.*   STRABO

T aking the trouble to compare Las Casas's text of the
diario with the biography of Columbus by Ferdinand
may well seem a fool's errand, given the textual history
of the latter. The *Historie* was first published in an Italian translation in 1571, more than thirty years after Ferdinand's death in
1539. To all appearances, the presumed Spanish original is lost. In the
absence of a manuscript or even a printed version in the original language,
it is far easier to note errors than to explain or attribute them. Almost
any alleged error may have been committed by Ferdinand himself, by
the purported translator, Antonio de Ulloa, whose scholarly repute is
dubious, or even by the printer.[1] The large number of typographical errors suggests that a greater burden of blame than usual is to be laid to
the last.[2]

The relationship among Las Casas, Ferdinand, oral tradition, and any
texts that may have been used is just another of the thorny issues that

1. For Ulloa see Cioranescu 1960b and Rumeu de Armas 1973a.
2. Cioranescu 1960a:68–69. Some of Las Casas's more bizarre errors in transcribing the diario (discussed elsewhere in this study) remind us, however, that not only
printers can be at fault. Luzzana Caraci (1989) is a comprehensive study of the *Historie*
that came to my attention too late to do more than cite it here. Her conclusion is that
in his *Historia* Las Casas borrowed from both the diario and the *Historie* for the first
voyage and from the *Historie* in other parts of the work. For a discussion of the
printing and translation errors, see Luzzana Caraci 1989:61–71.

bedevil the study of the sources for Columbus's first voyage. We know that Las Casas occasionally relied on some work of Ferdinand, but we can hardly measure the extent of that use, though as we will see, some have tried. We are not even certain what kind of work Las Casas meant. As far as the content of the diario is concerned, if the authenticity of Ferdinand's *Historie* is accepted, there are four possibilities: (1) that Las Casas copied from Ferdinand, (2) that Ferdinand used material gathered by Las Casas, (3) that each copied from the same Ur-text, or (4) that they used different copies of the log, one more "original" than the other. Although not equally likely, each of these possibilities has had adherents. The principal debate among those who believe that Ferdinand wrote most or all of the *Historie*, however, is between the first and second alternatives.

Given its checkered origins, it could only be expected that the *Historie* would come in for some rough critical treatment. In fact, for over a century a debate has raged, not over the reliability of the *Historie,* but over its very authenticity and textual integrity. Nowadays hardly anyone would agree with Caddeo, who, in his edition of the *Historie,* argued that the work "presents no interpolation or other intervention."[3] At that point, however, agreement promptly ceases, as each scholar identifies interpolations and explains them in different ways. Some have gone so far as to reject outright the idea that the *Historie* was an independently written and integral text by Ferdinand, based on his own observations and recollections and on written and manuscript sources he had collected or inherited.[4]

Three episodes in this century of skepticism stand out. The first was associated with Henry Harrisse in the 1870s, the next with Rómulo Carbia in the 1930s, and the third with Alejandro Cioranescu in 1960. Although each of these critics drew attention to anomalies and errors—often the same ones—each came to different conclusions to explain them, though all argued that Ferdinand was not the author of the text as we have it.

---

3. Colón 1930, 1:xxxix. A particularly hostile view of the reliability, though not the authenticity, of the *Historie*, is that of Jaime Cortesão in Ballesteros y Beretta 1947:664–73.

4. E.g., Mahn-Lot (1982:183–184), who supports Rumeu de Armas's arguments discussed below.

In 1872 Henry Harrisse, probably the most formidable Columbian scholar of his day, launched the earliest major assault on Ferdinand's authorship of the *Historie*. Following the lead of Gallardo, Harrisse wondered why the inventory of Ferdinand's effects made no mention of a manuscript biography and why no contemporaries appeared to have mentioned such a work.[5] Of course, Harrisse was struck by the egregious errors and inflated claims that festooned the *Historie,* and he drew particular attention to the numerous instances in which it expanded on events mentioned in the diario in unseemly grandiloquent style, as well as the uncharacteristically disputatious tone of the work, much in contrast to Ferdinand's reputation as a learned and gentlemanly humanist.[6] This led Harrisse to postulate that the *Historie* had been concocted by Antonio de Ulloa or that it represented under false colors a version of the then-lost work of Hernán Pérez de Oliva.

Arguments from silence are risky business, and in this case the worst happened—Harrisse's argument sprang from mistaken silence, and he was betrayed by it.[7] While it was true that no manuscript biography had been mentioned in the inventory, this document began and ended with declarations that, for various reasons, not all the contents of Ferdinand's estate had been tabulated, which undermined, without completely destroying, Harrisse's argument.[8]

Worse was to come. As noted, Harrisse relied heavily on the argument that incidents during the first voyage that were mentioned in the *Historie* had been heavily embellished compared to the diario, and he attributed this to the inventive faculties of the author of the *Historie,* whoever he may have been. These arguments had scarcely appeared before their refutation materialized in the form of Las Casas's *Historia de las Indias,* which was finally published in 1875 after languishing in manuscript for three centuries.[9] Virtually all the additions also turned up in the *Historia.*

5. Harrisse 1872; Gallardo 1863–89, 2:511. For Harrisse's career, see Sanz 1958.
6. Harrisse 1872:68–153 passim; Harrisse 1875:108–21. The latter was written partly in response to Avézac-Macaya 1873. For later aspects of the debate see Harrisse 1884–85 and Peragallo 1884.
7. On the argument from silence see Lange 1966 and Henige 1987b:65–69.
8. Ballesteros y Beretta 1945:68; Hernández Díaz 1941; Marín Martínez 1970:47, 74–75, 775–77.
9. Las Casas 1875–76.

To this contretemps Harrisse replied that while this negated his hypothesis of independently derived embellishments, it by no means established the authenticity of the *Historie*. In this Harrisse was correct, although most other Columbianists have disagreed. The majority view, as one of them put it, is that the correspondences between the *Historie* and the *Historia* are "the most definite proof against critics' suspicions."[10]

But while it might be true that such correspondences increase the probability of authenticity, no one could then (nor can they now) know whether Las Casas and the author of the *Historie* derived these details independently from a common source or drew on each other. It was just this uncertainty that led to further imputations of the *Historie*, on the premise that such correspondences cannot, in the absence of other evidence, establish the authenticity of all of them, or any of them at all.[11]

Inevitably, another debate on the authenticity of the *Historie* flared up, this time in the 1920s and the 1930s, and it proved to be even more rancorous. Its protagonist, Rómulo D. Carbia, was an Argentinian historian who appears to have been, as one observer put it, "an irredeemable hypercritic."[12] Carbia certainly used language more categorical than the evidence he adduced warranted. Moreover, in his doubts Carbia went farther than his predecessors, asserting that Las Casas wrote the *Historie* as a fraud designed to foster his polemic with Oviedo over the nature of the Indians. Carbia advanced the usual arguments of gross errors, specific attention to denouncing Oviedo, and an uncharacteristic (for Ferdinand) focus on the Indians.[13] In impugning Las Casas so directly, however, Carbia was regarded as having gone beyond the pale of civility as it was then (and to a large extent still is) defined. Carbia's willingness, if not

10. Ballesteros y Beretta 1945:70.

11. The best account of the twenty years' debate that followed Harrisse's arguments is Steffen 1892, but also see Rumeu de Armas 1973b:38–39. Steffen concluded that the *Historie* was "effectively" the work of Ferdinand, and he attributed the errors largely to the translator(s) and the printer (1892:146–48). Luzzana Caraci (1989:21–25) discusses the Harrisse episode.

12. Bayerri y Bertomeu 1961:80. For a brief overview of Carbia's career and writings, see Bayerri y Bertomeu 1961:76–82.

13. Carbia also professed to have detected anachronistic references in the *Historie* to events that occurred as late as 1552, thirteen years after Ferdinand died.

eagerness, to speak openly of "the frauds" of Las Casas was not quite the same as charging Ulloa with invention, and it hardly endeared Carbia to other historians, whose replies were often in kind.[14]

Carbia's portrayal of Las Casas the Pseudepigraphist was simply too harsh for most historians to tolerate.[15] Carbia's unequivocal—and on the basis of the evidence he presented, indefensible—characterization inevitably led to his arguments being peremptorily dismissed in favor of profitless ad hominem exchanges of argument by decibel, from which the vitriol fairly oozed. On these grounds Carbia was probably justified in observing, several years after the height of the furor, that despite his challenge, too little critical attention was being paid to the fundamental sources for the activities of Columbus.[16]

As far as the *Historie* was concerned, such attention would have to wait until 1960, when Alejandro Cioranescu launched the most serious, extensive, and effective attack on the authenticity of the work.[17] Cioranescu believed that Harrisse's arguments were "correct but poorly defended" and set out to strengthen them by means of a thorough textual analysis.[18] Cioranescu provided a detailed study of various kinds of errors in the translation—particularly false cognates but also errors of bad faith—and supplemented this with an extremely detailed comparison of the text of the *Historie* with that of Las Casas's *Historia*.[19] Cioranescu concluded that what had passed for the work of Ferdinand is really nothing more than "a first draft of the historical work of Las Casas."[20] Cioranescu identified this as a preliminary draft of the *Historia* completed by 1536 but

14. Relevant works include Carbia 1929, 1930a, 1930b, and 1931.

15. For works attacking Carbia's interpretations, see Jos 1931; Jos 1940; Jos 1942a; Jos 1942b; Jos 1944a; Jos 1944b; Jos 1952; Jos 1955; Bayerri 1961:78–82; Jos 1979: 15–25, 115–38; Gandía 1983. Morison gave the critics his usual short shrift (1942, 1:101n, 206–7, 289). Serrano y Sanz, who translated the *Historie* into Spanish, exemplified the popular view of Las Casas when he assured his readers (Colón 1932, 1:cxxv) that Las Casas was "absolutely incapable" of any form of dishonesty.

16. Carbia 1936. For a bibliography of the dispute engendered by Carbia's work, see Gandía 1942:24–40 and Jos 1944b:673–98.

17. A brief defense of the *Historie*'s authenticity appeared in Ballesteros y Beretta 1945:55–76 and in various works of Emiliano Jos cited above.

18. Cioranescu 1960a:25.

19. Cioranescu 1960a:198–222.

20. Cioranescu 1960a:198.

later revised and subsequently lost—or as Cioranescu argues, hidden.[21] Such a draft would have been in the nature of a compilation of documents as yet lacking much of the polemical fabric so obvious in the surviving version of the *Historia*.[22]

In developing this argument, Cioranescu had to overcome the recurring problem for those who would argue that Ferdinand never wrote an extended biography of his father: the explicit references to such a work in the *Historia de las Indias*. Cioranescu listed twelve instances in the *Historia* in which Las Casas cited Ferdinand a total of thirty-seven times and accepts them as clear evidence that Las Casas relied on Ferdinand at these points.[23] Cioranescu went on to show that these citations were clustered in suggestive ways. One referred to Columbus's alleged higher studies as a young man, another three to the second voyage, and the remaining eight to the fourth voyage, which Ferdinand accompanied.[24] In short, in most of the cases in which Las Casas credited Ferdinand as a source, it was because Ferdinand held a privileged position as an eyewitness rather than because he had written a synoptic biography. If he had, Cioranescu implied, would Las Casas not have cited him more frequently?

Cioranescu conceded that Ferdinand was probably "the author of some writings of a historical nature," possibly including the log of the fourth voyage but not of the published *Historie* attributed to him.[25] This false

21. Cioranescu 1960a:229–33. It is not generally admitted that Las Casas must have revised his *Historia*, perhaps continuously between 1527 and ca. 1560. Giménez Fernández (1949), however, argues for changes as late as 1563. See chapter 2 and 6.

22. Cioranescu 1960a:240–41.

23. Cioranescu 1960a:202–13.

24. Cioranescu 1960a:215–18.

25. Cioranescu 1960a:218, 220–21, following the argument first adduced by Harrisse, who had pointed out (1884–85, 1:113–15) that Las Casas referred vaguely to "writings" of Ferdinand. Modern editions of the *Historia de las Indias* play an unfortunate role here. In Book 1, chapter 104, Las Casas refers to Ferdinand's work and does so (at least in the fair copy manuscript of the *Historia* now housed in the Real Academia de la Historia in Madrid) by referring to it as the "historia." The first modern edition, based on the fair copy, rendered this as "Historia" (Las Casas 1875–76, 2:71), and the three modern editions based on the holographic copy of the *Historia* all render it as *Historia*, which is even worse (Las Casas 1951, 1:414; Las Casas 1957, 1:290; Las Casas 1986, 1:434). My thanks to Demetrio Ramos Pérez for kindly supplying me with a photocopy of the relevant folio of the fair copy manuscript. Un-

attribution resulted from chicanery on the part of Luis Colón—always a convenient scapegoat—into whose hands this earlier draft of Las Casas's *Historia* had fallen. Luis Colón sold this manuscript to an Italian publisher after Las Casas's death in 1566, and it began its dubious route to publication.[26]

Throughout the work, Cioranescu couched his argument in moderate terms, advancing hypotheses and treating them as such. In this he avoided the excesses of Carbia, who was wont to consider his own views as irrefutable. At the same time, by offering a scenario in which no blame accrued either to Ferdinand or to Las Casas, Cioranescu forced other scholars to dispute him on the grounds of his arguments, unlike Carbia, whom critics accused of destroying not only a source but also a reputation.

In fact, it was some time before there was any public reaction to Cioranescu's thesis. In 1973 Rumeu de Armas came to the defense of both Ferdinand and the *Historie*. He found Cioranescu's work stimulating, thought provoking, and "ingenious."[27] He did not think it probative, however, a point of view with which Cioranescu would probably have been the first to agree. Yet Rumeu de Armas's comments were hardly an answer to Cioranescu's arguments, because he mentioned them only briefly.[28] Using much the same approach as Cioranescu and employing virtually the same arguments, Rumeu de Armas came to precisely the

daunted, Varela (Varela/Columbus 1989:33) refers to the "book" of Ferdinand, and she is not alone.

26. Cioranescu 1960a:248–50. This barest outline can hardly do justice to the scope and subtlety of Cioranescu's arguments, which deserve greater attention and testing. See Cioranescu 1960b as well. Varela finds Cioranescu's work "splendid" but his conclusions "unconvincing," though she offers no rebuttal (Varela/Columbus 1982:xn). In turn, Arranz (Arranz/Columbus 1985:41n) mentions Cioranescu's work only in a footnote and does not discuss the debate later than Harrisse. Cioranescu's work also rates passing mention in Ezquerra Abadia 1988:670. See now Luzzana Caraci 1989:29–35.

27. Rumeu de Armas 1973b:42–43.

28. See Rumeu de Armas 1973b:122, 127–28, where the author remarks that Las Casas's "reiterated allusions" to the work of Ferdinand were "the major proof" that he relied heavily on him—this despite Cioranescu's demonstration to the contrary. Cioranescu receives equally short shrift in Luzzana Caraci 1976.

opposite conclusion. For him the *Historie* was, with one exception, "exclusively the work" of Ferdinand.[29] Books 1 through 15 of the *Historie* Rumeu de Armas attributed to "an anonymous biographer" because this section is riddled with errors and because it is "so virulent and aggressive" in tone.[30] By means of this preemptive amputation, he hoped to deflect much of the criticism of Ferdinand's accuracy by ridding him of this inconvenient growth.

According to Rumeu de Armas, in fact, Las Casas never laid eyes on the complete log but only an abstract that he copied literatim rather than abstracted in turn. But, he wrote, despite Ferdinand's unfortunate "zeal for condensing and abridging," the "parallelism" between the diario and the *Historie* is no less than "absolute" with respect to "chronological order, to the unfolding of events, and to the selection of details."[31] Ferdinand, then, must have had access to the log (in fact to the logs of all four voyages), whereas Las Casas had access only to secondhand materials and Ferdinand's own work.[32] Cioranescu's arguments were thereby turned on their heads without ever being confronted.

Most astonishingly, despite Cioranescu's emphasis on linguistic arguments in comparing the Italian edition of the *Historie* with any Spanish antecedent, Rumeu de Armas relied, with few exceptions, on a modern retranslation of the *Historie* instead of the indispensable Italian first edition.[33] By suppressing their counterarguments and by failing to seek out the original text in all instances, the arguments of Rumeu de Armas fail to convince. He disarmingly expressed a willingness to "accept resignedly" the role of "hypercritic" if that should be thrust upon him as a result of his work, but it seems safe to assume that he intended this as jest or irony, since he was so content to recycle old arguments and ig-

29. Rumeu de Armas 1973b:123.

30. Rumeu de Armas 1973b:92–118; Rumeu de Armas 1973a:132–35.

31. Rumeu de Armas 1973b:127, 150–51. Varela/Columbus (1989:33–34, 36–37) seems to agree. Of course only the last of these, the selection of details, is significant.

32. Rumeu de Armas 1973b:55–63.

33. That of Serrano y Sanz (Colón 1932). Throughout Rumeu de Armas 1973b he refers to Ferdinand's work as the *Historia del Almirante*, denying it even its proper title; see esp. Rumeu de Armas 1973b:30–34, 169–89. Cioranescu 1959:66–73 criticized the translation as it dealt with Columbus's stay in the Canaries prior to departing for America.

nore new ones in expressing a dominant ideology confidently endorsing itself.[34]

I

This latest stalemate between those who prefer to believe that Ferdinand was the sole or major author of the *Historie* and those who doubt this exemplifies the exiguity of the available evidence. Even so, all agree that there is a demonstrably close relationship between the text of the diario and those of the *Historie* and the *Historia*. While the nature of this relationship is disputed, there can be no doubt that ultimately each emanated in large part from the same source, either directly or indirectly, and that this source was probably the log of Columbus's first voyage, whether refurbished or not.

Let us assume, for the sake of argument, that Ferdinand was not, however, interested in reproducing his source as fully as Las Casas reproduced his and was frank enough to point out that he would mention only those matters he thought "necessary and proper" for exalting the accomplishments of his father.[35] Certainly his coverage of the first voyage is desultory and in places ambiguous, although we might not recognize this if we did not have the diario and the *Historia* for comparison. Ferdinand frequently telescoped the events of several days into a narrative framework that makes them seem part of a single day's activities. He also omitted most navigational details and displayed far less interest in the Indians than Las Casas's transcription of the diario suggests that Columbus himself did.

In five instances, however, Ferdinand included fairly extensive passages that he introduced with textual signals that they were verbatim extracts from his source, in much the same way as Las Casas did far more often in the diario. These occasions provide us with an opportunity to compare the direct citation of Ferdinand with the indirect discourse of Las Casas, and in one case to compare direct quote with direct quote. Doing so may shed some light on the working premises of both Las Casas and Ferdinand, as well as on those of modern editors and translators. It can serve

34. Rumeu de Armas 1973b:44. Luzzana Caraci (1989:37–40) discusses Rumeu de Armas's theories.

35. Colón 1930, 1:125; cf. Colón 1932, 1:142.

as well to test declarations like Morison's that the extracts in the *Historie* show that Las Casas "omitted nothing essential" in the diario.[36] Here I prefer to stress differences, because similarities speak for themselves and certainly have been spoken for often enough by others.

27 November 1492

Here Ferdinand must have been struck by the cascade of superlatives Columbus used to describe an area along the coast of Cuba.[37] Just before beginning direct quotation, Ferdinand mentioned that Columbus had named a certain harbor Puerto Santo, a point not included at this juncture in the diario.[38] According to Ferdinand, Columbus found the river emptying into the harbor to be eight fathoms deep only a boat's length upstream, and he proceeded to explore the river for a considerable distance ("buone pezza"). Here Las Casas is more elliptical but leaves the impression that Columbus ventured only about a boat's length inland.[39]

About two-thirds of that part of the entry that Ferdinand quoted is missing from the diario. While none of the omitted portions is particularly important, they constitute more than mere repetitions, as Morison would have it.[40] Along the way at least one discrepancy is of interest. Ferdinand has Columbus exclaiming that "my tongue" ("mia lingua," presumably "mi lengua" in the original Spanish) could not adequately describe the charming vistas, but Las Casas, not quoting, showed it as "a

36. Morison/Columbus 1963:42.

37. Colón 1930, 1:191–92; Alvar/Columbus 1976, 2:125–26; Dunn and Kelley/Columbus 1989:182–84.

38. Referring to the same place in the entry for 1 December, Las Casas wrote in the diario that he "believed" that Columbus had called it Puerto Santo; Alvar/Columbus 1976, 2:129; Dunn and Kelley/Columbus 1989:190–91. This suggests that he inferred this in the absence of any explicit testimony in his source. In the *Historia*, Las Casas also presented the information belatedly and expressed the same uncertainty (Las Casas 1951, 1:247).

39. It is possible—just—to interpret Ferdinand's account to mean that Columbus would have been satisfied to traverse the river for only a boat's length rather than that he did precisely that, and the grammar of his source may have misled Las Casas. In each case the language of the texts permits more than one interpretation, but not the same set.

40. Morison/Columbus 1963:106n10.

thousand tongues" ("mil lenguas") in the diario and repeated this in his *Historia*.[41] Rumeu de Armas suggests that this is a transcribing error—"mi" becoming "mil."[42] So far, so good, but a simple slip of the pen would not account for the necessary change from "lengua" to "lenguas." Rumeu de Armas attributes the error to his posited anonymous abstracter rather than to Las Casas, but is it not more likely that Las Casas misread the adjective and changed the noun to conform? Perhaps most likely of all is the notion that Las Casas simply outdid Columbus here in rhetorical flourish.[43] Just when Ferdinand stopped quoting Columbus here, Las Casas began. Why? Because, according to the diario, Columbus then began to wax eloquent about the convertibility of the Indians, the salubrity of the area, and its economic potential. Ferdinand had not a word to say about any of this.

Morison concluded that this passage "attests to the fidelity of the abstract of Las Casas [in the diario], who has done nothing more than transpose from the first person to the third person, and delete some of the repetitions."[44] While this is more true here than in the passages to be discussed next, Morison does not make it clear enough that by "some of the repetitions" he means two-thirds of the text, not all of which is repetitive, though it is admittedly of a kind, as so much of the diario is.

18 December 1492

By 18 December Columbus had reached Hispaniola, which struck him as even more wonderful than Cuba.[45] Here there seemed to be more Indians and, more important, more signs of gold. On this occasion a local *cacique* (whom Columbus called "the king of Hispaniola") came on board, and Ferdinand thought the matter interesting enough to quote. So did Las Casas, thus providing a unique opportunity for direct comparison of the two writers' methods. Modern scholarship finds the correspondence

41. Alvar/Columbus 1976, 2:125; Dunn and Kelley/Columbus 1989:182; Las Casas 1951, 1:243.

42. Rumeu de Armas 1973b:159–60.

43. See Morales Padrón/Columbus 1984:223n770a for a comment on another part of this passage.

44. Morison/Columbus 1963:106n10.

45. Colón 1930, 1:198–200; Alvar/Columbus 1976, 1:155–58; Dunn and Kelley/Columbus 1989:240–42.

close: for Caddeo the passage was "reported to the letter," and Morison wrote that "the same direct quotation is in Ferdinand's *Historie*." [46]

In fact there are a number of minor differences. For instance, Ferdinand and Las Casas reversed at least one sentence. Moreover, Ferdinand quoted somewhat more of his source than Las Casas did of his, and in doing so included a description of what happened after the cacique had returned to land. The sentence reads: "Afterwards a sailor who encountered the cacique told me that every one of the things I had given him were carried in front of him by a very respected man." [47] Las Casas, who was not quoting at this point, differs significantly: he presents the account not as hearsay but as eyewitness testimony, as though Columbus himself had seen all that he was reporting.

But the most interesting comparisons are not between the texts of Ferdinand and Las Casas but between those of the two modern translators, Keen and Morison. [48] Between a third and half of the wording of these modern editions is identical. Word after word, phrase after phrase, read alike in the two translations. Even the improbable word "pregustation" appears in both, once to translate Ferdinand's enigmatic phrase "per far la credenza" and once to render Las Casas's somewhat less cryptic "hazer la salva." [49] Is it possible, when working with an Italian translation of a Spanish text written by A and a Spanish text written by B, for such a high degree of replication to occur in word order and choice? Translation theory and common sense suggest that the probabilities are very low and that this verbal identity must be accounted for in other ways. [50] Whatever the case may be, comparing the modern English translations of the two passages can only suggest either that Las Casas and Ferdinand were

46. Colón 1930, 1:200; Morison/Columbus 1963:126n4.

47. Colón 1930, 1:200: "Poscia un marinaio, che lo trovò nella strada, mi disse che ciascuna delle cose ch'io gli aveva donate erano portate dinanzi a lui da un uomo molto onorato."

48. Colón 1959:78–80; Morison/Columbus 1963:124–26.

49. For this expression see Castro 1927 and Alvar/Columbus 1976, 2:156n319a.

50. In most cases the fit is better between the modern translation and Ferdinand's text (e.g., "wonderful dignity" for "gravità maravigliosa" in Ferdinand and "estado maravilloso" in the diario; "pleased" for "piacere" in Ferdinand, and "almarraxa" in the diario). Morison referred to Keen's translation several times, whereas Keen did not refer to Morison's translation of the diario, which, though published only in 1963, had apparently been in some state of completion since the late 1930s.

more careful than they could possibly have been or that they were in active collusion.

25 December 1492

Christmas was not a day of glad tidings for Columbus.[51] Overnight the *Santa María* had become grounded and had to be emptied and abandoned, and it is small wonder that Ferdinand thought it worth quoting his source on this occasion. The direct quotation begins with Columbus's mentioning that some of the crew had surveyed the coast and reefs three leagues "al Leste Soeste," a bastardized Spanish form lurking in Ferdinand's Italian text. In the context this can mean only "east southeast," since the fleet was moving in that direction. Las Casas has "leste sueste," but the phrase has caused some problems for modern editors. Keen translated it as an oxymoronic "east-southwest," while in his popularized version of the *Historie,* published several years after the scholarly edition, Caddeo simply transformed "Leste Soeste" into proper modern Italian: "Est-Sud-Est."[52]

In places, the two accounts resemble each other so closely that it is easy to suspect a common source, but discrepancies flare up nonetheless. Las Casas added a few touches, including several words and phrases not in Ferdinand's allegedly verbatim account.[53] As well, the timing of the arrival of the *Pinta* on the scene is differently phrased in the two accounts. According to Ferdinand, since "a great deal of the night had already passed" ("ed era già gran parte della notte passata"), Columbus decided to wait until morning to assess and rectify the damage.[54] Las Casas has it that "though much of the night still remained" ("aún quedaba mucho de la noche"), Columbus thought it prudent not to land with so much darkness left.[55] They agree that he waited until daylight but offer opposite

51. Colón 1930, 1:202–5; Alvar/Columbus 1976, 2:171–75; Dunn and Kelley/ Columbus 1989:276–78.

52. Colón 1959:81; Colón 1945:120.

53. E.g., Las Casas added "barlovento," or "windward," of the location of the *Niña,* on which basis Morison deduced that the *Niña* had "passed ahead" of the *Santa María* (1963:136n5). Las Casas also added "que era su gente" (who were his own men) to express the outrage that Columbus may have felt but which, at least according to Ferdinand, he did not express in writing.

54. Colón 1930, 1:203.

55. Alvar/Columbus 1976, 2:174; Dunn and Kelley/Columbus 1989:279.

reasons. Las Casas's account of the beaching of the *Santa María* is sequentially different and more confused than that of Ferdinand, as though he got lost in his paraphrasis and saw no point in finding his way out.

Apparently the Indians in the area were happy to help Columbus and his men discharge the cargo from the *Santa María*, but Ferdinand and Las Casas differ on the division of this labor. Ferdinand, still quoting his source, recorded that this work was either a joint effort or was accomplished entirely by the ships' crews, since he wrote "ascaricammo" (we unloaded). Las Casas shifted the credit from the crews to the Indians when he transcribed this as "descargó" (he [the cacique and his men] unloaded). To make his point a little more emphatic, Las Casas added a marginal note opposite this passage: "Note here the humanity of the Indians towards the tyrants who have since extirpated them."

To cite these differences is hardly to explain their provenance.[56] It is conceivable that the difference of opinion as to the time of night could reside in the Italian translation rather than in Ferdinand's original text, and it is certainly possible that the log had indicated that the Spanish stood idly by while the Indians unloaded the *Santa María*—scarcely uncharacteristic behavior. Other scenarios are possible too, but (and it is an important but) not one of them is demonstrably the case, leaving us with an option to ignore it all. After all, the differences are largely niggling and do not affect the "big picture" of what happened that Christmas day. On the other hand, they are numerous and troubling enough to undermine Morison's sibylline observation that a comparison of the two texts "shows that Las Casas merely transposed the story to the third person."[57] In a subtle way, Las Casas did more than that.

14 February 1493

According to both the *Historie* and the diario, perhaps the most serious crisis of the voyage occurred on 14 February, when a storm through

---

56. Keen does not come off too well here. In addition to translating "sabbato" as Sunday, he translated "le case" (the houses) as "two houses" and "uomini armati" ("armed men") as "two armed men." Ferdinand mentioned a "stringa" and Las Casas an "alujeta," both of which are most commonly translated as "shoestring," but both Keen and Morison chose the unlikely alternative of "lace point"; Colón 1959:82; Morison/Columbus 1963:136. For brief discussions of "alujeta," see Alvar/Columbus 1976, 2:64n135 and Lyon 1986:25n.

57. Morison/Columbus 1963:136n3.

which the tiny fleet was passing became so violent that Columbus momentarily lost faith in himself and in God.[58] Fearing that the *Niña* would be lost, he prepared a brief account of the discoveries and caused it to be thrown overboard in a cask.[59] There are at least nine discrepancies, not all of them minor, between the account of these events in the diario and that in the *Historie*:

1. The *Historie* credits Columbus with being much concerned that his "critics" ("contraddittori") be "convinced" that he had been right. Las Casas fails to mention this.[60]

2. The wording in the *Historie* makes it clear that the present danger caused the crews to "curse" Columbus and their own failure to force Columbus to turn around on the outward voyage. In contrast, Las Casas phrased his passages to suggest that any mutinous behavior had occurred only on the outward passage, and he even added a marginal note to that effect.

3. Columbus's worst fears, according to both accounts, were for his two sons back in Spain. If he were lost at sea, they would be, according to the *Historie*, "left without help" ("abbandonati di soccorso"). Las Casas gave this a different twist when he wrote that they would be "orphaned of father and mother" ("guérfanos de padre y madre"). Las Casas's statement has caused some perplexity, as well it might, since Ferdinand's mother was still alive.[61] Here Las Casas was technically wrong, but we cannot be sure whether to blame him or a thoughtless Columbus. Or it is possible that Las Casas transcribed accurately here but that Ferdinand rephrased his source, regarding its wording as a slur on his mother. We are left in doubt.[62]

4. Although Las Casas paraphrased most of this episode, or at least

58. Colón 1930, 1:222–24; Alvar/Columbus 1976, 2:222–26; Dunn and Kelley/Columbus 1989:370–72.

59. How he had time to do this under the circumstances is not addressed by any of the sources.

60. But see the fragment in Varela/Columbus 1982:138, which seems to say the same kind of thing. Morison 1939:236–37 states that this fragment came from a "notebook," and so does Varela. But does this not suggest that the contents of the diario were transcribed by Columbus himself into another form?

61. Cioranescu/Columbus 1961:422n421; Morison/Columbus 1963:166n9; Ferro/Columbus 1985:208n; Fuson 1987a:186n2.

62. Manzano (1964:400n) sees this as a case of "legal orphanhoods," while Ramos Pérez (1983b:36n) wonders if Columbus had concluded that Ferdinand's mother had

couched it in the third person, he did quote a brief passage saying that Columbus had written that his weakness and grief "would not let my spirit be made secure" ("no me dexava asensar la anima"), but this time there is no equivalent passage in the *Historie*.[63]

5. In a virtually impenetrable passage, Las Casas wrote (or seemed to write) that Columbus apparently believed that Ferdinand and Isabella would know (in fact "knew," "sabían") about the successes of the voyage from members of their household. This is probably not what either meant to say, and certainly we do not find its counterpart in the *Historie*. It must be regarded as an interpolation or mangling of the text either by Las Casas or an earlier transcriber.[64]

6. Las Casas mentions the Indies by name in this passage, while the *Historie* does not, confining itself instead to the vaguest generalities. This latter is the policy that Columbus himself is likely to have followed at this stage, when he was much closer to Portuguese territory than to Spain.

7. Another evident interpolation occurs in this passage. Las Casas includes a long sentence in which Columbus explicitly denies ("dize") the existence of tempests in the Indies because the grass and trees grew right out into the sea. None of this appears in the verbatim extract in the *Historie*. While this observation sounds very much like something Columbus might have said, the evidence suggests that here Las Casas said it for him.[65]

8. In his description of the contents of the letter Columbus placed in-

---

died while he was *en voyage*. Alvar (Morales Padrón/Columbus 1984:259n1657) elliptically comments that Columbus "appears to avoid" mentioning Ferdinand's mother.

63. "Asensar" is apparently an error for "asegurar"; cf. Las Casas 1951, 1:313. Alvar/Columbus (1976, 2:225n448), Navarrete/Columbus (1825, 1:152n), and Dunn and Kelley/Columbus (1989:371n) all think that Las Casas meant "asentar." In the diario Las Casas actually wrote "antes su flaqueza y congoxa no le dexava (diz que) asentar[?] su anima" and then crossed it out and after a few intervening words, rewrote it as "mas su flaqueza y congoxa (dize el) no me dexava asensar mi [crossed out and replaced by] la anima"; Dunn and Kelley/Columbus 1989:370; and Alvar/Columbus 1976, 1:233n917.

64. Cioranescu instead saw the statement as "the only indication we have that some of the marvelous circumstances concerning Columbus or his projects had been communicated" to Ferdinand and Isabella, but this—whatever it means—is hardly what the diario implies (Cioranescu/Columbus 1961:422n420).

65. Morison/Columbus 1963:166n10 regards this as "a *non sequitur*," since these grew only in sheltered areas, but the lack of logic is probably not Columbus's.

side the cask, Ferdinand mentioned that Columbus offered a reward of a thousand ducats to ensure that the message, if found, would be taken to the Spanish rulers. Las Casas did not include this interesting information in his transcription.[66]

9. The account of this eventful day ends in the *Historie* with a description of how Columbus placed high on the stern another cask (with yet another written account?) in order to double the chances that notice of his achievement would survive him. This passage too is missing from the diario, as though Las Casas regarded this hedge by Columbus as a lack of faith in divine providence.[67]

All in all, these differences are many and varied.[68] Most of them are probably interpolations that appeared later than the shipboard log but earlier than the diario, or the missing information may result from the adroit reticence of either Las Casas or Ferdinand. But however the modern historian chooses to deal with them, they need to be addressed as they occur. It is by no means enough to accept Morison's refrain that this day's record in the *Historie* "adds nothing but a few pious reflections, and again proves the honesty of this abstract by Las Casas."[69] It does nothing of the kind; most of the additional matter consists of inexplicable passages in the diario, not redundant piety in the *Historie*.

15–18 February 1493

This last verbatim extract in the *Historie* is the shortest of the five, and its very brevity is the source of its greatest perplexity for us.[70] During these days the *Niña* sighted Santa Maria, and probably São Miguel, in the Azores, and decided to land at one of them to recover from the effects of

---

66. Ferro/Columbus 1985:206n says that Las Casas "compressed" his source in this passage.

67. Varela/Columbus 1982:127–28n suggests that this second cask must have contained a message similar to the published letter addressed to Luis de Santangel. Cioranescu/Columbus 1961:423n423 goes even farther in hypothesizing that this was the very Santangel letter that Columbus recovered from the cask after the storm as unneeded.

68. With all due respect to, e.g., Asensio y Toledo 1891, 1:386, who regarded the Las Casas text as being copied "without doubt punctiliously."

69. Morison/Columbus 1963:166n7. Readers interested in the storm-at-sea motif in travel literature should consult Doiron 1989.

70. Colón 1930, 1:226–27; Alvar/Columbus 1976, 2:226–28; Dunn and Kelley/Columbus 1989:372–74.

the recent storm. The discrepancies in the account of these activities begin at once. According to the *Historie,* the ship "reached" ("io giunsi") an island as yet unknown to them on Saturday, 16 February, whereas Las Casas recorded that the *Niña,* although spotting an island—in fact two islands—lost sight of them and spent Saturday and Sunday toing and froing in search of them, finally "arriving" ("llegó") at one of them— Santa Maria—only on Sunday night. Then, according to the diario, the ship circumnavigated Santa Maria before coming to rest, losing an anchor in the process. The *Historie* mentions neither the circumnavigation nor the loss of an anchor.[71]

It is already obvious that Las Casas again provides details missing from the *Historie,* which purported to be quoting its source.[72] In fact, while the *Historie* devoted just a little over one hundred words to quoting Columbus, Las Casas expended over twice as many summarizing him! Even Morison, although he adverted to the fact that this material was "quoted in the first person" in the *Historie,* refrained from the obligatory claim that the *Historie* had once again made an honest copyist of Las Casas; but he also declined to explain how it did not.[73]

The idea that a paraphrase can be twice as long as, and can contain data that are not included in, the alleged original is nonsense. How, then, is the anomaly to be explained in this instance? Is it because, in his "zeal" for abridging, Ferdinand skipped over material even while he claimed (or had it claimed for him) that he was quoting verbatim? Were ellipses unknown to him? Or did Las Casas incorporate materials on this occasion from other threads of the memory of the voyage, perhaps from oral tradition? Unfortunately, none of these possibilities can be refuted, though it does not seem likely that Ferdinand would have passed over the episode of the lost anchor if he had encountered it in his sources. And Las Casas's account is once again sorely garbled, as if he tried, not quite successfully, to incorporate disparate and conflicting materials into a coherent whole.

71. Morison 1942, 1:424, even provides a reason for the loss of the anchor!

72. This is another instance of identical wording by Keen (Colón 1959:93) and Morison (Morison/Columbus 1963:167). Both translate the reference to Columbus's stiffness (arthritis?) in the two texts as "crippled in the legs from always being exposed to cold and [to, in Morison] water, and from eating little." Cf. Dunn and Kelley/ Columbus 1989:375.

73. Morison/Columbus 1963:167n3.

II

Where does this series of comparisons leave us? In most cases the differences between the two texts raise more questions than they answer. Our complete ignorance of their composition forces us to consider every possibility and only occasionally to discard any one of them. One such possibility is that both Ferdinand and Las Casas were faithful amanuenses, but of different redactions of the log. If so, Ferdinand's version is probably to be preferred since he is more likely to have had access to early transcriptions, although perhaps not to the original, which was securely in the hands of Spanish officialdom.

The garbled accounts of Las Casas for the events of Christmas 1492 and for 16–18 February 1493 underscore the real difficulty of paraphrasing accurately. These two entries in the diario impress the reader as unsuccessful efforts by Las Casas to extricate himself from a semantic maze at least partly of his own devising. The near absence of extensive corrections in the manuscript of the diario leads us to suspect that Las Casas was occasionally more willing to leave himself enmeshed than to fight his way out.

These comparisons certainly suggest that, with all due respect to Morison and others, Las Casas not only omitted some essential points but almost certainly added others, if they had not already been inserted into his *textus receptus* before he came into possession of it. Some of these passages are blatant anachronisms, and all serve to suggest that this state of affairs is more common among these texts than we would like to believe. Comparing the text of the *Historie* with that of the diario suggests that the latter, like all paraphrases, is a mixture of self and other, author and editor, text and intertext.

III

Finally, by way of an excursus, let us look at the letter that Columbus apparently composed on his return trip and that was destined for the Spanish court.[74] In this letter he tried to synopsize his activities, presum-

74. Any number of editions of the Letter have been published. I use the variorum edition in Ramos Pérez 1986:124–38, but also see Raccolta/Columbus 1892, 1:xxv–liv.

ably on the basis of the diario, his memory, and the urgency imposed on him by the travails that the reduced fleet (only the *Niña* remained with him) was undergoing at the time the letter is dated. The decision to write the letter is not directly mentioned in the diario, although as we have seen, at about the same time it records that Columbus wrote what must have been a similar document, consigned it to a cask, and threw it overboard in hopes that it would survive even if he did not.[75]

Obviously there are good reasons for comparing the testimony of the letter with its presumed major source, the shipboard log, which is also the presumed ultimate source of the diario. The view has generally been favorable. For Morison, and he is by no means alone, "on the whole, the Letter is an excellent précis of the Journal, and proves that Columbus had developed considerable skill in exposition."[76] This may be overstating the case because, while the diario often depicts the triumph of hyperbole over lackluster truth, parts of the Letter take Columbus's thinking well into the realm of fantasy.[77] More of this later, but first something on the peculiarities of the text of the Letter.

The problems begin at once. In all the extant editions the date reads 15 February, which is in the midst of the most severe storm the fleet encountered on the trip. Morison, for one, believes that the Letter should be dated earlier, but the matter must remain open.[78] It may well be, for example, that Columbus began the Letter on 15 February but was forced to postpone completing it until better weather. But there can be no doubt that the statement heading the Letter, to the effect that it was written "aboard the caravel [*Niña*], off the Island of Canaria," is seriously in error.[79] At least as obviously, the statement in the Spanish editions that the fleet required twenty ("veinte") days to cross the Atlantic westward is peculiarly wrong, perhaps intentionally so.[80]

The practice has been to seek convenient scapegoats for these errors

75. For other details see chapter 3.
76. Morison 1942, 1:414.
77. In this sense at least the diario and letter do "complement each other very nicely" (Heers 1981:229).
78. Among those who disagree is Jane 1930a:36n; cf. Ramos Pérez 1983a:23–24.
79. Cioranescu (1959:79–80) suggested that this was a deliberate error to avoid being accused of poaching in Portuguese waters.
80. The Latin edition of the Letter says thirty-three days but counts them from Cádiz, where Columbus had never been; Robbins 1966:8. Counting all the sailings from Palos to Gómera and then to Guanahaní comes to over forty days, and the

and others ("Ferrandina" for "Fernandina," "Isla Bella" for "Isabela," etc.) in the printers, but the incorrect date and place hardly constitute simple mechanical slips.[81] Even less do Columbus's wild overestimates of the ostensible east-west length and overall size of both Cuba and Hispaniola, which can only represent him at his hyperbolic best. He continues in this fashion when he describes sending reconnaissance parties into the interior of Cuba, where they were greeted by people "without number," hardly a fair characterization of the diario. Here we have Columbus crystallizing and intensifying his already frequently overstated views of the flora, fauna, population, and topography of his discoveries. As a result, these elements are in sharper relief in the Letter but are little different in substance.

The same cannot be said of several other descriptions, in which Columbus graduated from hyperbole to unadulterated fancy. Shortly after reaching Cuba, he mentions in passing in the diario a province called "Bafan" or "Basan."[82] In the Letter this province gains a slightly new name, "Avan" or "Anan," as well as purported dimensions (twenty-five to thirty leagues in length), and inhabitants with tails.[83] In similar fashion, in the Letter both Cuba and Hispaniola are said to have gold-bearing streams, mines of gold and other metals, and precisely those spices he expected to find in the Far East but which are not produced in the West Indies. In the process, Columbus's vague and expectant but unrealized statements in the diario become precise and real in the Letter.

Columbus's incurable trouble with numbers is clearly evident in the Letter. There he describes Hispaniola as being eighteen leagues east of Cuba, whereas in the diario it is said to be fifty-four miles, or 13.5 leagues, from Cuba.[84] In a brief postscript to the Letter, Columbus mentions that it was then the very day he sailed into Lisbon, which was

---

elapsed time to over sixty days. Ramos Pérez (1983a:26–27), thinks that the discrepancy is more than a printing error. For yet another permutation, see Varela/Columbus 1982:139–46.

81. E.g., Morison/Columbus 1963:187 considered every such error or discrepancy to be a "misprint."

82. Alvar/Columbus 1976, 2:93, shows "Bafan," while Dunn and Kelley/Columbus 1989:128, have "ba[s?]an."

83. See Morison/Columbus 1963:187n9 for comment.

84. Alvar/Columbus 1976, 2:135; Dunn and Kelley/Columbus 1989:202. See as well Dunn and Kelley/Columbus 1989:203n. It is no doubt merely coincidence that

4 March. The postscript itself, however, is dated 14 March. In this post-script he gives his return voyage as three or four days longer than it actually was and attributes the delay to "tempests," forbearing to mention that he had put into Santa Maria in the Azores.

Under the circumstances, it is small wonder that not all have been as glowing as Morison in their appreciation for the conformity of the diario and the Letter.[85] If the two were written by the same individual, the inconsistencies in the Letter can only highlight similar problems in the diario, and blaming them all on "misprints" only begs the question.[86]

Recently Demetrio Ramos Pérez, convinced that these errors and other anomalies cannot be laid simply to the carelessness of Columbus and/or his printers, has advanced a radical hypothesis: that the Letter as published in 1493 was really an amalgam of parts of a letter Columbus sent from Seville to the court, then at Barcelona, immediately on his return, and parts added by the Spanish court for political reasons.[87] Alarmed by the reaction of João II (discussed below) and wishing to enlist the support of the papacy at the earliest possible moment, Spanish officials, perhaps Luis de Santangel himself, altered for tactical advantage whatever Columbus had written. Unwilling to wait for Columbus to reach Barcelona, these officials made guesses regarding the place and date of composition that proved to be bad ones. The guess regarding place was based on ex-

---

eighteen leagues equals roughly fifty-four nautical miles but seventy-two of Columbus's miles.

85. For a view of the Letter by a literary critic, see Wilson 1977–78, which describes the Letter as Columbus's effort to stake a claim to the rewards promised him before he left. Wilson argues that "rather than a report about a landfall," the Letter was designed as a "testimony to the artistic skill and craftsmanship of Columbus" (1977–78:156). More recently Piedra (1989:47) refers to the Letter as "unedited," whatever that might mean.

86. Modern attempts to unravel the complicated and imperfectly known publication history of the numerous editions of the Letter include *Raccolta*/Columbus, 1:xxv–liv; Jane 1930a; Jane 1930b:cxxii–cxliii; Sanz 1956; Sanz 1958; Ramos Pérez 1986.

87. Ramos Pérez 1986:114–17 and passim. Ramos Pérez first bruited the idea in Ramos Pérez 1977, developed it in Ramos Pérez 1983a, and brought it to fruition in Ramos Pérez 1986. In this last work (pp. 124–38) he provides an extremely useful conspectus of modern efforts to transcribe and edit the Letter, in which the editions of Navarrete and Sanz fare especially poorly.

pediency, as part of an effort to tie the new discoveries as closely as possible to the Canaries, inarguably Spanish by terms of the Treaty of Alcá-çovas of 1479.

Although the matter is not susceptible to proof, Ramos Pérez builds a persuasive case that will be difficult to answer. In a detailed textual analysis, he illustrates how much of the Letter must have been based on Columbus's own testimony, and even his own words, since it dovetails so closely with the diario.[88] But if Columbus composed a chronological précis of the log, this was jettisoned by the court rewriters, who apparently were not interested in, or not alert to the implications of, adhering to such an arrangement. Conversely, as Ramos Pérez demonstrates, the major discrepancies between the Letter and the diario are all of a kind, intended to foster and legitimize Spain's undisputed claim to the new discoveries.

By this argument the contents of the Letter cannot be used to impugn or validate the accuracy of Columbus, or for that matter of Las Casas.[89] Even so, Ramos Pérez's argument allows us to use the Letter as a parable for the contents of the diario by illustrating the lengths to which Spanish officialdom was willing and able to go, and with great dispatch, to fabricate sources by manipulating other sources. The idea that the log may have changed its colors in many ways during its first few months in the tender clutches of the Spanish court will be discussed on several occasions below. These arguments should also be seen in the context of Ramos Pérez's arguments concerning the Letter.

88. Ramos Pérez 1986:69–86.

89. Milhou (1983:105n) exaggerates, though, when he argues that Ramos Pérez's analysis is "a weighty argument in favor of the total probity" of Las Casas as transcriber. See also Watts 1985.

4. Las Casas vs. Las Casas

*It is true during the analysis Hans had to be told many
things which he could not say himself, that he had to be
presented with thoughts which he had so far shown no
signs of possessing, and that his attention had to be turned
in the direction from which his father was expecting
something to come.*   SIGMUND FREUD

We have seen that apart from Ferdinand's *Historie*, Las Casas provided in his *Historia de las Indias* the only account of Columbus's first voyage that can conceivably
be based on anything resembling a shipboard log. There
are significant differences in the two accounts. That of Las Casas is much
longer, more detailed, and more personal. It is also tertiary, but in a most
peculiar way, since it represents his own reinterpretation and recasting of
his earlier interpretation and recasting of his source for the diario. In the
Historia, Las Casas is no longer distilling Columbus but himself. In a
very real sense Las Casas was the precursor of modern attempts to understand the diario, to rationalize it, to encompass its defects and incongruities in a narrative framework that makes sense. Looking at this first
attempt, then, is of particular value to understanding the process.

It is widely assumed that Las Casas was a faithful, even slavish, transcriber, first of the copy of the log and then of himself as he in turn
assimilated the diario into the *Historia*.[1] Here I both test this notion and
discuss the ways in which Las Casas reacted to the diario as a historical
source as he sought to transform it from raw document into both a work
of literary merit and an integral and contributing part of his *Historia*. I
do this by studying the additions, omissions, and other changes that Las
Casas introduced into his account in the *Historia* for the period from the

---

1. See chapters 2 and 3 for more on Las Casas's modern reputation as a transcriber.

evening of 11 October through sometime early in the morning of 16 October, when Columbus began to explore Fernandina.[2]

I

Las Casas's entire oeuvre illustrates the difficulties he had in containing himself, and this is never more obvious than in the text at hand, in which the account of Columbus's first voyage in the *Historia* is roughly twice as long as that in the diario.[3] The bulk of this inflation is vintage Las Casas: digressions in which he expatiated on matters he thought required explanation, defense, or merely greater detail. Sometimes it is fairly obvious when he did this. Often, in fact, Las Casas added such material marginally in the existing manuscripts of the *Historia,* where they can be seen as his afterthoughts as he tinkered with that work during the last years of his life after already tinkering with it for the previous thirty years or so. In many cases the additions are obvious—attacks on Oviedo's credibility, pious moralizing of the kind that Las Casas could only wish that Columbus had uttered, anachronisms, and spirited defenses—and occasional criticisms—of Columbus's behavior. Many of these run to several hundred words and in aggregate constitute the great bulk of the added matter.

On the other hand, Las Casas also interpolated material, sometimes at length, that is less obviously his own work. Generally these interpolations take the form of paeans to the lifestyle of the Indians or the salubrity of the Bahamas, comments that Columbus might well have made in his exuberance but apparently did not. For instance, in a long passage in the *Historia* Las Casas virtually recapitulates the Fountain of Youth notion without mentioning it by name.[4] In fact, this excursus was occasioned by Columbus's observation (which Las Casas quoted verbatim) that he had seen no old people on Guanahaní.[5] As an antidote to this alarming idea, Las Casas speculated that such elderly people must have stayed hidden,

2. For another approach, see Henige n.d.
3. The text of the diario runs to about 3,500 words, that of the relevant parts of the *Historia* to about 7,000 words.
4. Las Casas 1951, 1:203–5.
5. Columbus's statement is probably not to be taken as literally true (see Dunn and

because it was "known" that the islands were festooned with "very old men and women," who were "virtually unable to die" because of the remarkably healthy climate and diet.[6]

Paradoxically, it is the shorter and less obvious intrusions of Las Casas that create greater difficulties. Many of these clearly arose from Las Casas's attempt to interpret Columbus's actions to himself and to any expected audience. In describing the scene in the diario in which Columbus allegedly saw a light several hours before land was sighted, Las Casas added the phrase "de secreto" to explain how he thought Columbus had sought confirmation from Pero Gutiérrez and Rodrigo Sánchez.[7] He may well have done this to explain (if only to himself) why the incident seemed to have so little currency outside the sources based on the log and the despised Oviedo. At any rate, there is no clue in the diario that Columbus called to his colleagues sotto voce.[8] Columbus had described the light as rising and falling, and this prompted Las Casas to offer his own explanation—Indians with torches were going to and fro in answer to nature's call.[9]

Nor was Las Casas immune to adding a word here and a phrase there to suggest states of affairs not at all evident from the unvarnished diario. He wrote that it was "already afternoon" ("ya tarde") when Columbus returned to his ship after landing and claiming Guanahaní, thus allocating him six hours or more on the island.[10] In contrast, the diario implies that Columbus spent very little time there.[11] Accepting this slight addition of Las Casas would entail accepting that Columbus spent enough time on Guanahaní to explore it extensively, thereby enhancing the value of his descriptions of it. Maybe he did, but such information in the *Historia* has far less value than it would have in the diario.

Kelley/Columbus 1989:67n), but even if it were, it was recorded against the first day at Guanahaní and was belied by later statements.

6. Two days later Columbus did admit to seeing at least one old man. Alvar/Columbus 1976, 2:57; Dunn and Kelley/Columbus 1989:74–75.

7. Las Casas 1951, 1:198. See chapter 10 for more details on the situation.

8. The diario uses the term "llamó," or "he called," suggesting quite otherwise.

9. Las Casas 1951, 1:198. Cf. Alvar/Columbus 1976, 1:45–46; Dunn and Kelley/Columbus 1989:58.

10. Las Casas 1951, 1:206. See chapter 11.

11. Alvar/Columbus 1976, 2:48–49; Dunn and Kelley/Columbus 1989:64.

It probably does not matter much that in Las Casas's hands Columbus's "parrots" became "very attractive green parrots" or that he added the information that blancas were "money of Castile," but other apparently insignificant additions may be more consequential.[12] Whereas Columbus found some islands to be merely "very flat," Las Casas went a step further, declaring them in the *Historia* to be "as flat as fruit gardens."[13] Again, probably on the basis of his own observations at other times and in other places, Las Casas provided the information that the boats Columbus saw at Guanahaní were not only long enough to accommodate forty to forty-five men (à la diario) but were also "two cubits and more wide."[14] In the same fashion he added a wealth of detail to Columbus's account of the oars used to paddle these boats, again presumably from his own observations elsewhere.[15]

Las Casas was especially adept at plumbing the unexpressed feelings of the Indians on seeing and meeting and being kidnapped by the newly arrived Spanish, for in several places he vouchsafed just what these feelings were.[16] With regard to the Indians' use of signs to "tell" Columbus whatever he wanted to know, Las Casas added the peculiar remark that communications were conducted thusly "because the hands used to serve here for language" ("porque las manos servían aquí de lengua"), as if the Indians were a race of mutes.[17]

Some of Las Casas's more mischievous additions were his statements that Guanahaní was "fifteen leagues in length more or less" and contained a lagoon "of fresh water."[18] As we will see, these statements (the first repeated by Ferdinand) have caused no end of controversy among those who wish either to believe that Las Casas was mistaken or that he was

12. Las Casas 1951, 1:203–211. Cf. Alvar/Columbus 1976, 2:50, 63, and Dunn and Kelley/Columbus 1989:64, 84.

13. Las Casas 1951, 1:210. Cf. Alvar/Columbus 1976, 2:58, and Dunn and Kelley/Columbus 1989:76.

14. Las Casas 1951, 1:206. Cf. Alvar/Columbus 1976, 2:54. and Dunn and Kelley/Columbus 1989:68.

15. Las Casas 1951, 1:206; cf. Alvar/Columbus 1976, 2:54; Dunn and Kelley/Columbus 1989:68.

16. See, for example, Las Casas 1951, 1:201–2, 206, 211.

17. Las Casas 1951, 1:207. I take Las Casas's use of both the imperfect and "aquí" to mean that he was not rendering a general statement on semiotics.

18. Las Casas 1951, 1:200, 207. On the size of Guanahaní, see chapter 11.

actually providing invaluable data here that were not contained in (or originally transcribed by him from) the diario.

II

Given Las Casas's propensity for adding to the text, we might conclude that his omissions are less instinctive and therefore more important, and such, I think, is the case. Some omissions, generally those where he simply attempted to streamline the repetitiveness of the diario, seem to be no more than efforts to render the *Historia* intelligible enough to be instructive. More often, though, it is obvious that Las Casas had no compunction about suppressing or secreting textual matter that he felt reflected badly on Columbus or the Indians. He was fairly assiduous in this regard. We see, for example, that Columbus's ethnocentric obiter dictum "según la tierra" was dropped from the *Historia,* as was his uncomplimentary characterization that the Indians on Santa María de la Concepción fled from the Spanish "like hens." [19]

Columbus was rehabilitated in other ways as well. His remark in the diario that he would abscond with "all" the cotton he saw if it seemed to grow in any quantity was transcribed into the *Historia* without the "all," as though the original text presented a greedier Columbus than Las Casas preferred to see in his own mind's eye. [20] On the other hand, Las Casas abridged considerably Columbus's account of his releasing an Indian who had come aboard at Santa María de la Concepción. [21]

But if Las Casas was careful to shield Columbus from his own words, he was a great deal more insistent on protecting the Indians from some parts of the diario's account. At one point in the *Historia,* Las Casas professed to quote verbatim a very long passage from the diario, the passage in which Columbus described his initial impressions of the Indians. [22] By and large he did a fairly reasonable job of transcribing this except that right in the middle he omitted a fifty-four-word passage in which Colum-

19. Alvar/Columbus 1976, 2:54, 61; Dunn and Kelley/Columbus 1989:68, 80.

20. Las Casas 1951, 1:207; cf. Alvar/Columbus 1976, 2:56; Dunn and Kelley/ Columbus 1989:72.

21. Las Casas 1951, 1:201. Cf. Alvar/Columbus 1976, 2:61; Dunn and Kelley/ Columbus 1989:80–82.

22. Las Casas 1951, 1:204. For details, see chapter 11.

bus recorded that he saw wounds and scars on these Indians, which he thought had come from raiders from the mainland.[23] Instead, elsewhere in the *Historia* Las Casas tucked away a brief statement to the effect that the Guanahaní Indians sometimes used their "asagayas" to defend themselves from "other people, who *they say* come to do them harm."[24] Later in the diario Columbus reiterated that the inhabitants of "the islands to the northwest come to fight [the Guanahaní Indians] frequently."[25] This statement is absent from the *Historia* even though the statements preceding and succeeding it reside there untouched.[26]

Less obviously tendentious is the way in which Las Casas handled the disorderly text in which Columbus tried to account for his activities early on 15 October. In the diario these are described at some length, if not intelligibility, totaling some 125 words.[27] Las Casas massaged these out of existence in the *Historia*, where two words, "siete leguas," serve as an inadequate surrogate, as he jumped from the account of the preceding evening directly to that for the late afternoon and evening of 15 October.[28] Later in the text Las Casas included a few of the observations in the diario relating to the Indians for that day, but the passage containing the contradictory data on the distance, size, and number of islands Columbus saw, or may have seen, at the time, disappeared from the *Historia,* just as it did from Ferdinand's *Historie.*[29]

Wholesale omissions of this magnitude are rare in the *Historia,* in which elaborate additions are the rule. It seems that, in the missing 120 words or so we have Las Casas's unspoken admission that he was unable to make sense of the diario's account for that day. His editing skills, or at least his willingness to edit, are apparent enough from the account of the light, and we can conclude that he must have found the entry in question to be surpassingly impenetrable. His solution smoothed the way for his readers, but it deprived them of the chance to find their own meaning.

23. For more, see Henige n.d.

24. Las Casas 1951, 1:202, with emphasis added.

25. Alvar/Columbus 1976, 2:55; Dunn and Kelley/Columbus 1989:70.

26. Las Casas 1951, 1:207.

27. Alvar/Columbus 1976, 2:58–59; Dunn and Kelley/Columbus 1989:76–78. See chapter 16.

28. Las Casas 1951, 1:210.

29. Colón 1930, 1:172–73. Perhaps this is an argument for the mutual reliance of these sources on a single Ur–text.

III

In some cases Las Casas chose to modify the record rather than to em-
bellish or eliminate it. Take, for instance, the incident of the Indian whom
Columbus met in the channel between Santa María de la Concepción and
Fernandina. According to the diario, this Indian had in his possession
some bread, a jug of water, a piece of pulverized and kneaded bright
red earth, and "some dry leaves" ("unas hojas secas"), which Columbus
thought "must be something much appreciated among them" ("debe ser
cosa muy apreciada entr'ellos") since he had already been offered some at
Guanahaní.[30] In the *Historia* Las Casas mentions the bread (which he
glossed as "cazabí") and the water but described the other items simply
as "and other things of theirs" ("y otras cosas de las suyas").[31] His reasons
for this reticence are unlikely ever to be known.[32]

Occasionally Las Casas changed things to rescue Columbus from his
obscure prose. He begins by dismembering and rearranging the sequence
of events surrounding the account of the mysterious light.[33] Since the
Salve Regina was traditionally sung at sunset, it was sung at sunset in the
Historia, even though the diario is unambiguous in attributing a singing
of it to around 10:00 P.M. that night.[34] More interestingly, Las Casas
recast in almost pastiche form this peculiar text by changing other times
indicated in the diario. We recall that the diario began the episode by
relating that land was sighted at 2:00 A.M. on the twelfth but then reverts
to an unconvincing account of Columbus's having already seen its *ignis*

30. Alvar/Columbus 1976, 2:63; Dunn and Kelley/Columbus 1989:84.

31. Las Casas 1951, 1:211.

32. Still, for what it's worth, alchemists regarded red powder as an advanced mani-
festation in the long process that would lead to the fabrication of the philosopher's
stone, which in turn would allow lead and other base metals to be transformed into
gold. See Multhauf 1966:191–97; Read 1966:118–65; Ranque 1972; Sadoul 1972:
34–38; Pearsall 1976:46–57. The erudite Las Casas could hardly have been unaware
of the numerous alchemical treatises then in circulation (the matter may turn up more
explicitly elsewhere in his oeuvre), and he might have seen Columbus's statement as
evidence of unseemly dabbling in alchemy. Again, for what it's worth, at some point
the iguana was drawn into the alchemists' world (see Davidson 1987).

33. For the arguments concerning the text about the "light" see chapter 10.

34. Las Casas 1951, 1:198; cf. Alvar/Columbus 1976, 2:46; Dunn and Kelley/
Columbus 1989:60.

fatuus, the light, four hours earlier.[35] Las Casas appears to have concluded that this narration was essentially correct but that the time of Columbus's vision was given incorrectly, because he implies in the *Historia* that Columbus saw the light just before land was sighted.[36]

In his notorious preoccupation with the size of the Indian population, Las Casas made a habit of enlarging on Columbus's account of the numbers of Indians he met, which was itself probably a victim of Columbus's own illusion about having reached the Far East. Whereas the diario records only that on approaching Guanahaní Columbus saw "naked people" ("la gente desnuda"), in the *Historia* this bland statement mushrooms into: "the beach [was] all full of naked people, who covered all the sand and ground" ("la playa toda llena de gente desnuda, que toda el arena y tierra cubrían"), a far more impressive spectacle but one that Columbus seems to have missed.[37] The next day Columbus noted that "many of these men, all young ones" ("muchos d'estos hombres, todo mancebos") came to the shore, many of them swimming out to the ships to trade.[38] This account was apparently not quite enough to satisfy Las Casas's sense of the dramatic, for he wrote instead that "the beach appeared full of people" ("parece la playa llena de gente").[39]

During his last day at Guanahaní, Columbus and some of his men traveled along the coast to reconnoiter the island. Along the way, or so we read in the diario, they saw "people who all came to the beach calling to us and giving thanks to God" ("la gente que venía todos a la playa llamándonos y dando gracias a Dios").[40] The concept of unnumbered and unestimated groups of Indians never appealed to Las Casas; here he wrote of "a great number of people, both men and women" ("un gran número de gente, hombres y mujeres").[41] Two days later Columbus was to find Santa María de la Concepción disappointing despite the rave reviews of

35. Alvar/Columbus 1976, 2:46; Dunn and Kelley/Columbus 1989:60.

36. Las Casas 1951, 1:198.

37. Las Casas 1951, 1:200; cf. Alvar/Columbus 1976, 2:48; Dunn and Kelley/Columbus 1989:62.

38. Alvar/Columbus 1976, 2:53; Dunn and Kelley/Columbus 1989:68.

39. Las Casas 1951, 1:206. Note Las Casas's omission of "mancebos," or "young men."

40. Alvar/Columbus 1976, 2:57; Dunn and Kelley/Columbus 1989:72.

41. Las Casas 1951, 1:208.

the Guanahaní Indians. Although he met "many" people there, he found nothing else to detain him.[42] If Las Casas could make nothing into many, he could certainly make "many" into an "infinite" number, and this he proceeded to do. According to the *Historia*, Columbus saw nothing less on Santa María than "an infinite number of Indians" ("infinitos Indios"), who brought for trade "as much as they had" ("todo cuanto tenían"), another statement absent from the diario.[43]

If Las Casas was inclined to multiply the number of Indians Columbus reported seeing, he adopted the opposite stance with respect to the number of islands Columbus saw on the afternoon of 14 October. Columbus's "so many and so many" ("tantas y tantas"), truly an infinity, was reduced by Las Casas, who wrote merely that Columbus had seen "many islands" ("muchas islas"), a small but interpretively significant switch, and one that presaged innumerable modern attempts to come to grips with Columbus's words.[44]

Another equally important twist accompanied Las Casas's rewriting of this passage. In the diario we are told that Columbus first saw these islands and then was told by the Indians that there were more than one hundred of them, which they proceeded to name.[45] In the *Historia* another reshuffling takes place. Columbus asks about the islands even before departing from Guanahaní and is greeted with the litany of over one hundred names.[46] Then he sails and sees them, or many of them. However reasonable this set of events might seem, this was an editorial liberty not countenanced by the diario account.

Several other changes are either unaccountable or represent Las Casas's deliberate or random editing of the text in front of him. Among the former is his rendering of the "great urns of gold" ("grandes vasos de oro") as "many urns of gold" ("muchos vasos de oro"), where the difference in meaning is considerably more obvious than the reason for it.[47] As well, Las Casas changed the phrase "en el camino del nornordeste" into the

42. Alvar/Columbus 1976, 2:60; Dunn and Kelley/Columbus 1989:78.

43. Las Casas 1951, 1:210.

44. Las Casas 1951, 1:210. Cf. Alvar/Columbus 1976, 2:58; Dunn and Kelley/Columbus 1989:76. Also, see chapter 15.

45. Alvar/Columbus 1976, 2:58; Dunn and Kelley/Columbus 1989:76.

46. Las Casas 1951, 1:211.

47. Las Casas 1951, 1:207. Cf. Alvar/Columbus 1976, 2:55; Dunn and Kelley/Columbus 1989:70.

more specific but not necessarily more accurate "por el nornordeste."[48]
In the diario Columbus estimates the distance from Santa María de la
Concepción to Fernandina on different occasions as both eight leagues
and nine.[49] Las Casas simply combined these and recorded one rough
estimate: "about eight or nine leagues" ("obra de ocho leguas o nueve").[50]

IV

In the *Historia,* Las Casas exercised a historian's prerogative to paraphrase and tidy up his sources in order to support a particular narrative
thread or line of reasoning more effectively. In doing so he accepted the
concomitant onus of being judged on the extent to which he preserved
the meaning and "flavor" of these sources. It is important not to conduct
such an inquest anachronistically by applying to Las Casas the more exacting norms that have evolved in succeeding centuries. One way to assess
without judging is simply to inquire as to what degree our view of these
crucial days of Columbus's first voyage would differ if we had to depend
only on the *Historia* without the diario to supplement it.

In the first place, we would have a streamlined and rationalized exposition of incidents like that of the light, which would have the effect of
leading us to believe that Columbus actually saw it or was sensibly convinced that he had. In turn, this would appreciably affect our view of the
landfall, since it would require that those advocating an outer-rim island
do more than point out the incongruities of the primary text.

Of even greater effect would be to treat in isolation Las Casas's statement in the *Historia* that Guanahaní was fifteen leagues long. Without
the silence of the diario to challenge it, the statement could only wreak
havoc on nearly every proposed itinerary, particularly since it finds corroboration in Ferdinand's version. There is no hint whatever in the text
of the *Historia* that Las Casas did not derive this datum from the diario,
and his authority, combined with that of Ferdinand, would surely have
forced the debate along entirely different lines.

So too would the necessity of dealing with 15 October as a virtual

48. Las Casas 1951, 1:207. Cf. Alvar/Columbus 1976, 2:56–57; Dunn and Kelley/
Columbus 1989:70–72. For Columbus's itinerary during the morning of 14 October,
see chapter 14.
49. Alvar/Columbus 1976, 2:62; Dunn and Kelley/Columbus 1989:82.
50. Las Casas 1951, 1:211.

blank in the historical record, a necessity that would be imposed if only Las Casas's version as expressed in the *Historia* had survived. Lacunae of this nature have not impeded many interpreters from positing one route or another, but it would certainly have imposed an even greater burden on their ingenuity than does the diario along with the *Historia*.

Beyond the issue of the landfall is the matter of historical demography. A recently influential school of thought places much credence in Las Casas's numbers in the *Historia* and in his *Brevísima relación*, none of which is too large for its members to digest. We see Las Casas the demographer busily at work in the *Historia*, where he took every opportunity to create an impression of islands teeming with inhabitants, an impression that the diario seriously undermines.[51] By the same token, Las Casas is far more favorable to other aspects of Indian life than the diario permits. In terms of their pacificity, agricultural expertise, and numbers, the *Historia* distorts the record of the diario while retaining its form and hence its aegis.

Some might wonder whether these arguments are worth making. After all, we do have the diario, and we need rely on the *Historia* only infrequently for details of the first voyage. But we should remember that we lack many of the other sources on which Las Casas purported to base his *Historia*, and so, *faute de mieux*, we find it easy to believe that in the *Historia* we are viewing these sources only slightly removed. The inclination to treat paraphrased primary sources as originals is an entirely natural one but one that here would be too ingenuous by a healthy margin. In quest of the primary source, we need not shrink from scrutinizing each word of both the diario and the *Historia* in order to appreciate the nature and degree of any differences. This is not only an exercise in textual criticism, it is also a test of Las Casas's credibility in other respects. For we can hardly forget that he too was the author of the diario.

51. In the *Brevísima relación* Las Casas gave some precision to this notion by professing to believe that the Bahamas had had a population of "more than 500,000" people in 1492 (Las Casas 1982:73).

5. Modern Editors vs. the Diario

In short, the question is not what the Author might have
said, but what he actually said; it is not whether a different
Word will agree with the sense, and turn of the Period, but
whether it was used by the Author; If it was, it has a good
Title still to maintain its post, and the authority of the
Manuscript ought to be follow'd rather than the fancy of
the Editor.   WILLIAM BROOME

In 1939 Samuel Eliot Morison reviewed two editions and
five translations of the diario.[1] Pronouncing them all
wanting in various respects, he announced his own forthcoming translation. As Morison duly noted, his survey
was the first attempt to view modern editions and translations of the
diario critically and conspectively, and it turned out to be the last as well.
The time has come to attempt a similar exercise, but before doing so we
should look at Morison's own study, especially at the criteria he adopted
to distinguish good editorial and translating practices from poor ones.

Not unexpectedly, Morison's principal criterion was the way in which
editors handled Columbus's nautical and navigational activities. He was
surprised whenever an editor or translator with a naval background did
poorly in this regard, and even more astonished when a mere landlubber
(or "average scholar") managed to do well.[2] He was particularly critical,
for instance, of various translators' inability to intuit Columbus's mode
of expressing points of the compass and of their problems in correctly
identifying species of birds. Like others before and since, Morison found
it hard to speak kindly of Markham's translation even though Markham
"had served in the Royal Navy in the days of sail."[3]

---

1. Morison 1939b. For a list of the major, and many minor, editions, see Conti
1986:101–9, and Taviani/Columbus 1988: 2, 455–69.

2. Morison 1939b:243.

3. Morison 1939b:251. For other criticisms of Markham, see Diffie 1936; Bernstein
and Diffie 1937; Henige 1986b:297–98.

For our purposes, however, Morison's attitude toward the editions of Navarrete and de Lollis are of more interest. He found Navarrete's pioneering edition to be "carefully and faithfully made in accordance with the editorial standards" of its time, though he pointed out a few instances of mistranscription, dittography, and of course the inevitably incorrect bearings.[4] He complimented Navarrete on being better able to understand Columbus's nautical terminology because he was "nearer in thought, feeling, and experience to the seamen of Columbus's day" than any later editor, and moreover, he was prominent in the Spanish naval service.[5] But he found Navarrete's interpretations of Columbus's route largely faulty because he had had little or no direct experience in the West Indies. In regard to the text proper, Morison noted that Navarrete had expanded abbreviations, changed punctuation, modernized spelling, and spelled out all numbers, but apparently he found these procedures excusable, even desirable. As for the substantive changes Navarrete had made in the text, Morison considered them to have been "properly" done.[6]

Quite rightly, Morison regarded the edition of de Lollis in the *Raccolta Colombiana* as the best achieved to that time, both in the care taken with the transcription and in the textual apparatus de Lollis supplied, which among other things identified many differences between the text of the diario and Navarrete's transcription. Morison concluded, "If one accepts, as we do, the principle that old documents should be treated by this 'expanded' method, rather than printed with all their abbreviations and contractions *literatim et verbatim,* there is little to say in criticism of de Lollis's text."[7]

In sum, Morison, here the latitudinarian, favored an unrestricted editorial hand, changing the text to whatever extent was necessary to make it readable, including correcting obvious, and even probable, errors silently and ignoring all the scribal changes and additions in the manuscript of the diario as we now have it. Rather than calling for a diplomatic text, Morison seemed to regard such a thing as little more than an annoyance that would keep the "real" Columbus from interested readers.

Morison's own promised translation took nearly a quarter century to

4. Morison 1939b:240–43.
5. Morison 1939b:243.
6. Morison 1939b:241.
7. Morison 1939b:247. For more on the expanded method of historical editing see Morison's discussion in the *Harvard Guide* (Handlin et al. 1954:95–104).

appear.[8] Since then Alvar's juxtaposed quasi-diplomatic and modernized transcription has been published, as has the very similar Morales Padrón edition and Dunn and Kelley's diplomatic transcription with translation and concordance.[9] Presumably, Morison would not consider these to be useful, but in fact they are nearly two centuries overdue. Here I wish to look at various modern editions of the diario in ways that Morison would not have considered important. I argue that they are not only important but crucial, and in doing so I hope to put the modern editing history and practice of the diario into the larger context of the documentary editing discussed in chapter 2. Before doing this, however, it would be useful to discuss briefly the nature and value of a diplomatic edition of a text, because even though such editions of the diario are at long last available, their belated arrival says much about the attitude of modern editors toward the diario.

I

To coin a phrase, no text is an island. Even Las Casas's holograph of the diario—which has no extant antecedents, no self-expressed context of its own, and no known copies—can be viewed diachronically. Even as it survives it represents to its users a text on the way to being. Alvar, whose edition of the diario, supplemented by extensive annotation, will remain indispensable though no longer unique, lists more than a thousand changes in the text, occasions in which Las Casas added words or phrases, erased, crossed out, or otherwise changed what he had already written.[10] In addition, Las Casas added some 200 marginal notes. All of these—and the point cannot be emphasized strongly enough—are integral parts of the text of the diario, whose author is not Christopher Columbus but Bartolomé de las Casas.

8. Morison/Columbus 1963. In the meantime Jos (1950) provided an update to Morison, largely dedicated to criticizing Cecil Jane for criticizing the diario.

9. Alvar/Columbus 1976; Morales Padrón/Columbus 1984; Dunn and Kelley/ Columbus 1989. I have reviewed these in Henige 1990a. Add to those now Taviani/Columbus 1988 and Varela/Columbus 1989.

10. Alvar/Columbus 1976, 1:65–250. Whereas throughout this study I have relied on the second volume of Alvar's edition of the diario for transcriptions, in this chapter most of my citations will be to the first volume, in which Alvar discusses the text of the diario per se.

By definition, a diplomatic, or genetic, edition tries to capture a process as well as its results by providing access to all that survives of an author's thoughts as physically preserved in a text. It does this by trying to preserve to the extent possible the format of the original by reproducing the size, placement, and nature of all changes. It may include a facsimile of the original, but it is essentially a serious attempt to put the text within easier reach of a wider public.

The benefits of this approach can be seen by looking at the differences between Alvar's edition and that of Dunn and Kelley. In reconstituting the diario's text, Alvar took great pains to express in his footnotes the ways in which the changes had become part of the document. But he occasionally overplayed his hand, sometimes by being too punctilious, reminding us again that no amount of words can paint a picture.[11] In one sense, any genetic edition of the diario must differ from such editions of other texts. Ordinarily, a genetic edition earns its name by comparing existing manuscript variants of a text and seeking to establish from among them the one text that most truly represents the hypothesized "original" as conceived by its author. In the case of the diario, of course, this is not possible since it is a unique redaction.

It is extraordinary that until 1976 there was no serious effort to treat the text of the diario integrally. Even the *Raccolta* edition, for all its massive apparatus, allowed most of the 1,200 additions in the diario to pass unnoticed. In what follows I hope to show the effects of this procedure on interpreting the diario by discussing the practices of silent emendation and other, though less mortal, forms of editorial impropriety.

As an example of silent emendation it is appropriate to treat the edition prepared by Carlos Sanz as representative of many modern editions.[12] By providing the best published facsimile of the holograph diario to its time and by following it with a transcription that marches in lockstep with it line by line, Sanz's edition seemed to offer a chance finally to recapture the full text of the diario. It even included most of the substantive marginal notes of Las Casas.

The first hint that these hopes might not be fulfilled comes in the twenty-page introduction Sanz provided. Most of this is devoted to an appreciative recapitulation of Columbus's achievements; not a word is

---

11. In many cases, even a facsimile is no substitute for the original; see Tanselle 1989.

12. Sanz/Columbus 1962. See chapter 2.

said about the editorial policies and practices that shaped the edition that follows. These must be deduced from a collation of the transcription with the holograph text, and the results are by no means a testimonial to Sanz's care and consistency. The transcribed text was changed at will. For instance, Sanz's transcription disagrees with its own source on nearly 20 percent of the numbers used on the outward voyage, primarily because Sanz declined to use any Roman numerals at all. And of course, he expanded all contractions, modernized spelling and punctuation, added capitalization, and so forth. Furthermore, as a service to the reader he enclosed what he supposed to be direct discourse in the diario in quotation marks and italicized it as well. Other characteristics of the Sanz transcription will be addressed as the discussion proceeds.

Sanz's farrago of a text is no worse than most, and it is better than many, but the unabashed juxtaposition of modern editorial legerdemain with its supposed exemplar provides a particularly salutary example of the estrangement of modern editorial practice from widely accepted principles of textual editing, in which silent emendation is the cardinal sin. This is especially so, of course, when the "corrections" themselves are not justified.[13]

II

By presenting only the residue of the diario, most modern editions inevitably offer the impression of a manuscript unsullied by change, a finished product without blemish, and a transcriber who worked with astonishing perfection. In fact, as we have seen, Las Casas or someone else changed the original record more than a thousand times. The average of fifteen changes per double-sided folio is by no means excessive, but its aggregate is a substantial body of evidence that requires considerably more study than it has been accorded, which is virtually none at all.[14]

The changes include both corrections and additions to the text as first written, and they take three forms. Sometimes a word or phrase is

13. To make matters worse, modern editors are now silently emending their own predecessors. For instance, Vigneras (in Jane/Columbus 1960) made unacknowledged changes in Jane's translation as he re-edited it.

14. For the importance of placement and paleography in examining a text, see Bately 1988 and Boyle 1988. The study of erasures in textual criticism is exemplified by Moberg 1989.

crossed out and is followed immediately by a correction. In other cases, material is added in one of the margins. Finally, Las Casas very often changed the text by interlineating corrections above and near the point to which the interlineated matter refers. This pattern is suggestive, for it shows that he often failed to notice "errors" until after he had continued writing to the point where it was no longer possible simply to make the change immediately after the error.[15] In fact, it is quite possible that many of the marginal and interlineated corrections and additions were added long after the original transcription had been made.[16]

The most common forms of transcriptional error involve dittography (in which a word or phrase is inadvertently repeated, particularly at the end of one line or page and the beginning of the next) and haplography, or eyeskip (in which material is omitted). Las Casas seems to have been particularly prone to an acute form of the latter. Very often he began a word or phrase only to scratch it out. Frequently in these cases the word or words occur farther along in the passage, which suggests that Las Casas let his eye outrun his pen more often than many scribes. In some cases, a few of which will be noted later, he crossed out material that did not recur later in the text.[17]

In more than a dozen cases, Las Casas wrote and then crossed out most of a line or more. Three of these occur in the entries for the period from 22 to 30 September, when Columbus was apparently having much greater trouble controlling and mollifying the crews than the diario lets on.[18] The other instances are scattered throughout the text more haphazardly.[19] All seem to indicate Las Casas's substantial dissatisfaction with what he had written in paraphrase.

15. Only Dunn and Kelley/Columbus 1989 portray this process graphically. Alvar and others have done so through footnotes.

16. Perhaps a dozen times Dunn and Kelley suggest that a particular addition was an "insertion" or an "afterthought," but they attempt no discussion of the implications of this, which of course may well be much more widespread; see, e.g., Dunn and Kelley/Columbus 1989:121, 137, 141, 155.

17. He also had the habit of crossing out the repeated, rather than the repeating, word or phrase.

18. Alvar/Columbus 1976, 1:76n46; 76n49 (discussed below); 79n64; Dunn and Kelley/Columbus 1989:38, 40, 46.

19. Alvar/Columbus 1976, 1:82n78, 82n79, 126n250, 132n289, 133n295, 137n321, 171n527, 175n553, 180n585, 180n586, 180n588, 181n590, 183n614, 201n721; Dunn and Kelley/Columbus 1989:54, 156, 168, 170, 176, 244, 254, 264, 270, 304.

Modern scholars have often decried Las Casas's treatment of numbers in the diario, particularly when it suits their hypotheses to attribute errors to him in this respect. Viewed conspectively, though, Las Casas did not have a great deal of difficulty in recording either numbers or directions, at least as measured by how often he changed these in the manuscript. On the outward voyage he changed the distance traveled five times, or about one in twenty chances.[20] Only one of these cases seems unusual, when he substituted "XXX" for "quatorze" on 22 September.[21] For 7 December he made the opposite change: "diez y seis" for "XX."[22] And for 11 January "15" became "quinze" for no obvious reason.[23]

Twice Las Casas changed numbers in a way that suggests that the frequent conversions from leagues to miles in the diario resulted from his own calculations rather than those of Columbus. On 6 August he wrote "veynte" above a crossed-out "diez," and near the end of the voyage, "ocho leguas" became by interlineation "diez [y] ocho," to match the preceding "setenta y dos millas."[24] Such errors involving tens often occur in mental division, but it is anyone's guess whether they are errors Columbus made that went undetected until the time of Las Casas, errors that Las Casas made and quickly noticed, or errors someone else noticed and changed.

Morison and others have often attributed apparent errors in direction to Las Casas, but in only a few times in the diario did Las Casas change a direction already written to another, and in no case was the change significant. In fact, a few times it was no more than a matter of correcting a misspelling.[25]

Another charge frequently leveled at Las Casas is that he often confused leagues with miles. The record of changes on the diario is interesting here. Twelve times Las Casas changed "leguas" to "millas" but never

20. Alvar/Columbus 1976, 1:71n16, 72n23, 72n26, 73n34; Dunn and Kelley/Columbus 1989:28, 32, 34.

21. Alvar/Columbus 1976, 1:75n45; Dunn and Kelley/Columbus 1989:38.

22. Alvar/Columbus 1976, 1:154n430. Dunn and Kelley/Columbus 1989:210n indicates uncertainty as to the number canceled.

23. Alvar/Columbus 1976, 1:210n768; Dunn and Kelley/Columbus 1989:324.

24. Alvar/Columbus 1976, 1:68n5, 222n848a; Dunn and Kelley/Columbus 1989: 22, 348. See below, chapter 10.

25. Alvar/Columbus 1976, 1:83n85 (SW), 98n123 (SW), 98n127 (SW), 206n744 (E from W), 211n771 (NW); 223n854 (NW); 225n861 (NE); Dunn and Kelley/Columbus 1989:56, 94, 96, 314, 326, 352, 354.

the reverse.[26] In seven of the twelve cases the word "millas" is inter-lineated above "leguas," and in one it is added in the margin.[27] In four cases Las Casas detected the "error" immediately and made the change in the same line of the text (twice before "leguas" was even completed).[28] A pattern as consistent as this suggests that one of Las Casas's standard operating procedures was to compare all the numbers in his transcription with the copy he used. If so, we might well have reason to think that few errors remained—at least, few transcriptional errors—with regard to the distances recorded in the diario.

Las Casas had minor problems with days, dates, and times of day. For "13 setiembre" he first wrote "13 otubre," which is rather peculiar but perhaps no more than this.[29] In the combined entry for 11/12 October, Las Casas or someone else interlineated "viernes" to indicate that a new day had begun.[30] This appears to be a later inclusion, because if Colum-bus had noted the change of day as he wrote the log, he would certainly have begun a new entry. Finally, the heading for 22 November reads only "Jueves, 22," with the month missing.[31]

In two instances it seems that Las Casas corrected Columbus by first writing whatever was in his copy and then changing it to what he knew to be the case, a practice he usually reserved for his marginal notes. For 14 December the word "tjra" ("tierra") is crossed out and replaced by "isla" when Columbus was describing Tortuga.[32] Eight days later Las Casas wrote "yndias" and then changed it to "yslas," referring to places the Indians claimed were auriferous.[33] Since in both cases the changes were interlineated, any conclusions as to their significance must be tempered.

    26. On this matter, see Dunn and Kelley/Columbus 1989:10, 59n.
    27. Alvar/Columbus 1976, 1:70n14, 82n74, 83n80, 84n88 (marginal), 219n832, 224n859, 226n866, 227n868; Dunn and Kelley/Columbus 1989:28, 52, 54, 58, 342, 352, 356, 358.
    28. Alvar/Columbus 1976, 1:106n155, 149n400; Dunn and Kelley/Columbus 1989: 114, 200.
    29. Alvar/Columbus 1976, 1:71n17; Dunn and Kelley/Columbus 1989:30.
    30. Alvar/Columbus 1976, 1:85n94; Dunn and Kelley/Columbus 1989:60. On the date of the discovery, see below, chapter 10.
    31. Alvar/Columbus 1976, 1:131; Dunn and Kelley/Columbus 1989:164.
    32. Alvar/Columbus 1976, 1:162n478; Dunn and Kelley/Columbus 1989:226.
    33. Alvar/Columbus 1976, 1:179n581; Dunn and Kelley/Columbus 1989:262.

A particularly arresting set of changes are the three places where Las Casas wrote "es" (is) and then changed it to "era" (was) and the one case in which the reverse occurred, all within a three-week period. The first three examples occur in an admitted paraphrase, and "era" is in each case added above "es."[34] The fourth case is more involved. Here the word "es" is written very faintly in the margin, and it makes the relevant phrase read: "Mas es [replacing "era"] tanto y en tantos lugares y en esta misma isla Española, dize el Almirante, que es maravilla." ("But there is so much [gold] and in so many places and on this very island Hispaniola, the Admiral says, that it is marvelous").[35] It looks as though at some point either Las Casas or another copyist decided to harmonize the verbs in this sentence and chose to use the present tense for the purpose. But if it was intended to be a direct quotation, would Las Casas have written "era" in the first place?[36]

The vexing question of identifying direct quotations within the text has excited little attention. There seems to be a loose and unstated consensus in the matter, but it is not at all clear on what it is based. As noted, in his edition Sanz italicized those passages that he considered verbatim and enclosed them in quotation marks as well in another example of editorial overkill. Alvar frequently differed with Sanz's conclusions, especially after 1 November, where Sanz seldom used quotation marks at all. In this he was more in tune with Las Casas, who of course used no quotation marks at all since they were just beginning to evolve into the customary sign to indicate direct speech or exact borrowing.[37]

In short, Sanz and Alvar disagree on the matter, and both disagree with Las Casas, who is himself inconsistent, using several ways to indicate by both words and signs where he was beginning and ending what we would consider a direct quote.[38] The usual criteria for divining a direct quote in

34. Alvar/Columbus 1976, 1:159n462 (12 December), 169n518 (18 December), 189n649 (26 December); Dunn and Kelley/Columbus 1989:220, 240, 282.

35. Alvar/Columbus 1976, 1:196n693 (29 December); Dunn and Kelley/Columbus 1989:294; Sanz 1962:49r.

36. On the other hand, Morison/Columbus 1963:140 presents it as a direct quote, as does Cioranescu/Columbus 1961:137 and Varela/Columbus 1982:103.

37. See Henige n.d.

38. Morison/Columbus 1963 places about 5 percent more material within quotation marks than does Sanz/Columbus 1962. On quoting sources in early times, see McGurk 1961 and Romilly 1988.

the diario are for Las Casas to speak of "the very words" ("las palabras formales") of Columbus, to have Columbus apostrophize Ferdinand and Isabella, or simply to use the first person. In the above case, his use of the present tense would apparently serve the same end, although in truth Las Casas used many present tenses throughout the diario, whether purporting to quote or not.

In a few cases Las Casas made puzzling changes in text that he was allegedly quoting. For 14 October he first wrote "tierra," then crossed it out and wrote "cerca" above it, so that the phrase reads "que cerca toda aquella isla alrededor" ("that completely circled all that island [Guanahaní]").[39] For 3 December the phrase "ellos son gentes" (they are people) is crossed out and replaced by "los marineros," which is not even remotely similar.[40] The phrase recurs more than thirty words later, too distant even for Las Casas to have anticipated it. For the same date Las Casas first wrote "si era [sic] casa de oración" ("if it were a place of worship"), then crossed it out and replaced it with a similar—but different enough—"si hazían en ella oración" ("if they made prayer in it").[41] Finally, on 12 November Las Casas first recorded "niñas" and then replaced it interlineally with "chicas," both words meaning girls.[42] If Las Casas had been paraphrasing in these instances, such changes would mean little beyond indicating a few of his discursive predilections, but as he claimed to be quoting each time, it is necessary to ask where he came by the phrases he first wrote and then changed, as well as why these changes were made interlineally instead of on the spot if he were carefully reproducing the text in front of him.

In fact, the changes highlight one difference between the paraphrased text of the diario and that which is quoted. As might be expected, Las Casas generally made fewer changes in the latter. In the two folio pages of the prologue, there is but a single change.[43] In the extended verbatim

---

39. Alvar/Columbus 1976, 1:89n101. Dunn and Kelley/Columbus 1989:75n, read the replacement as "çerca."

40. Alvar/Columbus 1976, 1:147n385; Dunn and Kelley/Columbus 1989:196.

41. Alvar/Columbus 1976, 1:147n388; Dunn and Kelley/Columbus 1989:196.

42. Alvar/Columbus 1976, 1:122n223; Dunn and Kelley/Columbus 1989:146. Nowadays, "chica/o" is often more narrowly applied specifically to adolescents, but this cannot account for Las Casas's change.

43. Alvar/Columbus 1976, 1:65–67; Dunn and Kelley/Columbus 1989:16–20.

passage running from 12 to 24 October—a total of more than seventeen folio pages and three thousand words—Alvar recorded only fifty-two changes, or three per folio page. This is about 40 percent of the average for the whole work and even less of the average for the paraphrased passages only.[44] With a few exceptions, this pattern holds up throughout the diario. From this we can conclude that Las Casas either took a great deal more care in transcribing Columbus's own words or was content to let it appear that way. Alternatively, it would reinforce the view created by the high incidence of marginal and interlinear changes that at some later point Las Casas or another scribe returned to the text as it had been transcribed and introduced whatever changes were deemed necessary. Presumably, in doing this he would be less willing to tamper with the purported words of Columbus than with the rest of the text.

Much more needs to be done in the study of the changes effected in the holograph of the diario, a task rendered a great deal easier with the editions of Alvar, Dunn and Kelley, and others, which at last allow access to Las Casas as he transcribed. An early task of any such study should be to segregate intralineal, interlineal, and marginal changes from each other and to study them from the perspective of both their placement and their content.[45]

For 23 September Las Casas first wrote "la mar andava muy alta y sin viento" ("the sea was very rough and there was no wind") and then, perhaps recognizing the oxymoronic quality of his paraphrase, changed it immediately to "como la mar estuviese mansa y llana" ("since the sea had been calm and smooth").[46] This procedure is the most likely way in which a careful transcriber cum paraphrast would operate, yet this change is a rare example compared to the hundreds of similar changes that, because of their position in the manuscript, could have been made at any time after the completion of the original transcript, and not necessarily by Las

44. Alvar/Columbus 1976, 1:87n97–105n148; Dunn and Kelley/Columbus 1989: 64–112.

45. And their placement throughout the whole of the text as well. Nearly 60 percent are in the last half, and the changes per folio page are about twice as many from folio 24, which begins with 15 November. For similar thoughts on the Domesday Book, see Gullick and Thorn 1986.

46. Alvar/Columbus 1976, 1:76n49 (who omitted the interlineated "muy"); Dunn and Kelley/Columbus 1989:40.

Casas. Not to belabor the point, but this contamination of the text of the diario by what may have been various hands is diagnostically crucial in assessing its meaning, though the changes are adroitly brushed aside in modern editions.

III

The difference between apparent error and obvious error is often only in the eye of the beholder. Still, no one is likely to disagree that the entry between that dated "30 otubre" and that dated "1 noviembre" is glaringly misdated, for its heading reads "31 noviembre."[47] With the exception of de Lollis, Alvar, Alvar and Morales Padrón, Dunn and Kelley, and the latest edition of Varela, all modern editions have changed this date as a matter of course and without indication.[48] From Navarrete's copyist in the 1790s until the present, this entry stands dated as "31 otubre" and "31 October" in editions and translations, which, of course, it clearly should be in the real world divorced from the text and just as clearly is not in the text itself.[49] No doubt the assumption has been that this was simply a slip of the pen that for some reason Las Casas failed to notice, despite its egregiousness. Why he failed to notice it, or at least to change it, probably should have drawn more attention. After all, when Las Casas made other mistakes in dating entries, he usually changed them, perhaps almost as soon as he made them.[50]

Looking to the *Historia de las Indias* for this entry's counterpart there, we find Las Casas forgoing his only other opportunity to use the date of 31 October, and doing so with remarkable persistence. As noted earlier, two holographs of the *Historia* survive, one entirely in Las Casas's hand, the other by a copyist but with annotations and corrections by Las Casas for about two-thirds of the text. In both these manuscripts Las Casas

47. Alvar/Columbus 1976, 1:111n176; Dunn and Kelley/Columbus 1989:124.

48. Alvar corrected it in the second volume of his edition; see Alvar/Columbus 1976, 2:92.

49. Navarrete/Columbus 1971:53; Navarrete/Columbus 1825, 1:45; Sanz/Columbus 1962:19v; Varela/Columbus 1982:48; Arranz/Columbus 1985:112.

50. For example, Las Casas originally wrote "29 de hebrero" for both 1 March and 2 March before going back to correct them. Alvar/Columbus 1976, 1:143n974, 143n975; Dunn and Kelley/Columbus 1989:388.

wrote, or let stand, "el martes, 30 de otubre," followed by an account of the events of that day.[51] It was a busy day, so it was about 500 words later that he had occasion to go on to the next day, which he noted, was "el miércoles, 30 de otubre." Immediately following this he went on to say: "luego, jueves siguiente, 1° de noviembre."[52]

Perhaps the span of text between the two former dates permitted editors of the *Historia* to overlook this incongruity, and perhaps we should be grateful for that lest they, too, had silently emended Las Casas's text here to conform to reality. At any rate, there seems to be no doubt that, while Las Casas's dating of the last day of October in 1492 in the diario was an error, it was not an accident. While knowing this may not enable us to understand Columbus's activities any better, it does provide an intriguing glimpse into Las Casas, the prism between ourselves and Columbus. Just what that understanding is, I hesitate to say. It could simply be that in three distinct instances Las Casas coincidentally made the same very obvious and very peculiar error, but it would be a grand piece of credulity to accept this. Perhaps he had a deep-seated aversion to All Hallows' Eve; who can say?[53] But the inability to explain this anomaly satisfactorily is scarcely reason to ignore it. It is unlikely that any of the editors who changed it in the diario were aware of Las Casas's parallel practice in the *Historia,* but by changing it they closed the door on the question, standing between reader and text, obscuring the latter's complexity at the former's expense.

The diario entry for 16 October begins: "Partí de las isla de Sancta María de la Concepción" and goes on to describe the trip to the island Columbus called Fernandina.[54] The words "de las isla" represent a classic microcosm of the diario: they are self-evidently in error; they offer two

51. Las Casas 1875–76, 1:322; Las Casas 1927, 1:224; Las Casas 1951, 1:223; Las Casas 1957, 1:157.

52. Las Casas 1875–76, 1:325; Las Casas 1927, 1:226; Las Casas 1951, 1:275; Las Casas 1957, 1:158.

53. This dovetails with Gil's belief that Las Casas's eschatology prompted him to change the date of the discovery from 11 to 12 October. See Gil 1984:73–75, and below, chapter 10.

54. Alvar/Columbus 1976, 1:94 (who corrected it in the text); Dunn and Kelley/Columbus 1989:84, 85n. In his accompanying transcription Sanz rendered it as "de las islas" (Sanz/Columbus 1962:12v). See below, chapter 16.

choices, one the opposite of the other; and they provide no help whatever in deciding between them. The modern handling of this couplet is itself vivid testimony to the implications of silent emendation.[55]

The problem began at once. Navarrete's copyist rendered the phrase as "de las islas," and of course Navarrete followed suit in the first published edition of the diario.[56] Since all the editions and translations before 1892 derived from Navarrete rather than the holograph, all inevitably rendered the phrase as "de las islas," "from these islands," or "des îles."[57] After all, there is nothing downright implausible about considering the island or islands in question to have been many rather than one, particularly if the context is ignored. Later, in editing the diario for the *Raccolta Colombiana*, de Lollis noticed the discrepancy but treated it in the worst possible way, by rendering it as "de las isla[s]," thereby noting the dilemma and purporting to solve it at the same time.[58] By virtue of the *Raccolta* edition's authority, Las Casas meant to write—and Columbus did write—"islands," not "island." Later Alvar was to carry out the same restorative surgery.[59] Neither editor thought it necessary to explain his decision to lend explicit modern authority to the plural rendering. Morison, in turn, relying on the authority of the *Raccolta*, translated the phrase as "from these islands," and though we might expect some explanation since his Santa María de la Concepción was the single island of Rum Cay, he offered none.[60] More recently, Varela rendered the phrase as "de la islas" in her edition of the diario, with the usual lack of explication.[61]

There has also been a lesser tradition that translates the term in the singular. Both Markham and Jane spoke of "the island of Santa María."[62] Since neither consulted the holograph, both could have taken this option only because they believed that Santa María *was* a single island, namely, Rum Cay.

55. The matter is discussed in Fuson 1985:60, but the passage is omitted in Fuson 1987a:81–82.

56. Navarrete/Columbus 1971:17; Navarrete/Columbus 1825, 1:28.

57. La Roquette 1828, 1:58; Fox 1882:361. Becher, however, translated it as "the island" because for him Santa María de la Concepción was Rum Cay (1856:120).

58. Raccolta/Columbus 1892, 1:22.

59. Alvar/Columbus 1976, 1:94, as with Taviani/Columbus 1988:56, and Varela/Columbus 1989:61, both without comment.

60. Morison/Columbus 1963:71.

61. Varela/Columbus 1982:36.

62. Markham/Columbus 1893:45; Jane/Columbus 1960:154.

For more than a century and a half, then, we have had two strains of translation of the diario's "de las isla." One strand persisted in treating it in the plural. For this group Santa María was, at least once, a group of islands, even if this notion contradicted their own hypotheses about Columbus's route. The other strand ignored their own text in another way by translating the phrase in the singular, in deference to their views as to the identity of Santa María.

Writing in the early 1980s, Power was forced to recognize the self-contradictory nature of the phrase, but he turned it deftly to advantage by declaring that "Columbus has now mutated towards a pluralized form with the utilization of 'delas'." This happened, Power went on, because Columbus was "expanding the use of the name to include all the Caicos Islands that he had seen the previous day." In doing this, Power, like de Lollis and Alvar, simply adds an extra s to "isla" in brackets.[63]

Dunn takes the opposite point of view. Instead of seeking mutations, he points out that Columbus had previously (once or several times, depending on one's view of the number of islands Columbus mentioned in the entry for 15 October) used the singular to describe Santa María, this usage being the origin of Power's "mutation."[64] While this seems a more justifiable position, it is worth noting that any position requires a change in the text, which is palpably incorrect.

If only Navarrete's copyist had not taken it upon himself to decide the matter, the course of the discussion would probably have taken a different course from the beginning of the debate. However, it must be said that, from Washington Irving to at least Morison, those who have taken the text to mean "de las islas" have troubled themselves astonishingly little with the fact that this interpretation does serious violence to their own theories as to the identity of Santa María de la Concepción. Instead they prefer to overlook the matter, silently emending in their own minds before they silently emend on paper. Transcriptional theorists would hesitate to proclaim the likelihood of one error over the other—an extra "s" added or one accidentally omitted. Whether Las Casas made the error

63. Power 1985 : 163. Power then uses this (1985 : 164) to dismiss Rum Cay as Santa María de la Concepción on the grounds that it is "a solitary island that could not have inspired the use of the plural form 'delas'."

64. Dunn 1985 : 44–45. Lyon 1986 : 25 agrees with this. Cf. Dunn and Kelley/Columbus 1989 : 85n. For a discussion of Columbus's activities on 15 October, see below, chapter 16.

himself or simply transcribed an earlier error mindlessly, he can only be given a poor grade for inattention in this instance. Unfortunately, until recently no one has earned a better grade.

IV

At the same time that modern editors remove some materials from the diario, they add others. An example is the phrase "ciertos indios con nuevas" ("certain Indians with news"), which is found in the entry for 27 December in many modern editions even though it is absent from the diario.[65] The phrase derives from Las Casas's *Historia*, and it, or something like it, is needed to give sense to the passage, which in the diario reads "vinieron como la caravela pinta."[66] De Lollis, Sanz, Arranz, and Alvar all incorporated it within brackets, with a footnote to its provenance.[67] Varela is a little more adventurous: she dispenses with brackets and lets a footnote citation lead assiduous readers to the truth.[68] Arce, on the other hand, whose edition is not annotated, does the right thing in these circumstances and omits the four words entirely.[69] In his translation of the diario, Morison adds "[certain Indians with news]" to the text, together with a note that "Las Casas supplies the bracketed words in the *Historia*."[70] The question is: supplies them from where? Presumably this is a case of Las Casas meeting his own need and anticipating modern requirements as well by interpolating his own view of what the missing words must have been but not what they actually were, since it is unlikely, as we have seen, that when he was rewriting the diario into the *Historia* he had available to him anything more than his own transcription and his memory. The modern practice of using brackets to indicate Las Casas's later additions leads us to presume a closer textual relation-

65. Alvar/Columbus 1976, 1:194. Dunn and Kelley/Columbus 1989:293n, more properly mentions the matter only in an accompanying footnote.
66. Las Casas 1951, 1:284.
67. Alvar/Columbus 1976, 1:194; Sanz/Columbus 1962:48v; Arranz/Columbus 1985:173–74. De Lollis (*Raccolta*/Columbus 1892, 1:83) called his action a "reintegration"!
68. Varela/Columbus 1982:102.
69. Arce/Columbus 1971:140.
70. Morison/Columbus 1963:139.

ship than the evidence permits.[71] The best procedure would be to omit the offending words entirely and indicate with an accompanying note what Las Casas guessed was missing, thereby removing the implication that textually it is a part of the diario in some fashion. It is true that at this point Las Casas was paraphrasing his copy text, and it would seem reasonable to grant him a certain prerogative. But the fact remains that the words "ciertos indios con nuevas" are not in the diario.

Introducing extraneous wording into the diario can lead to farce as well. Take the passage in the entry for 31 December that reads in the diario: "y quexábase que todo aquel mal e inconveniente haberse apartado d'él la carabela Pinta" ("and [Columbus] complained that all that grief and inconvenience having left him the caravel Pinta").[72] All editors have agreed that something must be missing between "inconveniente" and "haberse." In the *Historia* Las Casas chose to recast the statement slightly: "Quejábase mucho de Martín Alonzo en haberle dejado, porque destos inconvenientes había sido causa" (He [Columbus] complained much about Martín Alonso [Pinzón] for having deserted him since [this] had been the cause of these troubles).[73]

The results of the loss of Las Casas's guiding hand are both amusing and bemusing. Navarrete set the tone by writing assuredly that the passage "lacks 'provenir de,'" and Varnhagen and de Lollis followed suit.[74] At this point things fell apart. Arce replicates the diario by having "haberse" follow "inconveniente" directly.[75] Arranz shows "[provenía] de" (came or resulted from) as though "de" were part of the holograph diario.[76] Sanz incorporates "provenía de" without the slightest hint that this is a modern device.[77] More forthrightly, Alvar interpolates "[provenía

71. Without the benefit of Las Casas's *Historia*, Navarrete's copyist (Navarrete/Columbus 1971:142) thought that only "nuevas" was missing, and so did Navarrete (Navarrete/Columbus 1825, 1:117) in the printed edition. Varnhagen (1864:75) followed suit. See also Varela/Columbus 1989:35.

72. Alvar/Columbus 1976, 1:198. Dunn and Kelley again and properly leave the issue to a note (Dunn and Kelley/Columbus 1989:299n).

73. Las Casas 1951, 1:289.

74. Navarrete/Columbus 1825, 1:118n; Varnhagen 1864:77; *Raccolta*/Columbus 1892, 1:86n.

75. Arce/Columbus 1971:142.

76. Arranz/Columbus 1985:176.

77. Sanz/Columbus 1962:49v.

de]," with a notation to the effect that the words "are [those] of modern editors."[78] Varela completes the cycle by preferring "[veníen de]" (came from), which certainly has as much authority—none at all—as the more popular "provenía de."[79] And there the matter lies. Modern editors have provided no fewer than three conjectural emendations for the edification of their readers, and these in a variety of formats.

V

The prevailing view that when we read the diario we are in effect reading the log of Columbus's first voyage is nowhere better exemplified than in modern editors' treatment of Las Casas's marginal notes as they survive in the manuscript. There are 199 of these, 147 substantive and the remainder the word No. The question has not been ignored entirely; some editors have acknowledged them, but once this token measure is applied, the practice has been to eliminate them from their editions. Only Alvar, Alvar and Morales Padrón, and Dunn and Kelley have included both forms of marginalia.[80] Otherwise the pattern is widely scattered. De Lollis printed most of the substantive notes but omitted all but a few of the Nos. In their editions Sanz and, surprisingly, Marañón included the substantive notes but also excluded all the No's. Varela's practice has been peculiar. In her first edition she rarely refers to the marginalia before 29 October and never quotes them, but after that date she quotes most of them verbatim in notes. The No's are not included, however. In her latest editions she includes them as "nota."[81]

In the only study devoted to these materials in their own right, Vázquez briefly indicates their nature and content.[82] Many of them are strategic, designed either to correct or to explain Columbus's errors or to lend a glossier patina to some of Columbus's activities that Las Casas could not bring himself to sanction outright. Others provide geographic and eth-

78. Alvar/Columbus 1976, 1:198n701. But in the modernized version (Alvar/Columbus 1976, 2:185) both brackets and note disappear.

79. Varela/Columbus 1982:104. Cioranescu/Columbus 1961:138 inserted "vénaient de" in brackets, while Morison/Columbus 1963:141 says "came" with no indication that Morison had interpolated it.

80. Although he missed a few of the "Nos" discussed below.

81. Varela/Columbus 1989; see also, and note 90 below.

82. Vázquez 1971:52–54.

nographic information not available to Columbus, while in a few cases Las Casas supplied a linguistic datum. Many, of course, were designed to highlight the activities and culture of the Indians in cases in which the text of the diario did not permit, even in paraphrase.

Many of the marginal comments eventually found their way into the text of the *Historia,* but their first and primary domicile is the diario, where they serve as internal glosses, a kind of minor subtext running along at the heels of the main text. Major or minor, they are intrinsic parts of what we know as the diario. Looking at a few examples can suggest their value for the study of the diario to the extent that they offer insights into the mind of Las Casas. Sometimes we find that that mind was simply confused by the obscurities of the text before it. Against the entry of 17 October, in the very midst of Columbus's meanderings through the Bahamas, Las Casas wrote: "Vuélvense a la Española" ("They return to Hispaniola"), when Hispaniola was as yet unknown to Columbus.[83] When Columbus wrote on 1 November that he thought Cuba was the eastern edge of the Asian continent, Las Casas observed, both surprisedly and surprisingly: "Esta algarabía no entiendo yo" ("I don't understand this gibberish").[84] Still, Las Casas's admiration for Columbus apparently extended to granting him a great deal of prescience, a view stated just three days later when he added marginally: "Debían mentir los indios" ("The Indians must have lied") because Columbus had written that they had told him that cinnamon and pepper were to be found in large quantities "to the southeast."[85]

One of Las Casas's more revealing marginal notes, and one that might be a parable for the modern study of Columbus's route, is entered against the entry for 6 December. The entry begins with Columbus's reporting that he found himself near a harbor that he named Puerto María. Before the day was out, Columbus had bestowed another name on what seems to have been the same place; this time he called it Puerto de San Nicolás in honor of the feast day.[86] Well might Las Casas insert against the second

83. Alvar/Columbus 1976, 1:98; Dunn and Kelley/Columbus 1989:94.

84. Alvar/Columbus 1976, 1:113; Dunn and Kelley/Columbus 1989:128. In his *Historia,* Las Casas (1951, 1:227) omitted this remark.

85. Alvar/Columbus 1976, 1:115; Dunn and Kelley/Columbus 1989:132. In the *Historia,* Las Casas (1951, 1:228) elaborated at needless length. More often he noted that Columbus had misunderstood the Indians or they him.

86. Alvar/Columbus 1976, 1:151; Dunn and Kelley/Columbus 1989:202.

baptism: "No entiendo como a este puerto puso arriba puerto María y ahora de San Nicolás" (I don't understand how this port was first named Puerto María and now San Nicolás).[87] If nothing else, this perplexed note suggests that here Las Casas read closely what he was writing, but his confusion must have continued, because when he came to record the incident in his *Historia*, he simply expunged Columbus's first naming of the harbor in question.[88]

Examining Las Casas's marginal notes therefore contributes toward a better understanding of how he processed his copy text as he prepared the diario, as well as how he viewed its content, but the extent to which these were simultaneous reactions is unclear. For instance, there is evidence that Las Casas wrote a marginal note against 25 November, crossed it out, and repositioned it against the previous day's entry, which indicates later touching up.[89]

Las Casas's many marginal *No*'s have raised some debate. Most editors take them as truncations of "Nota" and so to indicate points that Las Casas thought of special interest. But since Las Casas eventually absorbed almost all the diario, and then some, into the *Historia*, this procedure seems to have been unnecessary. Perhaps, however, these additions were made at the point at which Las Casas began to separate the material that ultimately became part of his *Apologética historia* from that part—the greater portion—that entered his *Historia de las Indias*. Varela has disagreed with the majority in this instance and writes that "often Las Casas expresses his disagreement with Columbus, intervening with a perfunctory 'Non' in the margin."[90] She does not sustain her view with an argument, and it seems unlikely that Las Casas would have disagreed with Columbus quite so often. Still, if true, the marginal notes on the holo-

---

87. Alvar/Columbus 1976, 2:135. To complicate matters, Las Casas first wrote "María" a second time and then replaced it with "San Nicolás." Neither Alvar (Alvar/Columbus 1976, 1:150n408) nor Dunn and Kelley (Dunn and Kelley/Columbus 1989:203n) guess at the identity of the crossed-out word. Morison/Columbus 1963: 113 had the answer: Columbus "promptly renamed" the harbor without bothering to mention his change of mind directly.

88. Las Casas 1951, 1:252–53.

89. Alvar/Columbus 1976, 1:133–34; Dunn and Kelley/Columbus 1989:172.

90. Varela/Columbus 1982:xixn. She has since changed her mind, but without indicating her earlier opinion beyond attributing it (without justification, as far as I can tell) to Alvar (Taviani/Columbus 1988:31; Varela/Columbus 1989:13).

graph would prove an even more valuable diagnostic tool and would at
the same time exalt Las Casas's scribal integrity.[91]

A convenient laboratory to test the exactitude with which modern editions have treated the text of the diario is the set of numbers it uses to
refer to the distances Columbus traveled on the outward voyage. There
are nearly a hundred of these, including both partial legs and the lower
numbers for daily distances traveled that Columbus purportedly fed the
crews. I have considered various aspects of these elsewhere.[92] Here I want
to concentrate on the way the numbers themselves appear in the manuscript and in modern editions.

In the diario these are entered in every possible way: some in words,
others in Arabic numerals, still others in Roman numerals. Modern editors have taken a remarkably cavalier attitude toward these numbers, preferring to interpose their own conceptions of what best serves the reader.
Only Alvar, Varela, and Dunn and Kelley have reproduced these numbers
exactly as they are in the diario. Even though Sanz published a facsimile
along with his own transcription, he failed to make the proper transfer in
nearly 20 percent of the cases. This attitude took shape early. Navarrete's
copyist, probably at his behest, rendered all the numbers as words, except
six three-digit integers. In the event, Navarrete found even this effort
unsatisfactory and proceeded to transform these six into words as well.
The result was, no doubt, an increase in one form of clarity but at the
cost of estranging himself from his source no less than 70 percent of
the time.

More recent editions have ranged from the single error in the *Raccolta*
to the 50 percent miss rate of Marañón. Most of these differences are to
be attributed to a latter-day reluctance to disfigure the text of the diario
with Roman numerals. Fifteen of Arce's sixteen differences, fifteen of the
seventeen in Sanz, and so on, result simply because these editors changed
Roman numerals either to words or to Arabic numerals, although without any consistency. Some might agree with them, and of course with
Navarrete, that to quibble over such matters is mere pedantry, that there

91. For other examples, see Gullick and Thorn 1986; Schwab 1988.
92. Henige 1990a; Henige and Zamora 1989; and below chapter 7.

is no important difference between "17" and "XVII," and if anything, "17" is preferable to "XVII" because it is seemingly less susceptible to transcriptional error and more readily intelligible to modern eyes.

These arguments are all quite valid, but at the same time quite without foundation. To take one example, we find that the Roman numerals are bunched in the earlier stages of the trip, whereas from 25 September nearly 75 percent of the numbers are expressed in Arabic numerals. Does this suggest a change in scribes about this time, even possibly on board ship? As discussed earlier, we know that the Spanish court set at least two copyists to work on the log, but even in the absence of this information, studying the recorded numerals closely would allow us, if not force us, to infer that very thing, as well as affording insight into the possible contribution of each scribe.

Other hypotheses develop from the study of the diario's numbers here. For example, very often the so-called lower count is expressed in a form different from the putative "true" distance for the same day. What are we to make of the peculiarity? Did Columbus do this himself in order better to distinguish the two or to confuse the men? Or did another hand add the lower numbers at some later stage for reasons that must escape us? While we can hardly answer this, accurately transcribing the numbers in the diario permits us at least to take the first step: asking the question. But if we turn to the editions of Sanz, or those of Arce or Arranz or Marañón, or worse yet to that of Navarrete, we would conclude that the only anomaly about these numbers is the perfect harmony with which Las Casas recorded them. But, as always, inconsistencies, incongruities, and contradictions are what matter and what instruct by inspiring doubt and study.[93]

VII

In addition to the many cases in which Las Casas corrected himself and the far fewer instances in which he failed to correct a painfully obvious error, there is a third category to consider: the hundreds of possibly minor errors, usually involving only a letter or two, that one or more modern editors have claimed to uncover. These are cases that, if true, must

93. For the transition from Roman to Arabic numerals in western Europe at about this time, see Hill 1915; Struik 1968; Swetz 1987:18–24. See also Develin 1990.

have escaped the attention of Las Casas and his emendators, if any, and even resisted any rereadings he may have given the text. By and large, these implied errors are negligible, but the task of identifying and "correcting" them is by no means simply a matter of mechanics. Quite the contrary, the hunt involves both paleographic and textual interpretation.

Since there seem to be as many anomalies as modern eyes are willing to see, I confine my attention here as a case study to the thirty-seven times that Alvar chose to correct a word in the text of the first volume of his edition by including his own rendering of the original text and specifying the "original" in a note. It is unclear why Alvar chose to do this in fewer than 4 percent of the changes he noticed while in other instances choosing quite a different means of proceeding (by indicating the change itself in the note). At any rate, employing this sample offers two advantages—one obvious, the other somewhat surprising. In the first place, it is a pre-selected sample immune from any biases I would inevitably bring to a selection of my own choosing. Second, it happens to provide a surprisingly wide variety of major and minor interpretive cruxes. Table 5.1 lists Alvar's sample and along with it the procedures of other editions, beginning with the *Raccolta*. The great majority of individual items in table 5.1 break down into broad categories and can be dismissed more easily than the disparate treatment given them by modern editors, a point I defer to the end of this discussion. The following are the broad categories of error found in table 5.1.

1. *Disagreement in number.* Cases 1, 2, 3, and 5 are those in which Las Casas failed to provide the required agreement between an adjective and its noun. In each of these cases, modern editors have done this for him.

2. *Transposition.* Transposing one or more letters or numbers is among the most common of scribal errors. For letters, the problem is usually obvious when it occurs, and it has proved so in the cases considered here (10 and 23).

3. *Misspelling by adding letters.* Although it is less common to misspell a well-known word by adding a letter than by omitting one, in this sample we have instances only of the first. In each case (8, 11, 16, 20) the error is egregious, and modern editions have noticed and corrected it.

4. *Misspelling by changing letters.* The eleven examples of this scribal error (9, 15, 19, 21, 22, 25, 27, 30, 31, 35, 37) form the largest category here. With the exception of 19 and 31, these have offered no editorial problems. Alone of the editors surveyed, Varela has retained the original

TABLE 5.1. *Sample of Thirty-seven Corrections Drawn from Alvar/Columbus 1976, Volume 1*

Case	Date of Entry	Location in MS	Alvar MS Reading	Alvar Correct Reading
1	9/17	4r/21	muchas (27)	mucha
2	9/17	4r/23	yerva (29)	yervas
3	9/19	4v/35	Canaria (41)	Canarias
4	10/7	7v/23	guesueste (77)	guesudueste
5	10/14	10v/18	venido (100)	venidos
6	10/15	12v/43	nombre (114)	hombre
7	10/16	12v/39	sorjas (116)	sonajas
8	10/19	14v/36	Yslabela (128)	Ysabela
9	10/21	15v/38	comigo (133a)	comido
10	10/29	19r/2	aryes (169)	aires
11	10/30	19r/45	linera (175)	línea
12	10/31	19v/1	noviembre (176)	otubre
13	11/6	22r/20	negros (211)	negras
14	11/15	24v/27	que que (247)	que
15	11/18	25v/12	suduesto (264)	sudueste
16	11/20	25v/32	lueguas (268)	leguas
17	11/24	27r/22	bevía (298)	benía
18	11/27	28v/7	los (325)	las
19	11/27	29r/32	soldar (338)	sondar
20	11/27	29v/31	gujnera (348)	guinea
21	12/4	32r/43	pozo (391)	paso
22	12/7	34r/48	entral (428)	entrar
23	12/11	35r/39	dizean (446)	dezían
24	12/15	37r/30	dl (482)	de
25	12/16	38v/2	descendir (499a)	descender
26	12/21	41v/16	dize (547)	hize
27	12/21	42r/9	von (551)	con
28	12/22	45r/4	estimaya (616)	estimaba
29	12/24	45v/42	ot° (629)	(o)tiro
30	12/24	46r/4	casjagos (630)	cascajos
31	1/5	52r/15	soldando (734)	sondando

Raccolta	Sanz	Varela 1982	Dunn and Kelley
mucha[1]	mucha	mucha[s]	muchas
yerva[s][2]	hierba	yerva⟨s⟩	yerva
Canarias	Canarias	Canaria⟨s⟩	canaria
guesu[du]este[3]	Ouese[du]este	Güesueste[4]	guesueste
venido[s]	venidos	venido"s"	venido
hombre	hombre	hombre	nombre
sonagas[1,2]	sonajas	sonajas	sonajas
"Isabela"[1]	Islabela	Isabela[1]	Islabela
comido[1]	comido	comido	comigo
ayres	aires	aires	aryes
línea	línea	línea	línea
otubre[1]	octubre	otubre	noviembre
negras[1,3]	negras	negro[s]	negros
que[1]	que	que	que que
sudueste	sudueste	sudueste	sudueste
leguas[1]	leguas	l[u]eguas	lueguas
bevía	venía	benia	bevia
los	las	los	los (aguajes)
sondar[1]	sondar	soldar	so[l?]dar
Guinea	Guinea	Guinea	guinea
pozo[2]	paso	pozo	pozo[5]
entrar[1]	entrar	entrar	entrar
dezían	dezían	dezían	dizean
d'él	de	de	dl
descendir[3]	descender	descender	desçendir
dize	hice	dizé	dize
con	con	con	con
estima ya	estimaba ya	estima ya	estima ya
tiro[1,2]	ot°	tiro	ot°
casgajos	cascajos	cascajos	casjagos
sondando[1]	sondando	soldando	soldando

TABLE 5.1. (*continued*)

Case	Date of Entry	Location in MS	Alvar MS Reading	Alvar Correct Reading
32	1/11	54v/8	del [dl] (763)	al
33	1/11	55v17	taob (783a)	tuob
34	1/11	56r6marg	nuevos (794)	uuevos
35	1/18	58r/35	ad (842)	al
36	2/7	60r/50	barlouiento/ barlomento (870)	barlovento
37	2/15	62v/10	ad (923)	al

¹ MS reading in notes.
² Reading by Navarrete in notes.
³ Reading in *Historia de las Indias* in notes.

"soldar" and "soldando," though without explanation even though neither seems to fit its context as well as "sondar" and "sondando."⁹⁴

5. *Disagreement in gender.* Cases 13 and 18 appear to be straightforward examples of the need to change an *o* into an *a* to conform to proper usage. But the situation may be more complex. In the first passage Columbus is describing the Indians of Cuba, of both sexes. After writing that both men and women went around "as naked as their mothers bore them," he added that in fact the women wore a small amount of clothing. Then he went on to say, at least in the opinion of modern editors: "Y son ell*a*s de muy buen acatamiento, ni muy negr*o*s, salvo menos que canari*a*s" (And they are exceedingly deferential and not very black, less so than the Canarian women). It is true that of the letters italicized above, the first and last look to be an *a* and that the second appears even more certainly to be an *o*, but in fact all three letters are smudged to a certain extent. This may hardly seem to matter at all, but is it not odd that, if we accept the view that the apparent *a o a* sequence should be *a a a*, then we must accept concomitantly that Las Casas was referring to the attitude and complexion only of the Cuban females?

94. Note, though, that Pontillo (1975:406) found a later instance in which "soldar" was used to mean "to touch bottom," which would be an acceptable alternative meaning in this case.

Raccolta	Sanz	Varela 1982	Dunn and Kelley
del	al	del	dl
tuob	tuob	tuob	taob
huevos[1]	huevos		uuevos
al[1]	al	al	al
barloviento	barlovento	barlovento	barlovento
al[1]	al	al	ad

[4] In her text Varela (1982:27n) annotates the word, but only to comment on possible reasons for a change in direction.
[5] Dunn and Kelley (1989:199n) think that "poso" was intended.

Perhaps Alvar and others were influenced by the fact that in his *Historia* Las Casas appeared to correct himself by writing "negras," but it would be dangerous to rely too heavily on this line of argument since in this same passage, though couched as direct quotation from the diario, Las Casas departed from the diario's exact text four times in the space of about fifty words.[95] In short, there seems to be at least a vestige of an argument for believing that the italicized letters above should be *o o o* rather than *a a a*.

Case 18 is a bit more complicated and brings forward the paleographical issues that plague the study of the diario. In the passage in question we find "los agua—," with the dash here representing some very light and indecipherable marks. The vowel in "los" is clearly an *o*, but the interpretation of the next word is very much open to question. As we see from table 5.1, both de Lollis and Varela concluded, probably not independently, that the word after "los" was "aguajes," a masculine noun with which "los" would be correct. Alvar, on the other hand, sees only an *s* after "agua" and ignores the light scratching that follows. Either interpretation may be correct, although it requires a certain determination to divine anything as specific as "jes" among the scratchings and even more to attribute them to Las Casas. On the other hand, in its favor "aguajes" has

95. Las Casas 1951, 1:231.

the slightly narrower and, as it happens, more appropriate meaning of current or wake in this context.[96] Still, as we know from the narrative for Guanahaní (see chapter 12 below) Columbus (and/or Las Casas) could use "aguas" in very nondescript ways. Unfortunately, we cannot let Las Casas cast a deciding vote since in the *Historia* he used neither "las aguas" nor "los aguajes" in his description of the occasion.[97]

6. *Repetition.* All scribes repeat themselves from time to time as a result of being distracted or interrupted or from inattentiveness. Elsewhere Las Casas wrote "Quisay" three times before crossing out the first two.[98] Here (case 14) he simply overlooked the more inconspicuous "que," and modern editors have caught him out.

7. *Contractions.* Las Casas was not prone to contracting words beyond the fairly generous custom of the time. In case 29 modern editors have deduced from the context that the slightly disguised contraction should be "tiro."[99]

8. *Anticipation.* Ordinarily Las Casas's use of "noviembre" for "otubre" could be attributed to his demonstrated penchant for anticipating the succeeding text. In case 12 there may have been other forces at work, as discussed earlier in this chapter.

9. *Misspelling by omission.* The case here (4) is not without problems. Modern observers have preferred "west-southwest" because it clearly fits the situation better and because "west-southeast" makes little sense in any context.[100] Thus it has been easy to visualize Las Casas as omitting a couple of letters in his haste. This line of reasoning, however plausible, must take into account that in both surviving manuscripts of his *Historia* Las Casas again wrote "guesueste" so if he is adjudged careless here, he was careless not once but three times.[101]

96. Pontillo 1975:87. Dunn and Kelley/Columbus 1989:178 gives this as "aguajes."

97. Las Casas 1951, 1:243–44.

98. Alvar/Columbus 1976, 1:113n189; Dunn and Kelley/Columbus 1989:128.

99. This is omitted in Las Casas 1951, 1:275–76.

100. E.g., Markham/Columbus 1893:33; Thacher 1903–4, 1:528; Jane/Columbus 1960:204n16. Navarrete/Columbus 1825, 1:18 began the process by giving this as "guesudueste" and was followed by McElroy 1941:224; Caddeo/Columbus 1968:43; Arce/Columbus 1971:44; Cioranescu/Columbus 1961:41; Morison/Columbus 1963:61; Arranz/Columbus 1985:87; Ferro/Columbus 1985:40–41; Kelley 1985:[81]; Fuson 1987a:71. Only Jane and Ferro noted the original text.

101. Las Casas 1875–76, 1:285; Las Casas 1951, 1:196.

10. *Calligraphic Problems.* All transcription is an act of interpretation, however low level such interpretation may usually prove to be. Decisions must be made on both contextual and calligraphic grounds, although the two inevitably overlap. In some of the cases here, Alvar has drawn conclusions that others have not—particularly for cases 6, 7, 24, 33, 34, and 36.[102] In each instance one need not be an apologist for Las Casas to grant him the same degree of latitude we permit ourselves when writing. Looking at the holograph manuscript, for instance, it is hard to agree with Alvar that Las Casas actually wrote (that is, intended at that moment to write) "taob" instead of "tuob," "nombre" instead of "hombre," and so on. These are clearly cases in which the benefit of the doubt, as well as the doubt itself, is called for.

We now enter a second realm of disparity and dispute, occasioned by the fact that the forms of the disputed letters are in words in the manuscript that look like other words that have meanings that are also possible contextually, even though not particularly similar in meaning. In fact, the four cases that follow exemplify how extraordinarily often words that look alike can excite differences of opinion.

Take case 17, "benía"/"bevía." Alvar concluded that Las Casas wrote "bevía" in the diario and equally certain that he intended to write "benía." De Lollis agreed that "bevía" was written in the diario, but he clearly believed that it was intended since he offered no gloss on the word.[103] Varela, although she modernizes the diario's language, still transcribes the term as "benía" when presumably she should have written "venía." As it stands in her edition, "benía" is an unintelligible hybrid. In his translation of the diario, Morison accepted that Las Casas meant to write, and did write, "bevía," and so he translated it—somewhat awkwardly, since it is in the singular—as "one drank."[104] The context of the word is: "y de más agua que hasta entonces habian visto, y que [bevía or benía] el agua dulce hasta la mar" (and with more fresh water than they had seen, and one [drank or went] until the sea). Both the mention of fresh water and the fact that in other cases near this passage Las Casas wrote "*venían*" leads us to suspect that in this case Alvar guessed incorrectly in changing the

---

102. By far the best account of the calligraphic issues surrounding the study of the diario is Dunn and Kelley/Columbus 1989:5–11.

103. *Raccolta*/Columbus 1892, 1:46.

104. Morison/Columbus 1963:101; Fuson 1987a:115 disagrees.

word. Even so, the diario's use of the singular and the image of the Spanish drinking fresh water as they sailed on give pause.

Another instance in which the evidence suggests a misreading, or rather a misinterpretation, by Alvar is case 26. Here Alvar purported to be quoting Columbus as follows: "y vi todo el levante y poniente que [dize or hize] por ir al camino de septentrión, que es Inglaterra" (and I saw all the east and the west, which [he said or I made] for having taken the route of the north, which is England). As usual, Las Casas did not distinguish by any signs that he had interrupted his verbatim transcription with the phrase that began "que hize/dize," and this must have led Alvar to believe that "hize" was meant because it is a first-person verb form. In several ways the difference between *d* and *h* is important. If Las Casas meant to write "dize" (and in the manuscript the word is clearly "dize"), then we have another case in which he insinuated his own comments into the text and almost into the mouth of Columbus, for the phrase stands squarely in the midst of verbatim matter.

But is it likely that Columbus would have glossed his own wording in the log this way by reminding himself where the route to the north led? If so, the passage would amount to a dialogue between the phrase beginning "que dize/hize" and that preceding it, as though Columbus needed to explain to himself what he meant by his own words. In his interpretation Alvar keeps company with Thacher, Cioranescu, and Sanz but with no other editor of the diario.[105] De Lollis transcribed the word in question as "dize" and rigorously excluded the passage in which it occurs from his quotation marks, while Morison also considered it to be an obiter dictum by Las Casas and translated it rather ponderously as Columbus's "way of saying that he had gone on the northern route to England."[106] Most recently, Dunn and Kelley come as close as possible with their rendering: "(which he says because of going on the route north to England)."[107] Varela's transcription as "dizé" puts her in a minority of one on the matter.

Case 28 is puzzling primarily in the inconsistency with which editors have handled it. The text indisputably reads "estimaya," which has no

105. Thacher 1903–4, 1:616; Cioranescu/Columbus 1961:120; Morales Padrón/Columbus 1963:128, 236n1091; Sanz/Columbus 1962:41v.

106. *Raccolta*/Columbus 1892, 1:71; Morison/Columbus 1963:128.

107. Dunn and Kelley/Columbus 1989:253; cf. Taviani/Columbus 1988:41.

meaning. Transcribing it as "estima ya" (I now estimate), as both de Lollis and Varela do, puts it in the present tense at a time when Las Casas was paraphrasing Columbus, not quoting him. Sanz's rendering simply transgresses the text without explanation. Moreover, granting "ya" the status of a separate word rather than a suffix brings in untestable assumptions about the circumstances under which Columbus was estimating, whether it was a revision of an earlier unrecorded estimate, and so forth.[108] In sum, Alvar was probably right in suggesting a scribal error by Las Casas.

Perhaps Alvar's most problematical emendation from this test set is his suggested substitution of "al" for "del" in case 32. His change is not entirely anticalligraphic; the word is written as "dl" in the diario, which might easily be construed as "al." However, Alvar's main inspiration is contextual. In order to demonstrate this, the passage must be quoted at length:

> A media noche salió del río de Graçia con el terral; navegó al leste, hasta un cabo que llamó Belprado, cuatro leguas y de alli al sueste esta el monte a quien puso Monte de Plata, y dize que hay ocho leguas. De allí [del/al] cabo de Belprado, al leste, cuarta del sueste, está el cabo que dixo del Angel, y hay diez y ocho leguas; . . . [109]

The punctuation here is Alvar's, slightly modernized but remaining faithful to Las Casas's own rather more haphazard style. More of this later. Taken literatim, the passage could be translated:

> At midnight he left from the Rio de Graçia with the land breeze; he sailed to the east until a cape which he called Belprado; and from there to the southeast is the mountain to which he gave the name Monte de Plata, and he says that it is eight leagues. From there, [from/to] the cape of Belprado to the east-southeast, is the cape that he named Cape del Angel, and there are eighteen leagues.

Grammatically speaking, using "del" in this construction makes "alli" and "Cabo de Belprado" in apposition and hence identical. In other words, both Monte de Plata and Cabo del Angel would be oriented from the same point, Cabo de Belprado, the first being eight leagues to its

---

108. Thus Morison/Columbus 1963:132, following de Lollis, translated it as "*now guessed*" (emphasis added).

109. Alvar/Columbus 1976, 1:210.

southeast, the second eighteen leagues east-southeast. Such an interpretation is competitively plausible, whereas by substituting "al" for "del" Alvar renders the statement unintelligible: "From here to Cape de Belprado, to the east-southeast, is the cape that he named Cabo del Angel." Thus "here" becomes a new and otherwise unmentioned point somewhere west-northwest of Cabo de Belprado. Rather than having one too many "dels," the sentence now has an extra "al," and one that cannot be explained away by apposition.[110]

Others have found this passage wanting in different ways. De Lollis, for example, attached "de allí" to the preceding sentence. Not only did this furnish that sentence with an exceedingly superfluous "de allí" but it also resolutely contravened Las Casas's own punctuation, for he placed "/." between "leguas" and "de allí."[111] Morison, Jane, and Fuson all translate the phrase using "del," although Fuson believes that the text's eighteen leagues should be eighteen miles.[112]

The diario continues, "y d'este cabo al monte de Playa ay un golfo y tierras las mejores y mas lindas del mundo" ("and from this cape to Monte de Plata there is a gulf [bay?] and the best and fairest lands in the world").[113] Theoretically, the unnamed "este cabo" could refer either to Cabo de Belprado or Cabo del Angel, both recently mentioned in the text, although the latter is more likely since Cabo de Belprado has already been described as "allí." On the other hand, a few sentences later Cabo del Angel is also cast into the discursive distance, for we read "del cabo del Angel" (from Cabo del Angel).[114] This is followed by a series of descriptions of headlands Columbus sighted that day. These are each introduced with "de allí" or "d'este," and while it is reasonable—almost nec-

110. Yet a minor consensus in favor of substituting "al" has developed in recent editions, e.g., Marañón/Columbus 1965:159; Arce/Columbus 1971:153; Arranz/Columbus 1985:186.

111. For another example in which confusing punctuation has impeded understanding, see Dunn and Kelley/Columbus 1989:101n. Another case is discussed in Miller 1935. A fascinating analysis of the ideological role of the lowly comma is Gilliard 1989.

112. Jane/Columbus 1960:144; Morison/Columbus 1963:149; Fuson 1987a:170.

113. Alvar/Columbus 1976, 1:210; Dunn and Kelley/Columbus 1989:324.

114. It is probably fatuous to advance arguments of this kind, because in this entry Las Casas oscillated between "este"/"esta" and "allí" to such a degree that it becomes impossible to determine what Columbus's real words were, where he was writing from that day, or if he was writing that day at all.

essary—to assume that each refers to its immediate predecessor, we can hardly be as certain as we would prefer.

In fact, by suggesting that "al" be substituted for "del," Alvar has, if inadvertently, reminded us that directions based individually on a series of unfixed points in succession rather than collectively on a single fixed point require unambiguous language. At this point Las Casas's unfortunate penchant for prolixity and oscillation between the past and present tense leaves us in some doubt. Whether Las Casas was recapitulating Columbus's itinerary for this day using Columbus's own words or attempting to cast it into his own, the effort is not wholly successful. Unfortunately, he abridged himself dramatically in the *Historia*, allowing no comparisons.[115]

VIII

Alvar's treatment of this set of supposed errors raises specific points that are broadly interesting, and instructive as well. At the same time, the alarmingly disparate treatment of these points by the editors discussed here raises other, more general considerations that need to be addressed. In the first place, by choosing to treat these cases as he did, Alvar departed from his policy of rendering the original reading in his text, sometimes in brackets to indicate a suggested change, and sometimes not. This departure is not necessarily a bad thing, but it creates a disconcerting inconsistency and raises procedural questions. Why, for instance, does Alvar show "de las ysla[s]" in the entry for 16 October yet deal with cases 1, 2, 3, and 5 in table 5.1 so differently? Was his decision mechanical, accidental, or epistemological?

More important is the disheartening range of editorial responses to these issues. Many of the original readings that Alvar questions have not been questioned by other editors. In many cases this is simply because other editors apprehended the text differently from Alvar, testimony to the unavoidable vagaries of ocular interpretation. De Lollis noted his own variances from the text only when he concluded that there might be ambiguity. Thus he felt no compunction about changing "Canaria" to "Canarias," "Guinera" to "Guinea," or "sudugueste" to "sudueste" without indicating that the text of the diario differs, but he balked at doing

115. Las Casas 1951, 1:302.

the same for several others, even for some (e.g., "lueguas" to "leguas") in which silent correction was, by his lights, no less justified. Varela's betrayal by her typography in cases 5 and 26 can only lead us to wonder about the problem in the rest of her text. Her unexplained preference for "soldar" and "soldando" over "sondar" and "sondando" likewise raises doubt.[116]

What emerges most clearly from this exercise is that the text of the diario is incredibly protean, shaping itself anew in the eyes of each beholder. This is largely a paleographic problem occasioned by the unavoidable incongruities and uncertainties of a hastily prepared handwritten text full of interpolations, corrections, oversights, and afterthoughts. Although only a handful of the examples here have historical consequences, the picture that emerges of a text that is physically immutable but psychologically mercurial can only be salutary. If nothing else, it serves to remind us that Las Casas must have had the same problems with his own exemplar, and the royal copyists theirs with the log.

A final pair of examples concludes this brief survey of modern editors' attitudes to the text of the diario as text. They occur within a few lines of each other in the entry for 7 December and have rather a common history. In each case, Navarrete's copyist got the ball rolling, Navarrete increased its momentum, and from there numerous twists developed.

The first occasion is in the passage that reads, "lo cual todo lo probó el Almirante aquel por la costa" ("all of which the Admiral learned about that along the coast").[117] Something is missing here, and all agree that it must be a noun after "aquel." Navarrete's copyist raised the issue by adding "Quizá falta *día* ("Perhaps lacks *day*") in the margin.[118] Navarrete obviously agreed, for he inserted "día" in the published text without indicating that it was his interpolation.[119] When his turn came, de Lollis placed "[día]" in the text of the *Raccolta* edition but failed to note the reason for the brackets, a procedure Alvar followed exactly.[120] Varela was unusually diffident, inserting nothing more than a symbol indicating that

116. In the second edition (Varela/Columbus 1984:34) "venido"s" was corrected to "venido<s>" but no other changes were made in these items.

117. Alvar/Columbus 1976, 1:153; Dunn and Kelley/Columbus 1989:208.

118. Navarrete/Columbus 1971:100.

119. Navarrete/Columbus 1825, 1:82.

120. *Raccolta*/Columbus 1892, 1:58; Alvar/Columbus 1976, 2:139.

"el texto resulta uninteligible."[121] Ferro was more forthcoming. He inserted "giorno" into the text with a note explaining that this is a case of eyeskip and that the word for "day" was indicated.[122] Perhaps so. All other editors and translators have simply added the appropriate word for "day" as if it had originally been a part of the text.[123]

A few lines later Columbus describes the circumference of what is now Cap S. Nicolas Mole in northwestern Haiti as being "en el cerco .34. millas" (about 34 miles).[124] The numeral *3*, shown below, was written in such a way that Navarrete's copyist wondered whether the figure ought not to be 24.[125]

$$34.$$

Navarrete changed the premise entirely by transcribing it as "tres ó cuatro millas" in the published edition but failed either to indicate or explain the change.[126] De Lollis followed suit by including ".34." in the text with a note that this actually should have been "3 ó 4."[127] With a few exceptions this has come to be accepted. In his translation Morison attempted to explain why. A distance of "'3 or 4 miles,'" he wrote, "is . . . about the correct circumference" of Cap S. Nicolas Mole.[128] This judgment conflicts with Morison's own map of the cape published in another of his works, in which the circumference is shown to be more like ten nautical, or twelve Columbian, miles.[129] It is particularly necessary here to take into account Columbus's chronic exaggeration in estimating sizes and distances all along the coasts of Cuba and Hispaniola.[130] Since it is Columbus's mental maps that matter here, not modern ones, we need to look at

121. Varela/Columbus 1982:75.

122. Ferro/Columbus 1985:122.

123. At least twelve modern editions include the word "día" without indicating its alien nature. Dunn and Kelley/Columbus 1989:209 shows "[day]."

124. Alvar/Columbus 1976, 2:139; cf. Dunn and Kelley/Columbus 1989:209n.

125. Navarrete/Columbus 1971:100.

126. Navarrete/Columbus 1825, 1:82.

127. *Raccolta*/Columbus 1892, 1:58. Most recently see Taviani/Columbus 1988: 152n; Varela/Columbus 1989:103.

128. Morison/Columbus 1963:114n6.

129. Morison 1939–41: between pp. 249 and 250.

130. For numerous examples of such overestimates, see Morison 1939–41.

the sketch map of this area of Haiti that is generally believed to be in Columbus's own hand.[131] On this he shows Cap S. Nicolas Mole as disproportionately large, almost half the length of the island of Tortuga, when in fact it is only about one-fifth as long. Columbus also overestimated the size of Tortuga on this map, as well as its distance from Hispaniola, by a factor of two or three.[132]

All this means that there is a great deal more reason to believe that Columbus wrote ".34." and meant it than to accept that Las Casas miswrote Columbus's "3 ó 4." What is undeniably clear is that the text of the diario does read either 34 or 24 (or 24 changed to 34) and that threequarters of the modern editions fail to let the reader in on what has become, through editorial emendation, something of a secret. It also suggests that, but for the lone exception of Navarrete's copyist, no modern editor has been concerned with the calligraphic aspects of this text. As we can see, the figure in the manuscript looks very much as if Las Casas had first written a 2 and then changed it to a 3. While this may not be especially significant in the larger picture, it is an integral and inseparable part of the history of the diario—far more so than the dubious notion that Las Casas's exemplar had "3 ó 4."[133] Whatever else, the incident symbolizes the habit of modern editors of the diario of attributing particular transcribing errors without cause.

IX

The critical stance adopted in this brief survey of modern editorial practices derives from the earlier discussion about the procedures and standards being adopted with greater effect by textual critics and documentary editors everywhere, particularly with respect to the deplorable practice of emending a text silently. Jenkinson did not exaggerate when she characterized silent emendation as "an insidious vice" and a scholarly crime.[134] Each time it occurs it tears the text farther and farther away from

---

131. Morison 1939–41:263; Morison 1942, 1:374, as well as numerous other places.

132. Morison/Columbus 1963:115–24, esp. 115n1 and 120n4.

133. The fact that Las Casas frequently amended numbers in his transcription militates against his making this kind of error. Yet again, in his *Historia* (Las Casas 1951, 1:253–54) he omitted this detail. Ferdinand (Colón 1930, 1:194–95) also had nothing helpful to say.

134. Jenkinson 1934:433.

the opportunity to study it carefully and thoroughly, and worse, it does so furtively. Silent emendation is a pernicious form of arrogance on the part of editors who, in doing it, assume time and again that they know better than both their texts and their presumed audience. In both instances they run the risk of being wrong.

The cost effectiveness and appropriateness of providing diplomatic or genetic texts has often been called into question, particularly if the body of materials involved is large—perhaps several published editions or thousands of letters—or its importance historically marginal. None of this is valid for the diario, which is a single, relatively short text of central importance, as the body of interpretation based on it so amply illustrates. All things considered, the treatment accorded this text is as extraordinary as it is condescending. Worst of all, it is symptomatic, almost as though pinning down the text of the diario was an end not so fondly to be desired after all.[135]

135. The treatment of the text of the *Peregrinação* of Fernão Mendes Pinto provides a parallel, though less grand, example; see Catz 1988.

6. Columbus Revised

Day by day and almost minute by minute the past was brought up to date. In this way every prediction made by the Party could be shown by documentary evidence to have been correct. . . . All history was a palimpsest, scraped clean and reinscribed exactly as often as necessary.

GEORGE ORWELL

In the prologue to the diario we find Columbus undertaking, among other things, to "write all this voyage very punctually, from day to day, all that I should do, see, and undergo, as will be seen in what follows . . . besides writing each night that which occurred during the day and each day whatever was sailed at night."[1] In this way, the text assures us, not only will the contents of the account that follows be a full rendering of the vicissitudes of the voyage but also they will be recorded promptly, even spontaneously. Students of the first voyage have generally allowed themselves to be comforted by these words. Even those who believe that the prologue was written after the voyage have seldom been inclined to doubt its sincerity in this respect.[2] This view was forcefully, if somewhat defensively, expressed by Morison in his statement, "Crackpot critics of Columbus always base their theories on a presumed going-over of the Journal by Columbus or Las Casas to iron out inconsistencies and play up the Indies." Morison was sure that, on the contrary, Columbus "always let his mistakes stand."[3]

1. Alvar/Columbus 1976, 2:17–18; Dunn and Kelley/Columbus 1989:18–20. For the expected characteristics of logs of the time, see Pinto 1989:100–132.
2. Cronau 1921:19; Stewart 1931:128; Olschki 1941:649; Verhoog 1954:1106–7; Jane/Columbus 1960:xviii; Jos 1979:119; Ferro 1987:101–2, 108–9. Cf. Morison/Columbus 1963:48n.
3. Morison 1942, 1:347, 350n11, referring primarily to Vignaud and others who believed that the diario was largely a forgery.

This ready acceptance is hardly surprising, because it offers at least two advantages. First, it encourages us to take the diario always at its word, certainly the preferred alternative in dealing with any source. Moreover, it lends to each statement in it an aura of immediacy, even artlessness—rare enough commodities in the historical record. But the very lure of these advantages requires that Columbus's statement be tested carefully before it can be taken as attaining, or even approaching, the status of truth, whether prospective or retrospective. Here I am particularly concerned with Columbus's promise that he would record events "from day to day" in his log, as well as the conclusions that researchers have drawn from this assertion.

I

Logically, at least, any difference between a shipboard log and the diario could result from changes Columbus himself made during or after the voyage; from transmissional errors or changes by any of the intermediate scribes between Columbus and Las Casas; or from changes that Las Casas himself introduced. Early in this century, Vignaud was among the first to argue against the quotidian character of the diario when he suggested that "the definitive editing" of the log occurred after the return of the expedition, perhaps well after its return.[4] He supported his argument by pointing out that Ferdinand and Isabella wrote to Columbus in early September 1493 requesting that he supply the "degrees" of "the islands and land" he had discovered, as well as those of his routes there and back.[5] Presumably this information was required in the delicate negotiations that eventuated in the Treaty of Tordesillas the following year. Nearly a year later, Vignaud pointed out, the rulers asked Columbus for similar information.[6]

The second of these letters seems irrelevant (except as an indication of Columbus's reticence) since it must refer to Columbus's second voyage, but it is odd indeed that in their first letter Ferdinand and Isabella would have been obliged to solicit this information some six months after

4. Vignaud 1911, 2:259–61.

5. Ferdinand and Isabella to Columbus, 5 September 1493, in Navarrete/Columbus 1825, 1:130–33.

6. Ferdinand and Isabella to Columbus, 16 August 1494, in Navarrete/Columbus 1825, 1:184–86.

Columbus had returned and five months after he had surrendered the log to them. Although some have tried to explain this away, it is difficult to imagine what else this could mean except that the log was, or was thought to be, deficient in this area. At first glance the diario—the log as we now have it—is replete with just such information, but it may be that the authorities expected even more from Columbus.[7] Or it may be that these data entered the chain of transmission only at this point. Whatever the case, this letter alone is too ambiguous to serve as the sole basis for Vignaud's charge, although it may exonerate Las Casas from the frequently leveled accusation that he omitted some of these kinds of data as he transcribed.[8]

But if Vignaud provided the wrong answers, he was asking the right kind of question about the genesis and nature of the log even before its gradual transmutation into the diario, for the diario is suffused with knowledge of the future. Amazingly, he has been followed in this by almost no one except those, like Carbia, who preferred to argue that the entire text is a forgery.[9] Yet the issue persists.

Of special concern must be the role of intermediate scribes. In this respect, our ignorance only begins with the question of how many copyists intervened between the log Columbus surrendered and the text Las Casas copied. About this we do not know enough even to guess, except that two scribes were set to the task of making the very first copy of whatever document Columbus turned over on his return.[10] Nor have we the slightest notion of what their purposes in transcribing might have been, beyond the reasonable, if untestable, inference that it served some role in the pre-Tordesillas jockeying.

There is an overwhelming abundance of evidence to demonstrate that, even when transcription takes place under "ideal" conditions, there inevitably and frequently occur slips of the mind and pen.[11] Of course,

---

7. Morison (1942, 1:206–7) argued that Columbus lacked the scientific skills to provide more complete information and concluded rather rashly that Ferdinand and Isabella's request must have sprung from the Prologue, which was therefore written before the log.

8. E.g., Morison 1942, 1:206; Saint-Lu 1981:126.

9. Carbia 1929, 1930a, 1930b, 1931, 1936.

10. Ferdinand and Isabella to Columbus, 5 September 1493, in Navarrete/Columbus 1825, 1:131.

11. See chapter 2.

these are usually detected only by comparing manuscript copies of the text in question, but the diario exists *in vacuo,* and most such slips must go either unnoticed or unattributed.

We come to Las Casas. Almost no one doubts that Las Casas intentionally wrought various changes in the manuscript as he copied and paraphrased it.[12] McElroy succinctly expressed the conventional wisdom in the matter when he wrote that the changes were "so few" and "so easy to detect" that any perspicacious student of the voyage need only root them out and exclude them from his or her reasoning.[13] The notion is appealing, and there has been a profusion of efforts to substantiate it. Vázquez's analysis is probably the most ambitious of these, pinpointing more than a dozen such interpolations in which Las Casas questioned, corrected, or chided Columbus within the text of the diario.[14] Numerous others have addressed the problem too, though on a smaller scale.

Certainly there are a number of exempla in the diario that are easily recognized as insertions. Sometimes Las Casas helped out by placing them within parentheses; at other times he provided information that could not have been known to Columbus or expressed what were clearly his own sentiments. But as Vázquez's study shows, if only incidentally, in many cases it is no more than modern inference that attributes certain passages to Las Casas or another scribe, so well have they been integrated into the text. In addition, we have already seen how Las Casas added some 200 marginal notes to his draft. While not denying that Las Casas interpolated intratextually, Saint-Lu regards these marginalia as a kind of safety valve by which Las Casas was able to intrude his views while protecting the integrity of his received text.[15] This is doubtless an effect of the practice, if not necessarily its intention, although it seems strange that Las Casas found it necessary to adopt both expedients so often.[16]

Be that as it may, the prevailing view of the diario is that Columbus did not refurbish his log, that intermediate scribes were virtually perfect

12. The exception is Rumeu de Armas (1973b, 1976).

13. McElroy 1941:211. See also Morison 1942, 1:156; Cioranescu/Columbus 1961:364; Saint-Lu 1981; Scammell 1981:301–2; Fuson 1987b:179.

14. Vázquez 1971.

15. Saint-Lu 1981:124–26; cf. Arce Fernández 1974:58–59.

16. In a sense his heavy use of marginal notes lends weight to Rumeu de Armas's generally weak argument that Las Casas was no more than a copyist, although not enough weight to cause us to accept it.

in their work, and that Las Casas signaled in one way or another all his own interjections.[17] The modern student need only strip away Las Casas's thinly disguised veneer in order to isolate pure Columbus—indeed the pristine shipboard log.[18] Such a view would not have embarrassed Dr. Pangloss, but the notion that Las Casas was always so maladroit as to reveal his handiwork is nothing more than an unusually virulent species of credulity. Worse yet, it is a position that can hardly be tested. Even so, I will discuss here five examples from the large number of cases in the diario that present anomalies that can best by explained by assuming that they were not originally part of the shipboard log.

II

The first of these is the episode of the light that the diario claims that Columbus saw several hours before land was sighted, a matter I take up from a different angle in chapter 10. Our knowledge of this incident derives largely from the entry for 11 October (see Appendix 1). The passage begins by granting that land itself was sighted by a member of the crew of the *Pinta*, the ship of Columbus's rival, Martín Alonso Pinzón. At first this might seem a wonderful example of Columbus's open-minded generosity, but that impression is squelched by what follows. Having let this cat out of the bag, the diario immediately reverts to telling the story of events that antedated the sighting, which is hardly characteristic of any log.

"Although" ("puesto que"), the diario continues in evident afterthought, Columbus himself had actually already seen, not land, but some kind of "light" ("lumbre"), something that was vague and intermittent, that soon disappeared, and that was seen by perhaps no more than one other Spaniard, perhaps none at all.[19] However peculiar it was, the tale proved plausible enough to secure Columbus the promised reward for sighting land, since the monarchs magnanimously conceded that the light

17. E.g., Martínez Hidalgo y Terán 1985:202–5; Taviani/Columbus 1988:58; Varela/Columbus 1989:28–29, 31.

18. This seems to be the underlying premise of Fuson's all-inclusive translation (Fuson 1987a).

19. For "lumbre" see Covarrubias Horozco 1611/1943:773; Corominas, 1954, 3:147.

was a divinely inspired metaphor for the land that was to be discovered only a few hours later.[20] One need not be unduly cynical to recognize the oddities of this passage and its probable intent: securing the reward. In fact, as we will see, both Las Casas and Ferdinand rearranged the sequence of events and added further details, as if struggling to make sense of the passage.[21] Basing his statements on a largely different set of informants, Oviedo offered a version that matched the diario in almost no respect at all.[22]

Textually, the problem has a double aspect—sequence and content. Even the most fervent admirers of the historical accuracy of the diario have found it hard to overlook the hindward nature of this entry, but many have chosen to believe, with Morison, that Columbus must have written it a day or two later while still in the frenzied thrall of a dream come true.[23] But if Columbus were keeping a log in the fashion he had promised, would he not have recorded the incident almost immediately rather than waiting for a day or more? Perhaps for the next four hours he was intent on seeking the source of the supposed light, but what about the several hours between the time land was sighted (2:00 A.M.) and dawn? The diario tells us that the fleet merely lay to during this interval, and one would expect that the potential financial implications of his good fortune would have impelled Columbus to get the story on record at the earliest possible moment.

Beyond the improbable sequence, there is also the matter of content. As I have suggested, the story is so skillfully told that it escaped refutation as easily at the time as it has since.[24] It was scarcely an apparition that all hands would have seen, and even from the first moment it was a matter of taking Columbus at his word. And, as Morison asked in another context: who would contravene the captain's word aboard ship?[25] It is true

20. Cédula dd, 23 May 1493, in Navarrete 1954–55, 1:326, to the point that they failed utterly to mention the light at all, a matter taken up in chapter 10.

21. Las Casas 1951, 1:198–99; Colón 1930, 1:159–63.

22. Oviedo 1851–55, 1:23–24.

23. Morison/Columbus 1963:63n2.

24. But who was there to refute it? Both officials whom Columbus asked (one said he had seen the light, the other had not) were left behind at Navidad, where they perished.

25. Morison 1942, 1:266.

that the diario recorded that, after the purported event, few believed that the apparition was a sign of land, but they did not question that there had been an apparition. Columbus begged to differ about its significance, and neither for the first time nor the last, the diario proved him correct in the midst of error.

If this entry is indeed a revision of the original log, it is no easier to suggest who might have done it than it is to pinpoint when it was done. Columbus could have done it as early as Morison suggested, but the maladroit way in which the rewriting was handled indicates a later date, perhaps during the generally uneventful homeward passage or after arrival in Spain.[26] Or someone else who was desirous of securing for Columbus every important prize on the voyage could have introduced the story. In any case, in its bizarre narrative configuration and its self-serving content, the passage cries out to be regarded as a later addition.

III

Wherever Columbus found himself at daybreak on 12 October, his instincts were firmly proprietary. His first recorded action was to disembark and claim this presumed outpost of the Far East for the Spanish crown. The scene that followed has inspired countless artistic renderings. Featured prominently in these are the banners the diario described:

> The admiral brought out the royal banner; and the captains [of the *Pinta* and the *Niña*] two banners of the green cross which the Admiral displayed on all the ships as a sign, with an F and a Y [and] above each letter a crown, one at one end of the cross, the other at the other.[27]

Then followed further details regarding the formalities of taking possession of the island and its lucky inhabitants in the time-honored fashion developed during the Reconquista and recertified in the conquest of the Canaries then still in progress.[28] At this point the first Indians appeared on the scene, and Las Casas promptly reverted to "the very words" of Columbus.

26. Or even later, to judge from the silence of the cédula noted above.
27. Alvar/Columbus 1976, 2:48; Dunn and Kelley/Columbus 1989:62. It is generally believed that the "F" stood for Ferdinand and the "Y" for Isabella, but for a different view see Gandía 1942:299–300.
28. For the background see Morales Padrón 1955 and Pescador del Hoyo 1955.

Our interest here is in these banners, or rather in the way in which the diario so lavishly and minutely describes them. Their provenance is nowhere stated, but both common sense and the use of the definite article make it reasonable to assume that they were known quantities that had been devised specifically for the expedition by the royal authorities or by Columbus with their approval.[29] The reference to them as "of the green cross" ("de la cruz verde") suggests that they were patterned after the banner of the military order of Alcántara, which consists of a green cross on a white field. At any rate, the casual reference to "*the* green cross" implies that these banners were well-known to the Spanish monarchs and their relevant officials. If so, we are obliged to consider the incongruity of this detailed description and ask why Columbus would have felt obliged to provide so detailed a verbal picture in his log, which he was compiling precisely for the eyes of the very persons from whom he had received the banners in the first place.

In the version of the log we now have, these banners, although well-known to the expected readers, are treated in exactly the same narrative fashion as the people and places of the West Indies. According to the diario, Columbus made no distinction, even though he was describing both things fully familiar and completely new things. In this sense the diario's description is not only superfluously detailed contextually but excessive in every respect. No matter how dazzled Columbus was at the moment—or rather at whatever moment he recorded this entry—we can hardly expect that he would have more than alluded to the banners, since they were simply a routine feature of a longstanding ceremony. In fact, it is more likely that, if his intent was to certify that he had followed the proper procedures, Columbus would have included more of the formalities themselves rather than concentrate on one of their lesser constituents. But the diario says otherwise, and in the circumstances we must suspect that its embarrassment of riches arose at a later stage as the log was on its way to becoming the diario. Las Casas is a possible candidate here but not an entirely likely one since this account is also in Ferdinand's *Historie*, although, interestingly, the description of the banners there differs

29. At least this is the import of Ferdinand's account (Colón 1930, 1:165), which referred to "the banners of the enterprise." Cf. Morison 1942, 1:166. It is impossible to imagine that Ferdinand and especially Isabella failed to exercise their royal prerogative in this matter.

slightly from that in the diario.[30] Perhaps a royal scribe, who would better have been able to provide the picturesque details, is more likely. In this instance, at least, Columbus is not a likely candidate. Whatever the case, this passage appears to represent an egregious instance of unbetokened but interpolated matter. In its excess and incongruity it seemingly invited unmasking at an early point in the study of the diario, but its career as an integral and accredited feature of the log continues unchecked.

IV

In the entry for 11/12 October, Columbus reported that he understood that the Indians of Guanahaní had been subjected to slave raiders, expressing the evidence in the following way:

> I saw some who had signs of wounds on their bodies and I made signs to them [asking] what it was, and they showed me how people from other islands that were nearby came there and wanted to take them, and they defended themselves. And I believed and [now] believe that they came here from the mainland ["tierra firme"] to take them captive.[31]

Two things about this passage immediately draw one's attention. The first is Columbus's (Las Casas claimed to be quoting him here) disparate references to Guanahaní, where he supposedly was at the moment, as both "here" and "there." This kind of slip would much more likely have been made at a later time when the revisionist was not at Guanahaní and so might instinctively refer to it as "there."

The other peculiarity is Columbus's use of the phrase "I believed and [now] believe" ("yo creí y creo"). What could he have intended by this construction? Surely he did not mean to imply that, as he entered the statement in the log on his very first day among the Indians of the New World he was still believing what they had told him only a few hours before? This juxtaposition of the past and present tenses for emphasis, although it exemplifies the dual tense emphatic used by some testators of the period, is unique in the diario, but this has drawn no attention.

30. Colón 1930, 1:165. Clearly, though, the description in the diario permits more than one graphic interpretation—even in its detail, the text confuses. Cioranescu/Columbus 1961:386n67 attributes the difference to a "misunderstanding" on the part of the translator of Ferdinand's *Historie*.

31. Alvar/Columbus 1976, 2:52–53; Dunn and Kelley/Columbus 1989:66. See Appendix 1.

One might be tempted to credit Las Casas with this little twist, but in his *Historia* Las Casas placed this passage elsewhere, even though he was actually in the midst of quoting Columbus at the time.[32] Clearly he was not inclined to preserve untouched for posterity this disagreeable view of one group of Indians enslaving another. Nor does there seem to be any reason why a transcriber would add one verb form or the other to the text. We are left with Columbus. Whether the Indians were in fact trying to tell Columbus what he thought they were telling him, it is easy to see why he would have been inclined to believe in such a state of affairs, since it offered a handy humanitarian impulse for future interference by providing the occasion to add God to gold.[33] On these grounds the repetition for emphasis would have been added at a later point as Columbus was crystallizing his plans for future activity in the area.

In fact, it is just the kind of minor revision that must be commonplace in the diario and its antecedents—occasions in which Columbus found it expedient to tie up loose ends or otherwise read into the diario knowledge gained from later experiences on the first voyage. The word "creí" is very much the type of interlinear addition that would idly be transplanted to the text proper by a scribe interested only in transforming the text before him into a thing of beauty and coherence, in much the same way as modern editors have in their turn treated the manuscript of the diario.

V

Expedience probably played an even greater role in the next passage to be discussed. The next day, 13 October, Columbus continued to record his impressions of the Indians as they came out to the ship, apparently in large numbers. In describing their complexions he observed that "they are in no way black, but rather of the color of the Canarians. Nor should anything else be expected since this [island is] east-west with the island of Hierro, on a line."[34]

32. Las Casas 1951, 1:204–5. See Henige n.d.

33. For the two recent views of Columbus's ability to understand the Indians at this stage of the game, see Szászdi 1985:17–19. Szászdi believes Columbus may have understood them. Hulme, in contrast, holds that it is all but impossible that he understood them (1986:17–43).

34. Alvar/Columbus 1976, 2:54; Dunn and Kelley/Columbus 1989:68. See Appendix 1.

The claim that Columbus thought that Guanahaní and Hierro were on exactly the same parallel has occasioned considerable modern comment, most concerned with establishing the identity of Guanahaní or appraising the navigational instincts of Columbus. In the former case, the statement has sometimes been taken to indicate a more northerly landfall, since Hierro's latitude (27° 46' N) is roughly the same as St. Petersburg, Florida, and is north of any of the Bahamas. More frequently the text has been used to gauge Columbus's accuracy as a sailor. The two points are hardly unrelated, of course, as Morison made clear when he announced that "there is only 3° 41' difference in their latitudes," attempting to minimize the difference in order both to argue that Watlings Island is Guanahaní and that Columbus was one of the finest dead-reckoning navigators of all time.[35]

Columbus's comment is not without context in the diario, in fact not without an apparently plausible context: the complexion of the Indians. But then we note that in the preceding day's entry Columbus had already described the Indians as "of the color of the Canarians."[36] To do so again was unnecessarily reiterative, even for the diario.[37] But when we look for other possible contexts for Columbus's insistence that Guanahaní and Hierro shared the same latitude we find that, while this emphasis may not have been necessary on 13 October 1492, it was decidedly expedient within a few months.

When Columbus was driven into Lisbon by a storm on his way home, he found himself once again in the jurisdiction of none other than João II, who grilled him in rather unfriendly fashion about his recent activities.[38] Rui de Pina, the Portuguese royal chronicler, tells us that João II was "outraged and aggrieved" to learn of Columbus's discoveries.[39] He was certain that Columbus had been poaching on territory assigned to Portugal by the Treaty of Alcáçovas, signed in 1479 and blessed by a papal bull two years later.

35. Morison/Columbus 1963:67n1. Watlings Island's latitude is 24° 06' N. Similar views have been expressed by, among others, Vidal Gormaz 1892:214n and Ferro 1987.

36. Alvar/Columbus 1976, 2:51; Dunn and Kelley/Columbus 1989:66.

37. For the duplications in the entries for these days, see chapter 12.

38. For this episode, see Alvar/Columbus 1976, 2:238–40; Dunn and Kelley/Columbus 1989:392–95; Las Casas 1951, 1:316–18; Colón 1930, 1:237–38 (more briefly and without the benefit of the Portuguese chroniclers' perspective).

39. Pina 1950:184; cf. Resende 1902, 3:20–22.

By this treaty Portugal had been granted rights to the region described as "qualesquier otras yslas que se fallaron o conquirieren de las yslas de Canaria *para baxo contra Guinea*" (what other islands which shall be found or conquered from the Canary Islands *down toward Guinea*).[40] This phrasing was interpreted, at least in the abstract, to mean that any lands to the south of the Canaries or any south of Cape Bojador (25° 06' N) on the west coast of Africa fell to the Portuguese monopoly.[41] But the wording was vexingly vague: Could not "para baxo" mean "west" (if there were a west) as well as "south"? And what exactly was encompassed by the phrase "ab insulis de Canaria ultra et citra et in conspectu Guinee" (from beyond the Canaries, and on this side of and in the vicinity of Guinea) in the papal bull *Aeterni Regis* of 1481?[42] For that matter, what constituted Guinea itself? Perhaps some of this did not matter, since both the treaty and the papal bull went on to limit Spanish expansion to the Canaries, which were itemized, and "all other Canary Islands conquered or to be conquered."[43] Because Columbus had taken possession of islands no less than thirty-three days' sailing west of the Canaries and had returned by way of the Azores, which were universally recognized to be Portuguese, João and his advisers had every reason to conclude that Portugal had a strong claim to the new discoveries, and they appear to have tried hard to convince Columbus of this.

Pina related that João had to resist the importunities of his counselors to assassinate Columbus, thereby cutting the incipient Gordian knot.[44] Although João dissembled and even managed to convince Columbus that he was "pleased" to learn of the new discoveries, he also informed Columbus that he "understood by the capitulation [of Alcáçovas]" that "the conquest belonged to him [João]," which probably serves to explain his delight as much as anything else.[45]

Columbus must have felt himself in rather a false position here, and he took refuge in pleading ignorance of the terms of the treaty. But he as-

40. Davenport 1917:38–44, with emphasis added.

41. For the Treaty of Alcáçovas and its aftermath, see Rumeu de Armas 1944; Bayle 1945; Pérez Embid 1948:214–20; Castañeda 1973:103–15.

42. Davenport 1917:51, 53.

43. Davenport 1917:38–51.

44. Pina 1950:185.

45. Alvar/Columbus 1976, 2:238–40; Dunn and Kelley/Columbus 1989:396. Las Casas (1951, 1:323–24) repeated this and added material from Resende. Useful accounts of the affair are Morison 1942, 1:436–42 and Davenport 1917:9–12.

sured João that Ferdinand and Isabella had forbidden him to go to any part of "Guinea." João replied "graciously," if somewhat ominously, that he was sure that the matter could be settled without the need for arbitration (the reigning pope was Spanish). João then handed Columbus over to the hospitality of the prior of Crato, but the next day he questioned him further, if still politely.[46] After a cameo appearance the following day, João then disappeared from the diario but certainly not entirely from the thoughts of Columbus, to whom the notion of relinquishing his discoveries to the ingrate Portuguese ruler must have seemed unbearably odious.

Within this context we can return to the passage. Columbus knew he was on safe ground in asserting that Guanahaní was not south even of the most southerly of the Canaries, for Hierro had been excluded by name from the Portuguese sphere. Moreover, he would not have been unaware that Cape Bojador, the other frame of reference, was still south of Hierro.[47] A question remains as to the extent he would have known that his statement about the latitude of Guanahaní was incorrect as well as expedient. Opinions as to his latitudinal navigational skills vary markedly.[48] Even so, he need only have consulted his log to realize that he had sailed many more miles to the southwest than to the northwest, and he must have concluded from this that Guanahaní was farther south than any of the Canaries, Hierro included.[49]

Columbus's letter to Luis de Santangel—dated 15 February 1493 and identified as being written in the Canaries, although Columbus was then in the Azores—suggests that he was having second thoughts about the need for damage control in specifying the locations of his new discoveries. At any rate, he described them (in aggregate, none in particular) as located at 26° N even though Cuba and Hispaniola are more like 20° N.[50] Thus he had already begun to edge them northward toward Hierro's lati-

46. Alvar/Columbus 1976, 2:240; Dunn and Kelley/Columbus 1989:396–98.

47. For Cape Bojador see the bull *Inter Caetera* of 1456: Davenport 1917:12, 29, 31, 81n.

48. On these see Morison 1942, 1:240–63; Laguardia Trías 1974:18–28 and passim.

49. This contradicts Ferro 1987:103–4.

50. Jane 1930b:15. Proponents of northerly landfalls (e.g., Molander 1985:120; Molander 1987:148; Winslow 1988; Winslow n.d.) find this placement significant, but it is just one of many offered by Columbus.

tude. The extent to which this contradicted any log entry in Columbus's mind is anyone's guess, although in fact 26° N is almost exactly the same latitude as that of Cape Bojador. It may be, then, that Columbus had already introduced the extraneous remark about Guanahaní's latitude into the log before he reached Portugal. If he had not, though, the situation in which he found himself there would have offered enough incentive.

As it happens, although Columbus escaped the enmity of the Portuguese court, the long arm of its diplomacy followed him to Spain. When he arrived at Barcelona scarcely a month after his return, he found the diplomatic ferment among Spain, Portugal, and the papacy already at full boil.[51] It is fairly certain that he retained possession of the log up to this time, so he could have adjusted it easily enough.[52] There is another, and perhaps even more likely, possibility. When the Spanish rulers wrote to Columbus in September, they apologized for the delay in returning a copy of the log to him, but the work of transcription had gone slowly, they said, because it was necessary to keep it hidden from the Portuguese officials at the Spanish court. What better time, and for what better reason, to introduce this clause into the text of the transcription, or even into the original? Whether or not these Portuguese officials were certain that the log existed, they might reasonably have inferred as much. If so, the Spanish authorities may have feared that it would be called into evidence during the negotiations already ensuing, and this provided a perfectly sound reason for bringing its data into line with their diplomatic aims.

In sum, the diario's comment on Hierro is a political statement rather than a geographical one, intent on telling its readers where Guanahaní was not rather than where it was. The reasons and opportunities for changing the diario in this respect were many. Columbus's letter to Santangel illustrates that the notion had already occurred to him, and this was shortly followed by experiences in Lisbon that must have seemed to him the prelude to a Barmecidal feast. Finally, the log was in the posses-

---

51. Dawson 1899; Vander Linden 1916; Morison 1942, 1:431.

52. Ferro (1987:103–4) concludes that latitude data had been gathered at Guanahaní, but then suppressed because Columbus realized that he might be trespassing on the Portuguese monopoly. Thus, when the log was surrendered, such data were "absolutely lacking" in it. For other views on Columbus's possible reasons for manipulating these data, see Magnaghi 1928:493–94, 553–58; Magnaghi 1990; Magnaghi 1933; Laguardia Trías 1974:18–22.

sion of the Spanish court for several months, during which its contents would have been seen either as potentially dangerous or as possibly useful, depending on just what they happened to be. In this ambiance the log had become a political document, not a scripture, and as such it may have been a candidate for a great deal of refashioning—even to the point, one might think, of producing a separate copy tailored to meet anticipated needs.

VI

Finally we come to the singular incidents of the casting of the chick-pea lots. During the return voyage the two remaining ships encountered storms so violent that Columbus feared for the expedition's survival. Clearly, it was the time for extraordinary measures, and no fewer than four times he adopted the standard procedure of the time of vowing to undertake a pilgrimage to a celebrated shrine in return for a favor granted. In each case, the diario tells us, it was decided to cast lots to determine which members of the *Niña*'s complement should accept the burden of carrying out this commitment. One chick-pea for each man aboard was placed into a cap. One of these had a cross cut into it, and the man who chose this pea was obligated to perform the pilgrimage.

On 14 February three such lots were drawn. In the first one, Columbus drew first and plucked out the marked pea. In the next lot, a certain Pedro de Villa found himself the fortunate pilgrim-in-waiting. In the final lot of the day, Columbus again drew the marked pea.[53] About three weeks later, another storm imposed the same measure, and . . . "the lot fell on the Admiral." In short, the diario informs us that Columbus was chosen by the peas three of the four times.

We realize instinctively that the likelihood of such a result occurring is extremely low, just how low depends on factors such as the number of peas in each lot and at what point in each drawing Columbus chose.[54] There were probably from twenty-two to twenty-five men on board the

53. Alvar/Columbus 1976, 2:223–24; Dunn and Kelley/Columbus 1989:364–66. Cf. Las Casas 1951, 1:312; Colón 1930, 1:221–22.

54. Alvar/Columbus 1976, 2:235–36; Dunn and Kelley/Columbus 1989:390. I am very grateful to Douglas Bates for help on calculating the probabilities here. Cf. Las Casas 1951, 1:321; Colón 1930; 1:232–33.

Niña during the return trip. We know from the diario only that on the first occasion Columbus drew first, though he may well have regarded this as his prerogative. On this assumption, and using the minimum figure of twenty-two peas, the probability that Columbus would have chosen the marked pea on all but the second occasion would be

$$.04545 \times .9555 \times .04545 \times .04545 = .0000895 \text{ or about 1 in 11,200}$$

cases.

However, the probability that Columbus would have chosen the marked pea on any three of the four occasions would be four times as great, or one in approximately 2,800, which is at least a token nod in the direction of plausibility.

If Columbus had chosen later in the last three drawings—say, tenth each time—then the odds for drawing the marked pea in the first, third, and fourth lots would be only about one in 5,000, assuming that he had the chance to draw in the second round, and again would be four times this, or about 1 in 1,250 for any three rounds. In other words, and with these assumptions, all undemonstrable but none implausible, the probability that the story of the chick-pea lots in the diario is accurate ranges from a low of one in 11,200 to a high of 1 in 1,250. Perhaps the episode of the chick-pea lots is not the most improbable in the diario, but it is the one most easily subjected to the acid statistical test of unlikelihood. As we see, it hardly passes that test.

Ferdinand noticed his father's luck and thought that the answer lay in a divine miracle rather than a statistical one. Discerning a supernatural hand in the proceedings, he piously observed that God was pleased to direct Columbus's hand to the marked peas "to show that the vows made by him were more pleasing than those [made by] others" ("dimostrare essergli più grate le promesse di lui che quelle de gli altri").[55]

One might expect that modern commentators not related to Columbus by blood would seek the answer elsewhere, but few have. Morison recognized the oddity and wondered: "Is it possible that some expert gambler among the men juggled the peas against him?"[56] The question best

---

55. Colón 1930, 1:233. Las Casas (1951, 1:312, 321) ventured no opinion but added a wry "as usual" ("como solía") after recounting the fourth drawing.

56. Morison 1942, 1:421; Granzotto (1985:181) follows Morison in looking for a gambler.

remains in the realm of the rhetorical. The more likely solution is that these episodes—or their outcome—were added to the log in order to cast a faintly virtuous light on the new Admiral of the Ocean Sea. Under the circumstances it is hardly possible to know whether Columbus himself felt the need or whether it was another, not excluding Las Casas. In closing, it might be noted that all three pilgrimage sites chosen by Columbus were in Spain, while poor Pedro de Villa found himself obliged to travel to Italy to redeem his pledge.[57]

VII

In the golden age of the movies, the Saturday serials flourished. Each week at segment's end the hero or heroine was brought to a perilous and seemingly inextricable pass. But at the beginning of the following week's episode, the impasse had become, as if by magic and certainly never on screen, ever so slightly diminished, the inextricable had become the barely extricable, and the story was allowed to recycle itself through a series of these metamorphoses for several weeks. So, too, with many modern efforts to rescue the diario from its contradictions and improbabilities in pursuit of historical certainty. In fact, these defects often turn out to be sows' ears that can be turned into silk purses.

The transformations begin with statements that deny reality. For instance, for McElroy the diario "shows no signs whatever of having been tampered with or even revised."[58] In like fashion, Didiez Burgos believes that "the distances, headings, and calculations [in the diario] are perfect," and "its facts follow along without interruption and without alteration."[59] Similarly resounding pronouncements reverberate through the literature.[60]

The next step, a form of sovereign remedy, is to suggest that the very contradictions (for even those who believe that we have discovered the log

57. Although Columbus promised to foot the expenses; presumably he felt he would not have the time to travel to Italy before beginning a new voyage and so declined to draw the marked pea.

58. McElroy 1941:210–11; cf. Arranz/Columbus 1985:63.

59. Didiez Burgos 1974:393.

60. For instance, that Las Casas was so "scrupulous" that he always added an "etc." or "indicated the reasons" why he did not reproduce material. Cioranescu/Columbus 1961:364–65. See Saint-Lu 1981:130 for a similar view. In fact there are only eight et ceteras in the entire diario.

reincarnate must admit to its contradictions) are proof of this uncorrupted state. Fox was one of the first to argue along these lines when he noted that Columbus "seems not to have overhauled his log to see whether it was at variance with itself."[61] This view has found a host of supporters.[62] How could it not, when virtually every entry provides another textual conundrum? Once this point in thinking is reached, a declaration of victory over the text usually ensues, and interpretative privilege is allowed to take possession of the battlefield.

In no small degree, this cozy orthodoxy springs from the fact that the diario has the format of a log and so purports to be a daily chronicle of events recorded as, or very shortly after, they occurred. As Fuson has recently put it: "We must assume that it was, *like other logs*, a true account of what happened *day by day*."[63] This instinct is entirely natural, but is it really easy to believe that Columbus never took time to reread and revise his log? At any rate, such a belief flies in the face of a rapidly growing body of evidence on other examples of the genre. In fact, thinking of the log Columbus surrendered on his return as a revised and reconstructed document puts it in ample and good company.

It may be surprising, but it is no less true, that some of the most famous "diaries" of all time, including the quintessential diary of them all, that of Samuel Pepys, were reprocessed by their authors before being consigned to publication or to the gaze of posterity.[64] The diaries of John Evelyn and Mary Boykin Chesnut underwent this refurbishing process, as did the *Anas* of Thomas Jefferson and the notes of James Madison on the Constitutional Convention.[65] In each case the revision did not extend to changing the format.[66]

---

61. Fox 1882:395.

62. Morison 1942, 1:206; Arce/Columbus 1971:17 ("written day by day with later retouching"); Saint-Lu 1981:126.

63. Fuson 1987a:xv, with emphasis added. Cf. Arranz/Columbus 1985:63.

64. Pepys 1970–76, 1:xlv lxvi–ix, xcvii–cvi; Latham 1974.

65. Evelyn 1955, 1:69–114; Lynn 1981; Faust 1982; Schachner 1951; Jefferson 1986:33–38; Cullen 1989; Farrand 1966, 1:xv–xix; Couser 1989:156–88.

66. Emonds (1941) provides an overview of discernible revising activity in the ancient world. One thread tying the sources together was the expectation that (like the diario) the work would be seen by others. More recent examples of the reconstructed diary include that of Anais Nin (Walters 1957; Nin 1968; Franklin and Schneider 1979:167–76; Black 1981; Tolstoy 1982; Scholar 1984:18–22; Sukenick 1976). A particularly minatory example is the printed edition of Gideon Welles's Civil War diary.

Perhaps the most famous of all modern diaries, that of Anne Frank, is similarly hybrid. Before her imprisonment she rewrote a large part of her original day-by-day account with the expressed ambition of ultimately having it published. Until recently no published version of her diary—or rather, diaries—took this into account by making any effort to include all or part of both recensions or even to indicate the nature of the problem. For our purposes it is important to note that the popular notion that Anne Frank's diary is entirely a spontaneous work compiled under the most trying conditions is an illusion.[67]

Nor were ships' logs themselves immune from the recasting process. In the seventeenth and early eighteenth centuries, for example, it was customary to publish journals of interesting voyages of discovery and piracy.[68] Almost invariably these were organized in the daily entry style and couched in the present tense. In one of the most famous of these, Woodes Rogers assured his readers that he had taken "the best method to preserve an unquestionable Relation of the Voyage, by having a daily Account kept in a publick Book of all our Transactions, which lay open to every one's View, and where any thing was reasonably objected against, it was corrected."[69] He went on to conclude: "This Method we observ'd during the whole Voyage, and almost in the same manner as you have it in the following Relation."[70] In fact, as he conceded, Rogers had "inserted" extraneous geographical and historical information "to oblige the Booksellers," and this constituted fully one-half of the whole.[71] Moreover,

---

In consulting the manuscript, Beale (1925) found that Welles made "an astounding number of emendations" at later dates, but the earlier published edition had assured readers that the diary had been "in no way mutilated or revised." See Welles 1960, 1 :xviii–xxxiv for more details. Studies of World War II fictional diaries include Young 1986–87; Young 1988 : 15–39; and Prüfer 1988. The genre of diary fiction has, in fact, been popular for centuries, for which see Stewart 1969, Abbott 1984, and Martens 1985. General studies include Späth 1987 and Hurlebusch 1987, while revised African travel journals are noted in Bridges 1986, Dawson 1987, and Helly 1987. See as well Plutschow 1982 and Campbell 1988. Another case is discussed in Terwiel 1989.

67. Frank 1989 : 59–77, 168–72.
68. Martens 1985 : 64–66.
69. Rogers 1712 : xxi.
70. Rogers 1712 : xxi.
71. Rogers 1712 : xvi.

another member of the same voyage had published his own account, and this gave Rogers an agenda: "to confirm the Truth of my Journal" against insinuations included in that version.[72] In these ways, esthetic and political considerations conspired to induce Rogers to produce a "journal" that was less a journal than a tract in journal form.[73]

Particularly unsettling is the fact that these tendencies toward revision usually have not been uncovered until long after the fact. The diagnoses are usually made possible by the inspection of successive manuscripts, the diarists' correspondence, or the handwriting, ink, and other physical characteristics of the original manuscript.[74] None of these diagnostic tools is available to students of the diario, which is several generations removed from the log and a primary source only by default. There is no paper trail to follow.

A natural consequence of this state of affairs is that the standard tools of textual criticism are blunted. Take, for example, the criterion of anachronism. For obvious reasons, this is regarded as the acid test by which textual scholars judge claims of immediacy in diaries, journals, logs, and the like. No one denies that the diario has its share of anachronisms, but these have customarily been debited to Las Casas's account. Las Casas endlessly glossed the text of the diario when he transferred it to the *Historia de las Indias,* and there certainly seems to be good reason to ascribe some of these anachronisms to him. He may even have been responsible for every one of them, but—and this is the point—we have no way of knowing, no foolproof litmus test. Columbus could very easily have introduced some of them later in the voyage. The only defense against this charge has been—can only be—that Columbus regarded the log as inviolate. As we have seen, this is not enough.[75]

72. Rogers 1712:xx. Cf. Cooke 1712. The introduction to Cooke's work included the same obligatory assertions of truth, and the work itself possessed the same diurnal format supplemented by great amounts of historical and geographical information for readers' edification.

73. For Rogers' work see Little 1960:151–59. The genre continues to this day; see Hassam 1988.

74. See esp. Pepys 1970–76, 1:xcvii–cvii for a discussion of the role of these factors.

75. Recently there has been much attention to the differences between the texts of Shakespeare's plays in the Folio and Quarto editions. The generally accepted view has been that these represent a form of "slippage" due to faulty memory on the part of

VIII

This discussion is not intended to condemn the log/diario by association so much as to urge the need to exempt it from the diplomatic immunity that so many critics have impulsively conferred on it. The diario offers a profusion of likely revisions beyond the few mentioned here: the double distances on the outward voyage, the fact that whenever positions were plotted Columbus was reported to be more correct than any of his pilots, and others.[76] Whatever the log was, and the diario is, it is much more than a terse and disinterested nautical account of passing events. It also served as a subterfuge to beguile the Portuguese, as a propaganda device and apologia in the service of Columbus, as a paean to a new world discovered as well as a testimony to the monumental illusions that it was really just another part of the Old World, and as an instrument for Las Casas to buttress his own worldview of the Spanish discovery and conquest and pass it along to others.[77] It will never be possible to cut through the results of this repeated editorial activity and recover the text of the log, which itself was probably never fixed. It is the argument here that Saint-Lu was no more than half right when he warned that "it is necessary

---

actors ("memorial reconstruction") or to changes emanating from repeated performance. Concomitantly, this logic holds, Shakespeare wrote with such facility and finality that the statement of two of his fellow actors that they had "scarce received from him a blot in his papers" was an accurate measure of his peculiar genius (Chambers 1930, 2:230). While time and oral transmission must have resulted in changes, the nature and extent of these has begun to lead several scholars to posit that Shakespeare made a practice of revising his *own* work from time to time, sometimes, as in *King Lear*, very markedly. For examples of this argument in context see Shakespeare 1986; Taylor 1986; Urkowitz, 1986a, 1986b; Everett 1988; Orgel 1988; Urkowitz 1988; Altman, 1989; Danson 1989; Honigmann 1989:188–221; Ioppolo 1989; Sams 1989. More generally, see Fisher 1988 and Higdon 1988.

76. E.g., Barata (1978:186) points out that Columbus would never have referred to the "roca de Sintra" (Alvar/Columbus 1976, 2:226, 236; Dunn and Kelley/Columbus 1989:373, 391) since at the time it was invariably called the Cabo da Roca. Other possible episodes are noticed in Ramos Pérez 1982 and Morales Padrón/Columbus 1984:220n675.

77. The mixed reception given Columbus on his return may also have played a role; for this see Ramos Pérez 1983b:7–43.

to guard against extreme positions that consist either of throwing everything into doubt systematically, or never posing questions at all."[78] In
fact, systematic doubt is the only legitimate methodology to apply to the
study of the diario.

78. Saint-Lu 1981:128.

7. Doubtful Distances
and Double Distances

In this distress I began to reflect on my former vanity, in imagining myself able to number the sand, to weigh the mountains, to sound the depth of the seas, and to measure the heavens.   JOHN JOHNSON

Despite Columbus's promise to provide all manner of detail regarding distances and courses traveled during his journey, such data for the first segment of the voyage are already sparse, as illustrated in the following table, in which one league is taken to equal three nautical miles and inferred distances are in brackets:[1]

Date	Leagues	Miles
8/3	15 + x	45 + x [49]
8/4	—	[94]
8/5	40 +	120 +
8/6	29	87
8/7	25	75
8/8	—	[94]

Although the diario does not specify when the counting should stop, Ferdinand is more helpful, saying that the fleet came within sight of the Canaries at daybreak on 9 August.[2] Regrettably, the island sighted is left unnamed, but both the diario and Ferdinand's account permit us to think

---

1. Alvar/Columbus 1976, 2:18–22; Dunn and Kelley/Columbus 1989:20–24. In his *Historia* Las Casas (1951, 1:179–82) did not include any of these figures, in fact ignored the details in the diario almost completely.

2. Colón 1930, 1:126–28.

that it was Gran Canaria, although both Lanzarote and Fuertaventura would likely have been seen first in the course of events.[3]

At any rate, we see from the table that Columbus provided specific information for only three days and part of a fourth. The average distance traveled on these three days was about ninety-four miles per day, and for the sake of argument, I have assumed that Columbus traveled about this distance on the other three days as well. On several grounds, using this average figure may be unduly generous. For instance, we learn from the diario that the *Pinta* had a rudder problem for several days, and Ferdinand tells us that this problem began the second day out and caused frequent delays.[4] Moreover, when this first happened Columbus could do no more than offer words of encouragement because of rough weather. The following day the makeshift repairs were damaged by high winds, and it was necessary to lay to and effect more repairs.[5] The diario mentions the need for repairs to the *Pinta* as well but assigns them (or so it appears) to different days than Ferdinand. It also notes, if more allusively, that Columbus could not come to the assistance of the *Pinta* "without danger to himself" ("sin su peligro").[6] The diario is unusually reticent about those travails, but several months later, when alluding to the tempest that forced Columbus to put into the Azores, it records that a similar storm had occurred "on the way to the Canaries" ("y lo mismo acaeció a la ida hasta las islas de Canaria").[7]

All in all, using an average of ninety-four miles per day for all six days is probably overstating the distances covered. Even so, the sum of that procedure, 564 miles plus the distance from sighting Gran Canaria to reaching it, falls far short of the actual distance from Palos, which is about 680 miles, with no detours allowed for contrary winds and storms.[8] To reach the higher figure, we must credit the fleet with having traveled

3. Colón 1930, 1 : 126–28. Alvar/Columbus 1976, 2 : 22–24; Dunn and Kelley/Columbus 1989 : 24–26. Apparently Lanzarote was the intended destination before the need for repairs forced a detour. See Cioranescu 1959 : 64–65, 73–75. Santiago (1955 : 350–78) is useful but less analytical than Cioranescu.

4. Colón 1930, 1 : 126–28.

5. Colón 1930, 1 : 126–28.

6. Alvar/Columbus 1976, 2 : 19–20; Dunn and Kelley/Columbus 1989 : 22.

7. Alvar/Columbus 1976, 2 : 231–32; Dunn and Kelley 1989 : 382.

8. U.S. Navy 1985 : 144; Fitzpatrick 1986 : 261; IATA/IAL 1986 : S322.

353 miles in the two and a half days that are not accounted for. This total is greater than the 327 miles recorded for one full day more. To put it another way, the daily average would be 48 percent greater than the known average for 3 1/2 days. In any circumstances this would be unlikely, and in the particular circumstances of the occasion it can only be considered impossible.

Yet both the diario and Ferdinand tell us that the three ships did reach the Canaries in this six-day period. Noting that the trip ordinarily took ten days, Morison observed that "Columbus's fleet was lucky to raise Grand Canary only six days out."[9] Judging only from the distances recorded in the diario, we have to think of it more as miraculous than lucky. The most obvious explanation is that the distances actually recorded in the diario were gross underestimates. Whatever the case, the dissonance between the figures recorded in the diario, the known events of the trip, and the actual mileage between Palos and Gran Canaria (and therefore necessarily covered) combines to bode ill for quantitative exercises regarding Columbus's first voyage that require both detail and precision. But perhaps this case is an aberration, the result of Columbus's or Las Casas's unwonted carelessness. Looking at data for other distances recorded in the diario might help us to decide.[10]

I

Few aspects of the testimony of the diario have raised more interest and presented more problems among students of the first voyage than the strange matter of the "double distances."[11] In the diario Columbus alleges several times that he provided two sets of figures for distances traveled daily—one a deliberately lowered set to allay the anticipated fears of the crews, the other the "true" set, designed for the inquiring eye of posterity. If it was actually carried into practice, the expedient created more mischief long after the voyage than during it. Some have been unkind enough to use these statements to highlight the underside of Columbus's

9. Morison 1942, 1:280.

10. For another discussion of the Palos–Canaries link see Díaz del Río Martínez 1986.

11. For more on the problem of the double distances, examined from a different angle, see Henige and Zamora 1989.

personality. Others see it as politic but impractical, while still others have found it both high-minded and feasible. At least one observer has suggested that it represented an act of altruism by Columbus to translate the figures from the shorter Italian mile he was using to Spanish measure to keep the men fully informed.[12]

It appears that there was more afoot than gulling the men. Typically, though, this other motive surfaced elsewhere in the diario, where, as late as 18 February 1493 we read: "And [Columbus] says that he pretended to have gone farther in order to confuse the pilots and sailors who were charting [the course], so that he would remain the master of that route of the Indies, as in fact he did remain, since not one of all of them drew his certain course because of which no one could be certain of his route to the Indies."[13] Columbus appears here to have been referring to his return route, more of which later, but it indicates his state of mind as to the value of his figures. Beyond that, as a defense it is singularly preposterous. Had Columbus wished to remain "master of that route of the Indies," he would have falsified directions rather than distances, especially if he thought that a mainland remained to be found just beyond his own discoveries. Citing public figures that were in the neighborhood of 20 percent less than the actual (or believed) distances would have little effect beyond making any imitators wonder a little longer as they kept heading directly for America.

Columbus provided at least two reasons for instituting double navigational bookkeeping. Both are implausible, but faith persists. Much of this I have addressed elsewhere. Here I want to notice only the extent to which the "true" and "false" figures survive their context. Table 7.1 synthesizes these figures as they appear in the diario and includes figures for the two occasions on which each of the pilots provided his own estimates of the accumulated distance from Gómera in the Canaries.

We will first look at the two sets of estimates of total distance traveled through 18 September for all three ships and then from 19 September

12. Kelley 1985:91–92.

13. Alvar/Columbus 1976, 2:228; Dunn and Kelley/Columbus 1989:374: "Y diz qui fingió haber andado más camino por desatinar a los pilotos y marineros que carteaban, por quedar él señor de aquella derrota de las Indias, como de hecho queda, porque ninguno de todos ellos traía su camino cierto, por lo qual ninguno puede estar seguro de su derrota para las Indias."

TABLE 7.1. *Recorded Distances for the Outward Voyage*

Date	Leagues Traveled Each Day	Accumulated Leagues	False Reckoning
A. 8–18 September			
8	9	9	x
9	45	54	x
10	60	114	48
11	40[+]	154[a]	16
12	33	187	x
13	33	220	30
14	20	240	x
15	27[+]	267	x
16	39	306	36
17	50[+]	356	47
18	55[+]	412	48

Estimate of the *Niña:* 440 leagues (28 more than recorded in the diario).[b]
Estimate of the *Pinta:* 420 leagues (8 more than recorded in the diario).
Estimate of the *Santa María:* 400 leagues (12 fewer than recorded in the diario).
Total of false reckoning: 225 + 5x[c]

Date	Leagues Traveled Each Day	Accumulated Leagues	False Reckoning
B. 19–30 September			
19	25	437	22
20	7.5	444.5	x
21	13	457.5	x
22	30	487.5	x
23	22[d]	509.5	x
24	14.5	524	12
25	21.5	545.5	13
26	31	576.5	24
27	24	600.5	20
28	14	614.5	13
29	24	638.5	21
30	14	652.5	11

Estimate of *Santa María:* 578 leagues (74.5 fewer than recorded in the diario).[b]
Columbus's estimate of "false" reckoning: 584 leagues (68.5 fewer than recorded in the diario).

TABLE 7.1. (*continued*)

Date	Leagues Traveled Each Day	Accumulated Leagues	False Reckoning

Columbus's estimate of "true" reckoning: 707 leagues (54.5 more than recorded in the diario).

C. 1–2 October

Date	Leagues Traveled Each Day	Accumulated Leagues	False Reckoning
1	25	677.5	20
2	39	716.5	30

Estimate of *Niña:* 650 leagues (66.5 fewer than recorded in the diario).[e]
Estimate of *Pinta:* 634 leagues (82.5 fewer than recorded in the diario).[e]

D. 3–11 October

Date	Leagues Traveled Each Day	Accumulated Leagues	False Reckoning
3	47	763.5	40
4	63	826.5	46
5	57	883.5	45
6	40	923.5	33
7	28	951.5	18
8	12	963.5	x
9	31.5	995	17
10	59	1054	44
11	49.5	1103.5	x

[a] The term "y más" (rendered as "+" in the table) is assumed to mean less than half a league, so four of them would equal one league.
[b] Recapitulated estimates are assumed here to be as of the end of the preceding day.
[c] See Morison/Columbus 1963:55n.
[d] Alvar (Alvar/Columbus 1976, 2:34) reads this figure as "xxvii."
[e] These figures are not in the diario but derive from Las Casas (1951, 1:193), who stated explicitly that these two estimates were made on "el miércoles siguiente," or 3 October.

to 30 September for the *Santa María* and from 19 September through 2 October for the *Niña* and the *Pinta*.

Santa María: from − 12 (18 September) to − 74.5, or a net lag of 62.5 leagues;
Niña: from + 28 (18 September) to − 66.5, or a net lag of 94.5 leagues;
Pinta: from + 8 (18 September) to − 82.5, or a net lag of 90.5 leagues.

We note first that, contrary to Morison, when the first round of comparisons was made, the pilot of the *Pinta* came closer to the figures in the diario than did the pilot of Columbus's own ship, the *Santa María*.[14] Further, if we assume that the count ran through 19 September, then the guess made by the pilot of the *Niña* would also be closer. If this seems peculiar, the second set of cumulated figures offers an even more bizarre result. If we assume (as I have here) that the figures reflect estimates as of the end of Sunday, 30 September, then Columbus overestimated his own daily figures in the diario by more than fifty leagues, and still by nearly thirty leagues if we include the next day's figure in the diario. The figure of the pilot of the *Santa María* is again at odds with Columbus, to an even greater degree than for the previous cumulated estimate. This implies either that Columbus could not add or could not read his figures correctly, or that the figures in the diario are in some respect different from those in the log.

But the problems with Columbus's allegedly false lower figures are greater still. For nine days before 1 October, no such figures are included in the diario, but they appear, at least silently, in the cumulative "false" figure of 584 leagues, since a total of only 361 "false" leagues are recorded in the diario to this point. The difference for the missing nine days, then, is 223 leagues (584−361), but the "true" distances listed for these nine days (8, 9, 12, 14, 15, 20, 21, 22, 23 September) total only 207 leagues. In other words, if we are to believe the figures, Columbus somehow had calculated a "lower" count that was more than 7 percent higher than the official count. While this makes no sense at all, it is enjoined by any belief in the figures available to us. As noted, the diario itself does not include the estimates of accumulated mileage provided by the pilots of the *Niña* and the *Pinta* on 3 October, but as if by magic Las Casas was able to produce these in his *Historia*.[15]

Rather than wasting time wondering how Las Casas came by these figures, we can look at their anomalies.[16] The pilot of the *Santa María* estimated that the fleet had traveled 178 leagues (578−400) in the twelve

14. Morison/Columbus 1963:55n3.

15. Las Casas 1951, 1:193. The figures—sometimes expressed in numbers, sometimes in words—are the same in all modern editions of Las Casas's *Historia*.

16. The figures for the *Niña* and the *Pinta* also appear in Ferdinand's account (Colón 1930, 1:152), which confirms that these estimates were offered a few days after that of the *Santa María*, but Ferdinand showed the *Niña*'s figure to be "DXL" or 540,

days from 19 September to 30 September inclusive, while the pilot of the
Niña estimated that the fleet had traveled a total of 210 leagues (650–440)
in a period of time two days longer, and the pilot of the *Pinta* thought
that the distance for the longer period was only a little more, 214 leagues
(634–420). Columbus, on the other hand, estimated that a distance of no
less than 240 leagues had been traversed, at least according to his day-to-
day figures in the diario, and a much higher figure, 271 leagues, if we
prefer to use his aggregated total of 707 leagues. Columbus's figure of 240
leagues is 14 percent higher than that of the average of the pilots of the
Niña and *Pinta* for two days longer and as much as 22 percent higher
than the distance calculated by his own pilot.

These discrepancies are not easily explained. Morison admits to "some
faulty arithmetic," though on different grounds, but brushes it aside as
the result of Las Casas's "drop[ping] some figures." [17] He then went on to
deduct 9 percent and to declare that the pilot of the *Santa María* was
correct. He leaves the matter there, disdaining to bring into his argument
Las Casas's puzzling figures for the other pilots.

If nothing else, these various sets of figures appear to deal a death blow
to the notion of a second set of figures, and even to a reasonably coherent
first set of figures. Neither Columbus nor the pilots are likely to have
derived their two sets of cumulative figures from anything but their own
logs, and in the case of the only version of raw data that survives, the
diario, we can make little sense of the figures when we pit them against
one another.

This can be explained logically only by attributing complete indifference to Columbus or by joining Morison in imputing mistranscriptions
along the way from the shipboard log to the diario. It hardly matters
which of the two choices we select unless we can show with a degree of
certainty that some figures are more likely to be correct than others.
Worse yet, this must be done without benefit of *petitio principii*, a procedure that would ordain that we agree with Morison that, whichever
figures happen to be incorrect, the ones that really matter are luckily
quite accurate.

---

instead of 650, as in Las Casas. It may be that Las Casas's source was Ferdinand, but
if so, he botched this particular figure by changing the *X* into a *C*.

17. Morison/Columbus 1963:60n1.

II

Those inclined to place credence in Columbus's ability to measure and aggregate distances, or in the diario's ability to convey these correctly, should pay close attention to the statement in the diario for 2 November. Columbus had reached the northern coast of Cuba several days earlier and had spent the intervening time coasting in search of the Great Khan. Las Casas ended the diario entry as follows: "And [Columbus] says that by his own calculation ("por su cuenta") he found that he had gone from the island of Hierro 1,142 leagues. And he still believes that [Cuba] is the mainland."[18] There has been scant interest in the provenance of this figure. How could Columbus have concluded that until that point he had traveled no more and no less than 1,142 leagues? Navarrete thought that "the true distance" was 1,105 leagues but offered no supporting argument, and most later students of the matter have been content either to repeat Navarrete's figure or to ignore the issue altogether.[19] Morison considered the point explicitly, agreeing with Navarrete that the figure in the diario was actually too large and that Columbus had arrived at it largely by calculating degrees and by dead reckoning.[20] Alvar, in turn, regards the figure of 1,142 leagues as representing Columbus's notion of the distance from Hierro to China, that is, that it was not a calculation but a conviction.[21]

18. Alvar/Columbus 1976, 2:95, Dunn and Kelley/Columbus 1989:130: "y [Colón] dize que por su cuenta halló que había andado desde la isla del Hierro mil y ciento y cuarenta y dos leguas, y todavía afirma que aquella es tierra firme." The figure is repeated in Las Casas 1951, 1:228, but is not in Ferdinand's account. While I have translated "cuenta" as "calculation," Dunn and Kelley render it as "account," and Morison (Morison/Columbus 1963:87) as "reckoning." Whatever the choice, it is clear that the term implies the manipulation of figures in some way.

19. Navarrete/Columbus 1825, 1:47n, repeated by Markham 1892:60; Winsor 1892:224; Thacher 1903–4, 1:557n; Cioranescu/Columbus 1961:69; and Varela/Columbus 1982:50n.

20. Morison 1942, 1:339, 349n10.

21. Morales Padrón/Columbus 1984:210n492.

22. That is, Columbus sailed from Gómera and, according to the diario (Alvar/Columbus 1976, 2:25; Dunn and Kelley/Columbus 1989:25), he avoided Hierro, the most westerly of the Canaries, because three Portuguese ships were in the area. Thus it might be necessary to add to these figures the distance from Gómera to the longitude of Hierro, but it is only a few leagues in any case. For whatever reason, Herrera (1934–57, 2:80), apparently relying on neither Las Casas nor Ferdinand, reckoned

But Las Casas said, to the contrary, that Columbus had "calculated" the distance, and he could have done so only on the basis of the figures in the diario—if he regarded them as credible. The distance from Hierro to the sighting of Guanahaní was, according to the diario (see table 7.1), just over 1,100 leagues, depending on how we interpret "Hierro."[22] As a figure, this cannot be wrong by more than four or five leagues—wrong, that is, as measured against Columbus's own sense of accuracy. They are, after all, supposed to be his own figures.[23] When Guanahaní was sighted, it was still two leagues distant. During the three days the fleet was at Guanahaní, Columbus sailed an indeterminate distance around the island, followed by a trip of at least seven leagues and probably more (see chapter 15) to Santa María de la Concepción. He then sailed more than ten leagues along its coast and then another eight or nine leagues to Fernandina, where he spent several days sailing to and fro before sailing off toward Isabela. On 19 October he sailed three hours before reaching there and then twelve leagues or more along one of its coasts. After three days at Isabela unsuccessfully searching for the island's putative ruler, Columbus left for Cuba on 24 October. The first day he recorded nineteen hours of sailing, with no distance specified. The next day the fleet sailed sixteen leagues, and two days later another seventeen leagues.

On reaching Cuba, Columbus first sailed west before turning back east. He entered into the log that they had covered more than fifteen leagues traveled on 30 October, the only day after 27 October for which any figures were recorded. Three days later he calculated that, all told, he had traveled 1,142 leagues.

It is easy to see that the numbers do not come very close to matching. At an absolute minimum, the distances actually recorded as numbers total 1,178 leagues (1,103 + 2 + 7 + 10 + 8 + 16 + 17 + 15) as well as some sixteen days of no, some, or much sailing. Thus the likely total must have been well over 1,200 leagues by 2 November. Several factors could lower this total. Perhaps, for instance, Columbus excluded the

---

Guanahaní to be 950 leagues from Hierro. Such an estimate would help bring Columbus's figure of 1142 leagues more into arithmetical alignment, though it has, of course, no apparent application to the diario.

23. The diario's use of "y más" after a distance in four cases, noted in table 7.1, introduces a slight ambiguity, but it is hard to imagine that this expression could have meant more than a fraction of a league.

westward loop off Cuba, writing it off as wasted leaguage. Or perhaps he calculated a certain small portion of the trip in the shorter so-called shore leagues, deftly juggling leagues of different values to reach his total. But even this improbable procedure would not explain the difference of 100 leagues or more.[24]

A third possibility is that Columbus was measuring only leagues westward, as Morison implied.[25] Such an assumption would undoubtedly help bring the figures into closer harmony, but it would also presume a number of unlikely contingencies. First, it would require that Columbus ignore the fact that Cuba was much to the south of Hierro, as though sailing west was sufficient to reach what he thought was the mainland of Asia even though he knew that he had not sailed only west. Second, it requires that Columbus apply a series of formulas to convert leagues traveled southwest, south-southwest, west-southwest, and any other direction into "net" leagues traveled west. Finally, it flies in the face of the text itself, which says only that Columbus reached his anchorage in Cuba by sailing for 1,142 leagues.

A further question relates to the provenance of the "count" itself. Where did Columbus get his figures—figures that allowed him to state a precise distance traveled? No matter how he interpreted them, he must first have had access to a series of addends that totaled 1,142. But there are no figures in the diario for at least sixteen days between 12 October and 2 November, and no other data could have been available to Columbus at the time.

Once again there seem to be only three reasonable possibilities to explain this contretemps: (1) Columbus could not count, (2) he could count but could not express the result intelligibly, or (3) a mistranscription occurred. Of these, the last would be the most probable were it not that, at least in the diario, the total is expressed in words. But whether we ascribe the discordance to Columbus, to intermediate scribes, or to Las Casas, it remains that the figure of 1,142 leagues blatantly and irremediably contradicts its constituents. It is another case in which the diario must be wrong in some respect, and another case in which we cannot show how or why it is.

24. For the shore league, see chapter 8.
25. Morison 1942, 1:350n10. As part of his argument, Morison stated that Puerto Gibara, his choice for Columbus's venue on 2 November, "is about 110 miles *west* of the San Salvador landfall"; emphasis added.

In a similarly based estimate made later in the voyage, Columbus fared better. The diario entry for 10 February ends with, "He [Columbus] said here that he went 263 leagues from the island of Hierro to the point that he saw the first weeds, etc."[26] Columbus had first reported encountering the Sargasso Sea on 16 September, prior to which he had traveled from Gómera slightly more than 267 leagues. The total would be 306 leagues if we include the traversal for 16 September, but there is no reason to withhold from Columbus the benefit of the doubt, and we can assume that he meant to exclude that day's run. The resulting disparity of four leagues could be held to represent his view of the distance from Gómera to Hierro, which it seems he chose consistently to ignore in his calculations.[27] This might lead us to eliminate the first alternative suggested above, that Columbus could not count.

III

Whereas on the outward voyage the diario provides information only on distances traveled, always expressed in leagues, these data for the homeward trip are for some reason very different.[28] In fact, they resemble what we might expect a log to contain in terms of detail. With only two exceptions, at least two distances, and sometimes as many as five, are provided for each day. As a result we have more than seventy separate estimates for the thirty-one days to 14 February, as opposed to only forty-five for the thirty-three days outbound.[29] Moreover, about half of these are expressed in both leagues and miles; most of the rest are expressed only in leagues. For two days we are even provided with full details on the *ampolletas,* or half-hourly watches.[30]

These computations sometimes disagree, most often in converting leagues to miles, an indication that at least part of this surfeit of infor-

26. Alvar/Columbus 1976, 2:221; Dunn and Kelly/Columbus 1989:360: "Dize aquí también que primero anduvo 263 leguas de la isla del Hierro a la venida que viese la primera yerba, etc."

27. It remains to be determined why Columbus interjected this information at this particular point.

28. *Pace* McElroy 1941:226: "We have the same sort of data in the Journal, and no more."

29. See Kelley 1985:[80–88]. Cf. Peter 1972:122–27.

30. Alvar/Columbus 1976, 2:210, 213; Dunn and Kelley/Columbus 1989:344, 348.

mation was provided by Las Casas or other scribes, not by Columbus. For instance, for 22 January Las Casas had to insert "ten" ("diez") to make "eighteen" ("diez [y] ocho"), the correct conversion in leagues for seventy-two miles.[31] Again, on 8 February Las Casas wrote "twelve" ("doze") and then crossed it out and replaced it with "thirteen" ("treze").[32] Las Casas also "corrected" figures when he transplanted them to his *Historia*. For 3 February the diario records that Columbus made ten miles an hour for eleven hours: "and thus, in eleven hours, 27 leagues."[33] In the *Historia* Las Casas emended this to read: "and in eleven hours he went *beyond* 27 leagues," since 110 divided by 4 is in fact 27 1/2 leagues.[34]

Las Casas was given to arithmetical synthesizing in the *Historia*. Most notably, he provided no daily details for the stretch from 22 to 31 January but summarized the data: "[Columbus] went, I say, 1050 miles, which amounts to 262 leagues."[35] This phrasing almost suggests that the diario's information for this period is primarily in miles, but the total of miles as miles there is only 713, and the total of leagues is only 232 1/2. Apparently Las Casas used the figure for leagues (which could vary, depending on how he calculated the day) and from that extrapolated miles.[36]

Columbus, however, appears not to have made any summary statements, and we are denied the opportunity to assess again his arithmetical skills. Even so, his figures are in conflict with the real distances between Hispaniola and the Azores, and between the Azores and Lisbon, the two legs of the return trip. The diario shows 1,060 leagues from the northeastern tip of Hispaniola to Santa Maria in the Azores and another 192 leagues plus two days unspecified from there to Lisbon, and these are markedly higher than the actual distances, at least if measured as the crow flies.[37]

These differences have led some to conclude that Columbus also over-

31. Alvar/Columbus 1976, 1:222n848a; Dunn and Kelley/Columbus 1989:348.

32. Alvar/Columbus 1976, 1:228n874; Dunn and Kelley/Columbus 1989:360. It should have been 13 1/2.

33. Alvar/Columbus 1976, 2:217; Dunn and Kelley/Columbus 1989:356.

34. Las Casas 1951, 1:309, emphasis added.

35. Las Casas 1951, 1:308.

36. On the differing means of calculating twenty-four-hour periods see Varela/Columbus 1982:xvii–xviii.

37. For the real distances, see U.S. Navy 1985:84, 142; Fitzpatrick 1986:197, 243; IATA/IAL 1986, L238. Peter (1972:126) estimates the missing figures as 12 1/2 and 10 leagues but only by reverse reasoning.

estimated distances on the return trip, this time by 15 percent, or even more than on the trip west.[38] In itself this argument is unexceptionable (though immensely rotund) and quite harmless so long as it remains a generalized statement.[39] In fact, it has been used to plot daily segments on the return trip by assuming that Columbus underestimated by the same amount every day and that, while he did this systematically with distances, he always managed to get the direction exactly right.[40] Neither of these contingencies is likely to be fully correct, and combined they become very implausible indeed.

Postulating repeated shortfalls carries with it the need to explicate Columbus's figures. McElroy attributed the overestimates to the fact that Columbus sailed back in the smaller *Niña* but failed to compensate for this and ended up by overestimating by about 15 percent.[41] While this hypothesis would help explain why Columbus misguessed every day, it portrays a rather witless Admiral of the Ocean Sea. Morison, on the other hand, emphasized "leeway," owing largely to adverse winds during the latter part of January.[42] While leeway probably was a mitigating circumstance and would exonerate Columbus from chronic inattention, it introduces an uncontrollable random factor into any calculations regarding the day-to-day progress of the fleet.

Militating against either of these explanations, the diario tells us that Columbus went about his business "calculating everything" ("tanteando todo") in computing his distances.[43] In some ways even worse, such arguments are ineluctably self-predicting and all-purpose. They can be applied with equal facility to any differential in the historical record. Whether Columbus had been 35 percent under reality in his estimates or

38. The figures proposed by McElroy (1941) and used by Morison (1942, 1:406–15). For the trip west, see below chapter 8.

39. On no authority at all McElroy (1941:209n), followed by Morison (1942, 1:408–9), asserted that on 25 January Columbus instituted "another series of 'phony reckonings'." Not a single ostensibly false figure for the return trip appears in the diario.

40. For such daily positions, see McElroy 1941:231–36; Peter 1972:122–27; Kelley 1985:[85–88].

41. McElroy 1941:226. McElroy also regarded leeway as a contributing factor.

42. Morison 1942, 1:414–15, unless, Morison wondered, Columbus allowed for it.

43. Alvar/Columbus 1976, 2:213; Dunn and Kelley translate the phrase more vaguely as "considering everything," a less precise definition than the verb "tantear" usually receives (Dunn and Kelley/Columbus 1989:350–51).

35 percent over would not matter at all. As explanations they have no cutting edge.

It might be possible, though, to look to the text in hopes of escaping this methodological impasse. We have seen that the detail for the return trip is much greater than for the westward voyage, and from this additional information a few points can be gleaned. A minor but chronic problem with regard to these computations is error in fractions and divisors.[44] As likely as not, Las Casas committed these errors. Interestingly, in several cases the diario provides only miles per hour for night runs, from which it appears that Las Casas (Columbus never used miles) calculated these totals.[45] Sometimes problems arose when, for instance, Las Casas originally wrote "53" miles in the entry for 12 February, only to replace it with "73" interlineally, which is correct if the figure for leagues—18 1/4—is itself accurate.[46] Together with the other examples of corrections in the text of the diario already noted, this forces us to wonder which of these data emanated from a shipboard log and which are in the diario solely by virtue of Las Casas's intervention. Less minor is the fact that in several cases the wording of the entries prevents us from knowing whether some figures supplement other figures for the same day or incorporate them.

A particularly vexing feature of the distances recorded for the return voyage is that so many of the figures for miles are tidily divisible by four, so that the resulting figures for leagues are integers. One would think that the probability that Columbus traveled a number of miles exactly divisible by four would be one in four for any particular case, but the diario tells us that Columbus defied these odds as remarkably as he did those against choosing the marked chick-peas three out of four times.[47] Before

44. Too minor for Morison to comment on (Morison/Columbus 1963:156–73). Cf. Fuson 1987a:177–92. Fuson does note the arithmetical errors.

45. Despite the fact that as early as 21 January Columbus noted that "the nights are longer because of the narrowing of the sphere" ("las noches ser más grandes, por el angostura de la esfera"), all the nights during the return trip are reckoned to be thirteen hours long except that of 26 February, when eight miles per hour during the night is made to total 100 miles. Alvar/Columbus 1976, 2:212n425, 234; Dunn and Kelley/Columbus 1989:348, 388. On the length of the "day" and of "daylight," see Laguardia Trías 1974:6–13, 64–66.

46. Alvar/Columbus 1976, 1:229n884; Dunn and Kelley/Columbus 1989:362, regard the canceled figure as being 63.

47. See chapter 6.

29 January, twenty-five of the thirty-one figures are divisible by four, instead of the expected eight cases. In fact, of these thirty-one numbers, only two, instead of fifteen or sixteen, are odd. From 29 January the pattern changes abruptly; twelve of the twenty-eight figures for miles are odd numbers, only six of them (less than would be expected) are divisible by four. For some reason, probability made great gains. Whether this change represents a change of procedure onboard, a change in scribes, or later revisions of the log is unknowable, but in the end the contrasting patterns can hardly serve to instill confidence in the accuracy or authenticity of the surviving figures.

IV

James Kelley recently concluded a computer simulation of Columbus's routes east and west across the Atlantic on his first voyage, using the data in the diario discussed in this chapter. Kelley concluded that his work "established that the *Journal* data are entirely consistent and highly credible in a quantitative sense."[48] In deciding which data to include in his exercise, Kelley naturally suspended judgment on the validity of individual items in favor of seeking to demonstrate the reliability of the whole. Clearly the argument of the present study has been different— that these data are frequently consistent neither with themselves nor with the real world outside the diario. It differs from Kelley's work and other such studies in another respect as well by declining to subordinate the text to the presuppositions imposed by software.

The examples adduced here can only suggest any number of unpleasant—and not mutually exclusive—possibilities: that Columbus was not as adept at estimating distances as we would prefer; that he could not count, or at least add; or that some numbers were changed or omitted at a later stage either intentionally or unintentionally. One or more of these must be true, whether or not we posit a whole series of explanations that involve correcting either Columbus's calculations or his words. But if there is an answer, it is not to be found in crunching the data in the diario on an electronic Bed of Procrustes.[49]

48. Kelley 1985:100.
49. Not that Kelley is alone in attributing healing powers to the computer; see Judge 1986:588–89 and Richardson and Goldsmith 1987.

8. When the Doctors Disagree

This is the dog,
That worried the cat,
That killed the rat,
That ate the malt,
That lay in the house
That Jack built.

From the nursery rhyme
"The House That Jack Built"

In the diario Columbus, and with him Las Casas, invited readers to view his new discoveries with him, but on the canvas his brush strokes were broad and occasionally discordant, while the viewing lens he offered was opaque. Still, the invitation has proved irresistible, and during the past two centuries, scores if not hundreds of students have tried to bring his tableaus to the contemporary world. All manner of scholars have joined in the effort—historians, geographers, linguists, archaeologists, and others. Over time, though, two well-differentiated groups have displayed a particular fascination with the diario.

On the one hand have been serving and former naval officers attracted to the issue as a problem in maritime history. Some of these have been of the armchair variety, while others acquired a more intimate knowledge of the Bahamas. Complementing these has been the group of residents and local historians of the area, whose principal strength has been a close and longstanding familiarity with local topography, weather and sailing conditions, and traditions. In this way, nautical expertise and local pride have combined in the quest for the four islands Columbus named San Salvador, Santa María de la Concepción, Fernandina, and Isabela.

The criteria by which members of each group have judged the historical record have varied. The naval historians' greatest interest has inevitably been in interpreting technical matters relating to course, sailing maneuvers, and seamanship. Conversely, those with local knowledge have tended to rely more on eye-of-the-beholder arguments sustained by their own repeated experience. Of course, there has been overlap between the two groups; for instance, Samuel Eliot Morison frequently congratulated himself on being able to advance arguments on both fronts.

One might expect that under the circumstances a high level of consensus would emerge within each of the interest groups. Quite the contrary has been true, however. Not only has agreement on larger issues failed to materialize, but on almost every supporting detail discord is so rampant that it strikes the observer almost as burlesque. This anarchy—and the term is not unjustified—calls for study and comment, and in the following discussion I look at several examples of the problem in hopes of throwing some light on the epistemological issues that underlie and bedevil the study of Columbus's first voyage. Many are treated from a different perspective and in greater detail later in this study, but bringing them together here is intended to highlight the degree and texture of the disagreement.

I distinguish three groups of studies. As noted, the first of these constitutes the work of the large group of naval men who have attempted to trace Columbus's route. Navarrete, Montojo, and Barreiro Meiro were all officers in the Spanish navy.[1] When Washington Irving sought to identify Guanahaní, he ceased to rely on his own judgment and called on his friend Alexander Slidell (later Mackenzie), who was an officer in the United States Navy.[2] Likewise, Becher and Markham served in the British navy, while Murdock was a member of the United States Navy, and Fox was a graduate of the Naval Academy and a former assistant secretary of the navy.[3] Verhoog and Roukema came from the ranks of the merchant marine.

Morison epitomized this cadre—he could, in fact, be considered its acme. Morison never let his readers forget that his formal training as a historian was supplemented by a longstanding interest in nautical matters, culminating with a rear admiralship in the navy.[4] When Morison took to Bahamian waters in search of Guanahaní, it must have seemed to many as though the millennium had arrived at last in the search for

1. Navarrete 1954–55, 1:vii–xlv; Morón 1842–46; Montojo 1892.
2. Mackenzie 1897.
3. Dunkin 1879:1–6; Markham 1917; Murdock 1931:268–69; Fuess 1931:568–69; Winthrop 1882–83:353–55.
4. Taylor 1977; Washburn 1979.

Columbus's landfall. Morison himself heartily espoused this view and wrote with great assurance, if not always with consistency.[5] In his writing the subjunctive mood is noticeably absent, as are qualifying clauses. To what extent this springs from his naval credentials is anyone's guess, but they unquestionably strengthened his case in the public eye.[6]

The naval officers were supplemented by other researchers, some of whom were residents of the Bahamas moved by local pride, others with an interest in yachting or island hopping, and eventually a few with historical training who saw the identity of the landfall as a problem worth solving. What distinguishes the members of this group is their familiarity with at least those parts of the Bahamas they suspected Columbus had visited. This contrasted with the naval men, only two of whom, Fox and Morison, had added eyewitness experience to their naval training.

The earliest of this latter group to publish an opinion on the landfall was George Gibbs in 1846, and he was followed by Henry A. Blake, governor of the Bahamas from 1884 to 1887.[7] While in office Blake took the opportunity, as he put it, to "sail around the islands with the diary of Columbus in my hands."[8] A few years later the German geographer Rudolf Cronau and the American author Frederick Ober did the same, and since then Stewart, the Links, and finally Judge and Power have all taken to retracing Columbus's steps in order to add the personal dimension to the textual.[9]

Coming eye to eye with Columbus, especially if it is done often enough, should lead to some consensus about what Columbus saw or thought he saw. Instead, a series of arguments has emerged that only emphasize the subjective nature of Columbus's own impressions. Here I will discuss some differences in ocular experience and technical opinion

5. Early in his Columbus career, Morison (1939a:2n) scoffed at "dryasdusts" who preferred to study Columbus's voyages from the armchair, and his later work is festooned with insider comments. See Fuson 1987a:xiii–xiv.

6. Style matters; for excellent and stimulating discussions of the ways rhetorical strategies are mobilized in aid of building, maintaining, and selling arguments, see Fahnestock 1989 and Veldink 1989.

7. For Blake, who later served as governor of Newfoundland, Jamaica, Hong Kong, and Ceylon, see *The Times*, 25 February 1918, 10b.

8. Blake 1892:541.

9. Ober, 1893:311.

as they relate to central points in the expression and interpretation of the diario.[10]

I

Under the date of 15 October, Columbus recorded his activities for the afternoon or evening as follows: "Cargué las velas por andar todo aquel día fasta la noche."[11] This statement has captured a good deal of attention over the years because interpretations of the distance Columbus traveled during the period in question necessarily play a central role in itinerary theory-building.[12] Becher began the sweepstakes in earnest by translating the sentence as "I made sail, continuing on until night."[13] Major, who accepted most of Becher's argument, seemed to accept this as well when he translated it as "started for the purpose of sailing all day."[14] Fox begged to differ, however, pointing out that the usual nautical interpretation of the term "cargar las velas," as evidenced in certain dictionaries, was "to clew up," that is, to furl sails.[15] Murdock quickly concurred, as did Cronau a few years later.[16]

Since then many others have done the same,[17] with two significant exceptions. In his translation of the diario, Morison reverted to Becher's phrasing and rendered the term as "made sail," largely because he had to get Columbus along the entire southern coast of Rum Cay in a very short time.[18] Regrettably, Morison offered no explanation for his departure.[19]

---

10. The analyses of the third group of students (Vidal Gormaz, Redway, Thacher, Gould, Tió, and Pérez) are excluded here since they fit neither category.

11. Alvar/Columbus 1976, 2:59; Dunn and Kelley/Columbus 1989:78.

12. See chapter 15.

13. Becher 1856:109.

14. Major 1871:71.

15. Fox 1882:358, 381, 391–92. In addition see O'Scanlan 1831:146.

16. Murdock 1884:467; Cronau 1921:34. Cf. Kahane, Kahane, and Tietze 1958: 152–53.

17. Among them Markham 1892:100–101; Link/Link 1958:13, 29; Fuson 1987a:80.

18. Morison/Columbus 1963:69, 71n2. In Morison 1942, 1:316, he paraphrased this as "coasted."

19. Roukema (1959:97n), emulating Morison as usual and in his haste to refute the Links, went even further, declaring that "the term is not ambiguous" and translating it as "crowded on sail."

Judge agreed with Morison by translating the phrase as "to crowd on sail" and felt obliged to explain why. Astonishingly, his explanation was that "in most translations [Columbus] says he had to crowd on sail."[20] Not only is this not the case, but in the very translation that accompanied Judge's advocacy of a Samana Cay landfall, Lyon rendered the phrase as "hauled in sails."[21] Not surprisingly, and not incidentally, Judge's reconstruction of Columbus's route also requires that Columbus "clip along at 5.2 knots" an hour.[22] Most recently Dunn and Kelley have agreed with Morison and Judge, and on contextual grounds have rendered the phrase as "spread sail."[23]

Other textual and contextual problems with this entry are discussed below, and these should have caused some hesitation on the part of anyone translating the phrase. But the issue that concerns us here is the tendentious way in which the statement has invariably been translated. While we cannot be certain just what Columbus had in mind, we need refer back only a few sentences in the diario to see the term unquestionably used to mean some form of making sail rather than the reverse, so those who translate this passage in the same way at least practice the virtue of consistency.[24] Even so, under the circumstances we are left with the suspicion that Columbus's use of technical nautical terms and his obscure phraseology have provided opportunities for circular reasoning.

Other examples from the period only reinforce this notion. When land was sighted on 12 October, Columbus wrote: "Amainaron todas las velas, y quedaron con el treo, que es la vela grande, sin bonetas, y pusiéronse a la corda."[25] The first impression offered by this sentence is that Columbus was trying to teach his grandmother to suck eggs and that it is not his but someone else's version that we have in front of us. Beyond that, there is the question of just what it means to say. Everyone but

20. Judge 1986:592.
21. Lyon 1986:19, 19n.
22. Judge 1986:591.
23. Dunn and Kelley/Columbus 1989:77, 77n.
24. Alvar/Columbus 1976, 2:59; Dunn and Kelley/Columbus 1989:76. See below, chapter 16.
25. Alvar/Columbus 1976, 2:47, 47nn.; Dunn and Kelley/Columbus 1989:63, translate this as, "They hauled down all the sails and kept only the *treo*, which is a mainsail without bonnets, and jogged on and off."

Morison has translated "pusiéronse a la corda" as "lain to" or "hove to."[26] In contrast, Morison argued that it meant "to jog."[27] The issue seems unbearably trifling until we realize that Morison's hypothesis that Columbus's anchorage was midway along the western coast of Watlings Island requires that the fleet cover many miles during the four hours between sighting and anchoring.[28]

Finally, there is the matter of whether Columbus's men rowed or sailed on their reconnaissance along the coast of Guanahaní on 14 October. In typical fashion the diario fails to specify this, but modern scholarship has not hesitated to fill the gap. Columbus spoke of using both the "batel" of the Santa María and the "barcas" of the other two ships, and the question becomes whether either (or both) of these would normally have been equipped with sails. Modern opinion divides tendentiously on the matter.[29]

Sightlines

Among the less ambiguous statements in the diario are several in which Columbus recorded that he saw islands ahead of him and that he saw them while at or on another island. These statements can hardly be ignored, although they are often misconstrued in modern reconstructions, which must necessarily, or so it would seem, follow a route with sightlines that match those mentioned in the diario. The procedure should be

26. E.g., Fox 1882:354; Murdock 1884:451; Fuson 1987a:75; Jane/Columbus 1960:148; Lyon 1986:9. Navarrete/Columbus 1825, 1:166n, went to some length to make this point.

27. Morison 1942, 1:xxxn, xliv, 298, 311. Yet in Morison/Columbus 1963:64 he contradicted himself by translating the passage as, "They handed all sails and set the treo, which is the mainsail without bonnets, and lay-to waiting for daylight." Emphasis added.

28. Dunn and Kelley/Columbus 1989:63, 63n, also translates it as "jogged on and off," which, unlike Morison, the editors take to mean "intentionally making no headway." They cite the diario entry for 13 November, in which Las Casas (presumably) glossed "a la corda" as "which is to go to windward and not to go anywhere." Dunn and Kelley/Columbus 1989:148. Cf. Alvar/Columbus 1976, 2:107; Morison/Columbus 1963:94n1. Alvar/Columbus 1976, 2:47n77, says simply that it means arranging "to make no progress." The question of whether Columbus attempted to make distance while he "jogged," if he jogged, remains moot.

29. See chapter 14.

simple enough: determine whether or not any island is visible, as required, from hypothesized landfalls. Thus, from Guanahaní there should be no islands visible; from Santa María there should be a large island visible to the west; and so on. Despite its apparent simplicity (and I overstate the case for effect), following these lines of reasoning has produced a ludicrously large number of permutations and contradictions.

In part, of course, these are inevitable, given the lack of precision in this aspect of the diario. For instance, Columbus never went so far as to state unequivocally that he could see no other islands from Guanahaní, although his silence has been taken as decisive. He did record that sometime after—apparently shortly after—leaving there he sighted a large group of islands, so numerous as to defy counting.[30] Leaving aside the issue of whether he was correct in thinking them to be islands, we turn to modern statements as to the visibility of other islands from one supposed Guanahaní, Grand Turk.

Navarrete, the first to advocate Grand Turk, had nothing to say on the matter, but another early proponent, George Gibbs—who should have known, since he lived on the island—categorically stated that East Caicos Island "is always visible" from Grand Turk.[31] Grand Turk's brief career as Guanahaní suffered an eclipse at this point, only to be revived recently when H. E. Sadler, another resident of the island, agreed with Gibbs: "the Caicos Islands are still visible from Grand Turk in clear weather, and they were even more discernible at the time of Columbus because of the greater vegetation which clothed the land."[32]

Not coincidentally, both Gibbs and Sadler misunderstood the diario to say that Columbus saw many islands *from* Guanahaní. With more of an eye for detail, Power did not make that mistake, but he stated in turn, and again certainly not incidentally, that "the Caicos Islands are not visible from Grand Turk."[33] Meanwhile, Slidell had written that the two were not visible from each other, while Ober was certain that they were.[34] More recently Taviani has asserted that "neither from South Caicos nor from East Caicos is it possible to see the Turks group."[35]

30. See chapter 15 for more details.
31. Navarrete/Columbus 1825, 1:25; Gibbs 1846:139, with emphasis added.
32. Sadler 1981:5.
33. Power 1985:160.
34. Irving 1828, 3:309; Ober 1893:92.
35. Taviani 1987b:216.

Each of these statements, except perhaps that of Slidell, was purport-edly based on observation, so the contradictions are hard to explain simply as differing visual perceptions. Seen in the context of the argu-ments that accompany them, though, we might justifiably see the visi-bility issue as less an ocular than an epistemological, or even ideological, phenomenon.

Things are not much different with respect to whether Long Island is visible from Rum Cay. The Watlings Island–Rum Cay–Long Island route is the most popular now afloat, and it requires both that Rum Cay not be visible from Watlings Island and that Long Island be visible from various points on Rum Cay. Wolper argued that under certain conditions Rum Cay is visible from Watlings, although she did not credit Columbus with seeing it from there.[36] This is only a modest breach in the solidarity of the Watlings Islanders' view that Rum Cay is invisible from there, or indeed from a long way off the southwest corner of Watlings.[37] But the visibility of Long Island from Rum Cay is another matter entirely. Blake was one of the earliest to comment when he wrote that Long Island was discernible from "about three miles north of [Rum Cay]."[38] Morison ex-pressed two views on the visibility question. He wrote first that "Mon-day, October 15, must have been an unusually clear day since from off the *southeast* point of Rum Cay [Columbus] 'saw another bigger [island] to the west.' That was Long Island, distant 22 miles."[39] Later he seems to have reconsidered. He conceded that Columbus "could not have sighted Long Island until he reached the *western* end of Rum Cay" and then went on almost immediately to retract even this by admitting that he himself could not see Long Island "even from a point about 3 miles S. of the western point" of Rum Cay.[40]

Cronau noticed that Columbus regarded the island to the west of Santa María as "very large" while he was still at Santa María, so he wrote en-thusiastically that "[n]ot only is Long Island plainly visible from . . . Rum Cay, but the long chain of its low ridges gird almost the whole western horizon and leave no doubt as to its extensive size."[41] Contrast

36. Wolper 1964:34.
37. Although Ober 1893:92, also thought so.
38. Blake 1892:550.
39. Morison 1942, 1:316, emphasis added.
40. Morison/Columbus 1963:71n2, 71n7, emphasis added.
41. Cronau 1921:35.

this with Morison's reconsidered view that at best Long Island is just barely visible from the extreme western end of Rum Cay.

It can be argued that the entire premise that modern sightlines can replicate and thereby confirm Columbus's experience is misconceived. Today's atmosphere is typically less clear than that of five hundred years ago, and some parts of some islands have been reduced in height to an unknown degree by deforestation. Beyond this, modern efforts at replication require an entirely unsuitable approach. It may be, as Wolper illustrates, that under just the right conditions and looking in just the right direction and knowing just what to look for, Rum Cay can be seen from the highest point on southwestern Watlings Island, but to begin with, we have no idea whether Columbus explored Guanahaní at all. Nor did Columbus have the advantage of knowing where to look and what to expect to find, an advantage endemic to every modern sightline experiment. As we have all learned, it is much easier to stack the deck and find something when we are looking for it in the first place.

For Columbus there was no right place, merely conjecture, hope, and the gesticulations of the Indians. To take Guanahaní as an example, Columbus does not tell us enough to know which parts of the island he visited and therefore in which seaward directions he could have spotted land—and therefore, of course, in which directions he could not have. From what we know of his general goals and his specifically stated intention, we might reasonably assume—provisionally and without textual support—that he sailed somewhere between south of west and west of south, and therefore that islands slightly west of north or east of south may have been visible to the keen observer. Beyond that, the bald assertions of visibility in the modern literature seem to have grown some hair.[42]

Graham's Harbour

Proponents of Watlings Island agree that Graham's Harbour, at the northernmost point of the island, is the reef-enclosed harbor so grandiloquently described by Columbus on 14 October. We might then expect that any disagreement on the candidacy of Graham's Harbour would

42. If we knew more, the altitude-visibility tables used by the Spanish navy reproduced in Luca de Tena 1968:248–49, as well as those in Manrique 1890:111–21, would be useful.

break along party lines, but this is not the case. There is remarkably little agreement among Watlings Islanders on any other aspect of Graham's Harbour. Two points concern us here: How large is it actually? and, Is this large enough to meet Columbus's qualification that it was capable of sheltering "as many ships as there are in Christendom"?[43]

At first glance, the former question would hardly seem worth asking; certainly it seems all too straightforward. In the event, it has not proved to be so. Over the past century, some half dozen estimates of the size of Graham's Harbour have been advanced. In 1892 Blake estimated that it was seven miles by four miles in extent.[44] About the same time, Cronau estimated it as about three and a half by four miles in size, or just half Blake's estimate.[45] Wolper, long a resident of Watlings Island, disagreed slightly, thinking it somehow smaller and less square, perhaps three by four and a half miles.[46] Finally, Morison offered two estimates: it was both three miles square and four to five miles square.[47] As was his custom, he felt no compunction about disagreeing with himself and showed no inclination to explain the difference of opinion. In sum, modern estimates by Watlings Islanders of the size of Graham's Harbour range from nine to twenty-eight square miles, with no agreement in either shape or size.

Given this disparity, one might expect a certain diffidence in deciding whether Columbus should be taken seriously in his own estimate as to the capacity, if not the size, of the harbor on Guanahaní. But no, opinions are regularly offered on the matter and as regularly disagree with each other. Blake, Cronau, and Stewart concluded that Graham's Harbour could indeed have sheltered every ship in Christendom in 1492.[48] Morison, Obregón, and Roukema asserted that Columbus's statement was an exaggeration produced by his excited imagination.[49] Others have not expressed an opinion. Any modern willingness to agree with Columbus can be nothing more than cavalier courtesy and would be useful only in underscoring how ready students of the voyage are to succumb to Columbus's blandishments.

43. Alvar/Columbus 1976, 2:57; Dunn and Kelley/Columbus 1989:74.
44. Blake 1892:550.
45. Cronau 1921:23, based on observations made in the early 1890s.
46. Wolper 1964:33.
47. Morison/Columbus 1963:69n; Morison/Obregón 1964:24.
48. Blake 1892:551-52; Cronau 1921:23; Stewart 1931:12b.
49. Morison and Obregón 1964:23; Roukema 1959:89.

Beyond that, it is remarkable that four modern students of the diario have chosen to take Columbus precisely in all forms of measurement while at the same time failing to agree among themselves on the measurements of a single small and more or less enclosed body of water. Could it be that Graham's Harbour is so undifferentiated from the surrounding sea that one person's opinion as to its extent is not much better or much worse than any others? If so, how can we ever expect to make sense of Columbus's view on the matter?

Streams

The diario is not replete with physical descriptions that are out of the ordinary. Columbus's reference on 17 October to seeing "the mouth of a river" on Fernandina might then seem to be a useful reference that could help establish the spot to which he was referring.[50] But Morison, for one, would have none of it. In fact he committed virtual lèse-majesté by proclaiming that Columbus "rather stupidly" was describing what was really "a shallow harbor," since there was a shallow harbor where Morison wanted him to be.[51] In truth, Morison stated, "there is not a single river or stream in the entire archipelago."[52]

Others, however, have disagreed with this sweeping verdict. Fox, Blake, and others have noted that there is at least one stream on Andros, and Blake added Crooked Island to the list.[53] Gibbs, in turn, reported that there had been creeks on Grand Turk as recently as the nineteenth century, when they silted up.[54] Some "deep creeks" are also attributed to Cat Island.[55] Finally, among those who disagree with Morison is . . . Morison, who in translating the diario rendered the phrase "muchas aguas" in the entry for 11/12 October as "many streams."[56] Most of the streams in question are tidal creeks, but for all we know Columbus may

---

50. Alvar/Columbus 1976, 2:69; Dunn and Kelley/Columbus 1989:92.

51. Morison 1942, 1:322.

52. Morison 1942, 1:318–19.

53. Fox 1882:387; Blake 1982:544; *Yachtsman's Guide* 1987:230 reports "dozens of streams" on Andros.

54. Gibbs 1846:142.

55. *Yachtman's Guide* 1987:334; Rigg 1973:220–22. Rigg (1973:239) even credits tiny Conception Island with a creek.

56. Morison/Columbus 1963:64.

have been describing such features himself. Our ignorance of his usage prevents us from drawing far-reaching conclusions based on the slender reed of modern topography.

Stones

While on Hispaniola Columbus noticed some stones that he described as follows: "many stones painted with colors, or a quarry of such stones, the work of nature, and very beautiful." Moreover, he added, they were "like those" he had "found on the islet of San Salvador [Guanahaní]."[57] Perhaps it is odd that he failed to mention these picturesque stones while actually at Guanahaní, but no matter. For Morison this was a precious clue that pointed to, and only to, Watlings Island. He argued that stones exactly like those Columbus described are found along the west coast of Watlings near Long Bay, his hypothesized site of Columbus's anchorage. Morison went on to say that "these naturally squared coral blocks . . . are unique in the Bahamas."[58]

Apparently the well-known axiom that it is difficult to prove the absence of something is again vindicated here. Navarrete had already suggested that certain formations on Grand Turk satisfied this description, and Gibbs added local familiarity in support of this case.[59] More recently Winslow has found similar stones on Great Harbour Cay that he feels "may be unique" to *that* island.[60]

Guanahaní's Reef

Columbus mentioned his fear of debarking at Guanahaní because of a reef that surrounded the island.[61] There are difficulties in accepting his statement as precise, but we can ignore those here in favor of seeing how modern students of the diario have used his statement to support their theories. Using Blake, Markham, Gould, Roukema, and Taviani as a sample of those who have addressed the issue, we find that they all agree that Cat Island is disqualified by this criterion, but with this, unanimity

---

57. Alvar/Columbus 1976, 2:190; Dunn and Kelley/Columbus 1989:308.
58. Morison/Obregón 1964:19–20, complete with photograph. Cf. Morison/Columbus 1963:145n2.
59. Navarrete/Columbus 1825, 1:125; Gibbs 1846:137, 141, 145.
60. Winslow 1988:18A.
61. Alvar/Columbus 1976, 2:57; Dunn and Kelley/Columbus 1989:74.

dissolves into discord.[62] Gould and Markham argue that Grand Turk pos-
sesses the required reef, but Blake and Roukema dispute this.[63] As far as
Samana Cay is concerned, Markham accepted that it has a surrounding
reef, and in this he is joined by Taviani.[64] But Gould and Roukema think
otherwise.[65]

The agreement over Cat Island is illusory because it does have a reef all
along its southern coast, which, its advocates argue, is where Columbus
anchored. If anything, Grand Turk seems to meet the requirement as well
as Watlings does. As for Samana Cay, a nonparticipant in the debate tells
us that it is "completely surrounded by coral reefs."[66]

Leagues and Miles and Circles

The final area of contention transcends group loyalties. The question of
the length of the mile and league as conceived by Columbus (or by Las
Casas) has exercised students of the diario from the beginning but has
taken on impetus with the recent application of computer methodologies
to Columbus's track.[67] The issue naturally divides into two parts: the
number of miles in a Columbian league and the length of these miles.
Combined, the question can be stated as: How many modern nautical
miles of 6,080 feet are represented by the term "legua" in the diario?[68]

Fox was the first to examine the matter closely, and he concluded that
Columbus used a mile of 4,842 feet and therefore that a league was 19,638
feet,[69] which is slightly more than 3.18 nautical miles. In one guise or
another, this figure has established itself as the predominant measure of a
Columbian league, ultimately being sanctified by Morison.[70] Recently,

62. Blake 1892:548–49; Markham 1889:108–17; Markham 1892:92–100; Gould
1927:412–13; Roukema 1959:86–89; Taviani 1987b:203, 213–24.
63. Gould 1927:412; Markham 1889:113; Blake 1892:548; Roukema 1959:87.
64. Markham 1889:117; Taviani 1987b:224.
65. Gould 1927:413; Roukema 1959:87.
66. *Yachtsman's Guide* 1987:361.
67. A further issue, not discussed here, is how often the diario reads "leguas" when
it "should" read "millas." For this see chapter 7.
68. This is itself part of the larger issue of linear distance measures in the Spanish
New World; see, e.g., Haggard 1941:78–79; Chardon 1980a; Chardon 1980b; and
for background, Morcken 1989.
69. Fox 1882:401–3.
70. Murdock 1884:465n; Nunn 1924; McElroy 1941:214–16; Morison 1942,
1:247–48, 260–61. Cioranescu/Columbus 1961:374n22; Obregón 1987a:189; Fuson

however, Kelley has suggested that Columbus's league consisted of four 4,060-foot miles, or the equivalent of 2.67 nautical miles.[71]

In fact, the matter has proved to be nothing so much as an interpretive gambit masked as mathematics. Most definitions of the Columbian league have been derived from calculating the leagues recorded in the diario, particularly for the outward trip, and dividing this figure into the number of miles by various routes from Gómera in the Canaries to whatever Bahamian island is deemed on the occasion to be Guanahaní.

But the exercise only begins with this step because, as Marden points out, using a conversion factor of 3.18 places Columbus "impossibly far to the west, west of present-day Miami."[72] All agree that this will not do and that some surgery is required. To deal with this, Marden concludes (not without some documentary evidence) that the length of an "Iberian sea league" was 2.82 nautical miles.[73] But wait; "the recomputed course, using a league of 2.82 nautical miles and incorporating current and leeway, because of the push of the current again came out too far west."[74] Marden clearly recognized that drastic measures were necessary, so he "found an excess of 9 percent," which he promptly deducted. The results were at last satisfying. "[W]e come to a position some ten miles east-northeast of Samana Cay," almost exactly where Marden and Judge wanted him to be.[75]

Albeit in emphatic form here, this practice of circular reasoning reinforced by a great deal of backtracking, has an unedifyingly long history. McElroy had already demonstrated the perverse charms of deducting arbitrary percentages from the figures in the historical record. By taking a

---

1987a:48. Fuson's statement (1987a:86) that Columbus's mile was between 4,060 ft. and 4,856 ft. seems the most that can be said with confidence, although he goes on to say that it was probably 4,284 ft.

71. Kelley 1985:105–7. Earlier (Cioranescu/Columbus 1961:37n22) had calculated a league of 5,920 meters, which Kelley (1985:106) calls "a Portuguese maritime league," that is, the league expressed by Columbus's pilots and one that was about 22 percent longer than Columbus's own notion. Peck (1989:6) accepts the 2.67-mile league.

72. Judge 1986:573.

73. Judge 1986:576–77. Richardson and Goldsmith (1987:4) accept this measurement in their reconstruction of Columbus's route, as do Fantoni and Ingravalle (1987).

74. Judge 1986:577.

75. Judge 1986:577.

league of 3.18 miles and deducting 9 percent for current, he too was able to place Columbus were he wanted him to be, "about 9 miles" south of Watlings Island.[76] When his turn came, Morison happily accepted McElroy's conversion factor and argued for an actual, if corrected, Columbian league of 2.89 miles.[77]

The invention of the corrected league and the mobilization of the computer stimulated landfall hunting because they eliminated all the limits imposed by Columbus's own evidence while permitting it to be used to support any conceivable landfall as long as it was east of Miami. Consequently, it is to be expected that the range of disagreement over the length of Columbus's league will shrink, to be replaced by frivolous differences of opinion over the error in his calculations introduced by current, wind, and the like.[78]

But the role of the league in landfall controversies does not quite end when Guanahaní is identified, because Columbus continued to use the term to indicate the size of other islands he discovered and the distances between them. Alas, his figures have proved troublesome, particularly to Morison. When he encountered Columbus's assertion that Santa María was five leagues by more than ten leagues (three to four times the size of Morison's candidate, Rum Cay), he blandly assured his readers that Columbus had at the very moment he penned this datum fallen into the habit of using "consciously or unconsciously, a league of about 1 1/2 nautical miles" to measure distances on land.[79]

Even for Morison this was audacious, and the newly minted league found no followers except Roukema, even among the staunchest champions of a Watlings Island–Rum Cay course. Generally, these researchers

76. McElroy 1941:216. McElroy's logic compelled him to postulate a "net" league of 2.82 miles on the outward voyage and one of 2.70 miles on the return trip. Later Fuson and Treftz (1976) also deducted 9 percent from the diario's total. However, in their reconstituted route Columbus ended up "ten nautical miles northwest of the Caicos Islands."

77. Morison 1942, 1:247–48.

78. Already Molander (1985) thought that the 3.18-mile league requires a 6 percent reduction to "fit."

79. Morison 1942, 1:316. Earlier in the work Morison (1942, 1:248) had stated that he was certain that it was "consciously" applied. Just a few years earlier Morison (1939–41) had failed to mention such a shore league, relying instead on transcription errors or "mere guess[ing]" by Columbus to explain the purported discrepancies.

have preferred the time-honored expedient of attributing visual overestimation to Columbus or transcriptional errors to Las Casas.[80]

II

In his search for the landfall, Glenn Stewart marveled at the ease of his task. "The accuracy of [Columbus's] descriptions," he wrote, "is a constant source of surprise and pleasure, authenticating the very things we were looking at."[81] Despite such roseate views, the preceding discussion suggests that an eye for the landscape is of little use without an eye for the text as well. Yet the floundering we have seen is almost inevitable, given all the information Columbus failed to provide. He begins by describing Guanahaní in perfectly nondescript terms, and once he departed from the island things only get worse. He fails to mention in which direction he sailed, how far or how long he had sailed before sighting a large group of islands, their bearing from his course, any distinctive characteristics of Santa María de la Concepción, and so on. Worse yet, the text of the diario is a series of detached impressions, a jumble of assertions that are seldom connected to each other in ways that matter. The text lacks statements of duration for specific activities, passes up countless opportunities to include an elucidating connective, avoids indicating that any place has already been referred to, and usually presents a slightly frenzied aspect for the journey through the Bahamas, in contrast to the greater care and detail that characterize its accounts of Cuba and Hispaniola. As a result, attempts to bridge these gaps fail to maintain contact with the text as they seek to impose order on chaos. The doctors disagree because the patient is unable to communicate its symptoms.

But the doctors also disagree for a less acceptable reason—their own preconceptions. Each is certain that the patient is suffering from a different disease, a disease created by their own predilections, a kind of hypochondria of the doctor rather than of the patient. The proportion of the arguments mentioned here that derives from disinterested attempts to match modern topographical features with the evidence of the diario is alarmingly low—and distressingly symptomatic, as we will see in the more detailed analysis of the landfall controversy that follows.

80. Markham 1892:84, 103; Roukema 1959:80–85.
81. Stewart 1931:128

PART II

The Historiographical Debate

9. The Identikit Island

Recently Timothy Severin, a journalist turned sailor, attempted to establish and retrace the itinerary of Odysseus as he slowly wended his way home after the Trojan war.[1] More than twenty years previously, Ernle Bradford, another journalist sailor, made a similar attempt.[2] Both tried to use the sailing distances and directions in the *Odyssey* and to match the topographical descriptions given there with modern-day features—or to explain why they did not match.[3] Both used the same translation of the poem. Both took a "hands on" approach, sailing around in small boats and making on-site inspections of the sites they favored. The result? The routes that the two latter-day Odysseuses eventually devised could hardly have been more different from one another.

The trouble may lie in the fact that, while both Severin and Bradford accept the testimony of the *Odyssey* as virtually unvarnished fact, most scholars, beginning with Eratosthenes, have suspected otherwise. For them the map used in composing (or compiling) the *Odyssey* was a mental map; the poet or poets now referred to as Homer exercised geographical as well as poetic creativity, perhaps at most basing parts of the *Odyssey* on vague folktales current at the time. Seeking Odysseus's route can be no more than a quest for a chimera since his adventures are unmistakably set in the realm of fantasy.

1. Severin 1987.
2. Bradford 1963.
3. Malkin and Fichman 1987.

If more hopeless than most, these two efforts to follow Odysseus around the ancient world do exemplify a longstanding genre of historical investigation.[4] Attempts to discover the route of Hannibal from Spain to Italy have occupied historians for over two millennia.[5] The itinerary outlined in the *Periplus Maris Erythraei* has exercised scholars for centuries, as various parts of the entire east coast of Africa have been postulated, often for no better reason than local pride.[6] More ominously, the credibility of Columbus's own inspiration, the record of the travels of Marco Polo, has been brought into question.[7]

The exploration of North America has been a very rich ground for seekers after routes. Despite the existence of three participant accounts, the exact route of De Soto is far from certain.[8] Coronado is ubiquitous in the historiography of the southwestern United States.[9] The expeditions of the La Vérendryes have also been subject to numerous interpretations, and even the study of the route of Lewis and Clark, so multiply documented in the journals of their expedition, has not yielded unanimous agreement.[10]

The relevant evidence for all these routes, and many others, is very much the same as for each of Columbus's voyages: distances, directions, and landmarks recorded in participant or subsequent accounts. As a result, the genre of travel itineraries is particularly well defined in both its structure and its focus. In addition to the homogeneity of the evidence,

4. Perhaps beginning with the journey of "Abraham" from "Ur" to "Canaan," and including as well the real voyage of Sinuhe and the imaginary trail of Aeneas from Troy to Latium.

5. Proctor 1971 is the most substantial of several recent studies. See also Walbank 1956; Lazenby 1978; Landucci Gattinoni 1984; Seibert 1986.

6. Mathew 1963:94–97; Mathew 1975; Huntingford 1980:77–100; Casson 1986; Kirwan 1986; Casson 1989.

7. For expressions of doubt see, among others, Olschki 1960:12–39; Haeger 1978; Heers 1984. For a recent survey, see Reichert 1988.

8. Interest in de Soto's route is mounting rapidly; a few of the studies on it are Smith 1976; DePratter 1983; Hudson et al. 1984; Brain 1985; DePratter et al. 1985; Weinstein 1985; Curren 1986; Williams 1986; Boyd and Schroedl 1987; Hudson et al 1989; Hudson 1990.

9. Riley and Manson 1983; Weber 1988:19–32 is particularly instructive on Marcos de Niza.

10. Smith 1980:67–94, 115–27; Moulton 1983; Moulton and Dunlay 1983–87. For an uncannily similar case to that of Columbus, see Rogers and Ballendorf 1989.

the study is characterized by nationalism and localism and thus has long tended to raise doubts as to its objectivity.

I
_____

If it is useful to set the study of Columbus's landfall into the relief of similar studies, it is no less important to bear in mind that much travel literature has turned out to be partly or wholly apocryphal.[11] Oddly perhaps, this has proved to generate its own brand of seductiveness. While no modern scholars have actually tried to follow Raphael Hythlodaeus or Pantagruel or Lemuel Gulliver or Frodo from place to place, many have continued to look for real geographical settings in which to situate the idea of their adventures.

The most important, though apparently not the most obvious, aspect of arguing about itineraries is the concatenated or multiplicative nature of the argument. While most historical arguments are necessarily interdependent, the extent to which this is true in this case is probably unparalleled. The argument must proceed remorselessly in serial fashion, with each component or link clearly distinguishable from all the others. At the same time, each depends irremediably on all those that precede it. Once a reconstructed itinerary goes astray, it can be reclaimed only by accident rather than by the force of argument. At the same time, since each successive step depends so heavily on preceding arguments, the probability that the entire line of argument is correct diminishes with each link in the chain. In this way the epistemological good health of reconstructed routes suffers a double burden and so requires an extra dose of rigor. Just the same, it is fair to suggest that no matter to what extent the evidence for the wanderings of Odysseus or the travels of Marco Polo is impugned, there will be those who will ignore their own doubts and the doubts of others and attempt to identify mountains, lakes, rocks in the ocean, and similar landmarks because a serene but unexamined belief in the actuality of the recorded past is necessary to an acceptable present.

The arguments that follow are designed neither to cast doubt on the reality of Columbus's first voyage nor to devalue its importance but

11. General and specific studies of the problem include, among a host of others, Moore 1941; Brachey 1944; Adams 1962; Châteaubriand 1969:xi–xxi; Galinsky 1977; Robinson 1979:129–43; Sherbo 1979; Parker 1981; Mezciems 1982; Adams 1983; Morgan 1985; Chipman 1987.

Florida

Abaco

Grand Bahama

Grand Harbour Cay

Andros

New Providence

Great

Bahama

Bank

Cuba

Nautical Miles

0 20 40 60 80 100

Hypothesized landfalls
are underlined

82° W   80° W   78° W   76°

74° W   72° W

N

The Bahamas

26° N

gg Island

Eleuthera
Cat Island
Conception
Watlings Island

24° N

Exuma
Rum
Cay
Long Island
Samana Cay
Crooked I.
Plana Cays
Ragged Is.
Fortune I.
Mayaguana
Acklins I.

22° N

East Caicos
Caicos
Bank
Grand
Turk

Great Inagua

20° N

Hispaniola

rather to provide an appropriate context for discussing the myriad arguments that swirl around the exact loci of its activities. The tendency has been to regard the view from the bridge as sufficiently relevant and rewarding rather than to cast a coldly critical eye on the only text that gives Columbus's first voyage its historical flesh. In reasserting the primacy of the text, the analysis of real voyages cannot be separated entirely from the overwhelming demonstration of the ability of imaginary voyages to fascinate and beguile both in their own time and after.

Toward the beginning of the first scramble for the landfall, Frederick Ober remarked that "One thing is certain; the first landfall of Columbus was an island in the Bahamas."[12] No one has yet disagreed with his assessment, but about no other aspect of the issue has there been universal agreement. To this turbulent historiography I now turn.[13]

12. Ober 1893 : 55. When I say this, I include Grand Turk and the Caicos, distinct from the Bahamas now only by the accident of colonial administrative history.

13. It is only fair to note that, stimulated by the quincentenary, this historiography is entering an intensified stage and this heightened activity may result in some advances over the present state of knowledge, although it may also partly mirror the existing literature in its ingenuity and tendentiousness. Readers are urged to consult *Encounters, Terrae Incognitae, Columbus 92,* and other journals devoted to the Columbian discoveries and to exploration in general.

10. Contradictions of Equal Weight?

As to the other tales contained in this work . . . I can make
but one observation; I am an old traveller. . . . My brain
is filled, therefore, with all kinds of odds and ends. In
travelling, these heterogeneous matters have become
shaken up in my mind . . . so that when I attempt to draw
forth a fact, I cannot determine whether I have read,
heard, or dreamt it; and I am always at a loss to know
how much to believe of my own stories.

WASHINGTON IRVING

After dealing with the latest disaffection on 10 October—
with a firm hand, according to the diario, by compromise and concessions, according to other sources—
Columbus found that the harbingers of land were grow-
ing more frequent and definite, which induced everyone to "breathe more
easily and become cheerful."[1] This time their hopes were not to be
dashed, as Columbus was at last proved a prophet.

The diario's account of the sighting of land and its preliminaries offers
a preview of the textual imbroglios that would accompany the journal
through the Bahamas during the next fortnight. It appears that land itself
was not sighted first but rather a light of some sort. Nor does the diario
tell us who first sighted it, or land, without a great deal of puzzling circumlocution. The account is fairly lengthy, but nearly every part of it
requires the most intensive scrutiny:

> After sunset he navigated on his former course to the west. They went
> about twelve miles per hour and until two hours after midnight went
> about ninety miles, or 22 1/2 leagues. And because the caravel *Pinta* was
> faster and went ahead of the Admiral, it found land and made the signals
> which the Admiral had ordered. This [land] was first seen by a sailor
> called Rodrigo de Triana. Although the Admiral, at 10:00 at night, being
> on the poop deck, saw a light ["lumbre"], although it was a thing so faint

---

1. Alvar/Columbus 1976, 2:45; Dunn and Kelley/Columbus 1989:56.

["cerrada"] that he did not care to assert that it was land. But he called to ["llamó a"] Pero Gutiérrez . . . and told him that there seemed to be a light ["lumbre"] and to look for it. And so he did, and saw it. He told Rodrigo Sánchez of Segovia as well, . . . who saw nothing because he was not in a place ["lugar"] where he could see it. After the Admiral said this, it was seen once or twice, and it was like a small candle of wax that was raised and elevated, which to few seemed to be a sign of land, but the Admiral was sure they were near land. Because of this, when they said the *Salve* [*Regina*], which all sailors are wont to say and sing after their own fashion, and all being there, the Admiral asked and admonished them to keep a good lookout on the forecastle and search well for land. And to him that first told him that he saw land, he would later give a silk jacket, besides the other rewards the sovereigns had promised, which were 10,000 maravedís' annuity to whoever first saw it. Two hours after midnight land appeared, about two leagues distant . . .[2]

In her study of the sources for crew members on the first voyage, Alicia Gould somehow believed that this account was so true to its original that she thought it "probable that if we changed the third person into the first person we would have the writing of Columbus." Similarly, Tió thought that the story was told with "great clarity."[3] Perhaps so, but if Columbus meant to tell the story of the most important moment in his life here, he failed badly, or Las Casas failed him, since in many ways the account is all but incoherent. Historically, the greatest importance has been paid to Columbus's seeing the "light" because this has been taken to be useful in determining the identity of Guanahaní, but we must begin with the assertion to which Columbus gave pride of place—that land was first sighted by a seaman on the rival *Pinta*.[4] The statement is unambiguous enough— a reason is even provided for the untoward circumstance—but it is followed by an account of what appear to be antecedent events. This has

2. Alvar/Columbus 1976, 2:45–47; Dunn and Kelley/Columbus 1989:58–62. See Appendix 1.

3. Gould 1984:205; Tió 1978:13.

4. Varela sees the dislocation as an example of the ancient rhetorical device *hysteron proteron*, or putting the last first for effect, designed in this case to "justify the assignment of the prize [for the first to sight land] to Columbus" (Varela/Columbus 1982:xv). Unfortunately, the effect is—and would be expected to be—just the opposite. One wonders to what degree Columbus would have been aware of ancient rhetorical devices in any case. See Gould 1984:205–6.

naturally caused it to be seen as anomalous in context as well as content, but the notion that land was first sighted by the Pinzóns was quickly squelched in the sources based on the diario. By relocating the passage in his *Historia*, Las Casas credited Pinzón with sighting land only after Columbus had seen its intangible equivalent, the light, thereby discursively preserving Columbus's priority as discoverer.[5] Ferdinand adopted the same strategy—first Columbus saw the light and then, several hours later, a sailor on the *Pinta* (which had "ranged far ahead") first descried solid land.[6]

We will return to this matter later; for the moment we can pick up the text of the diario where we left it. As we see, immediately on the heels of the statement about Rodrigo de Triana the diario launches into a rather long disquisition about a strange experience Columbus had had earlier the same night. The narrative begins oddly. Introduced by the conjunction "puesto que" (which often means "because" but can also mean "although," as it must here), it bears every aspect of a desperate obiter dictum, albeit one of inordinate length.

Under the circumstances, this can only lend credence to the idea that this entry is filled with one afterthought after another.[7] With only one exception, though, modern translators and editors of the diario have not commented on this intriguing incongruity.[8] To his credit, Morison felt obliged to draw readers' attention to it and even to offer an explanation. He was not inclined to blame Las Casas for the apparent muddle but believed that "it seems more likely that the atmosphere was so tense and the important events so many that Columbus put them down on the 12th or 13th just as they came into his head."[9] As a sovereign remedy

---

5. Las Casas 1951, 1:198–200.

6. Colón 1930, 1:159–60.

7. This topsy-turvy text is reminiscent of the entry for 9 August, while Columbus was at the Canaries. It seems more likely, though, that in the earlier case the problems arose from Las Casas's lack of success in summarizing a month of activity in a single entry. See Alvar/Columbus 1976, 2:21–24; Dunn and Kelley/Columbus 1989:24–27.

8. E.g., *Raccolta*/Columbus 1892, 1:15; Markham/Columbus 1893:35; Thacher 1903–4, 1:530; Jane/Columbus 1960:22; Cioranescu/Columbus 1961:42; Alvar/Columbus 1976, 2:45; Varela/Columbus 1982:88; Ferro/Columbus 1985:42; Dunn and Kelley/Columbus 1989:59. Fuson 1987a:73 omits much of the entry.

9. Morison/Columbus 1963n2; but he followed Ferdinand and Las Casas in rationalizing the report of the day's and night's events (Morison 1942, 1:296–98).

for finessing all manner of recalcitrant text, this is admirably encompassing, though hardly very convincing, even though the events for both the 11 and 12 October are combined into a single entry dated 11 October. It requires, for instance, that we accept that when Columbus harkened back to the events of the discovery, whether from the distance of a few hours or a few days, the very first thing that occurred to him was that Rodrigo de Triana had sighted land from the *Pinta*. Such an event is hardly conceivable, unless in fact Columbus's statement is true in the sense that it conveyed the actual sequence of events that night, which would certainly best explain the disjointed, even retrograde, unfolding of this narrative.

Besides the extraordinarily allusive wording, there are other hints that the text describing Columbus's sighting of the light is parasitic and that removing it would render the entry more, rather than less, comprehensible. For instance, at the end of the text (after long since noting that Triana had discovered land) we find Columbus urging the men to keep a sharp eye in order to claim the promised reward.[10] Yet by this time he had already provided justification for his own claim to that reward, a claim he later pressed successfully. Either the text is wrong at this point or Columbus was cynically encouraging his men with the promise of a reward to which he was in the very process of staking a claim.

I

One can hardly help but notice how assiduously and cleverly vague the description of the light itself is. It was an incident that would not bear checking, a tale for which an escape hatch was carefully provided. The object allegedly sighted, a "light" (presumably a fire), had but a momentary existence, so the whole matter would depend on Columbus's word. True, the text tells us that Columbus sought, and even secured, corroboration from one of the officers on board but that another, when asked, did not support Columbus's claim.[11] There was good reason for this,

10. Is it not peculiar that if the *Pinta* was already well ahead of the *Santa María*, Columbus would not have expected both that members of its crew would also have seen the light and that they would sight land first? That is, was there any point in "admonishing" the crew of the *Santa María* in this regard?

11. See Cioranescu/Columbus 1961:383n61. Tió (1978:15) has Sánchez's view obscured by "hills or trees."

however; he was not in a place where he could see the light. This is rather a peculiar statement. If Sánchez were not situated where he could see whatever there was to see, why was he asked? Or why did he not move to a more advantageous position? And for that matter, just where was this mysterious "place?" So, the story goes, Columbus had two witnesses and both supported his case, since the first claimed to have seen the light and the second did not see it only because he could not, which was nearly as good.[12] In the event, it scarcely mattered, because both men were left behind to perish at Navidad and were lost to history and its inquisitors.

Then there is the admittedly minor matter of the *Salve Regina* that the passage states Columbus had the men sing in honor of his seeing the light. As Morison and others have noted, this hymn was normally sung at twilight, and though it was not impossible that on this occasion they sang it as well much later in the evening, it must be regarded as out of the ordinary.[13]

But surely any untimely singing of the *Salve Regina* was far less extraordinary than the activity of the ships after Columbus saw the light. At this point the story within a story abruptly ceases, but in the preceding passage, Columbus—again anachronistically—provided the sailing schedule of the ships that day and night. According to this, they sustained a speed of "twelve miles each hour" between sunset and "two hours after midnight." To drive the point home, Columbus (or Las Casas) then noted that this equaled "ninety miles," the equivalent of seven and half hours' sailing. This leaves no room to doubt that after seeing the light Columbus blithely sailed on at a rather brisk pace for another four hours! Although such behavior can scarcely be said to make sense, it has, as we will see,

---

12. Young (1906, 1:160), Gould (1927:432), and others have blended the accounts of Ferdinand, Las Casas, the diario, and Oviedo to give the impression that the diario itself spoke of many on board seeing the light, whereas the diario requires us to believe only that two people on board the *Santa María*, Columbus and Gutiérrez, said that they saw the light.

13. Tió argues for a "special" *Salve Regina* in thanksgiving for the light (1961:571). In fact, on his third voyage Columbus ordered that the *Salve Regina* be sung at midday to celebrate the discovery of Trinidad. See Las Casas 1951, 2:9; Morison 1942, 2:246. Morales Padrón notes only that "in this instance the *Salve Regina* put an end to the day" as though Columbus had clairvoyantly postponed singing it at its normal time (Morales Padrón/Columbus 1984:189n209).

aroused little more than perfunctory interest on the part of the partisans of one landfall or another.[14]

Even so, the passage concerning the distances covered is wholly incompatible with that about the light. If the light had been directly ahead, where one might suspect that Columbus had been gazing the most keenly, then the fleet would have been obliged to heave to in order to avoid running into the light's habitat.[15] On the other hand, had the light been to port or starboard, surely at least the *Santa María* would have stopped or made course in the relevant direction even at the risk of losing sight of the *Pinta*. One would think that after nearly five weeks filled with growing apprehension and one false alarm after another, either a concern for safety (had the light been straight ahead) or simple curiosity (had it been off to either side) would have compelled Columbus not to sail onward for yet another thirty-five to forty miles.

On balance, we have little recourse but to conclude that the information on the course and distance indicts the story of Columbus's profitable apparition (or possibly vice versa). This uncongenial point has not been entirely lost on the students of the landfall, though the most fervent advocates of one site or another have scarcely mentioned the matter at all.[16] Gould, rather than assuming that the light emanated from Watlings Island, which he then supported as the landfall, was willing to admit that Columbus's continued sailing was "very surprising," but he offered no explanation.[17] Later he changed his mind and argued that Conception Island is Guanahaní, but his perplexity continued.[18]

Barreiro Meiro, another partisan of Watlings Island, went further and admitted that it would have been "suicide" for Columbus to proceed at full speed for four hours after sighting the light. For Barreiro Meiro this

14. For example, Morison breezily wrote that "this little light does not cause Columbus to alter his course. His ships rush on, pitching, rolling, throwing spray" (1974:62). In turn, Tió suggested that an easterly wind may have prevented Columbus from turning to explore the source of the light (1978:13).

15. Varela/Columbus 1982:89n42.

16. Didiez Burgos (1974:143) and Perez (1987:30) did notice, but Gaffarel (1892, 1:102), Charcot (1928:153–55), Gandía (1942:284–84), Morison (1942, 1:296–97; 1974:62–63), Taviani (1984, 1:50–53), and Granzotto (1985:138–39) all ignored the problem.

17. Gould 1927:417.

18. Gould 1965:83.

could be explained only if Las Casas "did not understand the text of Columbus," and he mentioned an earlier occasion in which Las Casas expressed doubt over the reading of the text.[19] Didiez Burgos followed Gould both in noting the problem and in declining to offer an explanation.[20]

Earlier, Markham seemed to have sensed the pitfall when he wrote that Columbus proceeded "under very easy sail" after sighting the light, a statement in flat contradiction to the text.[21] More recently, Roukema dismissed Gould's concerns by arguing that the sighting of the light was "wisdom after the event" and was inserted into the log later, the proof being that Columbus called on "two mere landsmen for verification and not the seasoned officer in charge of the watch."[22] Roukema is likely to be right, at least in his conclusion, though hardly in his reasons for it, even though he offered his comment without reflecting on its implications. For Roukema it was merely one more argument in support of his position that Watlings Island is Guanahaní for, as we shall see, the incident of the light has long been regarded as an embarrassing complication by the Watlings Islanders. My agreement with Roukema stems from the nature of the text itself. Either the statement as to distances traveled and times involved or the story of the light, or both, must be wrong. In sum, the passage bears every mark of being an ex post facto abuse of Columbus's monopoly of the log.

II

As noted, both Ferdinand and Las Casas apparently found the account for 11 October troublesome since both rearranged and otherwise glossed it.[23] Ferdinand had the night begin, as traditionally, with the singing of the *Salve Regina* and then proceeded much as in the diario but with a few added twists. He has Rodrigo Sánchez arriving too late to see the light; he has others see it as well; and he has them believing that the light ema-

19. Barreiro Meiro 1968:7, apparently assuming that the light was seen directly ahead.
20. Didiez Burgos 1974:143.
21. Markham 1892:80.
22. Roukema 1959:91.
23. As did Herrera (1934–57, 2:77–79), hardly surprisingly, since his account was based on both Las Casas and Ferdinand.

nated from "fishermen" or "travelers," or even from people "going from one house to another."[24] None of this is in the diario, whose evidence is especially inimical to Ferdinand's last assumption.[25]

Las Casas went even further. As was his habit, he dealt with material from the diario in his *Historia* and then added commentary of his own. He, too, has the *Salve Regina* sung at dusk, "as was the custom of sailors," and introduces an ambiance of high expectation and tension, all a departure from the text of the diario.[26] Seeing a light, Columbus calls "in secret" ("de secreto") to Pero Gutiérrez, tells him he sees a light, and asks for confirmation. To this leading question Gutiérrez supplies the right answer—he, too, sees the light. Rodrigo Sánchez, however, could not see it—no reason given—but it "was seen a time or two" by unnamed persons, perhaps just Columbus again. Las Casas then offered his own explanation of the light: It was carried by islanders bowing to the necessities of nature. All in all, Columbus and "some others" saw the light "three or four times."[27]

Unlike in the diario, Las Casas in the *Historia* mentioned no time for the sighting of the light, but he left every impression that it was virtually simultaneous with the actual sighting of land.[28] Perhaps he too wondered why Columbus would have sailed on for another four hours. Las Casas then digressed at some length on why Columbus not only received but should have received the promised reward.

Both these accounts, although following the diario reasonably well, are

24. Colón 1930, 1:160, in a chapter entitled "How the Admiral Found the First Land."

25. Or in the *Pleitos*, for that matter, for which see notes 41 and 42.

26. Oddly, when Columbus believed that land had been sighted on 25 September, he had the crew sing the *Gloria* even though it was at sunset. Alvar/Columbus 1976, 2:36; Dunn and Kelley/Columbus 1989:42–43.

27. Las Casas 1951, 1:198–99. Neither Las Casas nor later proponents of this interpretation explain why the Indians would have needed torches on a night brightly enough lit by the moon for Rodrigo de Triana to be able to spot Guanahaní more than six miles away.

28. Las Casas 1951, 1:198–99. Regarding the light as real, and hence as a sign of the discovery, Gil (1984:73–75) argues that Las Casas intentionally left this impression because of an eschatological aversion to the number eleven, since St. Isidore believed that the number eleven indicated "a transgression of the [sacred] law or the diminution of sanctity," a view taken up by later church authorities as well.

lapidary; both attempt to polish the many rough spots in the text.[29] Lacking any evidence independent of the diario, the sceptic would be inclined, and with good reason, to suspect that the passage referring to Columbus's lucky apparition is an interpolation by either Columbus or Las Casas, perhaps based on a tradition in the Columbus family designed to legitimate the award of the 10,000 maravedís.[30] But however tempting such a suspicion might be, it is seriously weakened by, ironically, the testimony of Oviedo, drawn largely from anti-Columbus sources.

Perhaps no one emended more than Oviedo, whose brief account of the first voyage is disparaged as noncanonical because it apparently derived from an entirely different body of sources. Regardless of matters of canon, it is worth quoting *in extenso* because so much of it differs from the diario and its derivatives in content and perspective. After describing the latest episode of discontent on 10 October, Oviedo presents his account of the moment of discovery:

And that same day Columbus knew for sure that he was near land by the appearance of the clouds in the sky. And he admonished the pilots that if perchance the ships became separated from each other through some misfortune, each should head in the arranged direction or course in order to come into convoy. And as night arrived he ordered that the sails be reduced, with only the foremasts lowered. And going thus, a sailor from those aboard the flagship [the *Santa María*] said: "Light ["lumbre"]! Land!" And then Columbus's servant, named Salcedo, replied, saying: "The Admiral has already said this, my lord." And immediately ["encontinente"] Columbus said: "A short time ago I said that and saw that light, which is on land." And so it was that on Thursday ["jueves"] at two hours after midnight the Admiral called to a grandee named Escobedo . . . and told him he saw the light ["lumbre"]. And the next day ["otro día de mañana"] at dawn, and at the hour that on the previous day Columbus

---

29. Gould (1984:205) regarded the texts of Ferdinand and Las Casas as "almost identical" so that either Las Casas copied from "the work" of Ferdinand or both "copied directly" from the log in one of its versions. Any identity can also be explained by the fact that there was only one way to rationalize the account, and both took it.

30. Perhaps it should be noted that the *cédula* formally granting the reward to Columbus, dated 23 May 1493, made no mention of a light. Rather, Columbus was credited with being the first who "saw and discovered" the new lands. Navarrete 1954–55, 1:326.

had said [foretold?], from the flagship was seen the island the Indians call Guanahaní, from the tramontane ["tramontana"] or part of the north. And he who first saw land when it was already day ["cuando ya fue de día"] was named Rodrigo de Triana, on the eleventh day of October in the said year of 1492.[31]

Oviedo added that the sailor on the *Santa María* who "first said" that he had seen a light on the land and who was "from Lepe" apostasized to Islam on his return to Spain out of a sense of outrage at being cheated out of his just reward. Oviedo also noted that on seeing land Columbus cried with joy and recited prayers in gratitude.

Oviedo's narrative seems even more garbled than the diario's account, but those who would discount its value overlook the fact that it compromises any hypothesis that Columbus did not see (or rather did not say he saw) a light in the distance. The significant differences between Oviedo's text and that of the diario and its offspring are that Oviedo said:

1/that Columbus had already ordered the ships to reduce sails before land (or a light) had been sighted and had made provision for regrouping in the event that any separation resulted;

2/that an unnamed sailor from the *Santa María* first shouted that he had sighted both light and land;[32]

3/that thereupon Columbus's page, and then Columbus himself, claimed that he had already seen the light "a short time" before and believed that it was "on land";[33]

4/that Columbus then—and only then—told Rodrigo de Escobedo (and not either Pero Gutiérrez or Rodrigo Sánchez) of his experience and that apparently he did not seek confirmation from him;[34]

5/that all this occurred not at about 10:00 P.M. on 11 October but at 2:00 A.M. earlier the same day;[35] and

31. Oviedo 1851–55, 1:23–24. For the Spanish text, see Appendix 2.

32. Identified by Gould (1984:275–76) as Pedro Izquierdo.

33. For the page, Pedro de Salcedo, see Gould 1984:350–65.

34. Oviedo combined the title held by Pero Gutiérrez with the name Escobedo, for whom see Gould 1984:412–23.

35. On this confused passage see, among others, Didiez Burgos 1974:391–92 and Gil 1984:73–74. Both argue for a discovery date of 11 October. Branchi (1937), on the other hand, argued for a date of 13 October. Various accounts in the *Pleitos* support a discovery date of 11 October. *Pleitos Colombinos* 1989:xl, 271.

6/that Rodrigo de Triana (whom he did not place on the *Pinta*) first saw solid land after daybreak, not at 2:00 A.M.

Oviedo closed his account of the discovery of America by noting that his sources for the Lepe sailor's apostasy (and probably for much of the rest) were Vicente Yáñez Pinzón and Hernán Pérez Mateus.[36]

These discrepancies are not insignificant, nor can they all be laid to the ravages of time or even to the differing perspectives of the actors. Clearly there was a firm recollection that someone, sometime had claimed that they had seen what they said was a light. At this Columbus admitted that he had already seen a light.[37] We can only wonder why he had been so intent on keeping this exciting information to himself. The impression is that, whatever his alertness and visual skills, Columbus was also an opportunist, a view no doubt also held by the sailor from Lepe.[38]

Other discrepancies (from which ship land was "first" sighted and the very aberrant chronology) can better be laid to declining memories and a narrower angle of vision at the time.[39] But whether we choose to believe that Columbus wilfully deprived one of his sailors of the profit and glory of the first sighting, it would now be difficult to argue that the notion that a light had been seen—probably before land itself—was not current on board the *Santa María* at the time.[40] But whether it was a light, an optical illusion, or the product of outright duplicity is open to debate. To the course of that debate we now turn.

III

The problematic nature of the diario entry for 11/12 October has in no way discouraged researchers from employing the light to determine the site of the landfall. Very early in the debate, Washington Irving (or rather

36. For these individuals, see Gould 1984:461–97, 510–20.

37. With apologies, but the semantic horrors of the sentence are required by the circumstances.

38. For a different view, see Gould 1984:209–10.

39. For example, the date of 11 October also appears in the testimony in the *Pleitos* (1892–94, 2:220).

40. Although the absence of any mention of a light in the *Pleitos* leaves open the possibility that Oviedo was repeating information that had evolved through being transmitted orally in the intervening twenty-five years.

Alexander Slidell) pointed out that believing in the reality of the light enjoins accepting that Columbus must have passed at least one island before reaching Guanahaní.[41] Partly as a result of this line of reasoning, Irving adopted Cat Island as the landfall, since it was an interior island in the Bahamas archipelago.

Some three-quarters of those who have addressed the issue have concluded that Columbus saw some kind of light, but in positing the nature of the apparition, unanimity vanishes. It is not hard to understand why. If we are to believe the diario, at 10:00 P.M. the *Santa María* was still as much as forty miles away from sighting land—a long way to see any light. Almost instinctively, then, proponents of the reality of the light have been forced to consider alternatives to its being on land, or rather on the landfall, or to the distance being as great as the diario so clearly implies.

The variety of responses is impressive. Becher thought it may have been a meteor.[42] Markham, followed by Cronau, suggested that the light originated from Indians fishing from canoes in the area, but others were quick to scoff at the notion that Indians would fish so far out in the open sea.[43] Manrique wondered if it had not come from the *Pinta*.[44] Another, and more ingenious, solution was that the light represented "luminous marine annelids of the genus *Odontosyllis*," but this has found favor only with Gould.[45] Fantoni thinks that Columbus was misled by a small star in Hercules or Serpens.[46]

For others, such as Irving, the light emanated from an island the fleet passed on its way to landfall.[47] For most Watlings Islanders, of course, this notion is anathema since there are no other islands to be passed. For them it has been easiest to regard the light as an apparition, the product

41. Irving 1828, 3:311. Tió (1961:318–19), the most recent advocate of Cat Island, has also drawn on this argument. Apparently, it has also served as an encouragement to local pride there, as suggested in Powles 1888:240–41.

42. Becher 1856:90.

43. Markham 1892:88; Cronau 1921:16.

44. Manrique 1890:111–14. Cf. Arranz/Columbus 1985:89n.

45. Crawshay 1935:559–60; Gould 1965:91. Perhaps the fact that this form of illumination can be seen for only about 200 yards accounts for the reluctance. Earlier, Blake (1892:539) had suggested "a floating Medusa, or flying-fish" as the source of light.

46. Fantoni 1989. Bertone (1987:174–75) thinks that clouds or sandbanks are the most likely answer.

47. Most recently, Tió (1978) (Watlings Island) and Winslow (1988) (Abaco).

of a fevered but prescient mind that turned out to be no more than four hours off target.[48] Murdock, Morison, and other influential supporters of Watlings Island adopted this view.[49] The fact that the belief was based less on the text than on the the problem the light posed for their theory became clear as soon as Wolper carried out an experiment in 1959 designed to show that under certain circumstances a fire lighted on the highest point of Watlings Island could be descried as far as twenty-nine miles out to sea.[50] This was enough for Morison, Obregón, and others to rush to a very different judgment.

Morison had regarded the light as "imaginary" in 1942 and still did so in 1955.[51] By 1963, however, he had softened his position, and by the following year he was quite willing to accept "the rational explanation" Wolper had provided.[52] Doing so allowed Columbus to be correct in seeing a light and Morison to be correct in espousing Watlings Island as the landfall and locus of the light. But more than the text was sacrificed along the way. In 1942 Morison had believed that "the fleet was *at least* 35 miles off shore" at 10:00 P.M. on 11 October.[53] There is nothing to suggest that he had changed his calculation (which was very much endorsed by the diario) in 1963, but by 1964 Mauricio Obregón and he had moved the fleet, with a certain heavy-handed charm, a little closer to Guanahaní. It was now "twenty to thirty miles from land."[54]

48. At least one supporter of Watlings Island has been ingenious in this respect. Morales y Pedroso (1923:57–61) posited a scenario in which Columbus saw the light on Watlings Island to port but kept sailing along until Triana spotted the heights of Cat Island. Then Columbus lay to but did not anchor, and as a result of both contrary drift and Columbus's desire to land where he had seen the light, the ships hovered between Cat Island and Watlings Island until daybreak, when Columbus decided to land on the latter, approaching it from the west. A special advantage of this argument is that, after all, Columbus was both technically and morally entitled to the reward.

49. Murdock 1884:484–856; Morison 1942, 1:296–97. The tone was set by Manrique 1890:113–21.

50. Wolper 1964:9–23. Oddly, even the lighthouse on Dixon Hill, 163 feet above sea level, can be seen for only nineteen miles. Rigg 1973:226; *Yachtman's Guide* 1987:396.

51. Morison 1942, 1:297; Morison 1955:48.

52. Morison/Columbus 1963:64n5; Morison and Obregón 1964:15. Morison repeated his claim in Morison 1974:62. Clearly by then the light was as real for Morison as he had come to think it was for Columbus.

53. Morison 1942, 1:297, with emphasis added.

54. Morison and Obregón 1964:15.

Although his progress toward Guanahaní seems more purposeful, Morison was by no means alone in having trouble situating the fleet that night. Other estimates range from sixteen miles by Didiez Burgos (who believed that the sighting of the light preceded the sighting of land by only one hour instead of four) to forty-eight or more miles.[55] Many discussions offer no estimate at all, probably wisely, yet the text of the diario is explicit and precise on just this point. If we accept that the Columbian league approximated three nautical miles, then he saw the light when he was thirty-six miles away from where the fleet was to be located four hours later. Furthermore, when land was sighted it was still two leagues (six miles) away, so that at 10:00 P.M. land was some forty-two miles from Columbus's eyes. Under the circumstances, any demonstration that the light of a bonfire on Watlings Island (or any other island) can be seen twenty-nine miles away is completely meaningless and should not have generated the intellectual pratfalls Morison exhibited.

The latter part of the entry covering 11 October permits us only to wonder or to apply any number of emendations, none of which can be countenanced by more than sanguine predisposition. Certainly the Gordian knot could be cut most quickly by finding a way to disavow the passage in which the mileage for the day is so starkly laid out, but this inevitably opens Pandora's box to all other such passages that are mined so intensively in postulating Columbus's route. In some way, the course of events depicted in the diario must be wrong, but determining what is correct seems an impossible task. It is hardly acceptable procedure, though, to adopt an engrossing interpretation that assimilates the account in the diario with those in Las Casas's *Historia*, Ferdinand's *Historie*, and Oviedo's *Historia* as if these were largely complementary rather than largely contradictory.[56]

Neither Columbus's character nor Las Casas's transcriptional skill fares well in this entry. Some may wish to join Lamartine in believing that Columbus was vouchsafed a personal preview of America, which he gen-

55. Didiez Burgos 1974: 136, 138–44; Irving 1828, 3:311 (48 miles); Valentini 1892:156 (44 miles); Cronau 1921:18 (48 miles); Luca de Tena 1968:185 (48 miles); Perez 1987:30 (close to fifty miles). Some of these estimates appear to be in statute rather than nautical miles.

56. This has been done, apparently casually, by Markham (1892:80); Montojo (1892:17); Morison (1942, 1:296–97); Link and Link (1958:20); Gould (1965:82); and Didiez Burgos (1974:140).

erously shared with a few others, but the skeptic will no doubt reserve the right to suspect that Columbus was at his opportunistic best in this episode.[57] The historian can only view these texts as inextricably confused and confusing, and not susceptible to the kinds of cosmetic surgery they have undergone time and again. Whether Columbus saw a light, thought he did, or simply took advantage of the chance to say he did is unimportant in the sense that it is undeterminable.[58] From this it must follow that identifying its nature and source is even more so. Whatever arguments are brought to bear on the identity of Guanahaní, the notorious incident of the "luz de la víspera" has no part in them. The refusal by researchers to accept this can be seen in the fact that opinions as to the reality of the light and the identity of the landfall have become interdependent variables, with the ontological status of the incident of the light depending directly and entirely on the choice of landfall site. Exponents of island x believe or disbelieve in the light *only* because they believe island x is Guanahaní. It is easy enough to see why this line of reasoning evolved among the Watlings Islanders in view of its exterior geographical position. Even Morison was willing to lay aside his hero worship for a moment in order to disbelieve in the reality of the light, but only until he could find a light on Watlings Island to believe in.

Those who prefer an interior island should feel no obligation to press for the existence of the light unless they can do so on grounds independent of their preference. After all, the chance of seeing such a light at any given time is minuscule, if not microscopic. Accepting the reality of the light solely to enhance an argument for an interior island can only serve to undermine that argument. In truth, the quasi-mystical element of both the incident and its telling are reason enough to divorce it from any landfall arguments.

57. Lamartine 1852/1942:74–75. Lamartine helped his own cause by asserting that Rodrigo Sánchez "did not hesitate any more than Gutierez in discerning a light on the horizon." Young (1906, 1:172) was equally lyrical.

58. Except to those interested in Columbus's integrity. Most have found ways to exculpate him. See, for instance, MacKie 1892:363–68, Cioranescu/Columbus 1961: 384n63, and with great casuistry, Markham 1892:88. More recently, Taviani (Taviani/ Columbus 1988, 2:285–88) and Mahn-Lot (1988:79–80) have adopted such a stance.

11. A Potpourri of Puzzles

It's really quite simple: every time you decide something without having a good reason, you jump to Conclusions whether you like it or not. It's such an easy trip to make that I've been here hundreds of times. NORTON JUSTER

L and at last having been sighted, the fleet finally lay to during the early hours of Friday, 12 October, and with the coming of dawn Columbus and the captains, together with a few of the grandees aboard, disembarked to take "possession" of what they had found. The interval between the sighting and the landing is treated in the diario with the usual limited detail. The fleet waited until daylight, and then the landing took place; no more is said.[1]

Modern treatment of this passage provides an example of the tendency to make a meal of the diario's many morsels. At this stage the words are Las Casas's, though he was soon to revert to "the very words" of Columbus. In revising himself in the *Historia*, Las Casas was only slightly more forthcoming. Amid a torrent of pious verbiage, he tells us there that "when day came . . . the three ships arrived at land, dropped anchors, and saw the beach full of naked people."[2] Ferdinand was even less revealing, if slightly more panoramic: "When day came they saw there was an island 15 leagues long, flat and without mountains."[3]

1. Alvar/Columbus 1976, 2:47; Dunn and Kelley/Columbus 1989:62 see also Appendix 1. Columbus had nothing at all to say about the matter in his Letter (Jane 1930b, 1:1; Ramos Pérez 1986).

2. Las Casas 1951, 1:200: "Venido el día . . . lléganse los tres navíos a la tierra, y surgen sus anclas, y ven la playa toda llena de gente desnuda."

3. Colón 1930, 1:163: "Venuto adunque il giorno, videro che era una Isola di XV leghe di lunghezza, piana e senza montagne."

All this hardly seems the stuff of grand theorizing. The sum total of the testimony from the three sources is that Guanahaní was sighted at 2 A.M. and that later in the day, presumably shortly after dawn, Columbus landed and ceremoniously claimed the island for the Spanish crown. Even so, speculation about the spot where Columbus first set foot in the New World has proceeded apace for nearly two centuries. The question is both separated from and hopelessly entwined with the issue of which part of Guanahaní Rodrigo de Triana first sighted. On neither matter has there ever been a consensus, as is demonstrated in the opinions expressed by Watlings Islanders over time. First I will look at the matter of the sighting and then of the landing proper.

The very first scholar to suggest Watlings Island, Juan Bautista Muñoz, assumed that Guanahaní was first sighted from the east, and this has proved to be the most popular choice ever since.[4] The notion seems to be that Columbus was lucky enough to strike land dead ahead as he sailed west, not necessarily the most probable alternative. A minority position, however, supports a northerly approach.[5] Although its proponents do not always admit it, such a view has the direct support of Oviedo, who provided the only precise statement on the matter when he wrote that "from the flagship was seen the island that the Indians call Guanahaní, from the tramontane or part of the north."[6]

While interesting enough for what it says, Oviedo's statement is even more intriguing for the way in which he expressed it. "Tramontana," the word he used in apposition to "norte" means "across the mountains" and is a peculiarly Italian expression. Its use here suggests that Oviedo's source was close to Columbus himself, who used the term on occasion.[7] In this regard, Oviedo's evidence is to be regarded as more than merely *faute de mieux,* as, for instance, Barreiro Meiro would have it.[8] In its expression and in the lack of any data to contradict it, it deserves to be accepted not only as the best evidence available but also as good evidence.

---

4. Muñoz 1793:86, followed by, among other works, Murdock 1884:477; Mc-Elroy 1941:217; Morison 1942, 1:299; and Roukema 1959:92.

5. The works supporting this position include Harrisse 1884–85, 2:441; Thacher 1903–4, 1:600; Cronau 1921:17–19; Stewart 1931:126; and Barreiro Meiro 1968:28.

6. Oviedo 1851–55, 1:24.

7. On Columbus's use of Italianisms, see Terlingen 1943 and Milani 1973. For "tramontana" in particular, see Terlingen 1943:228–29, and Milani 1973:116–18.

8. Barreiro Meiro 1968:28.

In contrast, Morison and his erstwhile collaborator, Mauricio Obregón, developed an argument for the southeasterly part of Guanahaní. As always, knowing more than his sources, Morison intoned that "Rodrigo de Triana . . . sees something like a white sand cliff gleaming in the moonlight on the western horizon, then another, and a dark line of land connecting them."[9] Recently Obregón has been quoted as extending this argument when, in affirming his belief that Watlings Island is Guanahaní, he asserted, "When Columbus made his first landfall, he came from the east and he saw white cliffs—and the modern San Salvador [Watlings Island] has white cliffs in the right place."[10]

These solemn statements do not have the slightest textual warrant. Although one of the deponents in the Pleitos did mention, nearly twenty-five years later, that Rodrigo de Triana had seen "a white head of sand" ("una cabeça blanca de arena"), this hardly seems to offer much consolation.[11] Columbus himself mentioned neither sand nor cliffs, nor did any of the other early sources. All of them, as we will see, described Guanahaní as flat. No doubt it is possible to argue that these descriptions of Guanahaní and the notion that Columbus saw the white cliffs of Watlings Island can be made not completely incompatible, but that task would best be left to those who care to make the effort.[12] The argument is unabashedly circular: Watlings Island has cliffs facing to the east; Columbus came from the east; Watlings Island is Guanahaní; therefore Columbus must have seen these cliffs. Only the first of these assumptions is demonstrably correct.

We can leave this whirling dervish of an argument and move on to the question of Columbus's anchorage and landing. Disregarding the diario and other early sources, most proponents of Watlings Island separate the point of sighting from that of anchorage and debarkation.[13] To take the

9. Morison 1942, 1:268. Cf. Morison 1974:62, Morison/Columbus 1963:65n2.

10. *New Yorker*, 1 September 1986, 25. Cf. Wolper 1964:11–18.

11. *Pleitos* 1892–94, 1:220.

12. To be fair, I might mention Fox 1882:388 for cliffs on Samana, and Link and Link 1956:5–6 for cliffs on East Caicos.

13. Harrisse (1884–85, 2:452–54) suggested that Columbus anchored at one island (Conception or Playa Cay) and disembarked at another (Acklins). As noted above, Morales y Pedroso (1923:57–61) made a similar argument for Cat Island and Watlings Island respectively.

diario literally—and in this case there is no reason not to—would be to believe that Columbus saw Guanahaní, landed at or as near to the point of sighting as possible, anchored there from the morning of 12 October to the afternoon of 14 October, then sailed away.[14]

The principal argument that Columbus did not do this is that there are but few places on Watlings Island where the fleet could safely have anchored, most obviously on the western or lee side. Moreover, because of reefs and wind, the eastern side is the most dangerous part of the island at which to attempt a landing. Supporters of a western anchorage often note the statement in the diario that on the morning of 11 October there was "much sea."[15] Moreover, the distances recorded as covered that day suggest a strong easterly wind. On the other hand, 12 October was another day, a day when the fleet was over 150 miles west of its position the morning before, and a day when the condition of the sea is nowhere noted. There are, then, no specific statements in the diario to suggest that Columbus felt obliged to disembark at a location different from that at which he sighted land. The statement that the Indians swam out to the ships in great numbers suggests a sheltered anchorage, but we do not know whether this resulted from a deliberate attempt by Columbus to seek one out or simply from the abating of any troublesome winds.[16]

Despite the preponderance of opinion among Watlings Islanders that the point of landing differed from the area of first approach, there is no unanimity as to just where the former was. The map of Watlings Island shows that students of the problem have favored positions all around the perimeter of the island. In contrast to later opinion, Becher favored an eastern anchorage *because* the winds were said to be light.[17] Montojo, on the other hand, inclined to a northern anchorage because Oviedo's evidence seemed to require it.[18] Small wonder that there are now on Watlings Island no fewer than four plaques or monuments commemorating the landfall of Columbus, each at a different spot.[19]

14. This is the argument of Rumeu de Armas 1968:312–16, 321–23.

15. Alvar/Columbus 1976, 2:44. Sealey (1987:8–9) is the most recent to make this argument.

16. Alvar/Columbus 1976, 2:50.

17. Becher 1856:192.

18. Montojo 1892:18n.

19. *Chicago Herald* 1891; Leicester 1980; Cappon 1986.

The arguments regarding the point of anchorage have become enmeshed with views as to the nature and direction of Columbus's reconnaissance on the morning of 14 October, a question taken up in detail
later. Be that as it may, the most common opinion among Watlings Islanders has come to be that Columbus sighted Guanahaní from the east,
rounded the island either at its northern or southern tip, and then anchored at or near Long Bay in the lee of its western side. This view was
pioneered late in the nineteenth century and has, with the impetus of
Morison's work, prospered and become the consensus, virtually the orthodoxy, during the past fifty years. However, as we have seen, none of
the premises that fuel this hypothesis finds any textual support.

I
_____

The chronic lack of effective context throughout the diario gives impetus
to doubts and hesitations about the meaning even of single words. We
have seen this already and will see it again, but here I would like to
underscore the effects of this condition by addressing briefly the controversy over the word "volviendo" in the entry for 13 October.

While anchored at Guanahaní, Columbus took the first of many opportunities to grill the Indians about the location of gold in larger quantities than he had seen so far. He recorded the outcome in the diario:
"And by [their] signs I was able to understand that, [by] going to the
south or by [volviendo] the island by way of [?] the south ("Y por señas
pude entender que yendo al sur o volviendo la isla por el sur")."[20] Perhaps

20. Alvar/Columbus 1976, 2:55; Dunn and Kelley/Columbus 1989:70.

WATLINGS ISLAND

Point First Sighted by Columbus	*Point of Columbus's Anchorage or Debarkation*
1 Barreiro Meiro, Cronau, Stewart, and Thacher	A Becher
2 Muñoz, Murdock, Roukema, and Wolper	B Blake
3 Morison	C Major and Markham
4 Blake	D Muñoz and Albertis
5 Taviani	E Barreiro Meiro, Cronau, Morales y Pedroso, Morison, Obregón, Roukema, Stewart, Taviani, Thacher, Vidal Gormaz, and Wolper
6 Morales y Pedroso	F Murdock

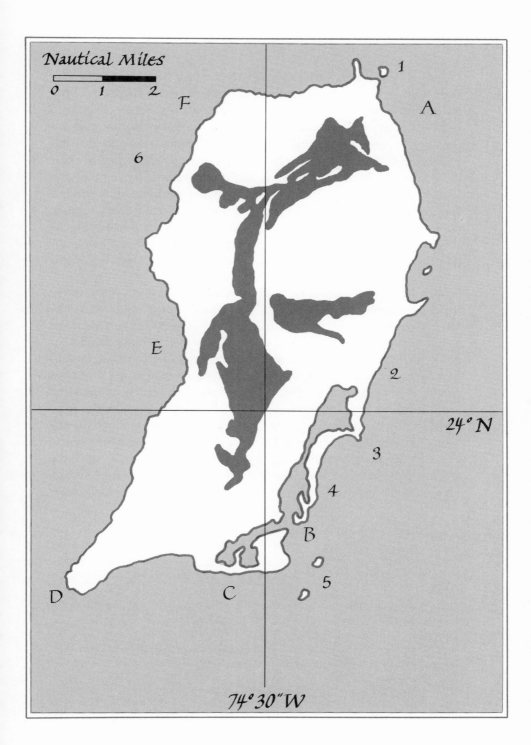

Nautical Miles

0   1   2

F

A

1

6

24° N

2

E

3

4

B

C

5

D

74° 30″ W

if Columbus had ended his thought after the first "sur," all would have been well, but the remaining clause has created much discussion, both about how to translate it and how to interpret it.

The simplest explanation is to believe that Columbus misread his ability to understand the Indians, as well as their ability to understand his questions, and he was simply befuddled. Apparently this view has never been adopted, though others have, and in abundance. By omitting the second clause from his translation, Becher did no more than emulate Ferdinand, who wrote simply that gold was to be found "in the part of the south" ("della parte de Mezzo").[21] Most others have accepted the reality of the wording and have attempted to deal with it.[22] The major question involves the most likely meaning of "volviendo"; did Columbus mean "turning" or "returning"?[23]

Most have assumed that he had "turning" in mind and take to translating "volviendo" as "doubling," "rounding," "going around," or the like. In contrast, Lyon, followed by Perez, has preferred to render the phrase as "returning (to) the island from the south."[24] While Lyon does not gloss his departure, Perez adds that this must mean that the Indians were telling Columbus that they would accompany him to the auriferous regions if he brought them back to Guanahaní.[25] Molander, on the other hand, is not discomfited by the apparent obscurity of the text. For him, "this clue makes immediate sense" because it indicates that the Indians were telling Columbus, then at Egg Island, that he would have to circle either Eleuthera or New Providence to find a deep-water route to Cuba, whereas from Watlings Island there is a direct deep-water route.[26] Others have used the expression to rule out certain points as anchorages for

21. Becher 1856:94; Colón 1930, 1:170.

22. Las Casas (1951, 1:207) followed the diario closely here, but in his edition Cioranescu inserted a "perhaps" after the first "sur," (Cioranescu/Columbus 1961: 46), while Fuson (1987a:78) inserts, "if I interpret them correctly," which is not in the diario.

23. A question arises over the meaning of "por" here. Notoriously in need of context because of its variety of meanings, "por" could well mean something other than "by way of" in this case.

24. Lyon 1986:15; Perez 1987:82. This meaning would require an "a" after "volviendo," which no doubt accounts for Lyon's parentheses.

25. Perez 1987:93n.

26. Molander 1987:145. Cf. Molander 1985:120–22.

Columbus.[27] Obviously, for instance, he could not have been on the south coast of Guanahaní at that time, for he could not then have doubled that same southern end and still proceeded southward.

Modern interpreters of the diario have been extraordinarily willing to grant that Columbus knew just what the Indians were telling him. For many, the idea of an extended interlocutory session between the newly arrived Spanish and the astonished Indians at this early stage would seem too preposterous to contemplate, no matter how ill-disguised Columbus's interest in gold may have been. Columbus himself seems to have had his doubts on this score on more than one occasion later in the voyage, but generally he exhibited little doubt that he could understand what the Indians were trying to tell him. Even more oddly, he appears to have been as certain that they understood his inquiries in the first place. Las Casas, it seems, was more skeptical, and on several occasions interpolated comments in his *Historia* questioning the diario on these points.[28]

Modern opinion is divided on the matter. Some have no doubt that Columbus and his surprised hosts were able to communicate effectively, but many have raised at least some doubt about the likelihood of this.[29] Studies of Indian mapmaking as late as the eighteenth and nineteenth centuries demonstrate that such doubts are not without foundation.[30] Even when it was not a matter of language, it was the more refractory problem of cultural difference, for the maps that the Indians constructed on request frequently showed how sharply their mental maps of their environment differed from the spatial images that characterize Western geographical notions. When Western cartography was imposed on Indian cartography, the results were—probably could only have been—considerably divorced from reality. Perhaps Garcilaso de la Vega, el Inca, should be granted the last word on this matter. In writing of De Soto's wanderings in the southeastern United States, he issued a caveat to his readers:

27. See, for example, Thacher 1903–4, 1:600–601; Cioranescu 1961:22.
28. Cf. Las Casas 1951, 1:287 and Alvar/Columbus 1976, 2:96.
29. Among them are Maury (1871:531–32), Lollis (1923:117), and Luca de Tena (1968). Pérez de Tudela agrees, but only to further his argument that Columbus had foreknowledge of the New World (1983:222–23). For a detailed discussion of the Spanish and Indians communicating "by signs," see Haensch 1984 and Romera Castillo 1989, as well as the sources cited there.
30. Allen 1987; Lewis 1987, and sources cited there.

"This is to give notice that this direction, and all others that appear in this history, are not to be taken precisely, lest I be blamed if anything different appear after, God willing, that land is won."[31]

11

With this in mind, and as we are about to look at Columbus's description of the first few islands he visited and modern interpretations of them, we must ask the unavoidable question: On just what experience are these descriptions based? In the diario entry for 13 October, Columbus offered a brief sketch of the physical characteristics of Guanahaní: "This island is fairly large and very flat and with very green trees and many waters and a large lagoon in the center, without any mountain, and all of it green, that it is pleasing to look at it."[32] Virtually every component of this sketch has been dissected and disputed by modern scholarship, and much of this is discussed in the following chapters. But before we look at the results of that scrutiny it is necessary to raise a few ancillary points.

The first of these is that Columbus appears to have deferred this overall description until he had already described the flora, fauna, and inhabitants of Guanahaní in some detail, as though the passage is out of place despite the fact that at this point Las Casas was quoting Columbus and had been for some time. In fact, in this respect it is of some interest that Columbus's priorities often mirror Las Casas's own. Columbus's strangely reiterative style at this juncture of the diario has evoked little comment, although it is hard to accept that it can possibly represent the unalloyed log. The degree to which the diario repeats information on the Indians is cloying, especially in contrast to the exiguous data on the island itself. Even the stylistic resemblances between widely separated passages are uncanny. The following table lists phrases in the entry for 11/12 October in the first column and those in the following day's entry in the second:

todos desnudos como su madre los parió	
muy bien hechos	muy bien hecha
de muy fermosos cuerpos	gente muy fermosa

---

31. Garcilaso de la Vega, el Inca 1605:51v. Hulme (1978) also expresses doubts, as does Todorov (1984:29–31).

32. Alvar/Columbus 1976, 2:55; Dunn and Kelley/Columbus 1989:70.

cabellos gruessos cuasi como
  sedas de cola de caballo y
  cortos
ellos son de la color de los
  canarios
son de buena estatura de
  grandeza y buenos gestos,
  bien hechos[33]

cabellos no crespos, salvo
  corredíos y gruesos, como
  sedas de caballo
y ellos ninguno prieto, salvo
  de la color de los canarios
de buena estatura[34]

As if to carry the practice to the point of caricature, under 13 October and within a few sentences of one other, the diario twice records that the Indians on Guanahaní had small pendants of gold hanging from their noses.[35]

It is unlikely that even Las Casas would have gilded the lily to this extent. It may well be that these passages are vestiges of one or more attempts to take the diario apart textually and then reconstitute it, during which some parts were repeated and others omitted. This would help explain the transcendent and paradoxical characteristics of the diario's description of Guanahaní—its uncharacteristic restraint and consequent exiguousness.

There may be another reason for this as well. Knowing Columbus's opportunities for extended close observation would improve our ability to judge the general and specific accuracy of these descriptive passages. Several modern commentators have assumed that Columbus and his men spent a great deal of time ashore during the more than two days that the ships were at Guanahaní. Robertson began the trend by having Columbus return to his ships "[t]owards evening" of the first day.[36] Morison was more specific and painted a pretty picture of the Spanish taking "shore leave," during which they "wandered into the natives' huts, did a little trading for the curios that all seamen love, and doubtless ascertained that the girls of Guanahaní were much like others they had known."[37] Others have drawn similar conclusions, if less lyrically.[38] In particular, many be-

---

33. Alvar/Columbus 1976, 2:51–52; Dunn and Kelley/Columbus 1989:64–66.
34. Alvar/Columbus 1976, 2:53–55; Dunn and Kelley/Columbus 1989:68.
35. Alvar/Columbus 1976, 2:55; Dunn and Kelley/Columbus 1989:70–72.
36. Robertson 1778, 1:93, ostensibly relying on Ferdinand and Herrera, although neither said as much. See comment of Las Casas discussed in chapter 4.
37. Morison 1942, 1:306, accepted *in toto* by Tyler 1988:55.
38. Link and Link 1958:7; Wolper 1965:20–27; Granzotto 1985:145.

lieve that Columbus "inspected" the harbor and its vicinity on Sunday morning by foot as well as by sea.[39]

Unfortunately for all these arguments, there is not a word in the diario to suggest that any of the Spanish ever set foot on Guanahaní after taking formal possession of the place, and there is a good deal to suggest otherwise.[40] As far as the trading is concerned, the last passage in the entry for 13 October reads: "as it was now night, all the Indians returned to shore in their dugouts" ("Agora como fue noche todos se fueron a tierra con sus almadías").[41] The entry for that day began by recording that the Indians appeared "on the beach," and followed this with an account of their coming out to the ships.[42] On the previous day as well the Indians had swum out to the ships to trade.[43] As for the harbor, Columbus mentioned only that he "saw all that harbor" ("yo miré todo aquel puerto") and made no mention of its environs, while the only land he described, at an indeterminable distance from the harbor, was a peninsula, which could readily have been observed from sea.[44]

To this relentless silence can be added the nature of Columbus's word pictures. These are cardboard, one-dimensional, almost surreal in quality. Guanahaní had a vague size, it was flat and well vegetated, and had various bodies of water. In fact, there is not a thing in Columbus's brief litany that he could not have included by looking at a painting of Guanahaní.

Almost the same is true of the Indians, despite any effort of Las Casas. Their persons are described, as well as whatever portable possessions they had, all of which Columbus could have gleaned without leaving the poop deck. But we learn nothing about the size and style of their houses, their domestic routines or social organization, or their diet or modes of production.[45] The only villages that make an appearance are obviously near

39. For example, Mitchell and Keegan 1987:91.

40. There is no hint in the diario as to the length of the possession ceremony, but it was probably brief, if formal.

41. Alvar/Columbus 1976, 2:56; Dunn and Kelley/Columbus 1989:72.

42. Alvar/Columbus 1976, 2:53–54; Dunn and Kelley/Columbus 1989:68.

43. Alvar/Columbus 1976, 2:48; Dunn and Kelley/Columbus 1989:64.

44. Alvar/Columbus 1976, 2:57; Dunn and Kelley/Columbus 1989:76. The translations of "miré" vary. Although the most popular seems to be "inspected," that of Dunn and Kelley/Columbus 1989:77, "looked over," is probably closer to the mark.

45. Columbus did venture that he "saw no beast of any kind but parrots" on Guanahaní." Some have taken this, as we will see, to rule out the existence of other fauna,

the shore and are mentioned rather than described. Either Columbus's vaunted observational skills were completely dormant, or he did not place himself in a position to observe, or he forgot virtually everything he saw before he could write it down, or all of the above. In what it says, in how it says it, and in what it fails to say, the diario permits only the conclusion that once he had duly claimed Guanahaní for the crown, Columbus was satisfied to view his new conquest from afar. With these points in mind we can proceed to join modern scholarship in sharing Columbus's vistas with him.

---

but under the circumstances the statement is fairly banal and without extrapolative value.

12. The Mismeasure of Guanahaní

Contrariwise, if it was so, it might be; and if it were so, it would be; but as it isn't, it aint. That's logic.

TWEEDLEDEE

in Lewis Carroll's *Through the Looking Glass*

Wherever he anchored and wherever he first set foot on Guanahaní, Columbus spent the next two and a half days at the island, about which he had several things to say. But before discussing the testimony of the diario, we must first look at one matter about which, extraordinarily, the diario has nothing at all to say—the size of the island. Columbus was not at all reluctant to offer numerical estimates of the sizes of places he saw; in fact, virtually the first information he offered about Santa María and Fernandina was a guess as to their size. For Guanahaní, on the contrary, there are impressions instead of estimates.

The first hint of Guanahaní's size is the use of the term "isleta" or "tiny island" in the diario.[1] At this point, however, Las Casas is still using indirect discourse, and there is every reason to think that the term is his rather than Columbus's, particularly as the diario goes on to describe Guanahaní, quite anachronistically, as "one of the Lucayos," or Bahamas. Moreover, in his *Apologética historia* Las Casas again refers to Guanahaní as "una isleta," no doubt appropriately so, viewing it from the Antilles.[2]

After the diario reverts to Columbus's own words, the first (and virtually only) intimation as to the size of Guanahaní is the characterization

---

1. Alvar/Columbus 1976, 2:47; Dunn and Kelley/Columbus 1989:62. This appears retrospectively in the entry for 5 January 1493; Alvar/Columbus 1976, 2:190; Dunn and Kelley/Columbus 1989:308.

2. Las Casas 1967, 1/1:9.

of it as "esta isla . . . bien grande."³ This is a decidedly middling description and rather tame, given Columbus's chronic lapses into the jargon of
the realtor rather than the chronicler. As we will see, it is a phrase that is
easily interpreted according to taste. Throughout the entries for 13 and
14 October, Columbus refers to Guanahaní as an "island" ("isla"), yet he
also refers to the small peninsula he described on 14 October that could
be turned into an "island" for defensive purposes as well.⁴ This would
suggest that, for Columbus, Guanahaní was larger than a "tiny island"
(whatever that may mean), whereas for Las Casas it was very small.

It is surprising to turn to the latter's *Historia,* then, and find there that
Las Casas added the information: "Esta tierra [Guanahaní] era y es una
isla de 15 leguas de luengo, poco más ò menos" (This land [Guanahaní]
was and is an island 15 leagues long, a little more or less).⁵ Thus, Las
Casas seems to tell us, Guanahaní was more than forty-five miles long.
Of course, Las Casas was second to none in his propensity for hyperbole,
and the tendency may be to dismiss his statement as fanciful. As attractive
as a notion like this may be in the circumstances, it is complicated by the
fact that Ferdinand also concluded somehow that Guanahaní was "an island of fifteen leagues in length."⁶ Of course, the likelihood that these
were independent conclusions is almost nil, but it remains for us to consider where this piece of information originated, as well as why both Las
Casas and Ferdinand believed it.⁷

Las Casas's little extra gloss ("poco más ò menos") seems to suggest
that, whether or not he followed Ferdinand in this, he had some personal
knowledge of whatever island was thought to be Guanahaní forty or fifty
years after it first came to the notice of the larger world. Thus, however
tempting it might be to dismiss this fairly precise datum in order to extend the bounds of special pleading, this can hardly be done with impu-
nity. By the same token, accepting it creates its own set of problems.

3. Alvar/Columbus 1976, 2:58; Dunn and Kelley/Columbus 1989:70.
4. Alvar/Columbus 1976, 2:58; Dunn and Kelley/Columbus 1989:70.
5. Las Casas 1951, 1:200.
6. Colón 1930, 1:163.
7. Herrera, not usually an independent witness in these matters, repeated the information (1934–57, 2:79). The only other written estimate I know of is that of
Alonso de Chaves in his *derrotero,* written probably in the 1530s but not published
until this century. There Chaves (Castañedo Delgado et al. 1977:38, 88) described
Guanahaní as being eight leagues long on a NW–SE axis and four leagues wide.

Modern attempts to put precision to "bien grande" while denying it to "fifteen leagues in length" have been both ingenious and ingenuous.

I

Not surprisingly, the advocates of Watlings Island are most affected by the evidence of Las Casas and Ferdinand, because the island falls far short of being forty-five miles long, or even around. Attempts of the Watlings Islanders to deal with the matter have not been helped by their own difficulties in expressing the size of the island. During the past century they have advanced at least ten different estimates, ranging from thirteen miles by five to seven miles to eighteen to twenty miles by six to eight miles.[8] To indicate the extent of this disagreement, we might notice that Morison first estimated Watlings to be thirteen by six miles, then sixteen by seven miles, and finally fifteen to sixteen by six to eight miles.[9]

One quickly notices how predictably various landfall advocates treat Las Casas's and Ferdinand's testimony. Those who favor Watlings, Samana, or Conception—all small islands—find it impossible to welcome these data into their arguments. With predictable unanimity they skirt the issue entirely. Although not the first (Markham and Murdock had preceded him in silence) Montojo set the tone by quoting from the relevant paragraph in Las Casas's *Historia* but adroitly omitting the reference there to Guanahaní's size.[10] This tactic proved appealing and begat a long line of imitators. One after another Cronau, Thacher, Gould, Morison, the Links, Wolper, Barreiro Meiro, Molander, Judge, Keegan and

8. Fox 1882:350 (13 × 5–7 miles); Manrique 1890:99 (14 × 4 1/2); Albertis 1898:43 (12 × 5); Ober 1893:65 (12 × 5–7); Thacher 1903–4, 1:598 (12 × 7); Cronau 1921:13 (13 × 6); Gould 1927:412 (13 × 6); Link and Link 1958:19 (13 × 7); Markham 1892:99 (13 × 5–7); Gould 1965:76 (13 × 6); Rigg 1973:223 (12 × 6); Taviani 1987b:203 (13 × ?). Oddly, the aberrant largest estimate is that of Wolper (1964:10), a longtime resident who judged it to be 18–20 x 6–8 miles. The *Yachtsman's Guide* (1987:345) gives 12 × 6. The discrepancies may be explained to some extent by the variant but undisclosed uses of statute and nautical miles.

9. Morison 1942, 1:300; Morison/Columbus 1963:68n5; Morison and Obregón 1964:16.

10. Montojo 1892:17n. Navarrete, however, though favoring the very small Grand Turk, mentioned that Ferdinand, Las Casas, and Herrera all described Guanahaní as fifteen leagues long; Navarrete/Columbus 1825, 1:cv.

Mitchell, and Sealey—most of them supporting Watlings Island but a few of them Egg, Samana, Grand Turk, or Conception—displayed what can only be described as avoidance behavior. Each discussed the size of Guanahaní as expressed in the diario and found ways to make Columbus's vague words (on which more below) suit their arguments, but not one of them saw fit to heed the only other evidence on the matter.

The extent to which proponents of small islands have gone in studiously ignoring Ferdinand and Las Casas can be encapsulated in the examples of Morison and Fuson. In his biography of Columbus, Morison cited Ferdinand for his information on the festivities on landing on Guanahaní, but he ignored Ferdinand's datum on its size, which appears only a few sentences earlier in his text.[11] Likewise Fuson, in advocating Samana Cay, left this information out of his translation of the "log" even though his explicit modus operandi was to incorporate data from both Las Casas and Ferdinand, a practice he freely adopts almost everywhere else in his work even when far less justified.[12]

Two stragglers, however (both supporters of Watlings Island), have faced the issue. Roukema mentioned the matter in passing and probably accidentally and then, as though in an afterthought, sought to explain it by mobilizing the "shore league," that wonderfully elusive and elastic expedient devised by Van der Gucht and Parajón and enthusiastically embraced by Morison.[13] Determined by shamelessly ex post facto reasoning to be about 1 1/4 to 1 3/4 miles long, the shore league was conjured up in hopes of keeping Columbus honest by reducing some of his more outrageous exaggerations.[14] This has generally and correctly been regarded as little more than a sign of extreme duress on the part of modern apologists.

More recently, Taviani has chosen a slightly different and equally beckoning alternative. He simply interpreted "leguas" as a slip of someone's

---

11. Morison 1942, 1:300–301.

12. Fuson 1987a:199. Elsewhere Fuson (1985:64–65) argues that fifteen leagues was the length of an island Columbus bypassed on 15 October on his way to Santa María and that this figure had became erroneously attached to Guanahaní at some early stage.

13. Roukema 1959:86–87. See above, chapter 10.

14. Gucht and Parajón 1943:38–42 and passim. For criticisms see, among others, Dunn 1985:45–46.

pen for "millas" and triumphantly concluded that the record shows how accurate Columbus was after all![15] In doing so he failed to notice that Columbus never used "millas" in any of the passages in the diario attributed to him verbatim. Conversely, advocates of larger islands have wasted no time in bringing Ferdinand's and Las Casas's fifteen leagues into full play. To cite just a few, Montlézun, MacKie, Valentini, and Tió (all of whom preferred Cat Island), and Verhoog and the Links (supporters of the Caicos), all found it wonderfully easy to pounce on these fifteen leagues and use them in their arguments.[16]

II

Any critical discussion of the size of Guanahaní must consider two points, among others: the intent of Columbus's description in the diario, and the provenance and character of the other references to Guanahaní's size. It is typical of the diario that instead of one precise datum we are offered two imprecise ones. Consequently we are obliged to consider not only what Columbus meant by "grande" but also what he wanted "bien" to convey. Translations of the phrase "bien grande" have inevitably been various and not a little tendentious. Some have translated it as "very large" even though "muy grande" would more naturally carry that meaning. "Tolerably large," "quite large," "pretty large," and "fairly large" also turn up, as well as minor variants. Some translate it in one of these ways and then go on to gloss it as "small."[17]

It is desirable, of course, to consider Columbus's own situation at the moment he presumably used the phrase. It seems to have been after some visual exploration of the island but not yet enough (or so it seems; see above) to know its full extent. Beyond this ignorance—his and ours—is the matter of Columbus's state of mind at the time. Certainly he wanted the island to be very large, perhaps about the size of Cipangu, so his saying so would not itself signify very much. If anything, his use of "bien grande" would argue in favor of Guanahaní's smallness, since the phrase lacks typical Columbian hyperbole.

15. Taviani 1987b:202–3.
16. Montlézun 1828:318; MacKie 1891:368–71; Valentini 1892:160; Verhoog 1947:28; Link and Link 1958:6; Tió 1961:313–14.
17. For example, Major 1871:197, 203; Markham 1889:103.

There is also the question of relativity. Taviani argues that the terms "isleta" and "bien grande" make sense even in tandem.[18] Columbus used the first because, compared to the Mediterranean islands, Guanahaní was indeed small (even though Las Casas thought it was forty-five miles long).[19] On the other hand, by the time Columbus got around to writing "bien grande" in his log a day or so later, he had encountered "the rocks, small islands, and cayos" around Guanahaní; in this new perspective, Taviani maintains, the latter now seemed fairly large. Such casuistry should be saved for better things.

Rumeu de Armas offers four logical possibilities to explain Ferdinand's and Las Casas's claim that Guanahaní was fifteen leagues long—logical, that is, in the context of his belief that Las Casas did no more than copy an existing abstract of the diario and that Ferdinand's manuscipt was the *fons et origo* of this portion of Las Casas's *Historia.* The four possibilities are (1) that the information was in the original log, which was not seen by Las Casas; (2) that it was personal knowledge that Ferdinand had gained during his travels with his father; (3) that it was in the original log but had been omitted by an early copyist; and (4) that Las Casas encountered it in his exemplar, deliberately omitted it as "devoid of interest," and later had a change of heart and reinstated it in the *Historia*.[20] Rumeu de Armas rejects the last alternative as the most unlikely and chooses the second as the best possibility.

In fact, all of the first three alternatives are reasonable, but to them I would add a fourth, that Las Casas acquired his information independently. His qualification, "a little more or less," seems entirely gratuitous unless he intended it to provide accuracy in place of precision. This is slight evidence, to be sure, and perhaps it is less important whether Las Casas knew this of his own experience than whether anyone knew. Although committed to no particular landfall, Rumeu de Armas clearly accepted the fact that Guanahaní was a large island, and I think that this

18. Taviani 1987b:201.

19. The first part of the argument is made persuasively in Fuson 1985:61–62. In his *Apologética historia* Las Casas (1967, 1/1:104) wrote that "many" of the Bahamas were from one and a half to three times the size of Gran Canaria when in fact only one, Andros, is much larger, while two others (Great Abaco and Great Inagua) are about the same size, reminding us how unreliable Las Casas is in such matters.

20. Rumeu de Armas 1968:18–21.

view is no more than one-half of a double possibility. Its counterpart, of course, is that the figure came to be exaggerated, as is the case with so much of the diario (and the *Historia*). Its absence from the diario suggests that it was never part of the original log, since it is very hard to accept that anyone would have omitted such an interesting piece of information when so many other less important quantitative data are included.[21]

As a series of possibilities, then, this takes us almost nowhere—either Guanahaní was large or it was not, either its size was part of the original log or it was added to the historical record later. But scanning the possibilities has the advantage of accumulating all the evidence and arraying it fairly. For many, its crippling disadvantage is that it is inconclusive and supports no particular argument about the size, and hence the identity, of the landfall.

Nonetheless, the paucity of evidence has not dissuaded many from drawing the size of Guanahaní into their arguments. We have seen that two aspects of this have been the exclusion of the testimony of Ferdinand and Las Casas from much of the debate and the interesting uses to which "bien grande" has been put. Another and more recent expedient has been to subject the terms "isla," "isleta," and "isleo," all of which appear in the diario, to searching scrutiny in hopes of escaping the bonds of such delightfully muddled thinking as that of Cronau, who asserted that Watlings Island "has just the size to permit the expressions of Las Casas and Columbus in speaking of Guanahaní at one time as of [*sic*] 'una isleta' (a small island), and at another time as 'bien grande' (moderately large)."[22]

Three recent studies, published simultaneously, exemplify this trend. Molander, so far the sole exponent of Egg Island, which is only 200 acres in size, naturally emphasizes the diario's use of "isleta."[23] Molander notes that Columbus used the term many times to describe the very small islands off the northern coasts of Cuba and Hispaniola, and he concludes that, by extension, Columbus must have been referring to another such tiny offshore body of land when he called Guanahaní an "isleta." Molander weakens his case by failing to note that at this point Las Casas was para-

---

21. Tió argues that the figure of fifteen leagues was "taken from the marginal notes" of Columbus and that "leguas," not "millas," was correct (1961:314–15).

22. Cronau 1921:13.

23. Molander 1985:118–19. This view has also been accepted by Keegan and Mitchell (1987a).

phrasing Columbus and that the first time Columbus is quoted directly he refers to Guanahaní as "bien grande."[24] But Molander believes that in using this latter phrase Columbus may have been referring either to Egg Island and Royal Island together or to their near neighbor, Eleuthera, even though the diario makes no distinction whatever between the objects of these two usages.[25] Verhoog, a partisan of the Caicos as the landfall, argues that "isleo," usually defined as a small island near a larger one or near a mainland, fits Little Inagua "exactly" even though this island is some thirty square miles in size, very much larger than the islands to which Columbus seems ordinarily to have applied the term.[26] These two arguments probably represent the polar extremes with regard to drawing Columbus's nomenclature for islands into arguments about the landfall. We see Molander willing to grant an island less than one-third of a mile in extent the description "bien grande," while Verhoog tries his best to persuade us that Columbus called another island, some one hundred times as large, an "isleo." A third paper, by Fuson, underscores the futility of these approaches. In it Fuson surveys briefly but devastatingly several examples (though not those of his fellow authors) in which modern scholarship has interpreted and translated Columbus's nomenclature out of all recognition and all in the service of particular landfall schemes.[27] At the same time, Fuson reminds us that Columbus was rather nonchalant in his use of various terms for bodies of land surrounded by water. Whatever Columbus's intentions, it seems inescapable that they were not carried out successfully enough for us to employ his terminologies as the crux of a larger argument. On the contrary, it is particularly for his statements about the size or populousness of the islands he was describing that we need most to recall his obsession with the belief that he was on the brink of discovering the Far East. Even without this consideration,

24. Elsewhere Molander (1985:148) argues that the fifteen leagues of Ferdinand derived from his belief that all of Eleuthera was Guanahaní. Cf. Molander 1987.

25. Molander (1985:122) further argues that Columbus made no estimate of Guanahaní's size since it was too small to warrant it.

26. Verhoog 1985:34. In contrast, the Links (1958:23), also supporters of the Caicos, considered Little Inagua much too large to be called an "isleo." More moderately, but no less categorically, Roukema (1959:95) asserted that "Little Inagua cannot ever have been called an *isla grandíssima*," referring in this case to the entry for 15 October describing Fernandina, which Columbus had also described merely as "grande."

27. Fuson 1985:61–62.

though, in its characteristic reticence the text of the diario forbids us to speculate fruitfully as to the size of Guanahaní.

<hr>

III

Islands have shapes as well as sizes, of course, and sometimes these can be of great use in identifying real islands with literary allusions. Regrettably, the diario says nothing about the shape of Guanahaní. In his *Apologética historia*, however, Las Casas reveals that "the said island [Guanahaní] has the shape of a bean [haba]."[28] Needless to say, modern scholars have seized on this datum with alacrity and have produced the usual scattershot effect. We will briefly look at some of these efforts and then attempt to surmise what Las Casas meant by "haba" and from where he drew his information.

It was only in the *Apologética historia* that Las Casas mentioned, and then in a throwaway fashion, that Guanahaní had the shape of a bean, but modern opinion frequently overlooks this provenance. Tió, for instance, asserted that Las Casas provided this information in the *Historia de las Indias*, or even that it is in the diario.[29] Fuson accepted that the statement appeared in the *Apologética historia* but went on to observe, erroneously, that "it was repeated by Ferdinand," who in fact emulated the diario by saying not a word on the matter.[30] In his turn Molander followed the mistaken spoor yet farther by arguing that the description is in the *Historia de las Indias*, that it was based on Columbus's own account, and that the bean was "a large bean."[31]

Added to the confusion over the textual home of the bean-shape reference is an even greater mystification as to what "haba" means, and this has resulted in some of the most labored arguments in the landfall debate. If advocates of small islands have assiduously ignored Las Casas's estimate of the size of Guanahaní, proponents of elongated islands have been at least as industrious in putting his "bean" to use, whether the island they favor is large or small. In these arguments, eye-of-the-beholder reasoning features prominently.

Although favoring Egg Island as the actual landfall, Molander is certain

28. Las Casas 1967, 1/1:9.
29. Tió 1961:568; Tió 1966:307.
30. Fuson 1985:65n.
31. Molander 1985:148–49; Molander 1987:149.

that its larger neighbor, Eleuthera, is the bean-shaped island of Las Casas, even though its elongation is very pronounced.[32] At the other extreme, Power, favoring Grand Turk, is no less sure that it best conforms to the shape of a beanpod and compares it with a diagram in an early work on legumes, ignoring other drawings that undermine his argument.[33] Tió, who favors elongated Cat Island, also draws on Las Casas's description for support.[34]

Nor have partisans of Watlings Island been silent on the matter. Cronau concluded that Watlings fit Las Casas's description "in the most striking manner" and argued that Grand Turk, among others, did not.[35] On the basis of plucking one map from among many, Barreiro Meiro asserted that cartography "confirmed" Las Casas's description and eliminated Cat Island, which has the shape of "a tall boot, never of a bean."[36]

Others have seen Watlings Island in a somewhat different light. Fuson, then supporting a Caicos landfall, believed both that "haba" meant beanpod and that the description could not possibly fit Watlings Island.[37] Verhoog (another proponent of the Caicos), Tió (supporting Cat Island), and Didiez Burgos (arguing in favor of West Plana Cay) all agree that Watlings Island bears no resemblance to a bean or a beanpod.[38]

In fact, Watlings Island might well be construed as resembling some kind of bean, and this observation leads us directly back to Las Casas's text. Of this we must obviously ask whether by "haba" Las Casas meant "bean" or "beanpod," and if the former, to what species of bean he was referring. To raise the question is hardly to answer it or even to suggest a reasonable answer to it, although as we have seen, modern advocates of landfall sites have seldom been averse to believing that they have managed to plumb Las Casas's reticence.[39]

32. Molander 1985:148–49; Molander (1987:153) states that Consuelo Varela "assured" him that Las Casas was describing "a green bean pod."

33. Power 1985:156–157; cf. Sadler 1981:5.

34. Tió 1961:568.

35. Cronau 1921:15; cf. Cronau 1892:212. Morales y Pedroso (1923:34) expressed a similar view.

36. Barreiro Meiro 1968:11–12. Most of the maps adduced by Barreiro Meiro for support show Guanahaní as cruciform or squarish. Didiez Burgos (1974:158–62) uses some of the same maps to argue for West Plana Cay.

37. Fuson 1961b:36.

38. Verhoog 1954:1107; Tió 1961:566–69; Didiez Burgos 1974:162.

39. Tió (1966:307) goes so far as to refer to the "oval form of a bean."

We can only look to other uses of the word at roughly the time
that Las Casas was writing. Boyd-Bowman provides several instances in
which "haba" was used to describe the shape of gold nuggets and emer-
alds, and there can be little doubt that "beanpod" was not meant in these
instances.[40] In his dictionary Covarrubias provided descriptions of several
varieties of beans known to him, ranging from garbanzo beans or chick-
peas to snap or string beans.[41] Modern dictionaries inevitably concur that
"bean" has numerous meanings. One of these ("haba de las Indias") is the
sweet pea, a far cry from the shape of a beanpod but a usage that Las
Casas, in his fascination with the products of America, might well have
employed.[42] But this is no more than conjecture, and it merely underscores the range of possibilities. These encompass shapes from the extremely elongated pod of the string bean to the roundish shape of the
chick-pea or the common pinto bean. In short, Las Casas's use of the
term leads nowhere because it leads everywhere.

Such a view is reinforced by discussing the possible sources of Las
Casas's knowledge, a matter that has not failed to produce its share of
angst and error. Power, for instance, suggests that Las Casas was vouchsafed the information by his father, who, he believes, "was a participant
in the voyage of 1492, and therefore privy to certain oral information
concerning it."[43] In fact, as Las Casas himself tells us, his father accompanied Columbus on his second voyage, by which time Guanahaní had
been effectively relegated to the margins of Spanish interest.[44] With more
imagination than is called for, Molander wonders whether the idea of a
bean-shaped island may not have originated with the tableau at the court
of João II on Columbus's return. In his otherwise undocumented account, Las Casas related in his *Historia* that one of the Indian captives
allegedly depicted the discoveries by arranging beans on a table.[45]

40. Boyd-Bowman 1987:2174–75.
41. Covarrubias Horozco 1611/1943:677–78.
42. For a more general discussion of the products of America and their impact, see
Alvarez López 1945.
43. Power 1985:156n16. Power leaves unanswered the question of why the elder
Las Casas would need to rely on oral rather than visual information.
44. Las Casas 1951, 1:347. On Pedro de las Casas, see Giménez Fernández 1971:
67–69.
45. Molander 1985:149. The incident is elaborately portrayed in Las Casas 1951,
1:325, where the description smacks of Las Casas's embroidery. Las Casas used
"haba" there as well. The incident is not mentioned in the diario, nor in Pina, Resende,

Rumeu de Armas is probably right in suggesting that Las Casas drew his inspiration from a map of the Bahamas he had seen, perhaps the map of 1536 by Alonso de Santa Cruz that Barreiro Meiro used.[46] If so, his conclusion that the evidence is of "very scant" value actually overstates the case. But even if Las Casas derived his information from another source, it remains of little value because his expression of it permits no precision at all, a fact all too amply illustrated by the unavailing efforts to transform "haba" into a Proteus capable of assuming almost any shape on demand.[47]

IV

Columbus described Guanahaní as "muy llana," or "very flat," and then, as though to emphasize the point, added that it was "without a single mountain" ("sin ninguna montaña").[48] This seems simple enough, but of course it has proved to be otherwise, as exponents of one island or another jockey to establish their favorite as flatter or lower than any of its competitors. The issue necessarily begins with a determination of just what Columbus meant by "llana" or even by "montaña." Does the former mean "flat," "low-lying," or "flat and low-lying"? And by "montaña" could Columbus really have meant something very high? If not, then more islands can be considered even while taking him seriously, even literally. Clearly Columbus meant "llana" to convey the image of "flat" since he added the comment about a lack of mountains, but he may also have meant to imply that Guanahaní was low-lying. After all, nearly all the Bahamas are, but enough of them are not to prevent us from being certain.

At this point the Watlings Islanders find themselves in a dilemma very much of their own devising. After arguing, as we have seen, that Columbus first sighted the hundred-foot-high "white cliffs" of the island, they are forced to explain how he could later describe Guanahaní as "llana," no matter what the term means. Their cause is not abetted by the

---

or Barros. See Pina 1950; Resende 1902; Barros 1945–46, 1:118–22. Each of these chronicles was written in the sixteenth century.

46. Rumeu de Armas 1968:324–25.

47. As noted above, it assumed many shapes on the maps of the period.

48. Alvar/Columbus 1976, 2:55; Dunn and Kelley/Columbus 1989:70.

fact that in his *Historia* Las Casas called Guanahaní "toda baja" (completely low-lying) a statement almost unsportsmanlike in its uncompromising language.[49] Ferdinand concurred, describing Guanahaní as "piana e senza montagne" (flat and without mountains).[50] Neither the sources, then, nor the topography of Watlings Island provide any opening for such statements as "the description of Watlings Island answers every requisition of the journal."[51] Worst of all, since Columbus's description is directly and centrally embedded in the diario, it has not been quite as easy for researchers to ignore this problem in the way they have the size and shape of the island.[52] The result has been an orgy of industrial-strength improvisation, both amusing and bemusing but on the whole less than edifying.

Inevitably, some Watlings Islanders have still found it possible to disregard Columbus's observation entirely.[53] Most, though, have faced the issue in one way or another. The most popular reaction is simply to regard the heights of Watlings Island as "low." Morison, for instance, wrote that "the highest hill [there] is only [*sic*] 140 feet above sea level."[54] Roukema aped him closely (and aped Gould even more closely) by calling Watlings Island "generally low, nowhere exceeding 140 feet."[55] Wolper and Cronau, forgetting that Columbus had entered the description after spending a day or more in the vicinity of Guanahaní, entreat us to believe that Watlings Island appeared flat as Columbus *approached* it from the east.[56] In Wolper's case, at least the assertion is belied by a series of photographs that she included as part of her argument that the "light" Columbus saw emanated from atop the cliffs of the island.

Slightly more imaginatively, if even less convincingly, Markham argued that the heights on Watlings Island were not visible from Columbus's anchorage while at the same time paradoxically implying that this was at

49. Las Casas 1951, 1:200.

50. Colón 1930, 1:163.

51. Becher 1856:103n, just the first of many similarly sanguine assertions.

52. See above, chapter 10.

53. Markham 1889:108; Montojo 1892; Vidal Gormaz 1892:210; Ober 1893; Thacher 1903–4; Barreiro Meiro 1968; Obregón 1987a.

54. Morison 1:305. Elsewhere Morison omitted the name and elevation of the highest point on Watlings Island on the same map on which he had once included it (Morison/Columbus 1963:66; cf. Morison 1942, 1:299).

55. Roukema 1959:89, quoting Gould (1927:412) but without attribution.

56. Wolper 1964:27; Cronau 1921:13.

a different location than the point of sighting.[57] Becher responded to the challenge even more lamely. Watlings Island, he pointed out, is "not mountainous."[58] Stewart was satisfied to assert that Watlings is "very flat."[59] For the moment we can leave behind the issue of the topography of Watlings Island, both real and imagined, by noting the opinion of that comparatively rare bird, the disinterested party. The most recent edition of the *Yachtsman's Guide* characterizes Watlings Island as "comparatively high by Bahamian standards."[60]

On the other hand, Cat Island is higher yet, one of the highest islands in the Bahamas, and its advocates have had an even more severe problem in squaring this with Columbus's description. The result is a dismally evasive record. Two French critics of Navarrete's Grand Turk hypothesis both favored Cat Island, but neither supported his choice by referring to Columbus's use of "muy llana."[61] In espousing a Cat Island landfall, Washington Irving was particularly equivocal. In the 1828 edition of his biography of Columbus, he pictured Guanahaní as "a large and very beautiful island . . . level and covered with forests."[62] By 1841 he seems to have had second thoughts, perhaps realizing that Grand Turk, then the principal competitor of Cat Island, presented a stronger case. At any rate, his description of Guanahaní now covertly differed: it was "a very large and beautiful island, covered with forests."[63]

At about the same time as Irving was changing his mind, Humboldt discussed the matter of the landfall at some length but gingerly managed to avoid mentioning that Columbus had described it as "muy llana."[64] Later in the century, Valentini, who also favored Cat Island, mentioned the description of Guanahaní as flat only to dismiss it as "commonplace."[65] The two most recent supporters of Cat Island have been less reticent. Luca de Tena mentioned flatness as a physical requirement of

57. Markham 1892:99; cf. Albertis 1898:43.
58. Becher 1856:105n.
59. Stewart 1931:125.
60. *Yachtsman's Guide* 1987:345.
61. La Roquette 1828, 2:339–45; Montlézun 1828:312–14.
62. Irving 1828, 1:283.
63. Irving 1841, 1:307.
64. Humboldt 1836–39, 3:160–222, esp. 169.
65. Valentini 1892:156, presumably implying that most of the Bahamas are flat and low-lying.

Guanahaní but left it at that.[66] Tió appears to be the only exponent of Cat Island to have addressed the problem squarely. Like Markham, he pointed out that the higher elevations there are in the extreme north, far from where Columbus must have anchored. Anyway, he argued, Watlings Island has "hills" of its own.[67]

The description of Guanahaní as "muy llana" must be considered as one of the more nondescript data in the diario. The characteristically and predictably tendentious patterns of avoidance and embrace suggest that supporters of various landfalls have exploited it well beyond its capacity to contribute to the debate. The matter seems to be one of subjectivity: What did Columbus mean by "muy llana" in these particular circumstances? Clearly there is little point in comparing the merits of one landfall candidate with another from the present perspective since Guanahaní was the first island Columbus saw. But it might not be entirely unfruitful to wonder about other bases of comparison at his disposal. Leyva pointed out that Liguria was "a rather mountainous region," but it seems more relevant to particularize about the topography of the islands with which Columbus was familiar, particularly perhaps, the Canaries, which provided his most recent point of reference.[68] The Canaries range in elevation from 2,000 feet to 8,000 feet, and any of the Bahamas would appear markedly low-lying in contrast. Or it might be that Columbus gained the impression that Cipangu and its environs were flattish, and his description was just another example of semantic wish fulfillment. Whatever the case, the diario fails to provide an entrée into Columbus's mind on this occasion. Nor can looking ahead in the diario provide much perspective, since Columbus was building new contexts each time he saw another island. Valentini was not wrong in characterizing Columbus's description as "commonplace." The numerous islands he reported seeing during the late afternoon of 14 October he thought were "muy llana" and "sin montañas."[69] A few days later he found Fernandina to be, likewise, "muy llana" and "sin montaña," and he went on to say that this was "just like that of Sant Salvador and Sancta María."[70] If by now we find this description stilted, we find welcome, though slight, relief when he reached

66. Luca de Tena 1968:215.
67. Tió 1966:310.
68. Leyva y Aguilera 1890:29n.
69. Alvar/Columbus 1976, 2:58; Dunn and Kelley/Columbus 1989:76.
70. Alvar/Columbus 1976, 2:62; Dunn and Kelley/Columbus 1989:82.

Isabela, which he said was "higher than the other islands found, and in it a small elevation, which can hardly be called a mountain, but something which beautifies the rest."[71] If nothing else, this slightly variant description of Isabela suggests that the previous three islands Columbus had stopped at were very flat and/or low-lying indeed.[72] Yet the *Yachtsman's Guide* describes the east coast of Long Island, the odds-on choice to be Fernandina, as "high, rugged, and inhospitable with many spectacular white cliffs alternating with sandy beaches along its length."[73] This hardly suggests a profile that is either flat *or* low-lying.

71. Alvar/Columbus 1976, 2:73; Dunn and Kelley/Columbus 1989:98–100.

72. If we accept that no matter what Columbus meant by "muy llana," he knew when one island was higher than another, then we must rule out Cat Island, by common consent the highest in the Bahamas, as Guanahaní.

73. *Yachtsman's Guide* 1987:330; cf. Owen 1838:33

13. Guanahaní's Elusive Lagoon

You can never jump away from Conclusions. Getting back is not so easy. That's why we're so terribly crowded here.

NORTON JUSTER

The diario offers its only particularly descriptive passage relating to Guanahaní when it mentions "a very large lagoon in the center" ("una laguna en medio muy grande"). Consequently, advocates of various landfalls have been quick to seize on this brief passage to aid their arguments. The Watlings Islanders have been especially ardent in pursuing a modern equivalent of this body of water. Together with Columbus's "muchas aguas," or "many waters," it constitutes the central tenet in their belief system.[1] For them these statements fit Watlings Island like the proverbial glove. Better yet, they seem at the same time to disqualify other contenders. Before turning attention to their arguments, and those of the proponents of other landfalls, we need to look more closely at Columbus's language and the trouble it has given modern translators.

Just after describing the taking-possession ceremony, Las Casas cited (he was not yet quoting) Columbus as speaking of "muchas aguas," and on the next day Columbus is quoted as writing "aguas muchas." The use of the plural is ambiguous and has stimulated translators to travel down many paths. Among those who have translated this portion of the diario in its entirety, only Jane and Lyon have rendered the two terms consistently, but Jane thought that Columbus meant "much water" while Lyon preferred "many waters."[2] Others have differentiated between the two.

---

1. See, for example, Murdock 1884:477; Winsor 1892:214–17; Ober 1893:89; Obregón 1987a:192.
2. Jane/Columbus 1960:23, 26; Lyon 1986:9, 15.

Thacher translated the first as "much water" and the second as "many waters," while Morison was more imaginative, using "many streams" and "many bodies of water" respectively.[3] Fuson omits the first reference entirely and translates the second as "several bodies of water."[4] Cioranescu used "des cours d'eau" for the first and, more accurately, "beaucoup de cours d'eau" for the second.[5] Finally, Dunn and Kelley translate the first phrase as "many ponds" and the second as "much water."[6] The two words, then, have managed to attract no fewer than eight different translations,[7] and there seems to be little pattern to this variety. One might, however, be tempted to see in Morison's two translations (and perhaps those of Dunn and Kelley) an implicit effort to draw the interior of Watlings Island into the argument, since there is no denying that it might well be construed as representing "many bodies [or ponds] of water."

Columbus's term "laguna" would appear to be less problematical, but this has not proved to be so. Of the translators of the diario, only Fuson has translated "laguna" by its most likely counterpart, "lagoon."[8] Thacher, Jane, Morison, Cioranescu, Lyon, and Dunn and Kelley have all translated it as "lake."[9] This virtual unanimity is not mirrored in the arguments about what kind of body of water Columbus meant by the term, which are impressive in their variety if not their plausibility. More on this later.

Two strategies dominate the discussion. The Watlings Islanders make the fact that the interior of this island is undoubtedly well-watered the centerpiece of their case and attempt to strengthen it by denying interior bodies of water to other possible landfalls. Proponents of these, on the other hand, generally concede a strong case to Watlings Island while attempting to demonstrate that their own preferences also meet this criterion.[10]

3. Thacher 1903–4, 1:532, 536; Morison/Columbus 1963:64, 67.

4. Fuson 1987a:78.

5. Cioranescu/Columbus 1961:43, 46.

6. Dunn and Kelley/Columbus 1989:63, 71.

7. The number is greater if we include partial translations, among them, Becher 1856:87, 95; Murdock 1884:451, 453; Cronau 1921:12, 13; Wolper 1964:20, 25.

8. Fuson 1987a:78. Cf. Fuson 1987a:200–201, and below.

9. Thacher 1903–4, 1:536; Jane/Columbus 1960:26; Cioranescu/Columbus 1961:46; Lyon 1986:10; Dunn and Kelley/Columbus 1989:71.

10. One of the more bemusing aspects of the matter is the varying amount of water shown on maps of Watlings Island. For the extremes, compare those by Didiez Burgos

Watlings Islanders have generally been satisfied to remark on the mention of "the very large lagoon" in the diario even when they call it a lake. Most would agree wholeheartedly with Major, who stated that he regarded it as "indispensable to the identification" of Guanahaní, which he believed was Watlings Island.[11] Frequently, though, defenders of Watlings Island have been inclined to solidify their case by trying to eliminate the competition entirely. Becher, Markham, Cronau, Manrique, and Roukema all looked at other suggested landfalls, and all concluded that in most cases these lacked the requisite central body of water.[12] Recently Taviani has carried this tactic to its logical, if indefensible, conclusion by robustly declaring that a large lagoon is "only found" on Watlings Island, though he acknowledges that the Caicos have many "modest" lagoons.[13]

Others have declined to accept the degree of Taviani's commitment to Watlings Island in this respect. On the contrary, every other postulated landfall has been credited with possessing the necessary lagoon, and we catch the flavor of the landfall debate at its most acute by looking at a few examples of the ebb and flow of the discussion.

Grand Turk

In first editing the newly discovered diario, Navarrete suggested that Grand Turk, a tiny island southeast of the Bahamas proper, was Columbus's landfall.[14] He founded his conclusion on the premise that Grand Turk "conformed" to Columbus's description of Guanahaní, "most notably" in having "in the middle a lagoon which is not found on the other [contenders]."[15] The issue was joined in 1827 and 1828, when there ap-

---

(1974:410), whose maps show very little water, with Thacher (1903–4, 1:599) and Cronau (1921:17), whose maps show large amounts of water.

11. Major 1871:204.

12. Becher 1856:87–95; Manrique 1890:63–64, 74; Markham 1892:94–99; Cronau 1921:12–13; Roukema 1959:86–87.

13. Taviani 1987b:201.

14. How tiny is in dispute: Gould 1965:76 (1 × 2 miles); Roukema 1959:86–87 (5 1/2 × 1 1/2 miles); *Yachtsman's Guide* 1987:368 (6 × 1 1/2 miles). *Yachtsman's Guide* (1987:351) describes it as 2 3/4 by 2 miles.

15. Navarrete/Columbus 1825, 1:cv, citing Las Casas, Ferdinand, Herrera, and Bellin, whose map (Bellin 1773:opp. p. 84) showed Grand Turk with a substantial body of water near its southern end.

peared no fewer than four responses to Navarrete's work. The lagoon was to figure prominently in these, which together constitute a marvelous microcosm of the problems that Columbus's "una laguna en medio muy grande" has generated.

In the first of these, an extended review of Navarrete's edition, Caleb Cushing confessed himself persuaded by Navarrete's identification of Grand Turk, "especially in the circumstance of there being a large lake in the middle of it."[16] The very next year, two contrary opinions appeared. Washington Irving defended Cat Island as the landfall and assured his readers that Grand Turk "has no fresh water; . . . neither has it any lake, but several salt ponds."[17] Simultaneously, a French translation of Navarrete's edition appeared in which one of the translators rejected Navarrete's choice of Grand Turk on the grounds that the waters there in no way answered Columbus's description.[18] Finally, Montlézun, who also favored Cat Island, wrote "in refutation of some historians . . . with regard to the first islands Columbus discovered."[19] In addition to finding Grand Turk too small to be Guanahaní, Montlézun argued that the island's only fresh water was rainfall and that one-quarter of Grand Turk was covered by "salt water."[20] In the circumstances, Montlézun thought it impossible that, as small and as saline as it was, Grand Turk could have supported the culture Columbus had described. The elusive lagoons or lakes on Grand Turk quickly reappeared. In 1846 George Gibbs supported Navarrete's thesis and disputed Irving by noting, among other things, that "there is a considerable lake" on the island, which until recently had been navigable.[21]

After this twenty-year rollercoaster ride, Grand Turk underwent a temporary eclipse. Markham conceded that the island had low-lying wet areas, but he was not impressed by them, while Manrique also dismissed

16. Cushing 1827:275. On Caleb Cushing as the author of this unsigned review essay, see Fuess 1923, 1:54.

17. Irving 1828, 1:307.

18. La Roquette 1828, 2:341–42, relying on Puységur (1787:68–69, 76–77), whose account is not as uncompromising as La Roquette seemed to believe.

19. Montlézun 1828:299.

20. Montlézun 1828:325, citing Bellin 1773:86 to just the opposite effect that Navarrete cited him. Bellin thought that the water that collected in the rocks "was always sufficient to serve for a very large number of inhabitants."

21. Gibbs 1846:142, 146.

Grand Turk as unsuitable.[22] In turn, Gould observed that Grand Turk had "large lagoons" but thought it too small to satisfy the other criteria of the diario.[23] Roukema offered no opinion on whether Grand Turk had suitable inland bodies of water.[24] Recently Sadler and Power have revived the long-dormant notion that Grand Turk is Guanahaní. Only Power has brought the presence (or absence) of interior bodies of water directly into play, but on Sadler's map the Great Salt Pan on Grand Turk has grown to be unprecedentedly large.[25]

Cat Island

By the early nineteenth century, Cat Island had gained recognition as the site of Columbus's landfall and had been christened San Salvador. Irving was happy to accept the precedent and by inference the idea that Cat Island had "an abundance of water, and a large lake in the center."[26] Becher was ready to concede that there was water on Cat Island but thought that it was fresh water and that Cat Island was therefore somehow ineligible to be Guanahaní.[27] But as time passed Cat Island seemed to dry up. According to Manrique "it lacks water," while Cronau asserted that water there was "so scarce that the inhabitants must subsist . . . on rainwater."[28] Gould and Roukema were more willing to grant Cat Island its share of water but not a central lagoon.[29] This view seems to conform to modern conditions, and Cat Island does not now appear to meet the description of the lagoon in the diario if it is to be taken at face value.[30]

Samana Cay

The first partisan of Samana Cay was Gustavus Fox, who referred in 1882 to "the flooding of low grounds [there] by excessive rains," which re-

---

22. Markham 1889:112–117; Markham 1892:94–99; Manrique 1890:63–64.
23. Gould 1927:412; Gould 1965:76.
24. Roukema 1959:86–88.
25. Power 1985:156–60; Sadler 1981:4–5.
26. Irving 1828, 3:307.
27. Becher 1856:95n.
28. Manrique 1890:74–75; Cronau 1921:14.
29. Gould 1927:412; Roukema 1959:86–87.
30. Tió disagrees, arguing that the water on Cat Island fits—or once fit—Columbus's description closely (1961:569–70; 1966:312–13).

sulted in "a row of ponds parallel to the shore."[31] Although this apparently satisfied Fox on the matter of the lagoon, it was not a particularly strong case, and no one since has made it stronger. Judge has recently tried, and in doing so he has presented the water situation on Samana Cay in a somewhat different light than Fox. For the latter, the ponds created during the rainy season were later "soaked up by the rock and evaporated by the sun."[32] Judge, on the other hand, finds evidence of "a long, linear lake" that breaks up "into ponds during the dry season."[33] Finally, Fuson presumes that "Columbus probably meant that [Guanahaní] had many small lakes and ponds . . . and a salt water lagoon in the middle . . . on the coast he was on," and goes on to argue that "[t]his description fits Samana, not Watlings."[34]

Unlike Cat Island, then, it appears that Samana managed to become somewhat wetter during the past century, at least in the eyes of its champions.[35] The appearance and disappearance of bodies of water on various Bahamian Islands is a topos in the landfall controversy.[36] Its use has been frequent and flexible but, I will argue, also irrelevant.

Watlings Island

Several questions arise as to the strength of the case for Watlings Island. Supporters of other islands reject the notion that taking Columbus at what appears to be face value strengthens the likelihood that Watlings Island is Guanahaní. Molander argues that Watlings Island has "dozens of independent lakes" rather than just one, which he believes is required by the diario's evidence.[37] Along the same lines, Perez, supporting Samana Cay, believes that referring to the interior waters on Watlings Is-

---

31. Fox 1882:387–88.

32. Fox 1882:387.

33. Judge 1986:586–88.

34. Fuson 1987a:79n.

35. Another advocate of Samana, Perez, is so unimpressed with its "lagoon" that he calls on climatic and topographical change to explain it away (1987:27).

36. On historical changes in the topography of the Bahamas, including the nature and extent of the water supplies, see Keegan and Mitchell 1987a:106, and Mitchell and Keegan, 1987:96–101.

37. Molander 1985:122. Later he reduced this number to "at least half a dozen" (Molander 1987:144, 162).

land as "una laguna en medio muy grande" seems "something of an understatement."[38] By these arguments Watlings Island—and probably Conception Island as well—suffers from fitting Columbus's description too well.[39]

Whatever one thinks of this line of reasoning, it does seem that supporters of Watlings Island have often failed to realize that it is immaterial that the central body of water there is the most impressive in the area. On 12 October Columbus probably had no basis of comparison other than the coast of Guinea at Elmina, where the Benya lagoon is about one mile square.[40] Consequently we can have no idea what "muy grande" meant to him at the time he wrote it. In competition Watlings Island would score well, but there was no competition; the description was a first reaction to a particular phenomenon in this newly found world (though it may also have been based on personal experience about which we know nothing). If we were to argue, for instance, that by "muy grande" Columbus meant the proportion of water to land, then Conception Island would be a more likely alternative.

The alternating dehydration and humectation of various landfall sites in the literature suggests an eye-of-the-beholder argument at its worst. The blame is partly to be attributed to the fact that so much of the ground water in the Bahamas is seasonal, and in most cases we have no idea when the observations underlying these variant conclusions were made. We do know, however, that Columbus reached the Bahamas toward the end of the rainy season there, which is at its height from August through October.[41] A few days after leaving Guanahaní, Columbus wrote that it had rained every day since he had arrived, and he later recorded several more heavy rainfalls.[42] Under the circumstances he must have seen any lakes, ponds, lagoons, and other bodies of water in the area at almost their maximal extent if the rainfall had been normal that year, and this would only increase the number of possibilities for fulfilling this criterion.

38. Perez 1987:26.

39. Tió (1966:313) disqualified Watlings Island on similar grounds—it has "dozens" of lagoons, whereas Columbus spoke of only one on Guanahaní.

40. Survey of Ghana 1:62500, Sheet 25 C.C. SW; Survey of Ghana 1:2500, Sheet 7, Elmina (Ref no. X2475/7).

41. Shattuck 1905:117–18. Morison wrote of the entry for 17 October that "the rainy season had set in" when in fact it was likely to be nearly over (1942, 1:324).

42. Alvar/Columbus 1976, 2:72, 81.

I

We have seen that there has been a fitful and often implicit discussion in the literature as to whether "lagoon" or "lake" is the more appropriate term to use for Columbus's "laguna,"[43] and this discussion is not usually connected to the landfall arguments of which it forms a part. The question of what manner of body of water Columbus meant by "laguna" is, of course, crucially important, but we can only surmise. Today at least, the term is applied both to a relatively narrow and relatively shallow body of water connected to the sea most of the time and protected by a low land barrier and to a "lake-like stretch of water enclosed in a coral atoll."[44] The former configuration is very common along the Guinea coast, as well as the Algarve in southern Portugal, and Columbus may well have formed the conception of the word from the lagoons there.

Judge has stated, on what authority is not clear, that "laguna" signified "a low-lying lake" in fifteenth-century Spain.[45] Perez, on the other hand, has argued that "in modern Spanish 'laguna' is a small lake or a large pond," so that a very large laguna "probably meant something closer to a lake than a pond."[46] Tió, in turn, believes that the "accepted" definition of a "laguna" is "a small lake."[47]

In his dictionary published in 1611, Covarrubias saw the crucial distinction between a "lago" and a "laguna" to be the difference in depth and hence in the permanence of the two. A "lago" is permanent, deep, and sometimes navigable, whereas a "laguna" is "a large pit" or ditch that catches runoff from higher elevations during the rainy season and dries up during the dry season.[48] Thus it is not necessarily low-lying but only lower-lying, and it was seasonal.

We have no reason to believe that Columbus was not using the term in essentially this fashion. In this case the "laguna" happened to be low-lying, but that was incidental. In some way he inferred that its extent, or even its existence, was seasonal. If the lagoon in question was in the center of Guanahaní, this would have been a remarkable, and entirely gra-

43. See chapter 8 for more examples.
44. Colombo 1977; Barnes 1980.
45. Judge 1986:586.
46. Perez 1987:26–27.
47. Tió 1966:313.
48. Covarrubias Horozco 1611/1943:748–49.

tuitous, observation based on no more than a brief view, or no view at all.[49] On the other hand, if the lagoon was actually an arm of the sea in the west African fashion, Columbus could have judged with a great deal more acuity.

This brings us to two further questions—the meaning of "en medio" and the nature of the water in the "laguna," or for that matter anywhere else on Guanahaní. The belief is nearly universal that in writing "en medio" Columbus meant the middle of Guanahaní as viewed from above, as the center of a doughnut—an assumption wholly supported by translating "laguna" as "lake." But, as Fuson implied, "en medio" can have a lateral as well as a vertical connotation, and since we know that Columbus viewed much of Guanahaní from offshore, and not necessarily any of it from onshore, it is more likely that he used the term horizontally—the lagoon was in the center of the island as he viewed it from sea level. By this argument Watlings Island loses its most appealing physical feature. At the same time no particular island gains, since it would be difficult to know now just what lagoon-like coastal features existed in 1492.

If the available water on various landfall sites, as interpreted in the literature, is bewildering in retrospect, the matter of whether Columbus was describing fresh water or salt water—or even both—is a virtual study in sophistry. Once again the diario is of no help, and the matter itself may be of only mild interest, but neither circumstance has deterred the champions of various islands from entering the lists.

The combat was initiated by the advocates of Grand Turk and Cat Island. In attempting to refute Navarrete, Irving argued that Cat Island had "an abundance of fresh water," whereas on Grand Turk there were only "several salt ponds."[50] At the same time, Montlézun, as we have seen, advanced the same argument—Grand Turk had no fresh water other than whatever rainfall might collect "in the hollows of rocks."[51] In his reply some twenty years later, Gibbs pointed out from local experi-

49. Valentini (1892:158–59) suggested that Columbus's information on the lagoon was garbled and based on testimony of the Indians rather than his own observation. If so—and it is by no means an unreasonable assumption—then it is sure to be unrecognizably changed. Keegan and Mitchell (1987b:7) argue that "the small size of San Salvador can be inferred from Columbus's observation of a lagoon in the *center* of the island" (emphasis in original), but such an argument presupposes far too much.

50. Irving 1828, 3:307.

51. Montlézun 1828:324–25. See the comment in Becher 1856:103–4.

ence that "in October fresh water always abounds, from the autumnal rains forming large fresh water ponds."[52]

Once set in train, the arguments proliferated, but before we discuss them we need to look at other early sources. Although Las Casas had nothing to say about Guanahaní as a place, he did happen to divulge that "in the middle of it was good fresh water that the Indians drank."[53] Ferdinand seemed to agree, if not so explicitly; there were "very good waters" ("bellissimi acque") on the island.[54] Relying on Las Casas and Ferdinand as he did, Herrera necessarily followed suit, mentioning "a large fresh lagoon in the middle" ("una gran laguna dulce enmedio").[55]

The earliest sources, then, present us with three differing statements. According to the diario, there was a lagoon in the "center" of Guanahaní, along with other water, but it does not identify any of this as fresh or salt water. Conversely, Las Casas categorically informs us that the lagoon was of fresh water but mentions no other waters (though he implies their existence by referring to "the widespread and verdant foliage"). Finally, Ferdinand intimates that there were fresh "waters" on Guanahaní but does not certainly include the lagoon among them. While these three scenarios are hardly mutually exclusive, they provide the stuff that nourishes argument.

Not surprisingly, the Watlings Islanders have been in the forefront of this dispute. Their cherished lagoon is brackish, and they have had trouble in reconciling this with the testimony of Las Casas. There is no need to rehearse the whole of their argument, but a brief survey may be helpful. In general, for most supporters of Watlings Island it is as if neither Las Casas nor Ferdinand had so much as mentioned the water on Guanahaní,[56] but recently Taviani has ventured his opinion on the issue. After asserting rather disingenuously that "Don Fernando, *and also Las Casas,* does not say that the lagoon was fresh water," he concludes that Las Casas's statement that the Indians drank from the lagoon was "an

52. Gibbs 1846:142, 146.

53. Las Casas 1951, 1:200: "en medio della estaba una buena agua dulce de que [los Indios] bebían."

54. Colón 1930, 1:163, adding "with a large lagoon in the center" ("con una gran laguna in mezzo"). Keen translated this as "abounding in springs" (Colón 1959:59).

55. Herrera 1934–57, 2:79.

56. For a particularly egregious case of studied silence, see Morales y Pedroso 1923:37, 60–61.

arbitrary addition."[57] The Gordian knot is cut not once but twice. But Taviani proceeds to betray the thrust of his assertion by reminding his readers that, "as is well-known—the big lagoon in [sic] San Salvador [i.e., Watlings Island] is sea-water."[58]

Few advocates of Watlings Island have been quite as elephantine in their arguments, but most of those who believe that any water in the center of Guanahaní must have been brackish cover their bets by drawing on the argument from silence. In the diario Columbus failed to record that his ships replenished their water supply at Guanahaní but did record that a few days later they did so at Fernandina.[59] For some partisans of both Watlings Island and Samana Cay, this is strong evidence that there was no fresh water available at Guanahaní.[60] This line of reasoning is not wholly without merit, but for several reasons Columbus's silence is not conclusive. First of all, of course, the diario teems with lacunae. Then too, Columbus may have concluded that venturing into the interior of this strange new island was a risk he preferred not to take, especially with the assurances of the Indians that more lands, and larger ones, were just over the horizon. Without knowing the state of his water supply, we are not in a position to estimate the degree of his desperation and hence the strength of any argument from silence.[61] Finally on 14 October he re-

57. Taviani 1987b:203, emphasis added. Taviani then quotes only the last six words from Las Casas's quotation cited with note 53 above, in the process adding a "de" before "buena."

58. Taviani 1987b:203.

59. Alvar/Columbus 1976, 2:71; Dunn and Kelley/Columbus 1989:92.

60. Becher 1856:95–96, 104; Fox 1882:387; Roukema 1959:90.

61. La Roquette (1828, 2:340–41) made too much of the notion that Las Casas would certainly have specified if Columbus could have replenished his water supply at Guanahaní. The experience of Vasco da Gama five years later may be instructive. After leaving Lisbon on 8 July 1497, his fleet took on water at the Cape Verde Islands about three weeks later. They reached the southwest coast of Africa in the middle of November, but there is no record that the fleet replenished its water supply until 7 December. By the end of December the water had dwindled to the point that rationing was imposed and cooking was done with seawater, but it was another fortnight before the fleet took on much-needed water. Finally, when additional water was required in the middle of March, the need was so acute that the Portuguese were willing to secure it against armed opposition at Malindi, even though there had been ample opportunity—or so it would appear—in the intervening weeks to secure it with less trouble. All this would suggest either that water was taken aboard but the fact not entered in

corded that the Indians brought them water and "other things to eat."[62] This alone should have muted this particular argument from silence.

On the basis of Columbus's description, Rumeu de Armas believes that there were "potable waters" on Guanahaní.[63] As a diagnostic tool, though, the presumed presence or absence of water is without value. As Gibbs pointed out so long ago, and as others have pointed out since, in October any island in the Bahamas will have some fresh water, stored either naturally or by its residents.[64] We must ask ourselves whether, if he had arrived in April, Columbus would have spoken of "a very large lagoon" or "many waters."

Of course, this can be only a rhetorical query, raised heuristically in order to underscore the exiguity of the evidence about the nature and extent of the waters on whatever island Columbus called San Salvador. By chancing to arrive at the end of the rainy season, Columbus robbed posterity of the opportunity to plumb his utterances more conclusively in this respect. There is no cause to consider any very large lagoon now existing as "the principal argument" for or against any island.[65] The diario, Las Casas, and Ferdinand may all have been right, and if they were, then Watlings Island is probably not Guanahaní. Beyond that little can be said.

---

the journal of the voyage or that da Gama was reluctant to do so for whatever reasons until restocking was absolutely necessary. For details, see da Gama 1945, 1:1–29.

62. Alvar/Columbus 1976, 2:57; Dunn and Kelley/Columbus 1989:72.

63. Rumeu de Armas 1968:326.

64. See, for example, Wolper 1964:20; Hoffman 1987a:240; Hoffman 1987b: 98–99.

65. Cioranescu/Columbus 1961:386n. Arguments that the population of Guanahaní indicated by Columbus could not be supported by collected rainwater (e.g., Didiez Burgos 1974:410, 413) labor under the incubus of begging questions about both the fertility and the population of Guanahaní that the diario cannot answer.

14. The Lie of the Land or the Lie of the Text?

How should I know what I am going to prove? This is an investigation. If I knew the result beforehand, I shouldn't want to perform the experiment. R. AUSTIN FREEMAN

Torquato Luca de Tena entertained a high opinion of the diario entry for 14 October. For him, "The Columbian text for this day describes the southern coasts of Guanahaní with such precision and with such an accumulation of data that the details he provided are today the major proofs of the investigator, not only for localizing the Island of Discovery, but for venturing, without much margin for error, the very point at which the Spanish first disembarked in America."[1] Luca de Tena's characterization of this portion of the diario is at once true and false. To take the latter first, it is hardly possible to characterize the text of the diario here as precise and substantial except in comparison with other parts, which are even more exiguous. Nor is it more than presumption to speak of "the southern coasts" of Guanahaní in this context.[2] The claim that the diario's content for this day can enable modern scholars to identify Guanahaní with little chance of error is nothing less than Panglossian. Even so, the entries for 14 and 15 October are crucially important for all exercises in landfall theorizing. Because of this, I look at them integrally and seriatim in the next three chapters, in contrast to the entries for the previous several days, and treat interrelationships as they occur.

The diario tells us that Columbus spent the morning of Sunday,

1. Luca de Tena 1968:191.
2. Luca de Tena's assumption regarding the "southern coast" of Guanahaní sprang from the fact that he was a closet supporter of Cat Island as Guanahaní.

14 October, exploring some part of the coast of Guanahaní and in doing so observed a few Indian villages, a large harbor, and a peninsula. As usual, the language of the passages is frustratingly vague, if not downright contradictory in places, and the account disagrees in part with that of Las Casas, and almost completely with that of Ferdinand.[3] Inevitably, each of these accounts has been used and abused to support a variety of conflicting theories. The relevant text of the diario (see Appendix 1) is about 500 words in length; here I concentrate on those passages that have drawn the most attention.

En amaneciendo mandé adereçar el batel de la nao y las barcas de la carabelas, y fue al luengo de la isla . . . The problems begin at once. Columbus speaks of using both the "batel" of the *Santa María* and the "barcas" of the other two ships but provides no information on the nature of these vessels. Were they equipped with sails, or were Columbus and his men forced to row along "al luengo de la isla" (the length of the island)?[4] If the latter, then prevailing opinion has it that either Guanahaní must have been fairly small or the Spanish were able to traverse only a small portion of its perimeter in the few hours available.[5] From all appearances, both types of craft were designed to provide a means of disembarking from offshore anchorages, and it seems unlikely that they would be equipped with sails.[6] Ferdinand seems to settle the matter when he writes that the men were "exhausted from rowing so much" ("la gente oggimai ere stanca dal remar tanto").[7]

Just the same, opinion varies widely, even among those inclined to believe that Watlings Island is Guanahaní. Guillén y Tato took "aderecar"

3. Las Casas 1951, 1:208–9; Colón 1930, 1:171–72. On this see, among others, Luca de Tena 1968:244–46.

4. For a discussion of the usage of the times, see Alvar/Columbus 1976, 2: 56nn107–8, and the sources cited there.

5. E.g., Rumeu de Armas 1970:533; Luca de Tena 1968:192. Just how many hours is another unknown, since Columbus is his usual vague self. Eight hours (6:00 A.M. to 2:00 P.M.) seems a reasonable maximum, and this would include the time consumed in trading and fraternizing with the Indians, exploring the harbor and the peninsula, and (probably) returning to the ships. Each of these points is taken up in greater detail in this chapter.

6. See, for example, Pontillo 1975:146–47, 153–54; Fuson 1985:63.

7. Colón 1930, 1:172.

to mean "arbolar" or "aparejar" (to raise sail), thereby denying to Columbus the ability to express himself precisely even on nautical matters.[8] On the other hand, Barreiro Meiro and Winter, among others, believe that the trip was accomplished by rowing.[9] Adopting a Solomonic approach, Rumeu de Armas temporized, concluding that both means of propulsion were employed: the "batel" had sails while the "barcas" were equipped only with oars.[10]

The whole matter is regarded as crucial, particularly by the Watlings Islanders, who generally agree that Columbus anchored somewhere along the western coast of the island, probably in its southern half, and that the harbor he described later in the entry is Graham's Harbour at the northernmost point of the island, thereby requiring a round trip of twenty miles or more. Gerace has recently tried to overcome the problem by arguing that "Columbus could have started at dawn as described in the log [sic] (6:00 AM), made the round trip, and returned to the ships by mid-afternoon (3:00 PM)."[11] Unfortunately, his calculation of rowing prodigies both fails to take into account the many time-consuming diversions that Columbus noted in the diario and extends the time available beyond reasonable limits.[12]

Perhaps sensing this, Gerace posits a round-trip expedition as a worst-case scenario and suggests that it was actually only a one-way trip—that the fleet followed along outside the reef and Columbus rejoined it immediately after completing the reconnaissance rather than rowing back to the original anchorage.[13] While this notion is appealing, it is also unverifiable. Against it is the fact that it is unlikely that Columbus would have

8. Guillén y Tato/Columbus 1943:55n68. Cf. Pontillo 1975:80–81.

9. Barreiro Meiro 1968:18–19; Winter 1987:317.

10. Rumeu de Armas concluded that the maximum distance possible was fourteen miles and that therefore Guanahaní was "tiny" (1968:337). Obregón thinks that a twenty-mile round trip would have been "no problem," forgetting perhaps that the slower form of transportation—in this case, rowing—would determine the pace (1987:192).

11. Gerace 1987:232.

12. Power (1987:158) suggests nine hours, while Valentini (1892:163–65) supports his advocacy of Cat Island by having the boats rejoin the fleet "at night-time." Montojo (1892:19) made the same assertion. Both are without foundation. Sealey (1987:9) more or less agrees with Power, suggesting "9 to 10 hours."

13. Gerace 1987:232. Cf. Becher 1856:104–5, and Dunn 1985:142.

permitted all his ships to sail along the reef, about which he expressed so much alarm (see below).

Conversely, proponents of smaller islands regard the trip as a rowing expedition and thus as a factor militating against the pretensions of islands as large as Watlings. Molander and Judge are only the most recent exponents of small islands to draw sustenance from this passage.[14] In fact, in its vagueness the text of the diario permits many arguments to be applied. Whether the case be for sailing or for rowing, for a short trip or a long one, or for a one-way excursion or a round trip, the diario neither supports nor disallows either choice.[15]

en el camino del nornordeste   No passage in the diario has been the object of more anguished, perplexed, and ultimately inconclusive controversy as this one. As it happens, the issue is strictly one of text and translation—context is unimportant. For landfall disputation the key word is "del," which can mean in this context, as in so many others, either "of" or "from" its object. In his critique of translations of the diario, Fuson discussed the matter at some length and concluded that he strongly favored the view that Columbus meant "on the route from the north-northeast."[16] In other words, Fuson believed that Columbus traveled in a south-southwesterly direction that morning.

But when his own translation of the diario appeared a few years later, Fuson had changed his mind and now rendered the phrase as, "I went along the island *to* the NNE."[17] Apparently, in the interval other students

14. Molander 1985:123; Molander 1987:145; Judge 1986:589–90. Cf. Power 1985:158.

15. This is especially unfortunate, because knowing the duration of the reconnaissance would have a ripple effect on other events of that day and the following day. Since the reconnaissance and the journey toward the next landfall seem to be all that occupied 14 October, the less time spent on one, the more on the other. More specifically, the conclusion that the reconnaissance lasted nine hours, or even longer, necessarily implies that the islands Columbus saw later that day were closer to Guanahaní, because they almost certainly were sighted before nightfall, or, say, 6:30 P.M. Of course, the converse applies as well.

16. Fuson 1985:63. Harrisse had earlier noted the ambiguity and decided that the issue was a nicety that belonged "to the philologists" (1884–85, 1:452).

17. Fuson 1987a:79, with emphasis added.

of Columbus's route had convinced him that the phrase "camino del" meant much the same as "camino al." More about this later.[18]

The debate was inaugurated by Las Casas, who, as we have already noted, was in the habit of introducing small but significant changes when he incorporated the diario into his *Historia*. In this case he changed "camino del nornordeste" to "y [Colón] comenzó a caminar por el luengo de la costa de la isla, por el nornordeste" (and [Columbus] began to travel along the length of the coast of the island for [?] the north-northeast).[19] While this might not be quite as unambiguous as, say, "para el nornordeste," it does manage to convey a north-northeasterly course more unequivocally than the diario itself. Some have regarded Las Casas's modification as decisive proof, but it represents no more than Las Casas's playing his own guessing game with the obscure text before him.[20]

In fact, a dissenter appeared promptly in the person of Ferdinand, who wrote that his father proceeded "verso il Norveste."[21] This has the advantage of meaning only "toward the northwest," but the concomitant handicap of indicating a course some 90° removed from either course expressed in the diario. In modern times Ferdinand's view has received some support, but the great majority of opinion holds that Columbus sailed north-northeast, while the view that has received the least attention is that he sailed south-southwest.[22]

We can deal first with the modern minority view, which accepts the version of Ferdinand. Valentini argued for this on the grounds that "at least at their northern end," none of the islands in the Bahamas "show[s] a trend to the north-north-*east*." He was forced to conclude that "a mistake has been committed either by Las Casas or his printers."[23] Rumeu de Armas, committed to the view that in all cases "the testimony of Hernando Colón has an equal or superior value" to that of Las Casas,

18. See below.
19. Las Casas 1951, 1:208.
20. See, for example, Barreiro Meiro 1968:18n; and Taviani 1987b:205. Margarita Zamora tells me that she would interpret this to mean that Las Casas thought that Columbus sailed along the north-northeast coast of Guanahaní.
21. Colón 1930, 1:171.
22. Herrera, when forced to decide between Las Casas and Ferdinand, chose to side with Ferdinand (Herrera 1934–57, 2:83).
23. Valentini 1892:161–62, emphasis in original.

necessarily opted for a northwesterly course without regard for other considerations.[24]

Generally, though, Ferdinand's testimony has been accepted or rejected solely on its convenience for a particular landfall theory.[25] Many who support Cat Island, for instance, have liked what they read in Ferdinand because they see it as strengthening their case, if only by weakening that of Watlings Island.[26] Watlings Islanders, on the other hand, are no less certain that, as Barreiro Meiro put it, the information in Ferdinand's *Historie* is "an erroneous transcription of the Diario."[27]

Here we have a classic instance of the confrontation of intractable sources. Since the direction in which the reconnaissance proceeded has no textual bearing on its activities, it is impossible to choose among north-northeast, north-northwest, and south-southwest on any grounds but the authority of their respective texts. Here that is not enough. There is no reason to assume that Ferdinand (or whoever else may have written the *Historie*) mistranscribed than to believe that Las Casas did the same in his transcription of the source text for his summary.[28]

Even so, the majority of those who have addressed the matter are satisfied that Columbus sailed to the northeast (per Las Casas in the *Historia*) and not to the northwest (per Ferdinand) or the southwest (per the diario?).[29] In some respects it is hard to view this interpretation of the question as anything but parrotry occasioned by estrangement from the principal source. Fuson's recantation can only strengthen the hand of the north-northeasters, and it is important to consider their argument that the phrase "en camino del" *typically* means "on the way of" or even "on the way toward."[30]

Of course, any alleged common usage is less important than knowing how Columbus himself was accustomed to using the phrase, since

24. Rumeu de Armas 1968:318–21, 341–43.

25. Sanz transcribed it as "Norueste" with no comment whatever (Sanz/Columbus 1962:10v).

26. For example, Tió 1961:566.

27. Barreiro Meiro 1968:13, 20. Cf. Sealey 1987:8.

28. For the calligraphy of the word "nornordeste" in the diario, see below.

29. In addition to Fuson, exceptions include Power 1985:158.

30. Taviani chides Fuson and deploys the irrelevant argument that three recent editions of the diario have preferred "to the NNE" (1987b:205).

he was frequently at odds linguistically with his time and place. Looking to other parts of the diario, we find that no fewer than nineteen times on the outward voyage the diario uses the phrase "camino al" or "camino el" to indicate the direction toward which Columbus was sailing.[31] Only once in this portion is the phrase "camino del" used for this purpose.[32] It is true, of course, that these entries are in paraphrase while that for 14 October purports to be in Columbus's own words, but this matters only if we are prepared to believe that in 95 percent of these cases the scribe or scribes changed "del" to "al" or "el" from sustained caprice.[33] Most will probably not set much store in this conceit.

Elsewhere in the diario there are nine instances in which "del" is used to mean "toward," and "al" or "el" are used for that purpose another nine times after the word "camino," excluding instances between 12 and 28 October, all of which are part of the problem rather than of the solution.[34] In sum, then, in about three-fourths of the relevant cases the diario does *not* use "del" to express the notion of "toward" when used in conjunction with "camino."[35]

On the basis of Columbus's own usage, we are forced to conclude that Fuson was correct in challenging the majority opinion as to the direction of the reconnaissance party on the morning of 14 October. Adopting the most likely interpretation of the text "en el camino del nornordeste" can lead us to believe that Columbus actually sailed south-southwesterly that day and that the harbor he saw at what appears to have been toward the end of his trip was at or near the southern end of Guanahaní.

Luca de Tena took an intriguing new line on the matter. He noticed that all modern editions of the diario transcribe the seventeenth word of the day's entry as "fue," the third-person singular form of the verb "ser" in the preterite. But since Las Casas claimed to be quoting Columbus here, the word should have been "fui," the first-person singular, present

31. Alvar/Columbus 1976, 2:26–44; Dunn and Kelley/Columbus 1989:26–56. Cf. Guillén y Tato 1951:44.

32. The variation between "al" and "el" probably indicates the work of two scribes.

33. For another example of "camino al," see Alvar/Columbus 1976, 2:200; Dunn and Kelley/Columbus 1989:326.

34. For these, see Dunn and Kelley/Columbus 1989:419.

35. This count disagrees with that in Dunn and Kelley/Columbus 1989:73n, which is twenty-five and sixteen respectively, but in order to avoid begging the question, I exclude all cases in which the context is insufficient to draw reasonably certain conclusions.

tense of the same verb. Luca de Tena consulted the holograph of the diario and found that Las Casas "always dotted his 'i's." From this Luca de Tena concluded that in this passage Las Casas has "interpolated ideas and details of his own invention" and thereby changed the text "substantially." In doing so he had carelessly slipped into third-person discourse.[36]

Although it indicates the importance of frequently neglected paleographical aspects of the diario's text, Luca de Tena's argument appears to be forced. The word in question appears in the diario as follows:

Unfortunately for historians and textual critics alike, the third letter of the word is neither clearly open, signifying an *e*, nor dotted, signifying an *i*. Despite Luca de Tena's claim, it is hard to say whether Las Casas would have been more likely to make one slip or the other and thus allow us to choose one of the alternatives. It is interesting, to be sure, and all too symptomatic, that all modern editors have decided to regard the letter as an *e*, but this can hardly be regarded as conclusive.[37]

It is difficult to accept that Las Casas would have carelessly slipped into the third person here—and only here—whether he was inventing or not. There seem to be no other instances of such a lapse for the period between 12 and 24 October, but a more thorough canvass of the entire text would be necessary before defensible conclusions could be drawn. After all, who among us has not, and often, failed either to open an *e* or dot an *i*?

To my mind, a more interesting paleographical crux concerns the word "nornordeste" itself, which falls several words after "fue" or "fui" and looks like this:

This looks very much as though Las Casas had begun writing a word beginning with "nor-" and then changed his mind, crossed out what he

---

36. Luca de Tena 1968:245–46.

37. The more important instances are Navarrete/Columbus 1825, 1:29; Sanz/Columbus 1962:10v; Navarrete/Columbus 1971:24; Alvar/Columbus 1976, 1:89; Varela/Columbus 1982:93; Dunn 1985:179; Lyon 1986. None seems to have noticed the possible anomaly. Oddly, the verb is invariably translated in the first person for consistency with the rest of the text.

had written, and then wrote "nordeste." Or perhaps he just had a problem with his writing instrument. Whatever the case, there seem to be grounds for asking whether "nornordeste" should simply be "nordeste."[38] While the navigational implications are quite trivial, the paleographical ones are not.

Finally, there is the matter of just what "nornordeste" (or "nordeste") meant to Columbus. Like Valentini, partisans of one island or another have tended to look for long stretches of coastline that trend in the direction they have sought, but we know only that Columbus *began* to sail in a particular direction, after which he may have been obliged to change course many times. To assume that we must locate a stretch of coastline that runs inexorably in one direction is also to assume that Columbus would have noted any change of course. On the contrary, we know better than this on the basis of the performance of the diario throughout, including an instance later this same day.[39] In fact, as we will notice, several students of Columbus's activities on this day have assumed that he actually circumnavigated Guanahaní, while at the same time they look for entire coasts that stretch in a single direction.

para ver la otra parte, que era de la parte del leste   Like its immediate predecessor, this clause has been made to fit many beds of Procrustes. Navarrete started the ball rolling by inserting an extra "otra" before the second "parte."[40] As a result, all the translations and editions published before the appearance in 1892 of the *Raccolta*—and even thereafter—incorporated this bit of dittography. Both the French translator of Navarrete and Harrisse decided that this was a peculiar circumlocution by which Columbus actually meant "west."[41] In his turn, Fox found difficulty in explaining it, and he was far from alone.[42] Becher joined

38. This has been taken up by no modern editor, not even Alvar, who is sometimes almost too punctilious in being concerned about matters of calligraphy (see above, chapter 5); see Alvar/Columbus 1976, 1:89. Cf. Dunn and Kelley/Columbus 1989: 72–73n, and Lyon 1986:16.

39. See below, chapter 15.

40. Navarrete/Columbus 1825, 1:24, following his copyist, as in Navarrete/Columbus 1971:24.

41. La Roquette 1828, 1:48n; Harrisse 1884–85, 1:444n.

42. Major 1871:205–6; Fox 1882:357, 388; Murdock 1884:454; Manrique 1890: 187–88; Montojo 1892:18; Vidal Gormaz 1892:217; and with less justification, Thacher 1903–4, 1:536.

La Roquette in inferring that Columbus wished to see the western side of Guanahaní.[43] Murdock contented himself with accompanying his translation of the passage with a question mark.[44]

Eventually Navarrete's intrusion became no more than a historiographical curiosity, but eliminating it scarcely improved matters. Even when transcribed accurately, the text is problematical. Almost all observers agree that, wherever he may have anchored, Columbus approached Guanahaní from the east, yet they find no contradiction in his wanting to explore the eastern coast again on Sunday morning, suppressing his anxiety to move on in favor of several hard hours of what amounted to retracing his route.

The use of "de" before "la parte" makes no more sense than the "que había" that ends the sentence. In sum, this passage is an interpretive thicket. When translated literally, it makes even less sense than it does when viewed contextually, and this is inevitably reflected in modern translations. Lyon, whose translation attempts to be very literal, writes: "the other part, which was the eastern part."[45] Morison, who also claimed to be attempting a literal rendition of the diario, wrote virtually the same thing but included the final phrase: "to see the other side, which was the eastern side, what there was there."[46] Fuson, who leaves literalness far behind in his translation, truncates the passage to read: "to see the other part of the east" and in so doing creates the impression that Columbus had already seen some part of the eastern coast of Guanahaní or was actually there when he began his reconnaissance.[47] Finally, Cioranescu rather tortuously translated it as: "la côte opposée, qui s'étendait vers l'est" (the opposite side [coast], which stretches to the east), which in its turn gave yet another impression of Columbus's mental map of Guanahaní.[48]

All in all, the modern experience with this passage, beginning with Navarrete and extending to the present, has not been a happy one, and it shows not only how elastic the text of the diario always seems to be but also how modern students disregard this.

---

43. Becher 1856:104–5; compare the discussion on the anchorage site in chapter 11.
44. Murdock 1884:477.
45. Lyon 1986:17.
46. Morison/Columbus 1963:68.
47. Fuson 1987a:79.
48. Cioranescu/Columbus 1961:46–47.

*yo temía de ver una grande restinga de piedras, que cerca toda aquella isla
alrededor . . .*   As Columbus rowed or sailed along the coast of Guanahaní, he recorded that the Indians constantly beseeched him to come
ashore but that he preferred not to do so for fear of a reef that surrounded
the island. For the diario this amounts to an emphatic, almost categorical,
statement. The Watlings Islanders have not been reluctant to make a meal
of this morsel because their choice of landfall is virtually surrounded by
the requisite reef.[49] Beyond that, many of them have used the statement
to eliminate other islands from contention. Blake concluded that it ruled
out both Grand Turk and Cat Island.[50] Markham, on the other hand,
believed that Grand Turk possessed the necessary reef, as did Samana
Cay, but he agreed that Cat Island was out of the running.[51] Gould credited Grand Turk with "an encircling reef" but rejected both Cat Island
and Samana Cay.[52] Roukema also ruled out both Samana and Grand
Turk, and regarded the Caicos as qualifying only in part.[53] This was
enough to satisfy Taviani, who included Samana but, like all the others,
excluded Cat Island.[54] On the other hand, proponents of other islands
have found it expedient to overlook or minimize this passage, either because their island of choice had no reef or because of its possible implications for the size of Guanahaní, of which more below.[55]

However unambiguous the statement is descriptively, in all other regards it offers the usual set of paradoxes. Most seriously, the statement is
belied by Columbus's testimony that he had gone ashore just two days
earlier, at which time he failed to mention any reef surrounding Guanahaní. Moreover, it is possible that, shortly after expressing his fear, he

49. For "restinga," see Alvar/Columbus 1976, 2:57n110.
50. Blake 1892:548–49.
51. Markham 1889:108–17; Markham 1892:92–100.
52. Gould 1927:412–13.
53. Roukema 1959:86–89.
54. Taviani 1987b:203, 213–24. Morales y Pedroso (1923:49) rejected Cat Island
on these grounds, as did Rigg (1973:222). Cat Island does have a reef along its southern shore, the area where most if not all of its advocates would place Columbus's
landfall.
55. E.g., Booy 1919:58–59, allowed this single statement to persuade him that
Guanahaní could not have been larger than 48 miles in circumference. Chaves described Guanahaní, in contrast, as "clear all around" ("limpia a la redonda") (Castañeda Delgado et al. 1977:88).

crossed the reef to view at firsthand the large harbor he saw, although, of course, he may well have done that from outside the reef.

Another puzzling aspect of this statement relates to the source of Columbus's observation. The statement definitely implies that he had seen all sides of Guanahaní, yet at that very moment he was engaged in a time-consuming expedition to investigate "the other part" of the island. Some have concluded that Columbus's information derived from the reconnaissance itself, which was able to circumnavigate the island in the time available. This in turn requires that Guanahaní be rather small and doubly damns Cat Island, which is over forty miles in length.[56] Given that the passage appears in the diario before Columbus's description of the larger harbor or the peninsula, this argument would appear to have little to recommend it. Despite the many reticences of the diario, it seems unlikely that Columbus would have failed to mention that he had made a complete circuit of the Spanish crown's newest possession.

What, then, are we to make of the statement? Is it vintage Columbian hyperbole? Or is it simply a device to explain why he preferred not to go ashore, perhaps to mask his fear not of the reef but of the possible hostility of the Indians? Major suggested that the covering statement was no more than "an inference from what [Columbus] saw."[57] This is by no means implausible, but to accept it is to enjoin a good deal of caution in interpreting any of Columbus's statements. But whether or not Major was correct, the concreteness of the statement is offset by its incongruity. The passage generously allows us to assume that Columbus's reconnaissance encompassed everything from an exploration of a short stretch of coast to a complete circuit of Guanahaní. Certainly it is not enough to rule islands in or out of contention.

y entremedias queda hondo, y puerto para cuantas naos hay en toda la cristiandad, y la entrada d'ello muy angosta. Es verdad que dentro d'esta cinta hay algunas baxas, mas la mar no se mueve más que dentro de un pozo. Moving on with Columbus, we reach the reef-encircled harbor

56. Montlézun 1828:313–14; Gibbs 1846:138, 146; Montojo 1892:19; Booy 1919: 59; Morales y Pedroso 1923:49; Taviani 1987b:219. Muñoz (1793:86) had Columbus circumnavigating Guanahaní even though Muñoz believed that it was fifteen leagues in length.
57. Major 1871:205.

that he described so grandiloquently—it was so capacious that it could shelter as many ships as there were in Christendom. The task seems to be first to strip this passage of its undeniable exaggeration, then to imagine what Columbus really meant, and finally to equate this harbor with a modern counterpart. For partisans of Watlings Island, the case is simple enough. The largest harbor there is Graham's Harbour at the northern end of the island.[58] Since Columbus reported that he discovered the harbor near the end of his reconnaissance, this could have begun only at or toward the southern end of Watlings and could have proceeded only northeasterly, since this is the general trend of parts of Watlings Island's east and west coasts.[59] There is no need to rehearse the permutations of this argument except to note that it has been reiterated to the point that it has achieved orthodoxy.

Devising such scenarios requires a penchant for accepting Columbus's descriptions as having at least marginal quantitative value and then measuring this value against possible candidates throughout the Bahamas.[60] In this quest it does not seem to matter much that this expression was virtually a topos with Columbus for describing the size of a harbor.[61] Nor is it important that Columbus's view of the size of the combined fleets of Christendom, even the extent of Christendom itself, is as unknown to us as its actual size was to him.

The late favorite in this sweepstakes, Graham's Harbour, is more of a bay than a harbor, but it may be large enough to have earned Columbus's encomium.[62] Certainly Morison and other advocates of Watlings Island

58. With a few exceptions. Morales y Pedroso, for example, preferred that it be at "the extreme southern end of the east coast" of Watlings Island (1923:49).

59. For disagreements over which parts of Watlings Island trend properly north-northeast and so must represent Columbus's point of departure, see, among others, Manrique 1890:63, 75; Markham 1892:99–100; Ober 1893:92–95.

60. See, for example, La Roquette 1828, 2:340 (Grand Turk); Gibbs 1846:143 (Grand Turk); Vidal Gormaz 1892:218n (Watlings Island); Cronau 1921:22–23 (Watlings Island); Verhoog 1985:32–34 (the Caicos); Keegan and Mitchell 1987b (Conception Island); Molander 1987:145 (Egg Island).

61. He may have picked it up from Marco Polo; see Polo 1928:169. For other examples of its use in the diario, see Alvar/Columbus 1976, 2:69, 106, 118–19; Dunn and Kelley/Columbus 1989:90, 146, 168.

62. For examples of harbor shopping, see Gibbs 1846:143; Stewart 1931:125; Verhoog 1947:55; Cioranescu/Columbus 1961:23; Tió 1961:577; Tió 1966:316–17; Judge 1986:589; Perez 1987:77; Taviani/Columbus 1988:49n13.

have expressed no doubt that it is the "puerto" in question even though they cannot agree as to its present size.[63] Nor does it seem to have "the very narrow entrance" Columbus attributed to it, but rather "several entrances."[64]

The area off Cat Island known as the Ensenada or the Bight has also been cast in the role of Guanahaní's large harbor. Large it certainly is, far larger than Graham's Harbour, but it too lacks a narrow entrance. In fact, Columbus's description of the entrance to his harbor has thrown a pall over efforts to select one harbor from the many available. The usual reaction is to presume that Columbus judged too hastily or perhaps was exaggerating the secure nature of the harbor from attack.[65] The exercise of identifying Columbus's "puerto," as well as the argument underpinning it, can only fail.[66] For Columbus, harbors, mountains, and islands had only scale, not dimensions, and from all appearances his conception of scale was his alone.

y vide un pedaço de tierra que se haze como isla, aunque no lo es, en que había seis casas. El cual se pudiera atajar en dos días por isla . . . With the "piece of land that is made like an island but is not one" we reach the last of Columbus's descriptions of features on Guanahaní. The area in question, we are told, contained six houses, and Columbus thought it could be converted into an island in just two days.[67] We might well suspect, then, that it was a small peninsula with a very narrow isthmus con-

63. It must be said that in this they appear to have the support of Alonso de Chaves, who in his *derrotero*, compiled in the 1530s, described Guanahaní has having "a harbor on the northeast shore" (Castañeda Delgado et al. 1977:88). His description of Guanahaní, however, is virtually identical to his description of a harbor on the island he called "Samana," suggesting dittography and necessarily weakening the corroborative value of this early testimony. For modern uncertainty as to the size of Graham's Harbour, see chapter 8.

64. Morison/Columbus 1963:69n2. Cf. Wolper 1964:13, 31.

65. Montojo 1892:18, was content to regard Columbus's "puerto" as merely the sheltered water between reef and land. In contrast, Sadler declared that the reef harbor south of Grand Turk is "the only one of its kind in the entire Bahamas which is capable of sheltering 'all the fleets of Christendom'" (1981:5). See also Winslow 1988; Winslow n.d.

66. See, for example, Wolper 1964:33–34.

67. Alvar/Columbus 1976, 2:57–58; Dunn and Kelley/Columbus 1989:74.

necting it to Guanahaní.[68] Cronau believed that a peninsula at the east end of Graham's Harbour was "proof almost as strong as holy writ of the identification of Watlings Island" with Guanahaní.[69] Both Luca de Tena and Rumeu de Armas seemed to agree, as they made much of the diagnostic value of this description.[70]

Nearly all the Bahamian islands have irregular coastlines and are rife with peninsulas of varying sizes and shapes, so by itself the account has little intrinsic value as a means of pinpointing any modern landform. In order to increase the odds, some, like Cronau, have concluded that Columbus saw the peninsula from the harbor and so look for these features in tandem.[71] In fact, the diario makes no such claim and even suggests ("me moví") that the two features were some distance apart, but this has tended to be overlooked in the race for laurels.[72]

The description of this peninsula did not escape its earliest exegetes unscathed. Although in the *Historia* Las Casas retained the account virtually intact amid a torrent of geographical asides, Ferdinand differed markedly.[73] Somehow he gained the impression that, even though it still contained only six houses, the peninsula was so large that it would take no less than three days just to row around it.[74]

In sum, and taking the diario at its word, we learn the following details about Columbus's activities during the morning of 14 October. Some time after dawn, Columbus and some of his men embarked on a reconnaissance of the island in boats that may or may not have been equipped with sails. They proceeded in a southwesterly or northeasterly direction along the coast of Guanahaní, conversing, trading, and playing God with the Indians along the way. At some point they saw a large harbor with a

68. For examples of putting the peninsula to use, see Fuson 1961b:36; Power 1985:158; Verhoog 1985:34; Winslow 1988. Valentini thought it was an island whose channel had silted up (1892:162–63; cf. Luca de Tena 1968:196–97).

69. Cronau 1921:26. Cronau actually used Columbus's two-day estimate to reject a rival candidate (1921:22).

70. Luca de Tena 1968:196–98; Rumeu de Armas 1968:334–35.

71. Valentini 1892:164; Stewart 1931:126; Luca de Tena 1968:196; Judge 1986: 589; Taviani 1987b:219–20.

72. See, for example, Manrique 1890:63, 75; Vidal Gormaz 1892:219n; Tió 1961: 566–67; Winslow 1988.

73. Colón 1930, 1:172.

74. Colón 1930, 1:172. Cf. Fuson 1985:61. In the case of the *Historie*, the problem could have developed in the process of translating from a Spanish text.

narrow entrance and an interior that appeared to be deep and calm. Sometime after this they saw a small piece of land that was connected to Guanahaní by a narrow isthmus. After this they either doubled back, finished circumnavigating the island, or rendezvoused with their ships, which may have followed along outside a reef that may have surrounded Guanahaní. At this point the fleet sailed off to yet another series of discoveries and controversies. Despite Luca de Tena's sanguine words cited at the beginning of this chapter, we can say no more without transcending, ignoring, or contradicting the diario.

15. Tracks Without Traces

When I use a word, it means just what I choose it to mean, neither more nor less.
                                                    HUMPTY DUMPTY
                                                in *Through the Looking Glass*

The imprecisions, the incongruities, and the contradictions that bedevil the text of the diario as it describes events at Guanahaní continue apace after Columbus left that island. Two passages, separated in the diario but brought together in historians' arguments, constitute the principal problem for the period immediately after Columbus departed Guanahaní. Rumeu de Armas has noted that the "conciseness and exiguity" of the diario at this point "surprise the reader," but in truth the problems stem more from what is present than from what is absent.[1]

The first of these passages appears about midway through the entry for the preceding day, 13 October, when, in discussing his plans, Columbus wrote: "I decided to wait until the next afternoon and then to depart for the southwest." He wished to do this, he went on, because he understood the Indians to have told him that in that direction (but also to the south and to the northwest) there were land, people, and best of all, "gold and precious jewels."[2]

The second passage ends Columbus's entry for 14 October. After viewing the harbor and peninsula on Guanahaní, he wrote that he re-

1. Rumeu de Armas 1968:344.
2. Alvar/Columbus 1976, 2:55; Dunn and Kelley/Columbus 1989:76: "Determiné aguardar fasta mañana en la tarde y después partir para el subdueste." Sanz/Columbus 1962:10r, rendered the unusual "subdueste" as "sudueste," as did Varela and even Navarrete, though his copyist had duly written "subdueste" (Varela/Columbus 1982:92; Navarrete/Columbus 1825, 1:23; Navarrete/Columbus 1971:23).

turned to the *Santa María,* spread sail, "and saw so many islands" ("vide tantas islas") that he did not know which of them to head for.[3] It is fair to observe that no other statement in the Columbian corpus has aroused as much interest, debate, perplexity, and futile ingenuity as this. Certainly it fairly bristles with anomalies, and the first question is just when it was written. The answer seems all too obvious: Columbus used "hago" (I am doing) to express his sailing toward the largest of the visible islands, and this would appear to fix the very moment at which he recorded the information, at least up to that point in the text. Columbus is effectively claiming to be writing these words as he was making his way from Guanahaní to this island in the distance. Oddly, translators of the diario have had trouble with "hago." Markham, then Jane, and finally Morison all translated it as "I did," as if Las Casas had written "hize."[4] Fuson omits the phrase entirely from his translation.[5]

The reasons for this seemingly pointless and innocuous usage are discussed below, but for the moment let us return to the previous day's passage, in which Columbus outlined his plans for the following day. Here Columbus unequivocally stated his intentions—he could hardly have done more—but at no later point in the diario—say, between the words "vela" and "y" in the second passage (". . . y di la vela, y vide tantas islas")—did he go quite so far as to say that he was actually carrying out his plans, which in itself is somewhat puzzling.[6]

Be that as it may, most historians routinely turn Columbus's stated intention to sail southwest into his unstated deed.[7] Since a southwesterly course is a sine qua non for those who advocate a Watlings Island landfall, and is convenient for several other reconstructions as well, Columbus's sailing in that direction has become a historical "fact" by dint of constant

3. Alvar/Columbus 1976, 2:58; Dunn and Kelley/Columbus 1989:76. For the entire entry, see Appendix 1.

4. Markham/Columbus 1893:42; Jane/Columbus 1960:28; Morison/Columbus 1963:68. Murdock (1884:454), Thacher (1903–4, 1:538), Cioranescu (Cioranescu/Columbus 1961:48), and Lyon (1986:19) all translated it correctly.

5. Fuson 1987a:80.

6. Las Casas was vaguer still, writing that after the Indians had told him about the gold "to the south, southwest, and northwest," Columbus decided to go "there" (allá) (1951, 1:207).

7. Even Rumeu de Armas (1968:341–42) and Luca de Tena (1968:205–7, 214) do this. Fuson would regard any other direction as "illogical" (1985:63; cf. Manrique 1890:100 and Taviani 1984, 1:39).

repetition.[8] Most recently, for instance, Mauricio Obregón has been reported as attempting to refute a Samana landfall by asserting that Columbus "said he went *southwest*" after leaving Guanahaní.[9] This confident
betrayal of the text is only the latest in a litany by students of Columbus's
route who accept, assert, or assume that Columbus followed through on
his plans.

While Columbus's setting of a southwesterly course from Guanahaní
has been an article of faith in most quarters, others have suggested routes
that require other directions. Those who have favored Grand Turk or
the Caicos Islands posit a west-northwest route, while the proponents of
Cat Island usually have Columbus sailing off to the south-southeast.[10]
Varnhagen and Didiez Burgos, advocates of Mayaguana and West Plana
Cay respectively, hypothesize a westerly direction, and Gould, who favored Conception Island, which is near Cat Island, found it necessary to
postulate a southerly course.

Despite having edited the diario, Navarrete found it possible to believe
that Columbus's path was "always west" from one island to the next until
he reached Cuba.[11] Gibbs, like Navarrete a supporter of Grand Turk,
ignored the question entirely, as did Power, the most recent to argue for
that island.[12] Supporting a Caicos landfall, Verhoog pointed out that
"Columbus states neither course nor bearing" on leaving Guanahaní, and
he helped his own cause by overlooking Columbus's stated intention to
sail southwest.[13] This line of argument allows Verhoog to conclude that
the island Columbus named Santa María lay "probably in a westerly direction" from Guanahaní.[14] In advancing Cat Island, Irving accurately
but disingenuously remarked only that the diario "does not tell us which
course" Columbus followed when he left Guanahaní.[15] Montlézun, who
also believed that Guanahaní was Cat Island, wondered if there were

8. Dunn 1985:43–44.
9. Obregón 1987b:6, emphasis in original.
10. As does Larimore, who favors a Samana Cay–Plana Cay route (1987:3).
11. Navarrete/Columbus 1825, 1:civ.
12. Gibbs 1846:141; Power 1985:160–61.
13. Verhoog 1947:26.
14. Verhoog 1947:30.
15. Irving justified his choice by arguing that "the current was against" Columbus
(itself a dubious assumption), and therefore he could only have been heading to the
east-southeast because "the current sets constantly to the W.N.W. among these islands" (1828, 3:309).

copying problems and suggested that in any event Columbus "at least sailed toward the south." He went on to criticize Navarrete for ignoring the text so blatantly.[16]

Varnhagen also managed to ignore Columbus's statement of intent and devised a route for him that had him sailing in a westerly direction.[17] Didiez Burgos did the same but, despite much prolixity, never managed to come to grips with his choice.[18] Gould changed his opinion from favoring Watlings Island to advancing Conception Island as Guanahaní and so perhaps felt obliged to support his new view more fully. At any rate, he justly pointed out that an expressed intention can hardly be construed as the father of a deed without independent evidence of the deed itself.[19]

The penchant for the half truth among proponents of directions other than southwest inevitably led to criticism of their conclusions, particularly, of course, by partisans of landfall sites (Watlings Island and Samana Cay) that permitted the intent to be father of the deed. Murdock rejected both Irving and Varnhagen on these grounds.[20] Roukema criticized Verhoog's and the Links' choice of the Caicos Islands on the grounds that their proposed route required a west-northwesterly course, though he failed to find fault with their lack of a fully contextualized argument.[21]

Even Rumeu de Armas, who did not feel disposed to posit a specific landfall site, concluded that Columbus did sail southwest because he had already carried out the first of his stated intentions (the coastal exploration), because he did not mention seeing any lands from Guanahaní that might have deflected him from his purpose, and because "as soon as" he did see more islands, he "registered joy" and thereby rendered his earlier silence decisive.[22] This is an argument of some desperation. We might suspect that Columbus formulated any number of contingency plans as he sailed through these uncharted waters and then abandoned them as new information or unanticipated physical circumstances intervened. In this case, for instance, tides, winds, or further information from the Indians (who had already offered two alternatives to sailing southwest)

16. Montlézun 1828:327–28.
17. Varnhagen 1864:vii–viii.
18. Didiez Burgos 1974:148–60.
19. Gould 1965:78.
20. Murdock 1884:466.
21. Roukema 1959:94–101.
22. Rumeu de Armas 1968:343. Cf. Rumeu de Armas 1970:589.

could have disposed Columbus to sail in another direction or to change direction once under sail. Only an argument from silence can be made in this case, and that argument would be that Columbus's failure to mention sailing in *any* particular direction is at once odd and crippling.

As a result, the notion is baseless that the text of the diario best supports a Watlings Island–Rum Cay sequence, or for that matter any northeast-southwest sequence. Despite the efforts of moderns to supply what Columbus did not, the text of the diario tells us only that he sailed sometime (that too is not specified) on 14 October.[23] In fact as well as in theory, he may have sailed in any direction, although most likely between due southeast and due west. It is worth noting in closing that neither Las Casas nor Ferdinand presumed that Columbus followed through on his stated intention. Both mentioned that Columbus sailed from Guanahaní and no more.[24]

I

We might ask whether greater precision can be reached by looking at Columbus's subsequent activities. As we have seen, Columbus wrote that after setting sail he espied "so many islands" that he scarcely knew which of them to make for.[25] The identity of these islands has aroused considerable interest. In fact, the matter has been the crux of most arguments about Columbus's route through the Bahamas after leaving Guanahaní and on the islands' bearing in relation to Columbus's course.

First, though, it is necessary to point out that Ferdinand specified clearly that Columbus could see these islands *from* Guanahaní.[26] His statement is unadorned and its source is unknown, and there is no overwhelming reason to accept his version, since it directly contradicts the sense of the diario. As the diario seems almost straightforward here, it is perplexing (and symptomatic of the landfall debate as a whole) that a

23. Probably in early to mid afternoon.
24. Colón 1930, 1:172; Las Casas 1951, 1:210.
25. There is a minor tradition that would translate "tantas islas" as "many islands." Las Casas began it by writing "muchas islas" even though he was apparently copying directly from the diario (1951, 1:210). Ferdinand was content to speak of "the other islands" (Colón 1930, 1:172). The differences are not minor, but the textual authority of the diario must be upheld.
26. Colón 1930, 1:172.

strikingly large proportion of the students of the landfall (perhaps one-third) have followed Ferdinand in this belief even while occasionally claiming the diario as their source. Beginning with Irving and continuing to this day, the assertion has been made time and again, often without referring to its only possible justification, the statement of Ferdinand.[27] No doubt the diario text (or Columbus) may be wrong in this regard, but the mistake would not be an easy one to make, and as long as there is no evidence for the view, we must assume that Columbus did not see these islands from Guanahaní (although we cannot assume along with it that they were not visible from there). The question then becomes: How long after leaving Guanahaní did he first sight them?

As the diario reads, the temptation is to conclude that Columbus saw these islands almost at once, since the phrase "I saw these islands" not only follows "I spread sail" immediately but is even part of the same sentence.[28] The assumption is reasonable but hardly susceptible to proof. Columbus may not have thought it worth mentioning that he had sailed through empty seas for an hour or two and so recorded merely what happened rather than what did not. In other words, the text permits several interpretations—ranging from several minutes to several hours—but enjoins none. At this point occurs the first of many lacunae in which Columbus fails to specify either distance, elapsed time, or course. These disjunctures effectively disrupt attempts to reconstruct Columbus's track without requiring one untestable inference after another.[29]

Advocates of various routes have circumvented this difficulty largely by ignoring it. There is hardly a need to pursue these chimeras tediously, but we should notice two instances that can give flavor to these comments. Morison informs his readers that Columbus saw Santa María de

27. Irving 1828, 3:309; Gibbs 1846:138–39; Becher 1856:108–9; Ober 1893:91; Verhoog 1947:29; Verhoog 1954:1107, 1110; Fuson 1961b:36; Sadler 1981:5; Power 1985:158; Verhoog 1985:34. Tió (1961:567) accepts Ferdinand's version because the Exuma group can be seen from his suggested landfall, Cat Island, and this is the reason that most of the studies cited here prefer Ferdinand to the diario.

28. Which is not to say that whatever islands he saw were *not* visible from Guanahaní. Columbus's point of observation, after all, was probably the *Santa María,* not Guanahaní itself.

29. The only hint the diario provides is Columbus's statement later in the entry calculating the distance of the largest of the islands from "this [island] of Sant Salvador," which leads one to suspect that Columbus could see both it and Guanahaní at the same time and probably was closer to the latter. See chapter 16.

la Concepción (Morison's Rum Cay) "when about 15 miles from San Salvador."[30] Taviani takes a slightly different tack, though hardly a more
justified one, by trying to turn Columbus's very vagueness to advantage.
According to Taviani, "some hours . . . certainly passed between the
event 'me bolví a lo nao' and the 'di la vela' one." Furthermore, he is
sure that "more hours might have passed" between "di la vela" and "vide
tantas islas." And a good thing too, since "one must cover 20 to 25 miles
[from Watlings Island] to arrive at a point where Rum Cay and Conception might be seen with all their surrounding cayos."[31]

These presumptuous readings of the diario's text are no more than two
of a kind. But from the diario we can deduce only a series of circumstances that may or may not have been connected with each other and
that tend to leave much of the Bahamas open to Columbus's initiative on
14–15 October.[32] As it happens, the indeterminacy of the absent text is
only reinforced by the oddities of the present text. After recording that
he had sighted many islands, Columbus went on to estimate their distance
from his position and in doing so used the future tense, "será." When
used for a meaning in the present, "será" indicates uncertainty and would
be translated along the lines of "it must be" or "it is probably."[33] Nowhere else in his meandering through the Bahamas did Columbus seem
to be in such doubt. Nowhere else before 24 October, when Las Casas
ceased to quote him verbatim, did he use the future tense to indicate size,
distance, or direction.

Luca de Tena suggested that in this case "yo miré por" meant, not that
Columbus was looking *at* these islands, but that he was looking *for* them
on the basis of information supplied by the Indians and that he found

30. Morison 1942, 1:315–16.

31. Taviani 1987b:207.

32. Thus even statements like that of Fuson that Rum Cay "is too far away" from
Watlings Island are not permissible (1987a:203). Sealey advances the interesting but
slightly treasonable idea that the reference to the "so many islands" may have been
made "much later" and refers in general to what happened in the several days *after*
Columbus left Guanahaní, not what happened *as* he left it (1987:7, 9). In other words,
the passage was ex post facto.

33. Thacher 1903–4, 1:538 ("may be"); Cioranescu/Columbus 1961:48 ("it appears that it must be"); Morison/Columbus 1963:68 ("is probably"); Fuson 1987a:80
("is probably"); Lyon 1986:19 ("would be"); Dunn and Kelley/Columbus 1989:77
("is about").

them only by the next day.[34] Luca de Tena did not bring the implications of Columbus's use of "será" into his argument, but when combined the two points would annihilate the text as a certain indicator of the distance of the islands from Guanahaní. With that we turn to their direction from the landfall.

II

The issue of which direction Columbus went on leaving Guanahaní is quite distinct from the issue of the direction the islands he first saw lay from there. If Columbus's own turn of phrase casts doubt on the distance of these islands from Guanahaní, what can we say about their bearing? To put it another way, are the odds in favor of these islands' being located southwest of Guanahaní even if Columbus happened to sail in that direction? Not at all. Columbus failed to mention just where he saw them along the arc in front of him as he sailed, and there is no reason to assume that they were dead ahead, or for that matter that they were at any particular bearing on a radius of, say, 180° across the direction in which he was sailing.

Let us say that the latter lay somewhere between 135°, or due southeast, and 270°, or due west, since these encompass the directions in which Columbus expected to find lands and riches. On this assumption the islands—or at least the largest of them—could have been located anywhere from 45° to 360°, or anywhere from due northeast around the compass to due north of Guanahaní. While the extremes of this scatter are proportionately less probable than its interior points, it remains that even this generous estimate is not bounded by the text of the diario, which in its stubborn silence allows us to bring the entire compass into play without fear of textual contradiction.

III

The remainder of this puzzling text abounds with oddities, largely now of commission rather than omission. Columbus begins by telling us, for neither the first nor the last time, that he already understood the Indians

34. Luca de Tena 1968 : 207.

well enough to learn that the islands he had spotted were "without number" but that there were enough to permit the Indians on board to call "more than one hundred" of them by name, an astonishing feat by any measure. Still, for some reason this has not struck many modern critics as either an exaggeration or an impossibility.[35]

Is it likely (or just lucky?) that the few Indians on board knew the names of so many islands? Even if they did, we must surely wonder how they conveyed this information to Columbus, not to mention how they sensed he wanted it. Did they all speak at random while Columbus somehow distinguished the eponyms and tabulated the score? Or did the Indians choose a spokesman, somehow versed in naming islands? Why would Indians have had names for so many islands, most of which would have been uninhabited and uninhabitable? In fact, no imaginable scenario goes very far toward convincing us that the statement (and/or Las Casas's understanding of it) can be remotely correct. With typical Renaissance disdain for verisimilitude, Columbus asked that his readers swallow a great deal on faith alone, and many have.[36] It is far more likely that, convinced by Marco Polo's claim that no fewer than 7,459 islands reposed off the east coast of China, Columbus interpreted the Indians' statements as a resounding attempt to begin naming what he was certain were there to be named.

Nevertheless, name these islands they did, the diario tells us, and Columbus went on to give the impression that a goodly number of them—maybe all one hundred or more—were in plain, or at least partial, sight. As if to emphasize this, Columbus describes them in wonderfully prescient detail. They were (all?) "very flat" and "without mountains," facts that he could probably have observed from shipboard, even at a distance, although it took him two days to record such details about Guanahaní. But then he went on to assert that they were also "very fer-

---

35. Taviani, for example, asserts that "the Indians, who usually exaggerated, didn't exaggerate in this occasion" (1987b:207). Rumeu de Armas (1968:344) and Vidal Gormaz (1892:219n) disagree. That the statement did not seem to strike Columbus as hyperbole suggests that what he saw in front of him came close to measuring up to the Indians' statement—or to his own presuppositions.

36. Or to put it another way, if we accept that the Indians did name more than a hundred islands, then any hypothesized route that does not account for these must be suspect. Conversely, if we choose to doubt Columbus on this point, do we not engross the privilege of doubting any statement that does not support a modern argument?

tile" and "all populated," rather more difficult to discern from a distance of fifteen miles or so, and in any case certainly untrue. But he went further yet by reporting that the people of these islands made war on each other, although they, like the inhabitants of Guanahaní, were "very simple" and "comely" people.

It hardly seems fatuous to wonder how Columbus could have known all these things while yet so far from the places he was purporting to describe in such detail. This time, at least, he did not attribute his remarkable foreknowledge to the Indians, nor would they have described their neighbors thusly in any case. There are two possible conclusions, one more reasonable (although not necessarily more probable) than the other. The first, and less reasonable, is that, as Pérez de Tudela has postulated, Columbus had previously spent some time in the West Indies and had been lucky enough to return to the very places he had come intimately to know then.[37] The more probable explanation is that this is one of those parts of the diario (or the log) that was rewritten and in the process was jumbled together, with present and past and future tenses, as well as new and old knowledge, all vying for center stage and events being recorded without regard for the original sequence. Whatever the case, the entry as it stands is inexplicable, and major or minor surgery cannot redeem matters without leaving the text in wreckage.

Even so, reconstructive surgery began at once. Ferdinand omitted much of the material but obscured matters, as we have seen, by claiming that Columbus had seen the islands from Guanahaní. He then went on to relate that they all appeared to be level, verdant, and well-populated, and that (and this could be Ferdinand rationalizing) the Indians "confirmed" that this was the case.[38]

Las Casas had much more to say, although much of it is extraneous commentary on Columbus's actions, of some of which he did not approve. Even though in the diario Las Casas had transcribed Columbus verbatim at this point, his account in the *Historia* rearranged and glossed the text shamelessly. According to this revised version, Columbus asked the Indians about "other islands that way" ("otras islas por allí") without specifying which way, and they responded "by signs" that there were "very many," to which Las Casas added marginally, even though this was actually in the diario, "and they named more than one hundred." This exchange appears to have taken place at Guanahaní because Las Casas has Columbus then setting sail, after which "he began to see many islands," which were "very fertile, very beautiful and as flat as fruit gardens [vergeles]." With that Las Casas ended his narrative for the day.[39]

IV

Innocent of the fact that the matter would assume such importance in later times, neither Ferdinand nor Las Casas thought it necessary to wonder about the very nature of these "islands." For them they were simply what the diario called them—islands. But many researchers have begged to differ with them on this point, and considerable debate has ensued as to what Columbus really meant by "islas" as well as by "tantas."

A century ago Cronau admitted that the words "I saw so many islands" were "an insurmountable obstacle" to the notion that Watlings Island was Guanahaní. He then proceeded to surmount it agilely by arguing that they were not islands at all but hills on Rum Cay.[40] Both before and after Cronau, Watlings Islanders, whatever their differences on other matters, have all agreed that Columbus's phrase is—must be—incorrect in one or all of its parts. Some would have the "islands" be clouds.[41] Others have been sure with Cronau that they were actually higher elevations on a single island, or even treetops.[42] Still others have been equally sure that the "so many islands" were no more than psychologically induced optical illusions or just plain pardonable exaggeration.[43] Despite stiff competition, the numerous and various attempts to explain, or explain away, Columbus's explicit reference to seeing "so many islands" has a strong claim to being the most bemusing of the entire landfall controversy.

Although not alone in desiring to wish away these islands, the Watlings Islanders have been more strenuous in their enterprise. Morison sur-

---

39. Las Casas 1951, 1:209–10. Verhoog (1985:34) and Taviani (1987b:206) follow Las Casas's lead in translating "tantas" as "many."

40. Cronau 1892:215–16; Cronau 1921:29–31.

41. Markham 1892:84; Markham/Columbus 1893:42; Gould 1927:414.

42. Vidal Gormaz 1892:219n; Stewart 1931:124; Morison 1942, 1:316; Roukema 1959:99; Didiez Burgos 1974:168; Obregón 1987a:192.

43. Becher 1856:109, 111; Link and Link 1958:9; Wolper 1964:34.

passed himself by blandly writing that Columbus "sighted what appeared
to be a string of six [*sic*] islands," relegating to a footnote (in one edition,
deleting it entirely in the other) the evidence that he was putting words
into the diario.[44] Taviani tries another, even more impudent, approach.
Dismissing "the doubts, arguments, and discrepancies" in this matter,
and others as well, as being "of no great importance," he concludes that
these "so many islands" were indeed six hills on Rum Cay, a conclusion
he regards as "neither wandering [sic] or [sic] arbitrary."[45]

Whatever their differences as to what "islas" meant, these attempts all
agree that Columbus was wrong in believing that he was seeing islands,
wrong in thinking that the Indians could and did name over one hundred
of them, and wrong time and again in describing in some detail what he
saw. Along the way, such modern exegesis has interpreted and reinter-
preted the text virtually out of existence.

The cavalier dismissal of Columbus as certainly wrong in some cases
and just as certainly right in others deserves some attention. We might
wonder, for instance, how Columbus could have been seeing hills when
he described the islands as "very flat" and mountainless. Could he possibly have described six (or any other number of) hill-like objects jutting
from the seas as "so many"?[46] For that matter, how did he come to know
of their fertility or the extent of their population and the characteristics
of their inhabitants? Morison was forced to advance the unlikely suggestion that eventually Columbus realized that what he at first thought were
numerous islands was really only one, Rum Cay, but that he was reluctant to go back and disturb the sanctity of the log. Surely, though, it is
more reasonable to believe that, once he had discovered his error, he
would have noted this in the log—in supplementary fashion if he sub-
scribed to Morison's notion of sanctity. In fact, there is no good reason
to disbelieve that Columbus was describing anything else but what he
says—"so many islands" spread across the horizon that he was in doubt
in which direction best to proceed.

The sustained efforts to metamorphose these islands into clouds or hills
or treetops should by now evoke little surprise, since taking the text at

44. Morison 1942, 1:316, 331n4. For more on Morison's methods, see Parker
1985:19; Henige 1988.
45. Taviani 1987b:207. Keegan discusses the problem just as cavalierly (1989:
39–40).
46. Wolper has him seeing no fewer than twenty-one hills (1964:34–35).

its word here practically nullifies any effort to track Columbus from Guanahaní to Cuba. Only Grand Turk, Cat Island, or Great Harbour Cay stand any chance if the text is taken *as written*.[47] But looking at the text, we find that no matter how garbled it is, there are no arguments, other than circular ones, that allow us to treat Columbus's words as anything but authoritative in this instance. Everything in this passage suggests that he wrote it after he had seen, and seen without the possibility of error, the "islands" of which he wrote—though how long after is another matter. The idea that he wrote "islas" and then discovered that they were something quite different is belied again and again by the text.

Even before Cronau had concocted the hill theory, Murdock had candidly observed:

> Another difficulty is found in the positive statement of Columbus that when he left San Salvador, so many islands came in sight that he did not know which to steer for, but finally chose the largest, although that was not the nearest. It is hard to imagine that he was deceived or that he construed clouds or indications of land into islands: but his language indicates the existence of an archipelago such as we cannot find anywhere on our maps of to-day, near the border of the Bahamas, except in the vicinity of the Caycos, and this cluster of islands is so situated that no track can be followed from them that agrees with any of the subsequent record. It seems better to admit that this passage cannot be understood, rather than to attempt any forced reconcilement. Columbus may have been deceived, or some error may have crept into the log later. As it stands, it is irreconcilable with modern charts.[48]

A century of effort since Murdock wrote this has served only to support the force of his argument. As long as this remains so, Watlings Island cannot easily be defended as Guanahaní unless we assume a very long interval between the moment Columbus sailed from there and his seeing these islands. Nor for that matter can any other island be proposed in its stead, given the lack of detail regarding this elapsed time.

Instead of deciding randomly when Columbus was "right" and when he was "wrong," perhaps it would be wiser to accept that this passage, and its continuation the next day, bear the hallmarks both of later recast-

---

47. For the argument that the Exuma Cays are the "so many islands," see Tió 1966:317–19, 322–23. Winslow (1988) suggests that they are the Berry Islands.

48. Murdock 1884:485

ing and of faulty transcription. This would seem to have been the view of Las Casas, in light of his attempt in the *Historia* to rewrite it. The lacunae, false starts, and other obscurities can best be understood as the result of a bungled transmission—whether by Columbus or another can only remain in doubt. No context exists that allows conjectural reconstruction that could be shown to be superior to the text as it stands. This hard truth has been demonstrated by the unceasing efforts to do just that. Unfortunately, as we move on to investigate the historiography of the next day's entry, we find that such activities have only redoubled.

16. One Day in the Life of the Diario

Those who only read [A. E. Housman's] books perhaps never knew to the full his gift for nonsense. "What's the evidence?" I asked him about some new theory which he was advancing. He answered very gravely: "It rests on something better than evidence." I opened my eyes and he went on gravely: "Conjectural emendation."

T. R. GLOVER

The textual imbroglios that infest the entry for 14 October reach a crescendo in the entry for the following day, which may be the most garbled and mystifying text in the entire document—no mean achievement. Perhaps the problem stems from the fact that about one-quarter of the way into the entry, Columbus refers to "today Tuesday" ("hoy martés"), that is, the following day, 16 October. Any flickering hope that at least some of the entry was recorded on the same day as the events it describes occurred is dashed from the very first words, which are ominously couched in the pluperfect. The unavoidable conclusion can only be that not a single word of the entry dated 15 October was actually written on that day, even in the first redaction.

To make matters the more conclusive, the last part of the entry refers to activities during the morning of the sixteenth. As we will see, there is more than enough evidence to suggest that all or part of this and other entries was cobbled together at various later stages. While this could be—and has been—construed as yet another example of Columbus's inveterate and ingenuous spontaneity, it perforce brings into consideration those matters that affect any reconstruction of the past: memory, expediency, confused sequences, and lacunae. Keeping this in mind will help us to understand the thrust of much of the following argument. The text of this day's entry is long, too long to present in full here, so the reader is referred to Appendix 1.[1] Instead, I will deal explicitly with several short

1. See Appendix 1. For a translation of these passages, see Dunn and Kelley/Columbus 1989:77–85.

passages that encapsulate the entry as a whole and that have served as the bases for much hypothesizing.

I
_____

Y como la isla fuese más lexos de cinco leguas, antes será siete ... In order to appreciate the import of the entry for 15 October, we must put it into a context that begins with the end of the entry for the previous day. As Columbus was proceeding toward the numberless islands that loomed before him, he wrote that he thought that the largest of them, and the one for which he had decided to sail, was distant "from this [island] of Sant Salvador five leagues" ("d'esta de Sant Salvador cinco leguas").[2] The wording here is peculiar but suggestive. Both in using Guanahaní as one pole of the measurement and in adopting the demonstrative pronoun "esta," Columbus implies that he was still near Guanahaní when he made his estimate—in fact, one would think, still in sight of it.[3]

There is no indication that Columbus stopped sailing at this point, only that he stopped recording.[4] His use of the phrase "and so I am [now] doing" ("y así hago") refers to the earlier verb "andar" or "to sail."[5] Withal, when the next morning came, he concluded (on what grounds we do not know) that his objective now lay closer to seven leagues away than five.[6] Moreover, it now seems that the distance to the island was to be measured from Columbus's ship rather than from Guanahaní. This permutation is constantly ignored in favor of identifying Columbus's Santa María de la Concepción by its distance—as well as direction—from a postulated Guanahaní.[7] This is a point that can scarcely be overemphasized because it represents another, and more serious, disjuncture in the

2. Alvar/Columbus 1976, 2:58; Dunn and Kelley/Columbus 1989:76.
3. This would seem to militate against Watlings Island's being Guanahaní and Rum Cay being Santa María because, as Morison concedes, "[no] islands can be made out from Columbus's anchorage at San Salvador or for many miles out to sea" (1942, 1:316). From this Morison concluded, in remarkably circular fashion, that these islands were sighted "about 15 miles" from Guanahaní.
4. Even so, Thacher (1903–4, 1:193) has him becalmed, while Roukema (1959:97) has him lying to as soon as the islands were spotted.
5. That he continued to sail is accepted in Link and Link 1958:13.
6. Alvar/Columbus 1976, 2:59; Dunn and Kelley/Columbus 1989:76.
7. Among others, Humboldt 1836–39, 1:197; Blake 1892:543; Montojo 1892:19; Morales y Pedroso 1923:49; Tió 1961:575, 577; Dunn 1985:44; Lyon 1986:32.

text. The island that Columbus was seeking was, early on the morning of 15 October, about seven leagues (roughly twenty-one miles) from his own position, which, with respect to Guanahaní, is entirely unknown.

Commonly this change in estimate is taken to be Columbus's conscious revision of his earlier estimate of five leagues. For instance, Thacher and Cioranescu translated the phrase as seven leagues "rather than" five.[8] Others have been led to believe that Columbus "corrected" his information at this point.[9] If so, he was careless in expressing himself; there is no hint in his phrasing ("and as the island was [sic] more than five leagues, rather about seven") that he was referring, even obliquely, to his earlier estimate. In fact, his use of "como" encourages us to treat this passage as quite distinct in Columbus's mind from his previous mention of an island five leagues distant from Guanahaní. The objective now at hand, whether it was the same island or not, is simply more than five leagues away from his point of observation, perhaps as many as seven.[10]

None of the other early sources is of help here. As we will see, in his *Historia* Las Casas was uncharacteristically reticent in transcribing the events of this day. Here he noted only that one of the islands (he used the singular verb form "estaba" but without a visible antecedent) was seven leagues from wherever Columbus was observing it.[11] In his *Historie* Ferdinand did exactly the same thing.[12] Because in this instance he depended on Las Casas and Ferdinand, Herrera might be expected to repeat their information, but in fact he added another twist by declaring that the island Columbus was to name Santa María de la Concepción was "seven leagues from the first" ("siete leguas de la primera"). By this Herrera seems not to have meant Guanahaní, which he would have mentioned by name, but one of the many islands Columbus had sighted during Sunday afternoon or evening.[13]

---

8. Thacher 1903–4, 1:538; Cioranescu/Columbus 1961:48.

9. Fox 1882:390; Verhoog 1947:21, 26; Tió 1961:575; Perez 1987:32; Fuson 1987a:80.

10. Dunn (1985:44) implies that Columbus corrected his earlier figure, but Dunn and Kelley translate the phrase as "and as the island was farther than five leagues, rather about seven" (Dunn and Kelley/Columbus 1989:77), wording that does not carry such a connotation. Jane used identical language (Jane/Columbus 1960:29).

11. Las Casas 1951, 1:210.

12. Colón 1930, 1:172.

13. Herrera 1934–57, 2:84. In the very next line Herrera mentions San Salvador

Juxtaposing the two passages has naturally proved troublesome, particularly for the Watlings Islanders. All might be well if they were allowed to accept Columbus's second estimate—and with it the conclusion that he was measuring from Guanahaní—and to reject the first, since Rum Cay, their choice for Santa María, lies about twenty miles southwest of Watlings Island, that is, between six and seven leagues away. But like other interpreters of the diario, no matter their preference in landfalls, they are forced to wonder how the island, if it was the same island, had receded into the distance overnight. Several have found inspiration in the immediately succeeding passage, in which Columbus speaks of being detained by a current.[14] This view could be seen as pressing matters somewhat, since Columbus used this explanation only to excuse his taking five or six hours to cover the seven leagues in question, ordinarily a much shorter trip.

Columbus himself apparently saw no reason to explain this puzzling discrepancy, but then it may have become a discrepancy only on the way from Columbus's mind to his log or from the log to the diario. Recalling that the entry was made no earlier than the next day, it seems appropriate to question its temporal and textual integrity and continuity. Can we be certain, for example, that Columbus was referring to the same objective in both cases? In the entry for 14 October he describes, however dubiously, the islands toward which he was making as "very fertile" and "populous," but this is not the impression he leaves when describing affairs on the island at which he eventually landed and dubbed Santa María de la Concepción. Admittedly, this is no more than conjecture, but it is reinforced when we look at the text more closely.

Columbus begins by noting that the ships lay-to overnight because he feared to approach land "without knowing whether the coast was free of

---

by name, so his anonymity in this case suggests that he had another place in mind. Herrera had the fleet arriving at 3 P.M., whereas neither Ferdinand nor Las Casas mentioned a time.

14. See, for example, Becher 1856:111; Link and Link 1958:12; Roukema 1959: 97; Wolper 1964:36. Roukema, never reluctant to pluck rabbits from hats, thought it was "a freak current" (1959:97). See the comments in Fox 1882:390–91. Winslow (1988:17A), who has Columbus in the neighborhood of Great Harbour Cay, thinks he was grounded on shoals.

shoals" ("por no saber si la costa era limpia de baxas").[15] By coupling this with the statement that the presumed coast in question was still some twenty miles or more off, he appears to be offering an example of caution too extravagant to take at face value. Then, as we have seen, it took Columbus several hours to reach the object of his desires. In brief, we have the following series of events:

1. During the evening of 14 October Columbus saw an island that he thought was about fifteen miles from Guanahaní, after which he apparently continued to sail toward it for an undetermined time.

2. Eventually Columbus anchored overnight rather than approaching this (?) island, for fear of running aground.

3. Some twelve hours later the (an?) island was now about twenty miles in the distance, apparently measured from Columbus's ship, which replaced Guanahaní as the point of reference.

4. When he sailed for the island on the morning of 15 October, Columbus required some six hours to cover the intervening distance.

In no credible fashion can this set of circumstances be made to fit into a congruent whole, though not for want of many efforts to do just that. Although it may not prove appealing, the possibility that the text most obviously invites us to consider is that Columbus was not talking about the same island throughout the entry—in short, that Herrera was right.[16]

Any sense of cognitive dissonance is only strengthened by remembering that Columbus described the "so many islands" as "very flat" and yet claimed the next day to be able to see his objective (one of them?) at a distance of twenty miles or more. Various attempts have been made to explain how this could be. Most often it is assumed that the islands Columbus saw were then heavily wooded, hence higher (yet somehow still very flat).[17] A better explanation would be that the island that Columbus approached during the morning of 15 October was not among those he

15. Alvar/Columbus 1976, 2:59; Dunn and Kelley/Columbus 1989:76: "Había temporejado esta noche con temor de no llegar a tierra a sorgir antes de la mañana." For the apparently redundant use of "no" in the clause, see Dunn and Kelley/Columbus 1989:77n1. Cf. Alvar/Columbus 1976, 2:59n115.

16. Several similar disjunctures disfigure the account of Columbus's voyage to the Canaries. See Alvar/Columbus 1976, 2:19–23; Cioranescu 1959; and above, chapter 7.

17. See, for example, Murdock 1884:470; Verhoog 1947:19, 58; Fuson 1961b:36; Link and Link 1958:10.

had described as flat. In fact, once on the scene he provided no description at all of Santa María, quite in contrast to his practice elsewhere.
Strangely, his impressions of the various islands seem all to have been
formed only when he was still at least fifteen miles away.

II

*Y fallé que aquella haz, que es de la parte de la isla de San Salvador, se
corre norte sur y han en ella 5 leguas. Y la otra, que yo seguí, se corría
lestegüeste, y han en ella más de diez leguas.*[18]   If few have been notably
concerned with whether the next island Columbus encountered was five
leagues or seven leagues from Guanahaní or from Columbus on the
morning of 15 October, nearly everyone has been forced to give attention
to Columbus's next statement, in which he estimates the position and size
of the island. Here we have the usual combination of apparent precision
that on inspection proves to be a will-o'-the-wisp. Almost without exception, both translations of the diario and interpretations of Columbus's
itinerary have treated the north or south coast of this island as "facing"
Guanahaní in some respect.[19]

It appears, in fact, that here Columbus forsook another opportunity to
be helpfully specific. If we accept that he meant to say that the island he
reached about noon had a north-south coast that faced Guanahaní, then
its most reasonable location would be roughly due west of Guanahaní.
And if the orientation of this coast was slightly northeast-southwest or
northwest-southeast, then the island would lie slightly north or south of
due west, and so on. In any case, the implication is that the island was
more to the west of Guanahaní than any other direction.

This is another blow to the interests of, among others, a Watlings
Island–Rum Cay route, for the eastern face of Rum Cay can hardly be
construed as "facing" Watlings Island in any customary sense of that
word. In fact, if Columbus proceeded from the southwest corner of Watlings Island directly southwest to Rum Cay, he would have found that, if
anything, the latter's north coast faces Watlings Island a little more directly. The dilemma has not entirely escaped the partisans of Watlings

18. See Appendix 1. Note the use of figures for one number in this phrase and
words for the other.

19. Markham/Columbus 1893:42; Thacher 1903–4, 1:538; Jane/Columbus 1960:
29; Cioranescu/Columbus 1961:48; Fuson 1987a:80. Cf. Colón 1930, 1:172–73.

Island, who have attempted to deal with it in various ways. Murdock, who was among the first to suggest that Rum Cay and Columbus's Santa María de la Concepción were one and the same, was uncharacteristically evasive, arguing that the east side of Rum Cay "lies towards San Salvador [Watlings Island]."[20] Earlier Major had attempted to meet the issue by suggesting that Columbus had meant "on the side approached by ships coming from San Salvador" but that could equally apply to the north coast of Rum Cay.[21]

In general, though, the Watlings Islanders have preferred to skirt the issue. After Murdock, none of them has dealt explicitly with the question. A few have mentioned Columbus's statement in passing,[22] others have quoted part of the passage but deftly omitted Columbus's observation,[23] but most have simply disregarded the matter entirely.[24] This last procedure is well illustrated by Morison, who, in his translation of the diario, was naturally forced to include the statement but managed to translate it, even more idiosyncratically than Murdock, as "the coast which lies over against the island of San Salvador."[25] In his note to the translation he merely observed that "the orientation" of Rum Cay fits Columbus's description, that is, that its coasts are roughly north-south and east-west on a 1:2 ratio.[26]

Advocates of other landfalls have done little better. In Irving's work Slidell had Columbus traveling southeast from Guanahaní and was obliged to ignore any statements that suggested otherwise.[27] The translator for Fox, who supported a southerly course from Samana to Crooked Island, rendered the passage as "towards," but Fox had nothing to add on the matter.[28] Perez, who favors much the same route—Samana to

20. Murdock 1884:476, with emphasis added.

21. Major 1871:198.

22. See, for example, Cronau 1921:34; Stewart 1931:126–27; Barreiro Meiro 1968:20.

23. Montojo 1892:19; Vidal Gormaz 1892:220–21.

24. E.g., Becher 1856:111–12; Markham 1889:100; Manrique 1890:100; Markham 1892:92; Gould 1927:417; Morison 1942, 1:315–16; Roukema 1959:94–99; Morison and Obregón 1964:30; Judge 1986:591–92; Taviani 1987b:206; Obregón 1987a:192.

25. Morison/Columbus 1963:69.

26. Morison/Columbus 1963:71n. Cf. Morales y Pedroso 1923:62.

27. Irving 1828, 3:312–13, on the basis of "contrary winds."

28. Fox 1882:358, 392.

Acklins—confronts the issue more squarely, if perhaps too ingeniously, by suggesting that Columbus meant "the side that runs in the direction toward the island of San Salvador."[29] In this way Perez advocates nothing less than a 90° shift in orientation between the two islands. Finally, Dunn and Kelley, who prefer a Watlings Island–Rum Cay route, translate "de la parte de la isla de San Salvador" as "in the direction of San Salvador," which, as noted, does not fit the east coast of Rum Cay well.[30]

The next impasse appears to be a relatively minor one; many interpreters of the diario have transformed Columbus's "more than ten leagues" into simply "ten leagues."[31] If we accept the premise that Columbus recorded this estimate as he sailed along the entire length of the coast in question, then it is not a matter of a coastline extending beyond view, as may have been true later for Fernandina. On the other hand, as discussed below, Columbus may not have completed his intended journey—he never said that he did. At any rate, the "more than" modifier forbids us to assume that Columbus was visiting an island just twice as long as it was wide; the difference may have been much greater.

Few islands in the Bahamas measure up to Columbus's dimensions, here some fifteen miles by more than thirty miles, forcing modern scholarship along any number of exculpatory paths. Four principal strategies have emerged in the process.[32] The first of these is the time-honored tactic of ignoring the problem entirely, or brushing it aside as trifling or frivolous. Taviani, a partisan of Watlings Island and Rum Cay, exemplifies this strategy when he hastens to assure us that there is no problem at all: "We do not worry about the question, as many other times Columbus gives wrong or inexact measurements, and sometimes even fantastic ones."[33]

For those less easily comforted but still looking for an easy way out of the dilemma, it is easiest to believe, not necessarily that the question is

29. Perez 1987:34. Redway, who proposed the same sequence, also addressed the matter but admitted to being perplexed (1894:190–91).

30. Dunn and Kelley/Columbus 1989:77.

31. Gibbs 1846:143; Morison 1942, 1:316; Tió 1961:575, 578; Judge 1986:591; Molander 1987:146; Taviani 1987b:206.

32. There are also two minor ones. Becher (1856:116) suggested that at this point the manuscript of the log had become "blotted or rotten," while Thacher (1903–4, 1:597) found the dimensions acceptable because the 2:1 ratio fit the shape of Rum Cay. Morales y Pedroso (1923:62) took a similar view: Rum Cay is "somewhat smaller than 5 × 10 leagues but it has the right shape."

33. Taviani 1987b:206.

unimportant, but that Columbus fell prey to pardonable exaggeration for any number of reasons, none of which either he or his interpreters ever expressed.[34] A third alternative, and probably the most inexorable, is to remember that the diario is at least a thirdhand transcription and to suggest that Las Casas, an intermediate scribe, or possibly Columbus himself made not one slip of the pen but two. In both cases, "leguas" was not meant at all, but "millas," which would conveniently reduce the size of Santa María by about two-thirds. The idea, bruited by Murdock only as a logical possibility, has been repeated since with ever greater certitude. It is undoubtedly an attractive alternative, not least for its precedential possibilities in other similar cases.[35] Yet it is scarcely an expedient that can bear sustained scrutiny.[36] In the diario the distances are always recorded in leagues, occasionally supplemented by the equivalent figure expressed in miles. It is difficult to imagine why in this one instance Columbus would have had recourse to miles, or for that matter why whoever "mistranscribed" the terms would have done so not once but twice.

Perhaps with this in mind, Morison broke new ground by introducing a fourth alternative designed to save Rum Cay from oblivion. Columbus, Morison decided, had at this very juncture "consciously or unconsciously" taken to measuring certain distances in what Morison christened a shore or land league.[37] Morison purported to have borrowed this concept from an earlier study of Columbus's route along the northern coast of Cuba, but it would not be churlish to suspect that the length he bestowed on it—about one and a half nautical miles—derived from dividing the length and breadth of Rum Cay by ten and five respectively and averaging these out. In any case, a star was born. To Morison at least, this expedient had the advantage of rescuing Columbus from his own

34. See, for example, Leyva y Aguilera 1890:32; Vidal Gormaz 1982:220; Ober 1893:92; Cronau 1921:34; Gould 1927:421.
35. Markham went from having some doubts to having none at all (1889; 1892:92, 103; 1893:42n). See also Murdock 1884:476; Stewart 1931:127; and Obregón 1987a:192. Dunn and Kelley imply as much in their introduction when, in discussing the instances where Las Casas substituted "millas" for "leguas," they note in support that "Rum Cay *is* about 5 by 10 miles in size" (Dunn and Kelley/Columbus 1989:10; emphasis in original). Keegan agrees and advocates "using either miles or leagues, on a case-by-case basis" (1989:39).
36. For criticisms, see Dunn 1985:46.
37. Morison 1942, 1:316.

exuberance and Rum Cay from its own size, but to most observers it seemed a ploy so desperate as to appear cynical. As a result, Morison's imprimatur has not managed to sway even many supporters of a Watlings Island–Rum Cay route.[38]

The Links, who favored Mayaguana as the island in question, accepted Columbus's estimate for the east-west coast but rejected his estimate for the north-south coast because it is "much too high" to fit Mayaguana. They conclude that Columbus must have guessed at that dimension from seeing only part of the coast in question.[39] Verhoog also favored Mayaguana and would like us to believe that its dimensions, 6 miles by 26 miles, are only "somewhat less" than those of Columbus's island.[40]

In advocating Conception Island, the tiniest of the contenders (only 1 1/2 by 2 miles), Slidell had no choice but again to ignore Columbus's plain description, which could not be made in the least congenial, whether expressed in leagues *or* miles.[41] Molander argues that the island in question was New Providence and describes this as 21 miles long and 7 miles wide. He concludes that these dimensions offer a "closer congruence" to the testimony of the diario "than any other island in the Bahamas," even though he uses a league length of 3.18 miles.[42] Molander fails to point out that New Providence is more or less diamond shaped and there are virtually no north-south coastlines at all. His suggestion that Columbus derived his north-south estimate from "Indian sketches" hardly deserves notice.

Conversely, and not unexpectedly, we find that the proponents of larger islands seldom fail to note with satisfaction Columbus's estimates. Gibbs, Sadler, and Power all favor one of the Caicos as the island Columbus was describing, and they all cite Columbus's estimate to argue that this island fits his bill rather nicely.[43] By the same token, those who over the years have favored Acklins Island or Crooked Island as Santa María

38. Even Obregón found it unpalatable and preferred to believe that "leguas" was written in error for "millas" (1987a:192). Dunn seems sympathetic to the possibility, though he agrees that exaggeration may have contributed (1985:45–46).
39. Link and Link 1958:10.
40. Verhoog 1947:37; Verhoog 1954:1108.
41. Irving 1828, 3:309, 312–13.
42. Molander 1985:126–27; Molander 1987:161.
43. Gibbs 1846:143; Sadler 1981:5; Power 1985:161.

de la Concepción have found Columbus's figures to be altogether congenial.[44]

Perez proves to be especially ingenious in urging an Acklins Island identification. Acklins is far longer than five leagues from north to south and much less than ten leagues from east to west, but Perez points out that the east coast of Acklins turns sharply westward and would not be visible for its entire length from the northern perspective he attributes to Columbus. But from this point Columbus could hardly have estimated Acklins's east-west northern coast as being more than ten leagues in length and this forces Perez to bring into play the firm ally of all interpreters of the diario, the mistranscription. Perez suggests that at some point the word "diez" was substituted for the "dos" that Columbus had actually written. Perez then concludes that "more than 'two leagues' is an accurate measurement of the north coast of Acklins. . . . The log is now [*sic*] perfectly clear and logical."[45] Of course, once the specter of mistranscription comes into play, all things become possible. It is even conceivable that Herrera was again correct when he construed Las Casas's "cinco" to be "cincuenta" and that the island in question was really, in Columbus's estimation, fifty leagues from north to south.[46]

III

Forcing ourselves to return to the diario as we have it, we can only conclude that, given the lack of credible evidence to the contrary, the island Columbus saw before him was, or he thought it was, about fifteen miles long north to south and more than thirty miles long east to west. Having said this, he tells us that he began to sail along the east-west coast but, as usual, he comes up short on detail and fails to specify whether it was along the north or the south coast. No matter; modern historiography has the answer.

Historians generally hold that Columbus approached the island from a direction between due north and due east, although as I have suggested, the probabilities are hardly overwhelming. At any rate, it seems more

44. Varnhagen 1864:viii; Fox 1882:390; Didiez Burgos 1974:171; Judge 1986: 590–92.

45. Perez 1987:32–37.

46. Herrera 1934–57, 2:84.

likely that he was estimating the length of the east coast rather than the west coast, so the question becomes: At what point along this coast did he make his observation and draw his estimate? The common view is that it was somewhere near the northeast corner of the island, but this position emanates solely from the unproven assumption that he approached it from the northeast.

Since Columbus thought of this coast as "facing" Guanahaní, and since he was able to estimate its entire length, it would not be entirely unreasonable to assume that he approached the coast centrally and then chose to move either north or south until he reached a coast running east and west. By this argument the odds are theoretically equal as to whether he eventually sailed west along the southern or the northern coast, but since we have every reason to believe that his goal lay to the south or southwest, it seems likelier that he would have headed south along this east coast.[47]

Morison, for one, had no doubt that Columbus sailed west along the southern coast of Rum Cay. Typically, he declined to justify his conclusion explicitly, but the reason is not hard to find. Morison believed that the island Columbus claimed to see next was Long Island, which cannot be seen from off the northeast corner of Rum Cay.[48] The circularity of his argument is oppressive, but it has been adopted by several of his epigones.[49]

Two factors militate against the view. The first is that the hypothesis requires that Columbus sailed along the entire east coast of Rum Cay before turning west, eschewing the opportunity to sail west as soon as he reached the island. This presumes too much. While it scarcely contravenes the testimony of the diario outright—there is no testimony to contradict—it remains another argument against silence rather than from it. Then too, although Morison argued that Columbus saw that other island—Long Island, he believed—"from off the southeast point of Rum Cay," the diario gives quite a different impression. In it we read that

47. Dunn agrees that a south coast anchorage is "certain" (1985:44). The north coast remains the more popular choice, being espoused by Murdock 1884:476, map opp. p. 480; Cronau 1921:33, 35; Verhoog 1947:30; Verhoog 1954:1108; Tió 1961: 578; Rumeu de Armas 1968:346; Perez 1987:35.

48. Morison 1942, 1:316–17. This is a rare instance in which Morison departed from his guide, Murdock.

49. E.g., Roukema 1959:99; Wolper 1964:36; Barreiro Meiro 1968:27.

Columbus sailed along the east-west coast, and since he was able to estimate its length more precisely than usual, perhaps along all of it.[50] Only
then did he record that he sighted another, larger island to the west. If,
as Morison supposes, the sighting of this island was the impetus for the
westward course in the first place, Columbus here would be reversing
cause and effect—not impossible, to be sure, but decidedly odd and in
need of explanation.[51] At this point, though, we become entangled in the
thorniest thicket associated with this day's entry—the extent to which it
permits us to determine how many islands Columbus referred to during
the course of his day's activities.

IV

Although no longer as widely held as it once was (for reasons to be discussed later) the notion that Columbus passed at least one island this day
without bothering to name it has an impeccably long pedigree. Juan Bautista Muñoz, the first to use the diario to reconstruct Columbus's voyage,
interpreted its text to relate that Columbus sailed to a small island but did
not stop there, instead continuing on to "another large one" he saw ten
leagues to the west.[52] This view was embraced, after a fashion, by Navarrete, who, misled by his copyist, believed that Columbus had referred
to Santa María as "las islas" when in fact the diario enigmatically reads
"las isla."[53] In the event, Navarrete equated Santa María with the numerous islands constituting the Caicos group. Thus, while his argument was
unabashedly textual, it happened to be based on a misreading. Humboldt, in turn, lent his considerable reputation to this view, although apparently without studying the matter very closely.[54]

Later during the nineteenth century, Becher and Major accepted the
idea of a bypassed and unnamed island. Both identified it as Rum Cay,

50. Perez (1987:35–36) and others assumed that Columbus estimated the north-
south and east-west coasts at the same time and did so visually, but there is no overwhelming reason to believe this, particularly since the text was written so much later.

51. Later Morison changed his mind as to the point at which Columbus saw Fernandina; for this, see above, chapter 8.

52. Muñoz 1793:87.

53. Navarrete/Columbus 1825, 1:26n28. Cf. Navarrete/Columbus 1971:33. See
above, chapter 5.

54. Humboldt 1836–39, 3:197.

but their conclusions were not based on the best evidence or its use.[55] Fox was the first to challenge this budding consensus by means of a fairly intensive exercise in textual analysis.[56] He first pointed out that "cargué las velas" did not seem ordinarily to mean "to make sail" but rather to "clew up sails" or "take in sails," as though to reduce speed in favor of safety. In short, Columbus did not spend the afternoon of 15 October impatiently sailing westward but instead coasted slowly along the east-west axis of the island he was later that day to name Santa María de la Concepción. To his case Fox added Columbus's statement that he intended to take possession of each and every island he encountered. Fox resoundingly concluded that, no matter how one groups the events of 14 to 16 October, "in every aspect they will outweigh the assertion that [Columbus] did not stop at that second island which he made for on the 14th, and strove for on the 15th."[57]

From all appearances, Fox's elaborate argument put a quietus to the view that Santa María de la Concepción was the third island Columbus saw, if only the second he named and visited.[58] At any rate, the hypothesis did not form a visible part of any attempt to reconstruct Columbus's route until 1958, when the Links resurrected it to support their notion that Columbus must have bypassed Mayaguana on his way from Grand Caicos to Samana Cay, their Guanahaní and Santa María respectively.[59] In doing so they had recourse to a commissioned translation of the text that they believed sustained their thesis.

Since then the idea has enjoyed a minor revival. In advocating New Providence as Santa María de la Concepción, Molander finds it necessary to identify the several small islands east of it as places that Columbus must have seen but chose to ignore.[60] Power, influenced by the arguments of the Links and by the fact that the idea was "very compatible" with his own projected route, identified the unnamed island as one of the Caicos.[61] Finally, Perez has identified the bypassed island as Acklins Island, and Crooked Island as Santa María. In the process, as we have noted, he sug-

55. Becher 1856:108–9, 112; Major 1871:198.
56. Fox 1882:358, 391–93.
57. Fox 1882:393.
58. Although Winsor (1892:220) still believed in it.
59. Link and Link 1958:13.
60. Molander 1985:126–28.
61. Power 1985:161–62.

gested that an original "dos leguas" became "diez leguas" at some point.[62] Lately Fuson has also argued that there was an unnamed island in or just below the surface of the diario's text.[63]

By and large, those who do not accept the premise of an unnamed island have been satisfied to remain silent on the matter, letting Fox continue to speak for them. Watlings Islanders, for whom the thesis is awkward, have had little to say, although Taviani has tried to refute the suggestion at some length.[64] For most observers, apparently, the diario is clear and explicit: only one island, Santa María de la Concepción, is involved, no matter how it might be identified with a modern equivalent. With this background in mind, the relevant text is worth examining clause by clause.[65] When not encumbered by a preconceived itinerary, such textual analysis may offer new perspectives. In this a few of the points already made in this chapter will be mentioned again, but only minimally.

V

Y como d'esta isla vide otra mayor al güeste   As we have seen, the majority view is that Columbus saw this larger island to the west as soon as he began sailing along the coast of the island he was then at, or even that he decided to sail in that direction because ("como") he had already seen this island. But in the diario Columbus reported seeing the larger island only after he had already mentioned that he had sailed along the coast in question ("Y la otra, que yo seguí"). The point seems obvious, but is constantly disregarded. At best for such theories, Columbus discerned the larger island during the course of the coastal voyage; at worst, only after he had sailed ten leagues or more. Neither of these alternatives can

---

62. Perez 1987:35–40.

63. Fuson 1985:54. Fuson goes on to argue that the size that Las Casas and Ferdinand attributed to Guanahaní—fifteen leagues—is a vestige of the account of this island in the log.

64. Taviani 1984, 2:56–60; Taviani 1987b:206. Wolper (1964:36) suggested that Columbus mistook the southwest corner of Rum Cay for another island, perhaps forgetting that the entry was written the next day.

65. To my knowledge, only Fuson (1985:64–65, 72) has addressed the problem outside the context of explicitly defending a particular route. Dunn and Kelley do address the issue but reject the possibility of a second island on some of the same textual grounds I have used in arguing for it, that is, Columbus's use of the phrase "otra isla grande" in the next day's entry (Dunn and Kelley/Columbus 1989:79n).

be preferred over the other, but either is preferable to the idea that he saw
first and sailed afterward.

cargué las velas por andar todo aquel día fasta la noche   We have already
noted the longstanding differences of opinion as to the technical meaning
of the phrase "cargar las velas" as used in this notorious passage.[66] Here
we are concerned with the term in the particular context of a diario entry
and even, as it happens, in the context of its own sentence. If the term is
interpreted as "to make sail" or even as "to crowd on sails," as it has been
many times, it would imply that Columbus found it necessary to go apace
to reach this second, larger island during the afternoon, and this would
lend weight to its separate existence as Santa María. On the other hand,
should the term be given the opposite meaning, "to reduce sail," it suggests a shorter trip and perhaps one fewer island.

Inextricably entwined with "cargué las velas" in the diario, but hardly
so in the discussion over the meaning, are the words that follow: "por
andar." Aggravatingly, the two possible translations of this phrase are as
polar as are the two possible meanings of "cargué las velas." When followed by an infinitive, "por" can mean either "in order to" or "because
of" and it is left to the context or to close knowledge of the style of the
writer to determine the meaning in specific cases.[67] This will hardly do
here. If we accept "in order to," we must conclude that Columbus intended to proceed to or toward the second island and set his sails accord-
ingly. By the same token, if we think that Columbus used "por" to mean
"because of," we strike the opposite intent—and opposite sequence of
events—and so the opposite definition of "cargué las velas." In other
words, the interpretation of "por" affects the meaning of "cargué las velas" as much as, if not more than, the reverse, but neither can be interpreted without reference to the other.

Those who prefer to translate "cargué las velas" as "hauled in sails" or
its equivalent have taken to rendering the following clause in the pluperfect in order to avoid overtones of the oxymoron. Thus Fox's translator
rendered it: "for I had gone all day until night."[68] Murdock followed suit
in every particular.[69] Markham joined the crowd: "I clued up sails, after

66. See chapter 8 above.
67. Nebrija 1516/1973:157; Hanssen 1966:303–7.
68. Fox 1882:358.
69. Murdock 1884:455.

having run all that day until night."[70] Others have done the same.[71] In these cases, the action with the sails followed the activity described by "andar."

When Morison was faced with translating this phrase, he must have found himself in a quandary, for he then had Columbus at the southeast corner of Rum Cay, from which Long Island, his candidate for Fernandina, was barely visible, if visible at all. So Morison reverted to translating "cargué las velas" as "made sail" and the following phrase as "to navigate all that day until nightfall."[72] In a note he let the proverbial cat out of the bag: "I suppose that Columbus had lowered sail when he reached the nearest point of Rum Cay, and had to make sail again to reach the western end. But he could not have sighted Long Island until he reached the western end of Rum Cay."[73]

With this Morison gave renewed impetus to the long-discredited translation of Becher but without accepting Becher's concomitant belief in an unnamed bypassed island because in Morison's scheme of things no such island was available.[74] Recently Lyon, apparently free from a predisposition for a particular itinerary, rendered the phrase as: "I hauled in sails to go all that day until night."[75] As it stands, this translation is either vague or contradictory or both, but in this it only emulates its original.[76]

There are at least three logical ways to translate this sentence, none of them palatable, none of them provable, and none of them very much more likely than the others. First, we can translate it as Lyon has done, though it seems to credit Columbus with a palpable non sequitur. Second, we might conclude that translating "por" as "in order to" requires us to accept that Columbus meant "cargué las velas" to mean "to crowd on sails."[77] Finally, we can join Fox, Murdock, and others by giving the meaning "because of" to "por," thereby having Columbus haul in sails *after* traveling all afternoon rather than *before*.

Only a few sentences earlier, Columbus had written "y en amane-

70. Markham/Columbus 1893:42.
71. See, for example, Fuson 1987a:80.
72. Morison/Columbus 1963:69. Cf. Dunn 1985:44.
73. Morison/Columbus 1963:71n2.
74. Becher 1856:111–12.
75. Lyon 1986:19, as does Larimore 1987:13.
76. Dunn and Kelley/Columbus 1989:77, 77n.
77. As have Dunn and Kelley (Dunn and Kelley/Columbus 1989:77, 77n).

çiendo cargar las velas."[78] As an independent clause in itself, it offers no direct hints, but it hardly seems possible to credit that Columbus began the day by hauling in his sails when there was so much to accomplish. Some have discerned the yawning trap and decided that in this instance "cargar las velas" means "intended to" haul in sails, implying that in the event Columbus did not do so.[79] Since this is espoused in the same translations that render "por andar" in the pluperfect, one can only suspect a desperate need to make the two uses of "cargar las velas" appear as consistent as possible, if only in the intent.

But it makes little sense to require that we believe that Columbus took the trouble the next day to write what he had intended but not what he did, since no one believes that he actually spent the morning merely observing an island in the distance. A reasonable conclusion, though one based less on text than on context, is that in both these instances Columbus used "cargar las velas" to express the meaning of "to make sail," whether or not this belied the normal usage of his time.

This encourages us to translate this passage as follows: "I hoisted sails in order to go all the rest of that day until night." This has the dual advantage of making grammatical as well as contextual sense, however much it might interfere with one hypothesis or another. Doing so necessarily lends support to the idea that the island that was five to seven leagues away at dawn was not the same island toward which Columbus sailed throughout the afternoon.

To close on a less apocalyptic note, we might point out that the phrase "aquel día" (that day) bears attention. Since the day in question was allegedly the day preceding the writing of the entry, alluding to it as "that day" seems a very remote form of address indeed, as though the day and the entry were actually separated by a great deal more than twenty-four hours. It is not a point to belabor, but it seems to be yet another incongruity in a passage already swarming with them.

porque aun no pudiera haber andado al cabo del güeste   Matters become even more entangled at this point, along with the prose of the diario. The issue revolves around the likely meaning of "aun" in this context. For reasons to be noted later, this has often been translated as "otherwise," but its more common, and almost polar, meaning is "still." However it is

78. Alvar/Columbus 1976, 2:59n116; Guillén y Tato 1951:49; Lyon 1986:19n31.
79. Fox 1882:358; Murdock 1884:454; Fuson 1987a:80.

translated, there is a dilemma.[80] If it is translated as "otherwise," the passage tells us that Columbus "cargué las velas" because he had no alternative if he was to cover an unspecified distance and reach what he called "the cape of the west" at some unspecified time, probably nightfall. On the other hand, translating "aun" as "still" allows us to make sense of "cargar" as "to haul in," but any such interpretation seems to be belied by Columbus's statement shortly afterward that he had reached "the said cape" shortly "before sunset."[81]

This "cape of the west" is intriguing in its own right. Its description underlines the retrospectivity of the text at this point, since Columbus would have recognized it as a "cape" only after he had rounded it. Beyond that is the real question: just where was it located? Was it on the island that was ten leagues or more in length or was it not? And how did it relate to the larger island apparently still looming to the westward? Again, there is nothing in the text to help us resolve any of these questions.

A la qual puse nombre la isla de Sancta María de la Concepción   At this point, when to judge from the text Columbus was sailing toward "the cape of the west," he casually recorded that he had bestowed the name Santa María de la Concepción on . . . what? As it is constructed, "la qual" cannot refer to "cabo" since it is feminine while "cabo" is masculine. But why use such an odd construction in any case, one without visible antecedent? Literally translated, always a good start, the text reads: "to which I put the name the island of Santa María de la Concepción." This is hardly a model of elegance and naturally has drawn rather free translations.[82] A typical translation is that of Jane, Lyon, and Dunn and Kelley: "to which island I gave the name of Santa María de la Concepción."[83] This may be what Columbus had in mind, but he fell short of saying it.[84] The questions remains as to the idiosyncratic use of "a la qual" and the antecedent of "qual."

80. Thacher 1903–4, 1 : 599 ("because"); Cioranescu/Columbus 1961 : 48 ("de toute façon"); Jane/Columbus 1960 : 29 ("otherwise"); Fuson 1987a : 80 ("otherwise"); Dunn and Kelley/Columbus 1989 : 79 ("[otherwise]").
81. Alvar/Columbus 1976, 2 : 59; Dunn and Kelley/Columbus 1989 : 78.
82. Becher 1856 : 113 ("qual" = "cape").
83. Jane/Columbus 1960 : 29; Lyon 1986 : 19; Dunn and Kelley/Columbus 1989 : 79.
84. In this case Morison/Columbus (1963 : 69) is more faithful to the original.

Another question demands attention as well: Why did Columbus wait until this point in the text to record this piece of information? On the one hand, if only one island monopolized his attention all day, he had seen and been sailing toward and along this island since the previous evening. On the other hand, he had not yet landed, which would have been a more natural time for christening activities. The very next day he named Fernandina—or at least recorded that he had done so—before disembarking there, in fact while only halfway to it. A few days later he did the same for Samoet/Isabela. Clearly, Columbus's habit was to name islands he intended to visit before the fact.[85] By any standard, then, the placement of this sentence is at least as odd as its wording.

y cuasi al poner del sol sorgía acerca del dicho cabo por saber si había allí oro This has the virtue of being the least ambiguous sentence of this portion of the entry for 15 October. Here Columbus actually ties one statement to another by using "dicho" (said) in referring to the cape, and for this we must be grateful. We could be even more grateful if he had located the cape or had described it in any way. In particular, we might appreciate more detail on what he meant by "acerca."

Con todo, mi voluntad era de no passar por ninguna isla de que no tomase possessión, puesto que, tomado de una, se puede dezir de todas This sentence has been the linchpin of all one-island theorists, who believe that here Columbus made a categorical statement to the effect that to see an island was to name it.[86] It is difficult, nonetheless, to understand the basis for such a belief, since the statement is not so much unambiguous as self-contradictory. To begin with, it is not clear why Columbus began his statement with "con todo" (nevertheless) unless he meant to say that he would claim even those islands populated by ungrateful Indians.

Taken as a whole, the statement is less a determination to claim (and name?) every island that crossed his path than an apologia for not doing so. At this point Columbus may have remembered his comprehensive plans and promises as stated in the prologue to the log. After all, he chose

85. Which lends weight to the belief that Columbus named more islands than are recorded in the diario.

86. Fox 1882:376, 393; Blake 1892:543; Thacher 1903–4, 1:597; Gould 1927: 417n; Roukema 1959:196; Keegan and Mitchell 1987a:104.

to use the past tense ("era") instead of the present ("es").[87] By going on to advance the synecdochic—and rather specious—argument that one island equaled every island in this respect, Columbus was in effect opening the door for *not* claiming one by one each of the islands he was passing.[88] Given the circumstances, it would have been an entirely pragmatic decision. Aiming for the mainland of east Asia, he must already have felt that a surfeit, perhaps potentially an infinity, of disappointing islands stood in his way. To claim each would have been time-consuming and frivolous.

In short, this statement is, if anything, license to believe that Columbus had bypassed, and presumably expected to bypass, any number of islands that he thought were sparsely populated or, worse yet, lacking in gold. If the statement is to be used, it can be mobilized only to support arguments that Columbus passed one or more islands during 15 October that he forbore to name.[89] He may well have intended to linger and baptize but abandoned the notion on seeing a larger island to the west. Remember that he had just the day before permitted the Indians to name a hundred islands or more for him, evidently without feeling obliged to resort to the litany of saints himself.

Y di luego la vela para ir a la otra isla grande que yo vía al güeste . . . Here we briefly exceed our warrant by passing on to the events of 16 October, though they were recorded as part of the entry dated 15 October. The passage above presents a pair of incongruities. It is odd that Columbus would refer at this point to "the other large island" to the west, a phrase he repeated several times later. Why "other" unless he was already at the first large island to the west, which he had spotted some time during the afternoon of the previous day?[90]

His use of "vía" reinforces the notion. If Columbus had any sense of verb tense (and if he did not, the diario can bear no scrutiny at all), he would probably have used the pluperfect here, "había visto," if he were referring to the same island he had seen the day before. In fact, Lyon

---

87. Fuson (1987a:80) translates "era" as "is," but all other translations use "was."

88. Dunn and Kelley reject the force of such an argument, though with some misgivings (Dunn and Kelley/Columbus 1989:79n).

89. Becher 1856:112; Link and Link 1958:13–14; Perez 1987:39–41; Ramos Gómez 1989:18.

90. With all due respect to Dunn, who believes that the use of "the" implies the island already mentioned (1985:44).

translates "vía" as "had seen" but this is unwarranted.[91] Referring to the morning of 16 October, Columbus said he "saw" to the west "the other island," and the straightforward past tense opens the door for believing that he had come to see it only recently—as though, for instance, it had been hidden by the cape at which he had anchored.[92]

Adopted literally, the reading of the diario inclines rather heavily to the view that Columbus reached an island about noon on 15 October and sailed along it until he spotted another large or larger island to the west, toward which he sailed, reaching it before nightfall. He then anchored overnight at a "cape" somewhere on this latter island. After a bit of visiting, he sailed the next day toward another, even larger ("grandísima") island, again to the west. The first island he neither landed at nor named; the second he named Santa María de la Concepción, and the third, apparently the largest of all, he was to baptize Fernandina.

While this much seems clear enough, if distressingly minimal, the entry is undeniably riddled with ambiguities, contradictions, false starts, and lacunae while being largely unadorned with time or sequence signs.[93] Las Casas already noticed this. Taviani, however, tries valiantly to wring support for a one-island theory by asserting that Las Casas "demolished" the notion of two islands in his *Historia*, "without leaving any space for doubts."[94] In fact, Las Casas's account there is one of the most foreshortened of any in the *Historia*, being confined to only a few words for activities on 15 October per se. Except as it related to the Indians, almost nothing survived Las Casas's editorial scalpel, as though he preferred to grasp Ariadne's thread rather than wander through the maze that is Columbus's prose. However, to take what Las Casas did manage to say as support for the notion that Columbus saw only Santa María and Fernandina on 15 October is outrageously disingenuous. Note, for instance, that Las Casas stated that Columbus "arrived" ("llegó") at the island he named

91. Lyon 1986:21, followed in this case by Judge (1986:592).

92. Morison translated "vía" as "saw" without drawing any conclusions (Morison/Columbus 1963:70). Other translations include Thacher 1903–4, 1:539 ("saw"); Markham/Columbus 1893:45 ("in sight"); Jane/Columbus 1960:30 ("saw"); Cioranescu/Columbus 1961:49 ("j'aperçevois," or the imperfect). Fuson (1987a:81) does not translate the word at all, perhaps because his scheme makes this island not visible to Columbus at this point.

93. The problem is mentioned in passing in Fuson 1985:68.

94. Taviani 1987b:206.

Santa María at sunset. By the one-island theory this would be the island Columbus had already set his course for the previous evening, yet the diario says that he arrived at *that* island about noon.[95] If Las Casas thought that it was the very same island along which Columbus had been coasting all afternoon, it would have been a very anticlimactic "arrival" indeed, and one that Las Casas would better have described as anchoring or debarkation. But he did not.

VI

Although I end my analysis of the diario and its interpretation at this point, textual and interpretative questions hardly abate. By way of illustrating the continuing nature of the problems, let me cite just a few of these in the remainder of the diario entry dated 15 October. Columbus expressed his overnight stay at the elusive "cape of the west" rather peculiarly as "I remained [there] until today Tuesday" ("estuve hasta hoy martés"), as though the stay had been of much longer duration. Later he referred to "de otro cabo" (from another, or the other, cape) as if it was a follow-up reference, but as far as we can tell, this cameo is the only appearance of this particular landform.[96] Perhaps more detail was in the log but had been transcribed out of existence along its way to becoming the diario.

Toward the end of the entry, Columbus recorded that he had left Santa María de la Concepción about 10 A.M., but the entry for the following day, which manages to duplicate much of this entry, has him depart about "midday" ("medio día"). In the long run, discrepancies of a couple of hours may not matter, but most attempts to follow Columbus around the West Indies find it necessary to put almost every minute to some use. Finally, in the entry for 15 October Columbus noted that the waters around Fernandina were always ("siempre") very clear, even near shore, and were too deep to measure as near as two lombard shots (500 to 600

95. Las Casas 1951, 1:210; Alvar/Columbus 1976, 2:59.

96. Some translators have evaded the issue by bestowing an idiosyncratic meaning on "cabo" in this case while translating it as "cape" or "point" elsewhere in the diario: Markham/Columbus 1893:43 ("another direction"); Jane/Columbus 1960:29 ("another direction"); Cioranescu/Columbus 1961:49 ("autre côte"); Molander 1985:129 ("another direction"); Lyon 1986:21 ("the other cape"); Fuson 1987a:81 ("another cabo").

yards?) offshore.[97] Yet in the following day's entry he admitted that he had still not arrived in time to anchor safely near shore.[98]

When Columbus left Santa María de la Concepción, there was a southeast wind, yet he was unable to traverse the distance westward between Santa María and Fernandina because "all that day it was calm."[99] Finally, according to the entry for 15 October, the large island was nine leagues due west of Santa María, but in the entry for the following day that distance had shrunk to eight leagues while the bearing had shifted slightly—it was now "almost due west."[100] The trouble with either observation is that it is extraordinarily unlikely that Columbus would have regarded Long Island (most people's Fernandina) as either "due west" or "almost due west" of Rum Cay. While it is true that its northerly tip is roughly due west, the body of Long Island runs in a large arc from due west to due south. Under the circumstances, Columbus's reiterated claims that Fernandina was ever west of Santa María de la Concepción makes little sense if we postulate that the latter was Rum Cay and the former was Long Island.

Throughout the day's entry, then, we are left wondering whether Columbus was continuously talking about the same two islands or whether more were involved. In any event the signs of the working and reworking of the text of the diario (and the log?) are unmistakable, as is the mangling that has resulted. It becomes pointless to use these entries to determine niceties of direction and distance, or even to take Columbus's descriptions of places and things as the basis for drawing reasonable inferences. Yet no entry in the diario has been ploughed more often and with greater determination—and with good reason, because more than any other it underlies the character of the further track of Columbus. It is a burden that this troubled text cannot bear.

97. The range of a lombard shot is disputed by modern authorities. I use the figures suggested in Dunn and Kelley/Columbus 1989:53n.

98. See the comment on the effects of Columbus's apparently being becalmed in Alvar/Columbus 1976, 2:64n134.

99. For various translations of this, see Markham/Columbus 1893:46; Thacher 1903–4, 1:541; Roukema 1959:107; Jane/Columbus 1960:32; Cioranescu/Columbus 1961:52; Morison/Columbus 1963:72; Lyon 1986:27; Fuson 1987a:83; Dunn and Kelley/Columbus 1989:87.

100. On the sightlines from Rum Cay to Long Island, see chapter 8 above.

17. The Deafening Sounds of Silence

The brightest flashes in the world of thought are
incomplete until they have been proved to have their
counterparts in the world of fact.   JOHN TYNDALL

Until this point I have been concerned with the written sources for Columbus's first voyage. These are all texts, of course, but the concept of Text has recently been expanded, notably by literary critics, to encompass a much wider range of objects—for instance, paintings, buildings, even entire cities. While it is hardly necessary to subscribe to the notion that all the material world is amenable to textual analysis, it is reasonable, in fact necessary, in closing to treat certain types of archaeological evidence as texts as well. Archaeologists' interest in contributing to the debate over the landfall and its associated events has increased measurably in the past decade and in the process archaeological data have become the latest sources for the first voyage. Determining their contextual and epistemological validity requires, then, much the same approach that has been applied to written documents throughout this study.

It is only to be expected that archaeology would become involved in the landfall debate since there is a widespread feeling among archaeologists that archaeological evidence and literary evidence can readily be made to complement and illuminate each other, despite a wealth of experience to the contrary. Several years ago, in referring to the outer limits of archaeological inference, Lewis Binford, one of the most influential contemporary archaeologists, said, "The practical limitations on our knowledge of the past are not inherent in the nature of the archaeological record; the limitations lie in our methodological naiveté, in our lack of principles determining the relevance of archaeological remains to propositions regarding processes and events of the past."[1]

The notion that students of the past are at the mercy of nothing more than their own presumably temporary shortcomings is no doubt immensely heartening, but serious grounds to sustain it are as absent as most evidence about the past. Even more than historians, archaeologists are limited both in the survival of things past and in their ability to uncover and make contextual sense of them. Archaeology is concerned with the fortuitous survival of evidence. As a result, we immediately face questions about the degree to which archaeological evidence can be objective, unambiguous, and most of all representative—large questions that have occupied the profession since its beginning without being resolved.[2]

Despite the growing interest, relatively little archaeological work has been carried out in the Bahamas, but this has not dulled scholars' enthusiasm for the results. At least one recent archaeological argument in this regard is a true argument from silence, while others are arguments that are overwhelmed by silence. In the first case, Power, who advocates Grand Turk as the first landfall, argues that Guanahaní was sparsely populated. Lo and behold, excavations on Grand Turk had turned up almost nothing which might suggest a substantial pre-Columbian settlement there, and Power proceeded to turn this apparent sow's ear into a silk purse by suggesting that this state of affairs actually lends credibility to his hypothesis.[3] Somehow it does not, since we have no idea of the population density of Guanahaní.

Not surprisingly, Watlings Island has so far been the object of greatest attention by archaeologists, and some finds have resulted. At one site some beads, buckles, and a coin have been unearthed, and these, the site's excavators argue, "correspond closely" to the trade goods mentioned in the diario, and they conclude from this that "the archaeological evidence is extremely persuasive as corroborative evidence" that Watlings Island and Guanahaní are one and the same piece of real estate.[4] Neil E. Sealey's

1. Binford 1968:23.
2. An excellent study of these aspects of archaeological reasoning is Salmon 1982, but see also Kelley and Hanen 1988:225–74 and passim. Shanks and Tilley 1987: 36–44, 110–15, is particularly trenchant on the inclination to tailor data to fit theory. Snodgrass 1989:36–66 also has some pertinent remarks.
3. Power 1985:156.
4. Brill 1987:266 and passim.

enthusiasm carries him much farther. He claims that the discovery of these artifacts "immeasurably improve[s]" the "case for Watlings Island" because the artifacts are reminiscent of those mentioned in the diario.[5] Charles A. Hoffman, on the other hand, examined materials unearthed on Watlings Island and found them wanting: "They did not include any-thing to support a conclusion that Columbus landed there." He did not indicate what would have.[6]

The idea that the archaeological evidence supports Watlings Island, which is extremely popular, would be valid only if three other things were true: that no other such trinkets were ever traded in the area; that, once traded, trinkets invariably remain *in situ*; and that alternative sites in the Bahamas had been thoroughly exacavated and found to harbor no such articles. In fact, of course, not one of the three is the case, nor ever can be. As the excavators readily admit, this is the first serious archaeo-logical exploration in the area, and they realize too that trade goods move easily from place to place so that, once other work is carried out, such caches may be found at several other sites. This is particularly to be ex-pected since, while the goods found on Watlings Island may "correspond closely" to the diario's description of the goods Columbus brought along to trade, this is only because they were the type of cheap and gaudy European trade goods that flooded the market in the New World and in Africa and Asia as well.[7] Their very lack of distinctiveness destroys their heuristic value.

Turning Power's argument on its head, Hoffman argues that Grand Turk must be rejected as the landfall because he "found no sites there."[8] As an argument from silence, this is slightly more appealing than that of Power but far from even mildly convincing, and indeed it is somewhat presumptuous in implying that such sites would necessarily have been discovered had they existed.

5. Sealey 1987:10.

6. Hoffman 1987b:96.

7. For the ubiquity of glass beads as a trade commodity in the New World, see Francis 1984. Fitzpatrick 1989 adopts the same argument in order to posit a Roman presence in the very north of Scotland. For an argument against such an approach in the case of the De Soto expedition, see Henige 1990b.

8. Hoffman 1987a:239. Sears and Sullivan (1978:10) and Taviani (1987b:215) re-peat the argument against Grand Turk.

As it happens, in a fine example of archaeological evidence reversing itself, both facets of this sterile argument have been shattered by the recent discovery of a small Lucayan site on the southern coast of Grand Turk.[9] This may have surprised some and chagrined others, but one thing that this discovery seems to indicate is the quite unsurprising fact that sufficiently intensive excavation is likely to locate relevant sites on virtually every Bahamian island and thereby to obviate all arguments from silence in this respect.

Hoffman concludes by arguing that Long Bay on Watlings Island is "a site of Spanish contact with American Indians" between 1492 and 1560 and goes on to close his discussion with what appears to be a rhetorical question: "If Samana Cay is the real San Salvador, . . . how did all those historic artifacts get on present-day San Salvador [Watlings Island]?"[10] If possible answers to this question elude Hoffman, they are not likely to escape others.

Archaeology has been deployed to support other postulated points along Columbus's route. Both Judge, who favors Samana, and most partisans of Watlings Island favor Long Island as Fernandina, Columbus's third named port of call. Signs of Lucayan occupation have been found on Long Island, and although this can hardly be called earthshaking, both Judge and Obregón take heart in the circumstance. For Judge it is no less than "a vital clue" that Long Island is Fernandina, and Obregón could hardly agree more.[11]

Very much the same kind of argument has been dragooned into the service of Conception Island. Extensive digging there recently turned up a shard from a Spanish olive jar, and the principal excavator, Steven Mitchell, believes that this must have been deposited on the island no later than 1512, by which time, report has it, the Bahamas had already been depopulated as a result of Spanish slave raids. Mitchell goes on to assert that Conception Island now "has to be considered more seriously as the first landfall" because of, among other things, "prehistoric Indian activity and the Spanish pottery."[12]

9. Keegan et al. 1990.

10. Hoffman 1987a:244. Keegan 1989:36 implicitly asks the same question for both Long Island and Watlings Island.

11. Judge 1986:597; Obregón 1987a:192–93.

12. Dumene 1988.

By the latter criterion, no island in the Bahamas would be exempt from such arguments. Two possibilities come readily to mind as possible alternative explanations. The first is that the inhabitants of most Bahamian islands came into possession of such standard Spanish trade goods quite independently of any Spanish visits to the particular locale. The other, even more likely, explanation is that the Spanish left behind such artifacts on various occasions after the landfall and Columbus's first voyage. For instance, on his trip to Florida, Juan Ponce de León stopped at several of the Bahamas, and there is no reason to assume that his itinerary was an unusual one for the time and place.[13] In any case, the depopulation of the Bahamas could have occurred only by means of Spanish visits to spirit away the inhabitants. To put it another way, whereas Columbus visited Guanahaní only once, there were certainly scores, if not hundreds, of visits to the Bahamas in the twenty years or so after that. To suggest in the circumstances that any piece of Spanish manufacture could possibly lend credibility to any given island being Guanahaní can only be ill advised.

Archaeology simply does not employ an "objective approach," as Keegan and Mitchell would have us believe.[14] The pattern of archaeological discoveries in the Bahamas, as elsewhere, primarily reflects, not the objective situation, but a course of action determined by historiographical contingencies outside the discipline. Properly conducted excavation is expensive and time-consuming and must exercise rigorous selectivity. Watlings Island has received more attention from archaeologists because it has long been the most popular candidate for Guanahaní, so archaeologists hope that exacavations there will present a better opportunity for success. Finding certain artifacts as the result of such excavations then becomes little more than a self-fulfilling prophecy. It is possible, even likely, that conducting similarly extensive work on other islands would produce much the same results. Until that work is done, it is fruitless to draw conclusions about the identity of Guanahaní based on the first results of archaeology.

In fact, Keegan and Mitchell go on to display a lack of objectivity by

13. To date, the best account of Ponce de León's expedition is Davis 1935, but James E. Kelley, Jr., has prepared for publication a new translation of the primary source, the account in Herrera 1934–57, 3:317–26.

14. Keegan and Mitchell 1987a:102.

suggesting that "evidence of Lucayan settlements reported by Columbus must be found in the appropriate locations," by which, of course, they mean locations posited by modern hypotheses.[15] They further speak of "areas that lacked villages" on the grounds that Columbus failed to mention any.[16] Such procedures carry with them a pair of assumptions that cannot be validated—that Columbus's failure to mention habitations is evidence that none existed, and that certain modern interpretations of Columbus's route are demonstrably accurate. The latter, of course, is the very point ostensibly being tested!

Keegan and Mitchell conclude by noting that the finding of Spanish ceramics on Long Island, Little Exuma, and Acklins Island "provides equivocal support" for the route postulated by Morison, "while demonstrating the possible influence of prehistoric exchange networks."[17] In this formulation the second phrase all but cancels the first, which itself offers nothing new or exciting. As a whole, the statement encapsulates well the meager and ambiguous, though ambitious, role archaeology sees itself playing in determining Columbus's landfall and subsequent route to Cuba.

But separating the two sets of arguments could only lead to inconclusive results, not least because the paucity of information Columbus provided allows only that possible archaeological correlations be suggested without permitting any measure of serious proof. The effort to identify *any* modern site with references in the diario is inevitably doomed to fail.

If archaeology is a science, it can only be the quintessential science of the silent. It operates on a dismayingly slender data base, even in the best of circumstances, and its own history demonstrates emphatically that one of its recurring and significant themes is the constant scramble to fit new discoveries, most of them quite unexpected, into existing theories. This

15. Keegan and Mitchell 1987a:102. Note that the very title of this paper, "The archeology of Christopher Columbus' voyage through the Bahamas, 1492," denotes a certain partisanship by eliminating Grand Turk and the Caicos from consideration.

16. Keegan and Mitchell 1987a:104.

17. Keegan and Mitchell 1987a:107. Along the way the authors assert that "conclusive evidence is provided by the identification of the Delectable Bay Complex of sites [on Acklins Island] as Samaot," that is, as Columbus's fourth named island, Isabela, certainly a non sequitur.

need for reshuffling seems to apply especially to settlement patterns and to dating.

The historiography of the Bantu expansion in Africa, as well as the peopling of the Indian subcontinent, the Pacific islands, and the Americas shows all too well the effects that unanticipated discoveries can have on theories postulated on the basis of previously known evidence. The best-known such case, though, is the role that archaeological evidence and interpretation have played in casting into doubt the Old Testament view of the Israelite "conquest" of Palestine.

Much the same has been true for archaeological dating, for which, if anything, the matter intensifies. In the past century both the absolute and the relative chronologies of the Ancient Near East have changed frequently, and ultimately dramatically, in order to conform time and again to new archaeological data. Opinions on the dating, configuration, and even the existence of several dynasties of early and medieval India have ebbed and flowed in light of the testimony of newly discovered epigraphic and numismatic materials. In yet another case, archaeology has shown that the once-accepted chronology of early Japanese history, supported in its turn by other archaeological evidence, actually begins nearly a millennium too early.[18]

These cases are only a few of perhaps hundreds of instances in which archaeological interpretations hastily built on shifting foundations have been overturned rather than confirmed by new information. Oddly, despite this archaeologists often overlook the experience of their own discipline when seeking to throw new light on the history of others.

I

The silences of the diario have naturally come in for explicit attention by those intent on using them to defend one line of reasoning or another.[19] The argument from silence is a legitimate weapon in the historian's arsenal and one that, if anything, has generally been underrated.[20] After all, si-

18. In most of these cases, the literature is too voluminous and well known to require comment. For the Bantu expansion, see Vansina 1975–76; for India, see Henige 1975; and for early Japan, see Kiley 1973 and Barnes 1988.

19. See, for example, chapter 12 on the question of fresh water.

20. Lange 1966; Henige 1987:65–69.

lence is always the majority voice from the past, and the diario certainly contains its full measure of unexpected and unexplained silences. But the argument is a technique that needs careful handling. Silence in the historical record is merely interesting unless and until it can be shown to be both intentional and incongruent with its environment. By no means is the absence of evidence necessarily the evidence of absence.

The task of demonstrating this is seldom an easy one, requiring as it does the scouring of masses of sources in the hope of finding nothing in them. Moreover, the argument from silence comes only with a limited-time warranty since, no matter how well constructed, it is always at risk of being overthrown. Unhappily, the instances in which the argument has been applied to the landfall problem serve only to emphasize its disadvantages.

Arne Molander, an advocate of Egg Island, loses no opportunity to point out that Guanahaní cannot be Watlings Island because Columbus wrote, "I saw no animal of any kind except parrots on this island" ("Ninguna bestia de ninguna manera vide, salvo papagayos en esta Isla").[21] While interesting, even emphatic, this observation hardly forecloses discussion, because Columbus incorporated it into his first entry in the New World, 12 October, when his surveillance of any fauna on Guanahaní was confined to the very short period of time—perhaps only a few minutes—he spent claiming the island for Spain.[22] No doubt there was much that Columbus had not yet seen by that time, in fact that he never saw, and so from this statement we dare conclude nothing.

Some might wish to suggest that Columbus would have corrected himself on this point if he later discovered other animal life on Guanahaní, but the diario offers numerous examples in which Columbus declined to do just that. In any case, it is quite possible that Columbus never did see any other forms of animal life there, but since he apparently confined his observing to the vantage point of shipboard, this signifies even less.[23] And, of course, animal habitats change over time just like other forms of

21. Molander 1981:6; Molander 1985:118–119; Molander 1987:144–45. Cf. Alvar/Columbus 1976, 2:53, 53n; Dunn and Kelley/Columbus 1989:68.

22. On the amount of time Columbus spent on (rather than at) Guanahaní, see chapter 13.

23. On the shifting definitions of iguanas and other exotic fauna of the New World, see Gerbi 1985:418–22.

life, a point Molander implicitly acknowledges.[24] Molander's approach is
the argument from silence at its most vulnerable.[25]

24. Molander 1987:151. Some (e.g., Morison 1942, 1:305) even believe that Guanahaní itself was named by the Indians in honor of the iguana.

25. Or perhaps not; Ober actually used Columbus's statement to support his own
choice of Watlings Island (1893:90). When Columbus first mentioned iguanas (alliga-
tors?) in the diario on 21 October, he was remarkably nonchalant if this was the very
first occasion on which he had encountered what was for him a very different species
of animal. He called it a "serpent" ("sierpe"), mentioned that it was about seven palms,
or five to six feet long, and that they had killed it and preserved its skin for royal
edification. This lack of descriptive detail contrasts starkly with, for example, the
wealth of such information on the royal standards discussed above.

18. Conclusion

The proper task of criticism is to unsettle; not to yearn for an end to interpretation, but to emphasize and take pleasure in all the contradictory and self-canceling notions that an unbound text inflicts on a reader.

LAWRENCE LIPKING

The approach I have adopted in this book has its own critical foundation, and while I find it effective and convincing, it is not the only method that can be cogently defended. Still, it is to be regretted how often similar views expressed in the past have been accorded the opprobrium of "hypercriticism" or even of outright heresy. Such reactions can only reflect a cozy conviction that the more congenial an argument happens to be, the less it needs to be inspected, or even that it is unedifying to try to differentiate among arguments that are tied firmly to the evidence, those that are no more than tethered, and those that barely keep the evidence in sight. In fact, the degree to which Columbian scholarship has polarized is astonishing, with one extremity attracting the persistent believers, the other the determined unbelievers. It is no more astonishing, however, than the degree to which the diario has been treated as some kind of alter ego of Columbus. In this scheme of things the diario has become invested with all the emotions and passions that Columbus and his discoveries have evoked. Here I have tried to remove the diario from this debilitating context by granting it a polite divorce from its own future.

Recently a reviewer criticized an author for attempting to destroy long-standing wisdom on a matter while being "feeble and vague" in "constructing an alternative hypothesis."[1] In the present study I have rejected the notion that any hypothesis, no matter how estranged from the weight of evidence, has a preemptive right to be preferred to an open mind and

1. Kennedy 1988:55.

to be allowed to claim allegiance in the intellectual marketplace by default, and even to become orthodoxy.

On the contrary, I find the position of Charles Darwin far more attractive when he wrote that "[t]o kill an error is as good a service as, and sometimes even better than, the establishing a new truth or fact."[2] Consequently I have adopted a Pyrrhonist skepticism in looking at the evidence available for Columbus's first voyage.[3] This holds that no seeker after truth should expect to be unencumbered by doubt and that a healthy skepticism and an eye for incongruities are indispensable tools in all historical inquiry. Pyrrhonist skepticism does not assert the impossibility of attaining certain knowledge, but it does question the adequacy of our grounds for holding *particular* beliefs. In doing so it assumes that, for those deprived of revelation, the truth can be reached only by dialectic and interrogation.

Inevitably, then, Pyrrhonist critics lay stringent standards on demonstrating success and prefer to suspend judgment until those standards can be met. It follows that they lay particular weight on understanding that, while inference can render a conclusion credible, it can never *require* that conclusion, because it is never possible to be sure that other evidence does not exist that would invalidate even the most persuasive hypothesis.

Pyrrhonists are disquieted when they encounter generalizations that cannot be tested. They regard it as illicit to make a series of less, or even least, likely assumptions, all supporting a given presupposition, for they recognize this as ideology in embryo. Nor can they accept far-reaching arguments derived solely from anecdotal evidence. Finally, they are likely to consider it both bad policy and bad manners to regard a lack of evidence against a hypothesis to be evidence in favor of it. And, while it would be too much to say that Pyrrhonism is a species of pessimism, most Pyrrhonists would marvel at the confident statements that honeycomb the literature on Columbus's first voyage.

Despite these reservations, the Pyrrhonian critic refrains from rejecting such attitudes, arguments, and practices out of hand because to do so would resemble too closely the very dogmatism that epitomizes them. Even so, they would surely recognize that the most worrisome aspect of the questions raised here is not that there are at present no answers to them but that there are no real prospects of answers. Of course, historians

2. Darwin to A. Stephen Wilson, 5 March 1879, in Darwin 1903, 2:422.
3. For Pyrrhonism see, most accessibly, Naess 1968.

should never feel that the unproductive experience of the past is sufficient reason to abandon the search for new evidence, but that experience scarcely permits us to proceed as if we have already found it.

We have seen how contrary this epistemological stance is to the course of the study of Columbus's first voyage. Three strategies underlie and sustain the latter. First, and on a heroic scale, there is the tendency to pick and choose testimony from the diario solely to satisfy particular modern predispositions and in subservience to grand designs. To that end this enterprise, buoyed up by a belief in what Columbus really meant to say,[4] routinely imputes mistranscriptions, misrepresentations, and misinterpretations to all and sundry in total disregard of the content and integrity of the text of the diario. With such a modus operandi it has become altogether too easy to declare victory over both the text and competing interpretations.

Inextricably entwined with this methodology is the habit of disregarding the fact that even false hypotheses elicit some true consequences while ignoring its unforgiving corollary that a single false consequence suffices to invalidate a hypothesis. Once this illicit conversion takes place, entire hypotheses are held to be validated by a single apparently true consequence. Associated with this insouciant approach is its apparently inseparable companion, the practice of taking *possible* consequences to be *true* ones.

A final kindred tactic is to assume that any assumption whatever is valid "in the absence of any contrary evidence."[5] In this extraordinary view of things, it is inevitable that these approaches result in displaying Columbus as possessed of uncanny skills in navigation and observation, and even in exposition. But a close and disinterested study of the text of the diario not only fails to warrant such flights of fancy, it reveals a text that is a composite of many hands, written and rewritten with many purposes in mind and transcribed far too frequently for comfort. Consequently, the diario resembles nothing so much as a kaleidoscope that with each turning glints with a different light and whose essence is inextricably

4. The exemplar of this approach is Roukema, who postulated two errors in a single sentence in the diario and went on to justify his procedure by asserting that "[p]resumably Columbus meant to say" what Roukema was to say for him (1959:105). As I suggested earlier, this habit of altering Columbus's statements must have begun no later than the first known transcription of the diario in the summer of 1493.

5. Cook and Borah 1979:152.

bound up with the perspective of the observer. And, like a prism, the diario not only refracts its source but also disperses it from a continuous entity to discrete parts. Or perhaps the diario more closely reflects Proteus, who was able to change shape at will in order to avoid answering unwanted questions until Menelaus, privy to special information, was able to extract the necessary answers from him.[6] Whatever metaphor one prefers to apply, it is clear that the diario has succeeded all too well in preserving its secrets, though it may yet meet its Menelaus.

6. For Menelaus and Proteus, see the *Odyssey* IV, 385–570.

The Text of the Diario, 11/12 to 15 October 1492

What follows is the full text of the diario from the
beginning of the entry for 11/12 October 1492 to the end
of the entry for 15 October. The text follows the
modernized Spanish in Alvar/Columbus 1976, 2 : 44–63.
Those interested in the diplomatic text should consult
Alvar/Columbus 1976, 1 : 84–93, or Dunn and Kelley/
Columbus 1989 : 56–85.

Jueves, 11.° de otubre.

Navegó al güesudueste. Tuvieron mucha mar y más que en todo el viaje habían tenido. Vieron pardelas y un junco verde junto a la nao. Vieron los de la carabela Pinta una caña y un palo, y tomaron otro palillo labrado a lo que parecía con hierro, y un pedaço de caña y otra yerba que nace en tierra y una tablilla. Los de la carabela Niña también vieron otras señales de tierra y un palillo cargado d'escaramojos. Con estas señales respiraron y alegráronse todos. Anduvieron en este día, hasta puesto el sol, 27 leguas.

Después del sol puesto, navegó a su primer camino al güeste; andarían doze millas cada hora; y hasta dos horas después de media noche andarían 90 millas, que son 22 leguas y media. Y, porque la carabela Pinta era más velera e iba delante del Almirante, halló tierra y hizo las señas qu' el Almirante había mandado. Esta tierra vido primero un marinero que se dezía Rodrigo de Triana. Puesto que el Almirante, a las diez de la noche, estando en el castillo de popa, vido lumbre, aunque como fue cosa tan cerrada que no quiso afirmar que fuese tierra. Pero llamó a Pedro Gutiérrez, repostero [8v] d'estrados del Rey, y díxole que parecía lumbre, que mirasse él. Y así lo hizo, y vídola. Díxole también a Rodrigo Sánchez de Segovia, qu' el Rey y la Reina enviaban en el armada por veedor, el cual no vido nada porque no estaba en lugar do la pudiese ver. Des qu' el Almirante lo dixo, se vido una vez o dos, y era como una candelilla de cera que se alçaba y levantaba, lo cual a pocos pareciera ser indicio de tierra, pero el Almirante tuvo por cierto estar junto a la tierra. Por lo cual, cuando dixeron la Salve, que la acostumbraban dezir y cantar a su manera todos los marineros, y se hallaban todos, rogó, y amonestólos el Almirante que hiziesen buena guarda al castillo de proa, y mirasen bien por la tierra. Y que al que le dixese primero que vía tierra le daría luego un jubón de seda, sin las otras mercedes que los Reyes habían prometido, que eran diez mil maravedíes de juro a quien primero la viese. A las dos horas después de media noche pareció la tierra, de la cual estarían dos leguas. Amainaron todas las velas, y quedaron con el treo, que es la vela grande, sin bonetas, y pusiéronse a la corda, temporizando hasta el día viernes que llegaron a una isleta de los lucayos, que se llamaba en lengua de indios Guanahaní. Luego vieron gente desnuda, y el Almirante salió a tierra en la barca armada y Martín Alonso Pinçón y Vicente Anes, su hermano, que era capitán de la Niña. Sacó el Almirante la bandera real; y los capitanes con dos banderas de la cruz verde que llevaba el Almirante en todos los navíos por seña, con una F y una Y: encima de cada letra su corona, una de un cabo de la + y otra de otro. Puestos en tierra vieron árboles muy verdes, y aguas muchas y frutas de diversas maneras. El Almirante llamó a los dos capitanes y a los demás que saltaron en tierra, y a Rodrigo d'Escobedo, escribano de toda el armada, y a Rodrigo Sánchez de Segovia, y dixo que le diesen por fe y testimonio como él por ante todos tomaba, como de hecho tomó, possessión de la dicha [9r] isla por el Rey y por la Reina sus señores, haciendo las protestaciones que se requirían, como más largo se contiene en los testimonios que allí se hizieron por escripto. Luego se ayuntó allí mucha gente de la isla.

Esto que se sigue son palabras formales del Almirante, en su libro de su primera navegación y descubrimiento d'estas Indias: Yo (dize él) porque nos tuviesen mucha amistad, porque cognoscí que era gente que mejor se libraría y convertería a Nuestra Sancta Fe con amor que no por fuerça, les di a algunos d'ellos unos bonetes colorados y unas cuentas de vidro que se ponían al pescueço, y otras cosas muchas de poco valor, con que ovieron mucho plazer y quedaron tanto nuestros que era maravilla. Los cuales después venían a las barcas de los navíos a donde nos estábamos, nadando. Y nos traían papagayos y hilo de algodón en ovillos y azagayas y otras cosas muchas, y nos las trocaban por otras cosas que nos les dábamos, como cuentezillas de vidro y cascabeles. En fin, todo tomaban y daban de aquello que tenían de buena voluntad. Mas me pareció que era gente muy pobre de todo. Ellos andan todos desnudos como su madre los parió, y también las mujeres, aunque no vide mas de una harto moça. Y todos los que yo vi eran todos mancebos, que ninguno vide de edad de más de XXX años. Muy bien hechos, de muy fermosos cuerpos y muy buenas caras. Los cabellos gruessos cuasi como sedas de cola de caballo, y cortos. Los cabellos traen por encima de las cejas, salvo unos pocos detrás que traen largos, que jamás cortan. D'ellos se pintan de prieto, y ellos son de la color de los conarios, y ni negros ni blancos, y d'ellos se pintan de blanco, y d'ellos de colorado, y d'ellos de lo que fallan. Y d'ellos se pintan las caras, y d'ellos todo el cuerpo, y d'ellos solos los ojos, y d'ellos sólo el nariz. Ellos no traen armas ni las cognoscen, porque les amostré espadas y las tomaban por el filo, y [9v] se cortaban con ignorancia. No tienen algún fierro. Sus azagayas son unas varas sin fierro, y algunas d'ellas tienen al cabo un diente de pece, y otras de otras cosas. Ellos todos a una mano son de buena estatura de grandeza y buenos gestos, bien hechos. Yo vide algunos que tenían señales de feridas en sus cuerpos, y les hize señas qué era aquello, y ellos me amostraron cómo allí venían gente de otras islas que estaban acerca y los querían tomar y se defendían. Y yo creí, y creo, que aquí vienen de tierra firme a tomarlos por captivos. Ellos deben ser buenos servidores y de buen ingenio, que veo que muy presto dizen todo lo que les dezía. Y creo que ligeramente se harían cristianos, que me pareció que ninguna secta tenían. Yo, plaziendo a Nuestro Señor, levaré de aquí al tiempo de mi partida seis a Vuestras Altezas para que deprendan fablar. Ninguna bestia de ninguna manera vide, salvo papagayos en esta Isla. Todas son palabras del Almirante.

Sábado, 13 de otubre.

Luego que amaneció vinieron a la playa muchos d'estos hombres, todos mancebos, como dicho tengo. Y todos de buena estatura, gente muy fermosa. Los cabellos no crespos, salvo corredíos y gruessos, como sedas de caballo. Y todos de la frente y cabeça muy ancha, más que otra generación que fasta aquí haya visto. Y los ojos muy fermosos y no pequeños. Y ellos ninguno prieto, salvo de la color de los canarios. Ni se debe esperar otra cosa, pues está lestegüeste con la isla del Fierro, en Canaria, so una línea. Las piernas muy derechas, todos a una mano, y no barriga, salvo muy bien hecha. Ellos vinieron a la nao con almadías, que son hechas del pie de un árbol, como un barco luengo, y todo de un pedazo, y labrado muy a maravilla según la tierra, y grandes en que en algunos venían 40 y 45 hombres. Y otras más pequeñas, fasta haber d'ellas en que venía un

solo hombre. Remaban con una pala como de fornero, y [10r] anda a
maravilla. Y si se le trastorna, luego se echan todos a nadar y la endereçan
y vazían con calabazas que traen ellos. Traían ovillos de algodón filado y
papagayos y azagayas y otras cositas que sería tedio de escrebir, y todo
daban por cualquiera cosa que se les diese. Y yo estaba atento y trabajaba
de saber si había oro. Y vide que algunos d'ellos traían un pedaçuelo
colgado en un agujero que tienen a la nariz. Y por señas pude entender
que yendo al sur o volviendo la isla por el sur, que estaba allí un rey que
tenía grandes vasos d'ello, y tenía muy mucho. Trabajé que fuesen allá, y
después vide que no entendían en la ida. Determiné aguardar fasta mañana en la tarde y después partir para el subdueste, que según muchos
d'ellos me enseñaron dezían que había tierra al sur y al sudueste y al
norueste; y qu' estas del norueste les venían a combatir muchas vezes, y
así ir al sudueste a buscar el oro y piedras preciosas. Esta isla es bien
grande y muy llana y de árboles muy verdes y muchas aguas y una laguna
en medio muy grande, sin ninguna montaña, y toda ella verde, qu' es
plazer de mirarla. Y esta gente farto mansa, y por la gana de haber de
nuestras cosas, y teniendo que no se les ha de dar sin que den algo y no
lo tienen, toman lo que pueden y se echan luego a nadar, mas todo lo que
tienen lo dan por cualquiera cosa que les den; que fasta los pedaços de las
escudillas y de las taças de vidro rotas rescataban, fasta que vi dar 16
ovillos de algodón por tres ceotís de Portugal, que es una blanca de Castilla. Y en ellos habría más de un arroba de algodón filado. Esto defendi-
era y no dexara tomar a nadie, salvo que yo lo mandara tomar todo para
Vuestras Altezas, si hobiera en cantidad. Aquí nace en esta Isla, más por
el poco tiempo no pude dar así del todo fe. Y también aquí nace el oro
que traen colga [10v] do a la nariz; mas, por no perder tiempo, quiero ir
a ver si puedo topar a la isla de Cipango. Agora como fue noche todos se
fueron a tierra con sus almadías.

Domingo, 14 de otubre.
En amaneciendo mandé adereçar el batel de la nao y las barcas de las
carabelas, y fue al luengo de la isla, en el camino del nornordeste, para
ver la otra parte, que era de la parte del leste; qué había. Y también para
ver las poblaciones, y vide luego dos o tres, y la gente que venía todos a
la playa llamándonos y dando gracias a Dios. Los unos nos traían agua;
otros, otras cosas de comer; otros, cuando veían que yo no curaba de ir a
tierra, se echaban a la mar nadando y venían, entendíamos que nos pre-
guntaban si éramos venidos del cielo. Y vino uno viejo en el batel dentro,

y otros a vozes grandes llamaban todos hombres y mujeres: Venid a ver los hombres que vinieron del cielo; traedles de comer y de beber. Vinieron muchos y muchas mujeres, cada uno con algo, dando gracias a Dios, echándose al suelo, y levantaban las manos al cielo, y después a vozes nos llamaban que fuésemos a tierra, mas yo temía de ver una grande restinga de piedras, que cerca toda aquella isla alrededor y entremedias queda hondo, y puerto para cuantas naos hay en toda la cristiandad, y la entrada d'ello muy angosta. Es verdad que dentro d'esta cinta hay algunas baxas, mas la mar no se mueve más que dentro de un pozo. Y para ver todo esto me moví esta mañana, porque supiese dar de todo relación a Vuestras Alteas, y también adonde pudiera hazer fortaleza, y vide un pedaço de tierra que se haze como isla, aunque no lo es, en que había seis casas. El cual se pudiera atajar en dos días por isla, aunque yo no veo ser vecessario, porque esta gente es muy símplice en armas, como verán Vuestras Altezas. [11r]

De siete que yo hize tomar para les llevar y deprender nuestra fabla y volvellos. Salvo que Vuestras Altezas cuando mandaren pueden los todos llevar a Castilla o tenellos en la misma isla captivos, porque con cincuenta hombres los ternán todos sojuzgados. Y los harán hazer todo lo que quisieren. Y, después, junto a la dicha isleta están güertas de árboles, las más hermosas que yo vi, y tan verdes y con sus hojas como las de Castilla en el mes de abril y de mayo, y mucha agua. Yo miré todo aquel puerto y después me volví a la nao y di la vela, y vide tantas islas que yo no sabía determinarme a cual iría primero. Y aquellos hombres que yo tenía tomado, me dezían por señas que eran tantas y tantas que no había número y anombraron por su nombre más de ciento. Por ende yo miré por la más grande, y aquella determiné andar, y así hago, y será lexos d'esta de Sant Salvador cinco leguas; y las otras, d'ellas más; d'ellas menos. Todas son muy llanas, sin montañas y muy fértiles y todas pobladas, y se hazen guerra la una a la otra aunq' estos son muy símplices y muy lindos cuerpos de hombres.

Lunes, 15 de otubre.

Había temporejado esta noche con temor de no llegar a tierra a sorgir antes de la mañana, por no saber si la costa era limpia de baxas; y en amaneciendo cargar velas. Y como la isla fuese más lexos de cinco leguas, antes será siete, y la marea me detuvo, sería mediodía cuando llegué a la dicha isla. Y fallé que aquella haz, que es de la parte de la isla de San Salvador, se corre norte sur y han en ella 5 leguas. Y la otra, que yo seguí, se corría lestegüeste, y han en ella más de diez leguas. Y como d'esta isla vide otra mayor al güeste, cargué las velas por andar todo aquel día fasta la noche, porque aun no pudiera haber andado al cabo del güeste. A la cual puse nombre la isla de Sancta María de la Concepción, y cuasi al poner del sol sorgía acerca del dicho cabo por saber [11v] si había allí oro, porque estos que yo había hecho tomar en la isla de San Salvador me dezían que ahí traían manillas de oro muy grandes a las piernas y a los braços. Yo bien creí que todo lo que dezían era burla para se fugir. Con todo, mi voluntad era de no passar por ninguna isla de que no tomase possessión, puesto que, tomado de una, se puede dezir de todas. Y sorgí y estuve hasta hoy martes, que en amaneciendo fue a tierra con las barcas armadas; y salí, y ellos, que eran muchos, así desnudos y de la misma condición de la otra isla de San Salvador, nos dexaron ir por la isla y nos daban lo que les pedía. Y porque el viento cargaba a la traviesa sueste, no me quise detener y partí para la nao. Y una almadía grande estaba a bordo de la carabela Niña; y uno de los hombres de la isla de Sant Salvador, que en ella era, se echó a la mar y se fue en ella; y la noche de antes, a medio echando el otro, y fue atrás la almadía, la cual fugió, que jamás fue barca que le pudiese alcançar, puesto que le teníamos grande avante. Con todo, dio en tierra y dexaron la almadía; y alguno de los de mi compañía salieron en tierra tras ellos, y todos fugeron como gallinas. Y la almadía que habían dexado la llevamos a bordo de la carabela Niña, adonde ya, de otro cabo, venía otra almadía pequeña con un hombre que venía a rescatar un ovillo de algodón, y se echaron algunos marineros a la mar, porque él no quería entrar en la carabela, y le tomaron.

Y yo, qu' estaba a la popa de la nao, que vide todo, envié por él y le di un bonete colorado y unas cuentas de vidro verdes, pequeñas, que le puse al braço y dos cascabeles, que le puse a las orejas, y le mandé volver a su almadía, que también tenía en la barca, y le envié a tierra. Y di luego la vela para ir a la otra isla grande que yo vía al güeste, y mandé largar también la otra almadía que traía la carabela Niña por popa, y vide después en tierra, al tiempo de la llegada del otro a quien yo había dado las cosas susodichas y no le había querido tomar el ovillo de algodón, puesto qu' él me lo quería dar. Y todos los otros se llegaron a él y tenía a gran maravilla, y bien le pareció que [12r] éramos buena gente, y que el otro que había fugido nos había hecho algún daño y que por esto lo llevábamos. Y a esta razón usé esto con él de le mandar alargar, y le di las dichas cosas porque nos tuviese en esta estima, porque otra vez cuando Vuestras

Altezas aquí tornen a enviar no hagan mala compañía. Y todo lo que yo le di no valía cuatro maravedís.

Y así partí, que serían las diez horas, con el viento sueste, y tocaba de sur para passar a estotra isla, la cual es grandíssima, y adonde todos estos hombres que yo traigo de la de San Salvador hazen señas que hay muy mucho oro, y que lo traen en los braços en manillas, y a las piernas, y a las orejas, y al nariz y al puescueço. Y había d'esta isla de Sancta María a esta otra nueve leguas leste güeste, y se corre toda esta parte de la isla norueste sueste. Y se parece que bien habría en esta costa más de veintiocho leguas en esta faz. Y es muy llana, sin montaña ninguna, así como aquella de Sant Salvador y de Sancta María. Y todas playas sin roquedos, salvo que a todas hay algunas peñas acerca de tierra, debaxo del agua, por donde es menester abrir el ojo cuando se quiere surgir y no surgir mucho acerca de tierra, aunque las aguas son siempre muy claras y se vee el fondo. Y desviado de tierra dos tiros de lombarda, hay en todas estas islas tanto fondo, que no se puede llegar a él. Son estas islas muy verdes y fértiles y de aires muy dulces, y puede haber muchas cosas que yo no sé, porque no me quiero detener por calar y andar muchas islas para fallar oro. Y pues éstas dan así estas señas, que lo traen a los braços y a las piernas, y es oro, porque les amostré algunos pedaços del que yo tengo, no puedo errar con el ayuda de Nuestro Señor, que yo no le falle adonde nace. Y estando a medio golfo de estas dos islas—es de saber de aquella de Sancta María y d'esta grande, a la cual pongo por nombre la Fernandina—fallé un hombre solo en una almadía que se passaba de la isla de Sancta María a la Fernandina, y traía un poco de su pan, que sería tanto como [12v] el puño y una calabaça de agua, y un pedaço de tierra bermeja hecha en polvo y después amassada, y unas hojas secas, que debe ser cosa muy apreciada entr' ellos, porque ya me truxeron en San Salvador d'ellas en presente. Y traía un cestillo a su guisa en que tenía un ramalejo de cuentezillas de vidrio y dos blancas, por las cuales cognoscí que él venía de la isla de Sant Salvador, y había passado a aquella de Sancta María y se passaba a la Fernandina, el cual se llegó a la nao. Yo le hize entrar, que así lo demandaba él, y le hize poner su almadía en la nao y guardar todo lo que él traía; y le mandé dar de comer pan y miel y de beber. Y así le passaré a la Fernandina y le daré todo lo suyo, porque dé buenas nuevas de nos, por a Nuestro Señor aplaziendo, cuando Vuestras Altezas envíen acá, por aquellos que vinieren resciban honra y nos den de todo lo que hobiere.

Oviedo's Account of the Sighting of the "Light"

The following abstract is from Oviedo's Historia, *libro 2, capítulo 5 (Oviedo 1851–55, 1:23–24), based on information from members of the Pinzón faction, whose information, in more fragmented form, is also found in the Pleitos.*

E aquel mesmo dia que el almirante Colom estas palabras dixo, conosçió realmente que estaba çerca de tierra en semblante de los celajes delos cielos; é amonestó á los pilotos que si por caso las caravelas se apartassen por algun caso fortuito la una de la otra, que passado aquel trançe corriessen hácia la parte ó viento que les ordenó, para tornar á reduçirse en su conserva. E como sobrevino la noche, mandó apocar las velas y que corriessen con solos los trinquetes baxos; é andando assi, un marinero de los que yban en la capitana, natural de Lepe, dixo: *lumbre!* . . *tierra!* . . E luego un criado de Colom, llamado Salçedo, replicó diciendo: Esso ya lo ha dicho el almirante, mi señor; y encontinente Colom dixo: Rato ha que yo lo he dicho y he visto aquella lumbre que está en tierra. Y assi fue: que un jueves, á las dos horas despues de media noche, llamó el almirante à un hidalgo dicho Escobedo, repostero de estrados del Rey Cathólico, y le dixo que veía lumbre. Y otro dia de mañana, en esclaresçiendo, y á la hora que el dia antes avia dicho Colom, desde la nao capitana se vido la isla que los indios llaman Guanahani, de la parte de la tramontana ó norte. Y el que vido primero la tierra, quando ya fue de dia, se llamaba Rodrigo de Triana, á onçe dias de octubre del año ya dicho de mill é quatroçientos y noventa y dos. Y de aver salido tan verdadero el almirante, en ver la tierra en el tiempo que avia dicho, se tuvo mas sospecha que él estaba çertificado del piloto que se dixo que murió en su casa, segund se tocó de suso. Y tambien podria ser que viendo determinados á quantos con él yban para se tornar, dixesse que si en tres dias no viessen la tierra se volviessen, confiando que Dios se la enseñaria en aquel término que les daba, para no perder trabajo é tiempo.

BIBLIOGRAPHY

ABBREVIATIONS

CC   Burkhardt, Frederick. 1986. *A Columbus casebook: A supplement to* "Where Columbus found the New World." (Judge 1986). Washington, D.C.: National Geographic Society.

CW   *Columbus and his world.* Edited by Donald T. Gerace. Fort Lauderdale, Fla.: Bahamian Field Station.

IWC   *In the wake of Columbus: Islands and controversy.* Edited by Louis De Vorsey, Jr., and John Parker. Detroit: Wayne State University Press. (Also published as volume 15 [1983] of *Terrae Incognitae.*)

EDITIONS

Because of the multiplicity of modern editions of the diario, usually with very similar titles, I have included the OCLC database number in each case.

ALVAR/COLUMBUS

1976   *Diario del descubrimiento.* Edited by Manuel Alvar. 2 vols. Gran Canaria: Cabildo Insular de Gran Canaria. [4439323]

ARCE/COLUMBUS

1971   *Diario de a bordo de Cristóbal Colón.* Edited by Joaquín Arce and Manuel Gil Esteve. Alpignano, Italy: Tallone. [6808777]

ARRANZ/COLUMBUS

1985   *Diario de a bordo.* Edited by Luis Arranz. Madrid: Historia 16. [12712614]

CADDEO/COLUMBUS
1968   *Giornale di bordo di Cristoforo Colombo (1492–93).* Edited by Rinaldo Caddeo. Milan: Bompiani. [4984061] .

CIORANESCU/COLUMBUS
1961   *Oeuvres.* Edited and translated by Alexandre Cioranescu. Paris: Gallimard. [10119036]

DUNN AND KELLEY/COLUMBUS
1989   The Diario *of Christopher Columbus's first voyage to America, 1492–1493.* Edited and translated by Oliver Dunn and James E. Kelley, Jr. Norman: University of Oklahoma Press. [17775574; 17548381]

FERRO/COLUMBUS
1985   *Diario di bordo: Libro della prima navigazione e scoperta delle Indie.* Edited and translated by Gaetano Ferro. Milan: Mursia. [13399943]

GUILLÉN Y TATO/COLUMBUS
1943   *El primer viaje de Cristóbal Colón.* Edited by Julio Fernando Guillén y Tato. Madrid: Instituto Histórico de Marina. [8910238]

JANE/COLUMBUS
1960   *Journal.* Translated by Cecil Jane and edited by L. A. Vigneras. New York: C. N. Potter. [19721197]

MARAÑÓN/COLUMBUS
1965   *Diario del primer viaje de Colón.* Edited by Antonio Vilanova and Gregorio Marañón. Barcelona: Ediciones Nauta. [5457647]

MARKHAM/COLUMBUS
1893   *The journal of Christopher Columbus.* Edited by Clements R. Markham. London: Hakluyt Society. [3615973]

MORALES PADRÓN/COLUMBUS
1984   *Libro de la primera navegación.* Edited by Manuel Alvar and Francisco Morales Padrón. 2 vols. Madrid: Testimonio Compañía Editorial. [13040376]

MORISON/COLUMBUS
1963   *Journals and other documents on the life and voyages of Christopher Columbus.* Edited by Samuel Eliot Morison. New York: Heritage Press. [692582/5977424]

NAVARRETE/COLUMBUS
1825   *Colección de los viages y descubrimientos que hicieron por mar los Españoles.* Vol. 1. Edited by Martín Fernández de Navarrete. Madrid: Imprenta Real. [1515897]
1971   *Colección de documentos y manuscriptos compilados por Fer-*

nández de Navarrete. Vol. 2. Nendeln, Lichtenstein: Kraus-Thomson. [1516224]

RACCOLTA/COLUMBUS

1892   *Scritti di Cristoforo Colombo.* Edited by Cesare de Lollis. Vol. 1, part 1. Rome: Ministerio della pubblica istruzióne, 1892–94. Part of larger collection entitled *Raccolta di documenti e studi pubblicati della R. Commissione Colombiana.* [792542]

SANZ/COLUMBUS

1962   *Diario de Colón: Libro de la primera navegación y descubrimiento de las Indias.* Edited by Carlos Sanz. Madrid: n.p. [1085075]

TAVIANI/COLUMBUS

1988   *Il giornale di bordo: Libro della prima navigazione e scoperta delle Indie.* Edited by Paolo Emilio Taviani and Consuelo Varela. 2 vols. Rome: Istituto Poligrafico e Zecca dello Stato. [20098093]

VARELA/COLUMBUS

1982   *Textos y documentos completos.* Edited by Consuelo Varela. Madrid: Alianza Universidad. [9096495]

1984   *Textos y documentos completos.* Edited by Consuelo Varela. 2d ed. Madrid: Alianza Universidad. [11648336]

1989   Diario del primer y tercer viaje de Cristóbal Colón. In *Obras completas de Fray Bartolomé de las Casas,* edited by Consuelo Varela. Vol. 14. Madrid: Alianza.

STUDIES

AARSLEFF, HANS

1985   Scholarship and ideology: Jean Bédier's critique of Romantic medievalism. In *Historical studies and literary criticism,* edited by Jerome J. McGann, 93–113. Madison: University of Wisconsin Press.

ABBOTT, H. PORTER

1984   *Diary fiction: Writing as action.* Ithaca, N.Y.: Cornell University Press.

ADAMS, CHARLES KENDALL

1891   Some recent discoveries concerning Columbus. *Annual Report of the American Historical Association,* 89–99.

ADAMS, PERCY G.

1962   *Travelers and travel liars, 1660–1800.* Berkeley: University of California Press.

1983   *Travel literature and the evolution of the novel.* Lexington: University of Kentucky Press.

ALBERTIS, ENRICO ALBERTO D'
1898 *Crociera del* Corsario *a San Salvador.* Milan: Fratelli Treves.

ALLEN, JOHN L.
1987   The illy-smelling sea: Indians, information, and the early search for the Passage. *Man in the Northeast* 33 : 127–35.

ALMODÓVAR MUÑOZ, CARMEN
1986   *Antología crítica de la historiografía Cubana.* Havana: Editorial Pueblo y Educación.

ALTMAN, JOEL B.
1989   The practice of Shakespeare's text. *Style* 23 : 466–500.

ALVAREZ LÓPEZ, ENRIQUE
1945   Las plantas de América en la Europa del siglo XVI. *Revista de Indias* 6 : 221–88.

ANDRIEU, J.
1950   Pour l'explication psychologique de fautes de copiste. *Revue des Études Latines* 22 : 279–92.

ARCE FERNÁNDEZ, JOAQUÍN
1974   Problemi linguistici inerenti il diario di Cristoforo Colombo. In *Atti del I Convegno Internazionale di Studi Colombiani,* 51–90. Genoa: Civico Istituto Colombiano.

ASENSIO Y TOLEDO, JOSÉ MARÍA
1891   *Cristóbal Colón: Su vida, sus viajes, sus descubrimientos.* 2 vols. Barcelona: Espasa.

AVÉZAC-MACAYA, ARMAND D'
1873   Le livre de Ferdinand Colomb: Revue critique des allégations proposées contre son authenticité. *Bulletin de la Société de Géographie de Paris,* ser. 6, 6 : 380–403, 478–506.

BALLESTEROS Y BERETTA, ANTONIO
1945   *Cristóbal Colón y el descubrimiento de América.* Barcelona: Salvat.
1947   *Génesis del descubrimiento.* Barcelona: Salvat.

BARATA, JOÃO DA GAMA PIMENTEL
1978   The Rock of Sintra: Columbus' landfall. *Mariner's Mirror* 64 : 186–87.

BARBÓN RODRÍGUEZ, JOSÉ A.
1985   Una edición crítica de la "Historia Verdadera de la Conquista de la Nueva España" de Bernal Díaz del Castillo. *Jahrbuch für Geschichte von Staat, Wirtschaft und Gesellschaft Lateinamerikas* 22 : 1–22.

BARNES, GINA L.
1988 *Protohistoric Yamato: Archaeology of the first Japanese state.* Ann Arbor: University of Michigan Center for Japanese Studies.

BARNES, R.S.K.
1980 *Coastal lagoons: The natural history of a neglected habitat.* Cambridge: Cambridge University Press.

BARREIRO MEIRO, ROBERTO
1968 *Guanahaní.* Madrid: Instituto Histórico de la Marina.

BARROS, JOÃO DE
1945–46 *Asia.* Edited by Hernani Cidade. 4 vols. Lisbon: Agência geral das colonias.

BARROS ARAÑA, DIEGO
1892 El proyecto de canonizar a Cristóbal Colón. *Anales de la Universidad de Chile*, special issue. 53–87.

BATAILLON, MARCEL
1959 "Estas Indias" . . . hipótesis lascasiana. *Cultura Universitaria* [Caracas] 66/67:97–104.

BATELY, JANET
1988 Manuscript layout and the Anglo-Saxon Chronicle. *Bulletin of the John Rylands University Library* 70:21–43.

BAYERRI Y BERTOMEU, ENRIQUE
1961 *Colón tal cual fué: Los problemas de la nacionalidad y de la personalidad de Colón y su resolución más justificada.* Barcelona: Porter.

BAYLE, CONSTANTINO
1945 Las bulas Alejandrinas de 1493 referentes a las Indias. *Razón y fé* 572/73: 435–43.

BEALE, HOWARD K.
1925 Is the printed diary of Gideon Welles reliable? *American Historical Review* 30:547–52.

BECHER, A. B.
1856 *The landfall of Columbus on his first voyage to America.* London: J. D. Potter.

BELLIN, JACQUES NICOLAS
1773 *Description des débouquemens qui sont au nord de l'isle Saint-Domingue.* 2d ed. Versailles: Imprimérie de Département de la Marine.

BENJAMIN, S.G.W.
1877 Contemporary art in Germany. *Harper's New Monthly Magazine* 55 (June): 1–22.

BERNSTEIN, HARRY, AND BAILEY W. DIFFIE

1937   Sir Clements R. Markham as a translator. *Hispanic American Historical Review* 17:546–57.

BERTONE, GIORGIO

1987   L'occhio, l'ancora, la scrittura, lo sguardo dell'Almirante. In *Columbeis II*, 153–80. Genoa: D.AR.FI.CL.ET.

BEVINGTON, DAVID

1987   Determining the indeterminate: The *Oxford Shakespeare*. *Shakespeare Quarterly* 38:501–19.

BINFORD, LEWIS R.

1968   Archaeological perspectives. In *New perspectives in archaeology*, edited by Sally R. Binford and Lewis R. Binford. Chicago: Aldine.

BLACK, LYDIA

1981   The daily journal of Reverend Father Juvenal. *Ethnohistory* 28:33–58.

BLAKE, HENRY A.

1892   Where did Columbus first land in 1492? *Nineteenth Century* 32 (October): 536–52. Also published in *Eclectic Magazine* 119 (November): 673–83, without map.

BOOY, THEODOOR DE

1919   On the possibility of determining the first landfall of Columbus by archaeological research. *Hispanic American Historical Review* 2:55–61.

BOWERS, FREDSON

1967   Old wines in new bottles: Problems of machine printing. In *Editing nineteenth century texts*, edited by J. M. Robson, 9–36. Toronto: University of Toronto Press.

BOYD, C. CLIFFORD, JR., AND GERALD F. SCHROEDL

1987   In search of Coosa. *American Antiquity* 52:840–44, with comments, 845–56.

BOYD-BOWMAN, PETER

1987   *Léxico Hispanoamericano del siglo xvi*. Madison, Wis.: Hispanic Seminary of Medieval Studies.

BOYLE, LEONARD E.

1988   "Epistulae venerunt parum dulces": The place of codicology in the editing of medieval Latin texts. In *Editing and editors: A retrospect*, edited by Richard Landon, 29–46. New York: AMS Press.

BRACHEY, FREDERICK

1944   The maps in *Gulliver's Travels*. *Huntington Library Quarterly* 8:59–74.

BRADFORD, ERNLE

1963   *Ulysses found*. London: Hodder and Stoughton.

BRAIN, JEFFREY P.

1985   The archaeology of the Hernando de Soto expedition. In *Alabama and the borderlands from prehistory to statehood*, edited by R. Reid Badger and Lawrence A. Clayton, 96–107. University, Ala.: University of Alabama Press.

BRAMBILLA AGENO, FRANCA

1986   Gli errori auditivi nella trasmissione dei testi letterari. *Italia Medioevale e Umanistica* 29:89–105.

BRANCHI, CAMILLUS E.

1937   *The birth of America*. New York: Vigo Press.

BRIDGES, ROY

1986   David Livingstone's journal entry for 26 March 1866. In *Essays in religious studies for Andrew Walls*, 57–61. Aberdeen: University of Aberdeen Department of Religious Studies.

BRILL, ROBERT H., ET AL.

1987   Laboratory studies of some European artifacts excavated on San Salvador island. In *CW*, 247–77.

BRODSKY, LOUIS D.

1988   William Faulkner's 1962 Gold Medal speech. *Studies in Bibliography* 41:315–21.

BROOME, WILLIAM

1739   *Poems on several occasions*. 2d ed. London: Henry Lintot.

BRUFORD, ALAN

1986–87   Oral and literary Fenian tales. *Béaloideas* 54/55:25–56.

BRUMBLE, H. DAVID, III

1988   *American Indian autobiography*. Berkeley: University of California Press.

BURKHARDT, FREDERICK

1986   Editing Darwin. *Proceedings of the American Philosophical Society* 130:367–73.

1988   Editing the correspondence of Charles Darwin. *Studies in Bibliography* 41:149–59.

CALLCOTT, GEORGE H.

1959   The sacred quotation mark. *Historian* 21:409–20.

CAMPBELL, MARY B.
1988   *The witness and the other world: Exotic European travel writing,
         400–1600.* Ithaca, N.Y.: Cornell University Press.
CAPPON, LESTER J.
1973   American historical editors before Jared Sparks. *William and Mary
         Quarterly* 30 : 374–400.
CAPPON, MASSIMO
1986   Ma dov'è l'America di Colombo? *Epoca,* no. 1885 (21 November): 96–102.
CARBIA, RÓMULO D.
1929   La superchería en la historia del descubrimiento de América: Co-
         municación preliminar. *Humanidades* 20 : 169–85.
1930a   Fernández de Oviedo, Las Casas y el señor Caddeo. *Nosotros*
         70 : 90–95.
1930b   Fernando Colón, el P. Las Casas, un señor Caddeo, y yo. *Noso-
         tros* 68 : 59–73.
1931   La historia del descubrimiento y las fraudes del P. Las Casas. *No-
         sotros* 72 : 139–54.
1936   *La nueva historia del descubrimiento de América: Fundamentos
         de la tesis según la cual estaría comprobada la falsedad de la ver-
         sión tradicional acerca del extraordinario suceso.* Buenos Aires:
         Coni.
CARPENTIER, ALEJO
1980   *El arpa y la sombra.* Mexico City: Soler.
CASSON, LEONARD
1986   The location of Tabai (*Periplus Maris Erythraei* 12–13). *Journal of
         Hellenic Studies* 106 : 179–82.
1989   *The* Periplus Maris Erythraei: *Text with introduction, translation,
         and commentary.* Princeton, N.J.: Princeton University Press.
CASTAÑEDA, F. PAULINO
1973   El Tratado de Alcáçovas y su interpretación hasta la negociación
         del Tratado de Tordesillas. In *El Tratado de Tordesillas y su pro-
         yección,* 1 : 103–15. Valladolid: Seminario de Historia de América.
CASTAÑEDA DELGADO, PAULINO, MARIANO CUESTA, AND PILAR
HERNÁNDEZ APARICIO
1977   *Alonso de Chaves y el Libro IV de su "Espejo de Navegantes."*
         Madrid: n.p.
CASTRO, AMÉRICO
1927   Hacer la salva. In *Mélanges de philologie et d'histoire offerts à*

M. Antoine Thomas par ses éléves et ses amis, 89–94. Paris: Honoré Champion.

CATZ, REBECCA
1988   A translation of three chapters from the *Peregrinaçao* of Fernão Mendes Pinto. *Portuguese Studies* 4:55–83.

CENTER FOR EDITIONS OF AMERICAN AUTHORS
1972   *Statement of editorial premises and procedures.* Rev. ed. New York: Modern Language Association.

CHAMBERS, E. K.
1930   *William Shakespeare: A study of facts and problems.* 2 vols. Oxford: Clarendon Press.

CHARCOT, J. B.
1928   *Christophe Colomb vu par un marin.* Paris: Flammarion.

CHARDON, ROLAND
1980a   The elusive Spanish league: A problem of measurement in sixteenth-century New Spain. *Hispanic American Historical Review* 60:294–302.
1980b   The linear league in North America. *Annals of the Association of American Geographers* 70:129–53.

CHÂTEAUBRIAND, FRANÇOIS, VICOMTE DE
1969   *Travels in America.* Translated and edited by Richard Switzer. Lexington: University of Kentucky Press.

CHICAGO HERALD
1891   There landed Columbus. 4 July, pp. 1, 9, 10.

CHIPMAN, DONALD E.
1987   In search of Cabeza de Vaca's route across Texas: An historiographical survey. *Southwestern Historical Quarterly* 91:127–48.

CIORANESCU, ALEJANDRO
1959   *Colón y Canarias.* La Laguna de Tenerife: Cabildo Insular de Tenerife.
1960a   *Primera biografía de C. Colón: Fernando Colón y Bartolomé de las Casas.* Tenerife: Aula de Cultura de Tenerife.
1960b   El traductor italiano de las *Historias* de 1571. *Estudios Americanos* 20:33–39.
1966   La 'Historia de las Indias' y la prohibición de editarla. *Anuario de Estudios Americanos* 23:263–76.

CLEMENTS, WILLIAM M.
1990   Schoolcraft as textmaker. *Journal of American Folklore* 103:177–92.

COLOMBO, G.

1977   Lagoons. In *The coastline: A contribution to our understanding of its ecology and physiography in relation to land-use and management and the pressures to which it is subject*, edited by R.S.K. Barnes, 63–81. London: John Wiley and Sons.

COLÓN, FERNANDO

1930   *Le* Historie *della vita e dei fatti di Cristoforo Colombo*. Edited by Rinaldo Caddeo. 2 vols. Milan: Edizioni Alpes.

1932   *Historia del Almirante don Cristobal Colón por su hijo don Hernando*. Translated by Manuel Serrano y Sanz. 2 vols. Madrid: Victoriano Súarez.

1945   *La vita e i viaggi di Cristoforo Colombo*. Edited by Rinaldo Caddeo. Milan: Fasani.

1959   *The life of the admiral Christopher Columbus by his son Ferdinand*. Edited and translated by Benjamin Keen. New Brunswick, N.J.: Rutgers University Press.

CONNELLY, THOMAS L.

1977   *The marble man: Robert E. Lee and his image in American society*. New York: Knopf.

CONTI, SIMONETTA

1986   *Un secolo di bibliografia Colombiana, 1880–1985*. Genoa: Cassa di Risparmio.

COOK, SHERBURNE F., AND WOODROW W. BORAH

1979   *Essays in population history*. Vol. 3: *Mexico and California*. Berkeley: University of California Press.

COOKE, EDWARD

1712   *A voyage to the South Sea and around the world*. London: Lintot and Gosling.

COROMINAS, JUAN

1954   *Diccionario crítico etimológico de la lengua Castellana*. 4 vols. Madrid: Gredos.

CORTESÃO, JAIME

1947   *Los Portugueses*. Buenos Aires: Salvat. Bound with Antonio Ballesteros y Beretta, *Génesis del descubrimiento*.

COUSER, G. THOMAS

1989   *Altered egos: Authority in American autobiography*. New York: Oxford University Press.

COVARRUBIAS HOROZCO, SEBASTIÁN DE

1611/1943 *Tesoro de la lengua Castellana o Española*. Barcelona: S. A. Horta.

CRANE, ELAINE FORMAN

1988   Gender consciousness in editing: The diary of Elizabeth Drinker. *Text* 4:375–83.

CRANE, STEPHEN

1988   *The correspondence of Stephen Crane.* Edited by Stanley Wertheim and Paul Sorrentino. 2 vols. New York: Columbia University Press.

CRAWSHAY, L. R.

1935   Possible bearing of a luminous syllid on the question of the landfall of Columbus. *Nature* 136 (5 October): 559–70.

CRONAU, RUDOLF

1892   *Amerika: Die Geschichte seiner Entdeckung von die altesten bis auf die neueste Zeit.* 2 vols. Leipzig: Ubel and Müller.

1921   *The discovery of America and the landfall of Columbus* and *The last resting place of Columbus.* New York: R. Cronau.

CULLEN, CHARLES T.

1989   Casual observer beware: The need for using scholarly editions. *Prologue* 21:68–73.

CURREN, CALEB

1986   *In search of de Soto's trail: A hypothesis of the Alabama route.* Camden, Ala: Alabama-Tombigbee Regional Commission.

CUSHING, CALEB

1827   New documents concerning Columbus. *North American Review* 53:484–89; 55:265–94.

DANSON, LAWRENCE

1989   The flexible bard. *Nation,* 16 October, 429–32.

DARWIN, CHARLES

1903   *More letters of Charles Darwin.* Edited by Francis Darwin. 2 vols. New York: D. Appleton.

DAVENPORT, FRANCIS G., ED.

1917   *European treaties bearing on the history of the United States and its dependencies to 1648.* Washington, D.C.: Carnegie Institution.

DAVIDSON, JANE P.

1987   "I am the poison dripping dragon": Iguanas and their symbolism in the alchemical and occult paintings of David Teniers the younger. *Ambix* 34:62–80.

DAVIS, T. FREDERICK

1935   History of Juan Ponce de León's voyages to Florida. *Florida Historical Quarterly* 14:1–49.

DAWSON, MARC H.
1987   The many minds of Sir Halford J. Mackinder: Dilemmas of historical editing. *History in Africa* 14:27–42.
DAWSON, SAMUEL E.
1899   The line of demarcation of Pope Alexander VI in A.D. 1493 and that of the Treaty of Tordesillas in A.D. 1494; with an inquiry concerning the metrology of ancient and mediaeval times. *Proceedings of the Royal Society of Canada* 5:467–546.
DE PRATTER, CHESTER B., CHARLES M. HUDSON, AND
MARVIN T. SMITH
1983   The route of Juan Pardo's explorations in the interior Southeast, 1566–1568. *Florida Historical Quarterly* 62:125–58.
1985   The Hernando de Soto expedition: From Chiaha to Mabila. In *Alabama and the Borderlands from prehistory to statehood*, edited by R. Reid Badger and Lawrence A. Clayton, 108–27. University, Ala.: University of Alabama Press.
DEVELIN, R.
1990   Numerical corruption in Greek historical texts. *Phoenix* 44:31–45.
DÍAZ DEL CASTILLO, BERNAL
1982   *Historia verdadera de la conquista de la Nueva España*. Edited by Carmelo Sáenz de Santa María. Madrid: Instituto Gonzalo Fernández de Oviedo.
DÍAZ DEL RÍO MARTÍNEZ, ANGEL
1986   Derrotas de las naves de Cristóbal Colón en las islas Canarias en el viaje del descubrimiento. *Revista General de Marina* 211:303–15.
DIDIEZ BURGOS, RAMÓN J.
1974   *Guanahaní y Mayaguain: Las primeras isletas descubiertas en el Nuevo Mundo*. Santo Domingo: Editora Cultural Dominicana.
DIFFIE, BAILEY W.
1936   A Markham contribution to the *leyenda negra*. *Hispanic American Historical Review* 16:96–103.
DOIRON, NORMAND
1989   Les rituels de la tempête en mer: Histoire et voyage au seuil de l'âge classique. *Revue des Sciences Humaines* 90:43–70.
DUFF, CHARLES
1957   *The truth about Columbus and the discovery of America*. London: Jarrolds.
DUMENE, JOANNE E.
1988   Looking for Columbus. *Naval History* 4 (Fall): 33–37.

DUMVILLE, DAVID
1985   On editing and translating medieval Irish chronicles: The *Annals of Ulster*. *Cambridge Medieval Celtic Studies* 10 (Winter): 67–86.

DUNKIN, EDWIN
1879   *Obituary notices of astronomers, fellows and associates of the Royal Astronomical Society*. London: Williams and Norgate.

DUNN, OLIVER
1985   Columbus's first landing place: The evidence of the *Journal*. In *IWC*, 35–50.

DUVIOLS, JEAN-PAUL
1985   *L'Amérique espagnole vue et rêvée: Les livres de voyages de Christophe Colomb à Bougainville*. Paris: Promodis.

EASSON, ANGUS
1987   Reviewing editions: Letters, journals, and diaries. In *Literary reviewing*, edited by James O. Hoge, 44–67. Charlottesville: University of Virginia Press.

ELIAS, ROBERT H.
1987   Eighteenth-century thorns, twentieth-century secretaries, and other prickly matters. *Text* 3:347–53.

EMERTON, J. A.
1987–88   An examination of some attempts to defend the unity of the flood narrative in Genesis. *Vetus Testamentum* 37:401–20; 38:1–21.

EMONDS, HILARIUS
1941   *Zweite Aufläge im Altertum*. Leipzig: Harrassowitz.

ERASMUS, DESIDERIUS
1974–87   *The correspondence of Erasmus*. Translated and edited by R. A. B. Mynors, D.F.S. Thomson, and James K. McConica. 7 vols. Toronto: University of Toronto Press.

EVELYN, JOHN
1955   *The diary of John Evelyn*. Edited by E. S. de Beer. 6 vols. Oxford: Clarendon Press.

EVERETT, BARBARA
1988   New readings in *Hamlet* (and some principles of emendation). *Review of English Studies*, n.s. 39:177–98.

EZQUERRA ABADIA, RAMÓn
1988   Las principales colecciones documentales Colombinas. *Revista de Indias* 48:661–91.

FAHNESTOCK, JEANNE
1989   Arguing in different forums: The Bering Crossover controversy. *Science, Technology, and Human Values* 14:26–42.

FAHY, CONOR

1988   More on the 1532 edition of Ariosto's *Orlando Furioso*. *Studies in Bibliography* 41:225–32.

FANTONI, GIROLAMO

1989   La scoperta dell'America: Il primo avvistamento dell'isola di San Salvador. *Rivista Marittima* 380 (May): 69–82.

FANTONI, GIROLAMO, AND MARIO INGRAVALLE

1987   Alla ricerca della lega di Cristoforo Colombo. *Rivista Marittima* 361 (October): 65–89.

FARRAND, MAX, ED.

1966   *The records of the federal convention of 1787*. 4 vols. New Haven, Conn.: Yale University Press.

FAUST, DREW G.

1982   In search of the real Mary Chesnut. *Reviews in American History* 10:54–59.

FERRO, GAETANO

1987   Columbus and his sailings, according to the 'Diary' of the first voyage: Observations of a geographer. In *CW*, 99–113.

FIELD, LESLIE

1989   *Thomas Wolfe and his editors: Establishing a true text for the posthumous publications*. Norman: University of Oklahoma Press.

FISHER, JOHN H.

1988   Animadversions on the text of Chaucer, 1988. *Speculum* 63: 779–93.

FITZPATRICK, A. P.

1989   The submission of the Orkney Islands to Claudius: New evidence? *Scottish Archaeological Review* 6:24–33.

FITZPATRICK, GARY L., AND MARILYN J. MODLIN

1986   *Direct-line distances*. International edition. Metuchen: Scarecrow Press.

FOX, GUSTAVUS V.

1882   An attempt to solve the problem of the first landing place of Columbus in the New World. In *Report of the Superintendent of the U.S. Coast and Geodetic Survey . . . during the fiscal year ending with June 1880*, 346–417. Washington, D.C.: Government Printing Office.

FRANCIS, PETER, JR.

1984   Bead report XII: Beads and the discovery of America, II: Beads brought to America. *Ornament* 8/2:24–27.

FRANK, ANNE

1989   *The diary of Anne Frank: The critical edition.* Edited by David Barnouw and Gerrold van der Stroom. New York: Doubleday.

FRANKLIN, BENJAMIN, AND DUANE SCHNEIDER

1979   *Anaïs Nin: An introduction.* Athens: Ohio University Press.

FREEMAN, R. AUSTIN

1912   *The mystery of 31, New Inn.* London: Hodder and Stoughton.

FREUD, SIGMUND

1952–66 Analysis of a phobia in a five-year-old boy. In *Standard edition of the complete psychological works of Sigmund Freud,* edited by James Strachey, 10:148–52. London: Hogarth Press.

FUESS, CLAUDE M.

1923   *The life of Caleb Cushing.* 2 vols. New York: Harcourt Brace.

1931   Gustavus Vasa Fox. *Dictionary of American biography* 6:568–69.

FUSON, ROBERT H.

1985   The *diario de Colón*: A legacy of poor transcription, translation, and interpretation. In *IWC,* 51–75.

1987a   *The log of Christopher Columbus.* Camden, Me.: International Marine Publishing.

1987b   The Turks and Caicos Islands as possible landfall sites for Columbus. In *CW,* 173–84.

FUSON, ROBERT H., AND WALTER H. TREFTZ

1976   A theoretical reconstruction of the first Atlantic crossing of Christopher Columbus. *Proceedings of the Association of American Geographers* 8:155–57.

GAFFAREL, PAUL

1892   *Histoire de la découverte de l'Amérique.* 2 vols. Paris: Arthur Rousseau.

GALINSKY, HANS

1977   Exploring the "Exploration Report" and its image of the overseas world: Spanish, French, and English variants of a common form type in early American literature. *Early American Literature* 12:5–24.

GALLARDO, BARTOLOMÉ JOSÉ

1863–89 *Ensayo de una biblioteca española de libros raros y curiosos.* 4 vols. Madrid: M. Rivadeneyra.

GALLOWAY, PATRICIA

1981   Dearth and bias: Issues in the editing of ethnohistorical materials. *Newsletter of the Association for Documentary Editing* 3 (May): 1–6.

GAMA, VASCO DA

1945   *Diario da viagem de Vasco da Gama.* Ed. Damião Peres. 2 vols. Pôrto, Portugal: Livraria Civilizaçao.

GANDÍA, ENRIQUE DE

1942   *Historia de Cristóbal Colón: Análisis crítico de las fuentes documentales y de los problemas colombinos.* Buenos Aires: Editorial Claridad.

1983   Emiliano Jos y la génesis del descubrimiento Colombino. *Investigaciones y Ensayos* 34:15–45.

GÁRATE CÓRDOBA, JOSÉ MARÍA

1977   *La poesía del descubrimiento.* Madrid: Ediciones Cultura Hispánica.

GARCILASO DE LE VEGA, EL INCA

1605   *La Florida del Ynca . . .* Lisbon: Pedro Crasbeeck.

GEARY, JOHN S.

1983–84   The Fernán González epic: In search of a definitive text. *Olifant* 10/3:118–31.

GERACE, DONALD T.

1987   Additional comments relating Watlings Island to Columbus' San Salvador. In *CW,* 229–33.

GERBI, ANTONELLO

1985   *Nature in the New World: From Christopher Columbus to Gonzalo Fernández de Oviedo.* Translated by Jeremy Moyle. Pittsburgh: University of Pittsburgh Press.

GIBBS, GEORGE

1846   Observations tending to show that the Grand Turk Island, and not San Salvador, was the first spot on which Columbus landed in the New World. *Proceedings of the New-York Historical Society,* 137–48.

GIL, JUAN

1984   Tres notas colombinas. *Historiografía y Bibliografía Americanistas* 28:73–91.

1985   Pleitos y clientelas Colombinas. In *Scritti in onore del Prof. Paolo Emilio Taviani,* 3:183–99. 3 vols. Genoa: Edizioni Culturali Internazionali.

GILLIARD, FRANK D.

1989   The problem of the antisemitic comma between 1 Thessalonians 2.14 and 15. *New Testament Studies* 35:481–502.

GILMAN, WILLIAM H.

1971   How should journals be edited? *Early American Literature* 6: 73–83.

GIMÉNEZ FERNÁNDEZ, MANUEL

1949   *El estatuto de la Tierra de Casas.* Seville: Edelce.

1971   Fray Bartolomé de las Casas: A biographical sketch. In *Bartolomé de las Casas in history,* edited by Juan Friede and Benjamin Keen, 67–125. DeKalb: Northern Illinois University Press.

GLOVER, T. R.

1943   *Cambridge retrospect.* Cambridge: Cambridge University Press.

GÓMARA, FRANCISCO LÓPEZ DE

1954   *Historia general de las Indias: Hispania Victrix.* Edited by Pilar Guibelalde and Emiliano M. Aguilera. 2 vols. Barcelona: Obras Maestras.

GOULD, ALICIA B.

1984   *Nueva lista documentada de los tripulantes de Colón en 1492.* Madrid: Real Academia de la Historia.

GOULD, RUPERT T.

1927   The landfall of Columbus: An old problem re-stated. *Geographical Journal* 69:403–29.

1965   *Enigmas: Another book of unexplained facts.* New Hyde Park, N.Y.: University Books.

GRAFTON, ANTHONY

1985   Renaissance readers and ancient texts: Comments on some commentaries. *Renaissance Quarterly* 38:615–49.

GRANZOTTO, GIANNI

1985   *Christopher Columbus.* Garden City: Doubleday.

GREENWAY, DIANA

1986   Henry of Huntingdon and the manuscripts of his *Historia Anglorum. Anglo-Norman Studies* 9:103–26.

GUCHT, J. VAN DER, AND S. M. PARAJÓN.

1943   *Ruta de Cristóbal Colón por la costa norte de Cuba.* Havana: P. Fernández.

GUILLÉN Y TATO, JULIO FERNANDO

1951   *La parla marinera en el diario del primer viaje de Cristóbal Colón.* Madrid: Instituto Histórico de Marina.

GULLICK, MICHAEL, AND CAROLINE THORN

1986   The scribes of Great Domesday Book: A preliminary account. *Journal of the Society of Archivists* 8:78–80.

HAEGER, JOHN W.

1978   Marco Polo in China? Problems with internal evidence. *Bulletin of Sung and Yüan Studies* 14:22–30.

HAENSCH, GÜNTHER

1984   La comunicación entre Españoles e Indios en la conquista. In *Estudis en memòria del professor Manuel Sanchis Guarner*, vol. 2: *Estudis de llengua i literatura*, 157–67. Valencia: Universitat de València.

HAGGARD, J. VILLASANA

1941   *Handbook for translators of Spanish historical documents.* Austin, Tex.: Archives Collections.

HALL, FREDERICK

1913   *A companion to classical texts.* Oxford: Clarendon Press.

HAMMOND, ANTONY

1986   Review of *Ulysses: A critical and synoptic edition.* Edited by Hans W. Gabler et al. [New York, 1984]. *The Library* 6:382–90.

HANDLIN, OSCAR, ET AL., EDS.

1954   *Harvard guide to American history.* Cambridge, Mass.: Harvard University Press/Belknap Press.

HANKE, LEWIS

1951   The *Historia de las Indias* of Bartolomé de las Casas. In *Essays honoring Lawrence C. Wroth*, 143–50. Portland, Me.

1952   *Bartolomé de las Casas, historian: An essay in Spanish historiography.* Gainesville: University of Florida Press.

HANSSEN, FEDERICO

1966   *Gramática histórica de la lengua castellana.* Paris: Les Presses du Marais.

HARRISSE, HENRY

1872   *Fernand Colomb: Sa vie, ses oeuvres; Essai critique.* Paris: Tross.

1875   *L'histoire de Christophe Colomb attribuée à son fils Fernand.* Paris: Martinet.

1884–85   *Christophe Colomb: Son origine, sa vie, ses voyages, sa famille, et ses descendants.* 2 vols. Paris: E. Leroux.

HASSAM, ANDREW

1988   Literary exploration: The fictive sea journals of William Golding, Robert Nye, B. S. Johnson, and Malcolm Lowry. *Ariel* 19:29–46.

HAWTING, G. R.

1984   "We were not ordered with entering it but only with circumambulating it": *Hadith* and *fiqh* on entering the ka^{c}ba. *Bulletin of the School of Oriental and African Studies* 47:228–42.

HAY, LOUIS

1988   Does "text" exist? *Studies in Bibliography* 41:64–76.

HEERS, JACQUES

1981   *Christophe Colomb*. Paris: Hachette.

1984   De Marco Polo à Christophe Colomb: Comment lire le *Divise-ment du monde? Journal of Medieval History* 10:125–43.

HELLY, DOROTHY O.

1987   *Livingstone's legacy: Horace Waller and Victorian mythmaking*. Athens: Ohio University Press.

HELM, E. EUGENE

1989   The editorial transmission of C. P. E. Bach's music. *Early Music* 17:33–41.

HENIGE, DAVID

1975   Some phantom dynasties of early and medieval India: Epigraphic evidence and the abhorrence of a vacuum. *Bulletin of the School of Oriental and African Studies* 38:525–49.

1980a   "Companies are always ungrateful": James Phipps of Cape Coast, a victim of the African trade. *African Economic History* 9:27–47.

1980b   "In the possession of the author": The problem of source monopoly in oral historiography. *International Journal of Oral History* 1:181–94.

1982   *Oral historiography*. London: Longman.

1986a   If pigs could fly: Timucuan population and Native American historical demography. *Journal of Interdisciplinary History* 16:701–20.

1986b   Primary source by primary source? On the role of epidemics in New World depopulation. *Ethnohistory* 33:293–312.

1987a   In quest of error's sly imprimatur: The concept of "authorial intent" in modern textual criticism. *History in Africa* 14:87–112.

1987b   The race is not always to the swift: Thoughts on the use of written sources for the study of early African history. *Paideuma* 33:53–79.

1988   Samuel Eliot Morison as translator and interpreter of Columbus' *diario de a bordo. Terrae Incognitae* 20:69–88.

1990a   Edited . . . and not precipitated: Three recent editions of Columbus' *diario. Terrae Incognitae* 22.

1990b   Proxy data, historical method, and the de Soto expedition. Paper presented at the Symposium on de Soto in Caddo Country, Fayetteville, Ark.

n.d.   To read is to misread, to write is to miswrite: Las Casas as transcriber. Unpublished paper in possession of the author.

HENIGE, DAVID, AND MARGARITA ZAMORA
1989   Text, context, intertext: Columbus' *diario de a bordo* as palimpsest. *Americas* 46:17–40.

HERNÁNDEZ DÍAZ, JOSÉ, AND ANTONIO MURO OREJÓN
1941   *El testamento de don Hernando Colón.* Seville: Gavidia.

HERRERA Y TORDESILLAS, ANTONIO DE
1934–57   *Historia general de los hechos de los Castellanos en las Islas y Tierra-*
            firme del Mar Océano. Edited by Angel de Altolaguirre y Duvale.
            17 vols. Madrid: Tipografía de Archivos.

HIGDON, DAVID L.
1988   Conrad, *Under Western eyes,* and the mysteries of revision. *Re*
            view of English Studies, n.s. 39:231–44.

HILL, GEORGE F.
1915   *The development of Arabic numerals in Europe.* Oxford: Clarendon Press.

HOFFMAN, CHARLES A.
1987a   Archaeological investigations at the Long Bay site, San Salvador,
            Bahamas. In *CW,* 237–45.
1987b   The Long Bay site, San Salvador. *American Archeology* 6/2:
            96–101.

HOLMES, FREDERIC L.
1987   Scientific writing and scientific discovery. *Isis* 78:220–35.

HONIGMANN, E. A. J.
1989   *Myriad-minded Shakespeare.* London: Macmillan.

HOUSMAN, A. E.
1988   *Collected poems and selected prose.* Edited by Christopher Ricks.
            London: Allen Lane.

HUDSON, CHARLES
1990   *The Juan Pardo expeditions.* Washington, D.C.: Smithsonian
            Institution.

HUDSON, CHARLES, MARVIN T. SMITH, AND CHESTER B. DE PRATTER
1984   The Hernando de Soto expedition: From Apalachee to Chiaha.
            Southeastern Archaeology 3 (Summer): 65–77.

HUDSON, CHARLES, MARVIN T. SMITH, CHESTER B. DE PRATTER,
AND EMILIA KELLEY
1989   The Tristán de Luna expedition, 1559–1561. *Southeastern Ar*
            chaeology 8:31–45.

HULME, PETER

1978   Columbus and the cannibals: A study of the reports of anthro-
            pophagy in the *Journal of Christopher Columbus. Ibero-Amerika-
            nisches Archiv,* n.s. 4:115–39.

1986   *Colonial encounters: Europe and the native Caribbean, 1492–
            1797.* London: Methuen.

HUMBOLDT, ALEXANDER VON

1836–39   *Examen critique de l'histoire de la géographie du nouveau conti-
            nent, et des progrés de l'astronomie nautique aux 15me et 16me
            siécles.* 5 vols. Paris: Gide.

HUNTINGFORD, G. W. B., ED.

1980   *The Periplus of the Erythraean Sea.* London: Hakluyt Society.

HURLEBUSCH, KLAUS

1987   "Relic" and "tradition": Some aspects of editing diaries. *Text*
            3:143–53.

IATA/IAL

1986   *Air distances manual.* 13th ed. London: IATA/IAL.

IWC   *In the wake of Columbus: Islands and controversy.* Edited by
            Louis De Vorsey, Jr., and John Parker. Detroit: Wayne State Uni-
            versity Press, 1985. Also published as volume 15 [1983] of *Terrae
            Incognitae.*

ILLUSTRATED LONDON NEWS

1987   Pictures that lie. No. 4043 (August): 49–52.

IOPPOLO, GRACE

1989   "Old" and "new" revisionists: Shakespeare's eighteenth-century
            editors. *Huntington Library Quarterly* 52:347–61.

IRVING, WASHINGTON

1828   *A history of the life and voyages of Christopher Columbus.* 3 vols.
            New York: G. and C. Carvill.

1841   *History of the life and voyages of Christopher Columbus.* 2 vols.
            Philadelphia: Lea and Blanchard.

1849   [Crayon, Geoffrey]. *Tales of a traveller.* Rev. ed. New York:
            George P. Putnam.

1981   *The life and voyages of Christopher Columbus.* Edited by John H.
            McElroy. Boston: Twayne.

JACKSON, DAVID H.

1986   The Stanford *Falesá* and textual scholarship. *Review* 8:79–92.

JANE, CECIL

1930a   The letter of Columbus announcing the success of his first voyage.
            Hispanic American Historical Review 10:33–50.

1930b   *Select documents illustrating the four voyages of Columbus.* London: Hakluyt Society.

JEFFERSON, THOMAS

1986   *The papers of Thomas Jefferson.* Vol. 22: *6 August 1791 to 31 December 1791.* Edited by Charles T. Cullen. Princeton, N.J.: Princeton University Press.

JENKINSON, HILARY

1934   The representation of manuscripts in print. *London Mercury* 30: 429–38.

JOHNSON, JOHN

1794   *A mathematical question, propounded by the vice-regent of the world, answered by the king of glory.* Windsor, Vt.: Alden Spooner.

JOS, EMILIANO

1931   Supuestas falsificaciones del P. Las Casas en la historia de Colón. *Revista de Occidente* 31:217–24.

1940   Fernando Colón y su historia del Almirante. *Revista de Historia de América* 9:5–29.

1942a   En las postrimerías de un centenario colombino poco celebrado. *Estudios Geográficos* 2:513–63.

1942b   Enfermedad de Martín Alonso e impugnaciones a la "Historia del Almirante." *Revista de Indias* 3:85–110, 189–221.

1944a   La *Historia del Almirante* y algunos aspectos de la ciencia colombina. *Revista de Historia* 10:1–17.

1944b   Investigaciones sobre la vida y obras iniciales de don Fernando Colón. *Anuario de Estudios Americanos* 1:525–698.

1950   El libro del primer viaje: Algunas ediciones recientes. *Revista de Indias* 10:719–51.

1952   El diario de Colón: Su fundamental autenticidad. In *Studi Colombiani,* 2:77–99. Genoa, S.A.G.A.

1955   Las Casas: Historian of Christopher Columbus. *Americas* 12: 355–62.

1979   *El plan y el génesis del descubrimiento Colombino.* Valladolid: Seminario Americanista de la Universidad de Valladolid.

JOYCE, JAMES

1984   *Ulysses: A critical and synoptic edition.* Edited by Hans Walter Gabler. 3 vols. New York: Garland.

JUDGE, JOSEPH

1986   Where Columbus found the New World. *National Geographic* 170 (November): 568–99.

JUSTER, NORTON

1967   *The phantom tollbooth*. New York: Random House.

JUYNBOLL, G. H. A.

1983   *Muslim tradition*. Cambridge: Cambridge University Press.

KAHANE, HENRY, RENÉE KAHANE, AND ANDREAS TIETZE

1958   *The* lingua franca *in the Levant*. Urbana: University of Illinois Press.

KAISER, RUDOLF

1987   Chief Seattle's speech(es): American origins and European perceptions. In *Recovering the word: Essays on Native American literature*, edited by Brian Swann and Arnold Krupat, 497–536. Berkeley: University of California Press.

KAMINSKI, JOHN P.

1987   The records of a productive summer. *Documentary Editing* 9 (September): 16–20.

KEEGAN, WILLIAM F.

1989   Columbus's 1492 voyage and the search for his landfall. In *First encounters: Spanish explorations in the Caribbean and the United States, 1492–1570*, edited by Jerald T. Milanich and Susan Milbrath, 27–40. Gainesville: University of Florida Press

KEEGAN, WILLIAM F., AND STEVEN W. MITCHELL

1987a   The archeology of Christopher Columbus' voyage through the Bahamas, 1492. *American Archeology* 6/2: 102–8.

1987b   The Columbus landfall question—yet another viewpoint. *Encuentro*, 2 (Spring/Summer): 6–7.

KEEGAN, WILLIAM F., MAURICE W. WILLIAMS, AND GRETHE SEIM

1990   *Archaeological survey of Grand Turk, B.W.I.* Gainesville: Florida Museum of Natural History.

KELLEY, JAMES E., JR.

1985   In the wake of Columbus on a portolan chart. In *IWC*, 77–111.

KELLEY, JANE H., AND MARSHA P. HANEN

1988   *Archaeology and the methodology of science*. Albuquerque: University of New Mexico Press.

KENNEDY, HUGH

1988   Review of Patricia Crone, *Meccan trade and the rise of Islam*. *Middle East Studies Association Bulletin* 22: 55.

KENNEY, E. J.

1974   *The classical text: Aspects of editing in the age of the printed book*. Berkeley: University of California Press.

KENYON, NICHOLAS, ED.
1988   *Authenticity and early music.* Oxford: Oxford University Press.

KIDD, JOHN
1988a   An inquiry into *Ulysses: The corrected text. Papers of the Biblio-graphical Society of America* 82:411–584.
1988b   The scandal of *Ulysses. New York Review of Books* 35 (30 June): 32–39.

KILEY, CORNELIUS J.
1973   State and dynasty in archaic Yamato. *Journal of Asian Studies* 33:25–49.

KIRWAN, L. P.
1986   Rhapta, metropolis of Azania. *Azania* 21:99–104.

KLINE, MARY-JO
1987   *A guide to documentary editing.* Baltimore: Johns Hopkins University Press.

KNOLLENBERG, BERNHARD
1940   *Washington and the Revolution: A reappraisal.* New York: Macmillan.

LAGUARDIA TRÍAS, ROLANDO A.
1974   *El enigma de las latitudes de Colón.* Valladolid: Casa-Museo de Colón.

LAMARTINE, ALPHONSE DE
1852/1942 *Christophe Colomb.* Edited by Antoine Velleman. Geneva: Editions de l'Ecole d'Interprètes.

LANDFALL
1926   The landfall of Columbus. *Geographical Journal* 68:338–39.

LANDUCCI GATTINONI, FRANCA
1984   Annibale sulle Alpi. *Aevum* 58:38–44.

LANGE, JOHN
1966   The argument from silence. *History and Theory* 5:288–301.

LARIMORE, CHRISTOPHER C.
1987   The Columbus landfall question: Could this be the true route? *Encuentro* 3 (December): 12–13.

LA ROQUETTE, J. B. M. A. DEZOS DE
1828   *Relations des quatre voyages enterpris par Christophe Colomb pour la découverte du Nouveau-Monde de 1492 à 1504.* 3 vols. Paris: Treuttel and Würtz.

LAS CASAS, BARTOLOMÉ DE
1875–76   *Historia de las Indias.* Edited by Marqués de la Fuensanta del Valle and José Sancho Rayón. 5 vols. Madrid: Miguel Ginesta.

1951   *Historia de las Indias*. Edited by Agustín Millares Carlo. 3 vols. Mexico City: Fondo de Cultura Económica.

1957   *Historia de las Indias*. Edited by Juan Pérez de Tudela and Emilio López Oto. 2 vols. Madrid: Ediciones Atlas.

1965   *Tratados*. Translated and edited by Manuel Giménez Fernández, Juan Pérez de Tudela Bueso, Agustín Millares Carlo, and Rafael Moreno. Mexico: Fondo de Cultura Económica.

1967   *Apologética historia sumaria*. Edited by Edmundo O'Gorman. 2 vols. Mexico City: Instituto de Investigaciones Históricas.

1982   *Brevísima relación de la destruición de las Indias*. Edited by André Saint-Lu. Madrid: Ediciones Cátedra.

1986   *Historia de las Indias*. Edited by André Saint-Lu. 3 vols. Caracas: Biblioteca Ayacucho.

1989   *Brevísima relación de la destrucción de Africa: Preludio de la destrucción de Indias*. Edited by Isacio Pérez Fernández. Salamanca: Editorial San Estebán/Instituto Bartolomé de las Casas.

LATHAM, ROBERT
1974   Publishing Pepys. *Scholarly Publishing* 6:51–57.

LAZENBY, J. F.
1978   *Hannibal's war*. Warminster: Aris and Phillips.

LEICESTER, L. ANTHONY
1980   Columbus's first landfall. *Sea Frontiers* 26 (Sept.–Oct.): 271–78.

LEWIS, G. M.
1987   Misinterpretation of Amerindian information as a source of error on Euro-American maps. *Annals of the Association of American Geographers* 77:542–63.

LEYVA Y AGUILERA, HERMINIO C.
1890   *Descubrimiento de América: Primer viaje de Colón; Estudio acerca del primer puerto visitado en la Isla de Cuba*. Havana: La Propaganda Literaria.

LINK, EDWIN A., AND MARION C. LINK
1958   *A new theory of Columbus's voyage through the Bahamas*. Smithsonian Miscellaneous Collections, vol. 135, no. 4. Washington, D.C.: Smithsonian Institution.

LIPKING, LAWRENCE
1981   Literary criticism. In *Introduction to scholarship in modern languages and literatures*, edited by Joseph Gibaldi, 79–97. New York: Modern Language Association of America.

LITTLE, BRYAN
1960   *Crusoe's captain*. London: Odhams Press.

LOLLIS, CESARE DE

1923   *Cristoforo Colombo nella leggenda e nella storia.* 3d ed. Rome: Fratelli Treves.

LUCA DE TENA, TORCUATO

1968   *Los mil y un descubrimientos de América y otros ensayos.* Madrid: Ediciones de la Revista de Occidente.

LUDWIG, H.

1980   Zwischen tradition und fortschritt. *Weltkunst* 50 (15 May): 1394–97.

LUZZANA CARACI, ILARIA

1976   Nuova luce intorno al problema delle "Historie" Colombiane. *Bollettino della Società Geografica Italiana* 10/5 : 503–12.

1989   *Colombo vero e falso: La costruzione delle historie fernandine.* Genoa, Edizioni Culturali Internazionali.

LYNN, KENNETH

1981   The masterpiece that became a hoax. *New York Times Book Review* (26 April): 24–26.

LYON, EUGENE

1986   The diario of Christopher Columbus, October 10–October 27, 1492. In *CC,* 5–45.

MACBAIN, WILLIAM

1987   Remembrance of things still to come: Scribal memory and manuscript tradition. *Manuscripta* 31 : 77–88.

MCCARTER, P. KYLE, JR.

1986   *Textual criticism: Recovering the text of the Hebrew Bible.* Philadelphia: Fortress Press.

MCELROY, JOHN W.

1941   The ocean navigation of Columbus on his first voyage. *American Neptune* 1 : 209–40.

MCGANN, JEROME J.

1983   *A critique of modern textual criticism.* Chicago: University of Chicago Press.

MCGURK, PATRICK

1961   Citation marks in early Latin manuscripts. *Scriptorium* 15 : 3–13.

MACHAN, TIM WILLIAM

1989   Scribal role, authorial intention, and Chaucer's *Boece. Chaucer Review* 24 : 150–62.

MACKENZIE, A. S.

1897   Alexander Slidell Mackenzie. *National Cyclopaedia of American Biography* 4 : 527–28.

MACKIE, CHARLES P.
1891   *With the Admiral of the Ocean Sea*. Chicago: A. C. McClurg.

MAGNAGHI, ALBERTO
1928   I presunti errori che vengono attribuiti a Colombo nella determinazione della latitudini. *Bollettino della Società Geografica Italiana* 65:459–94, 553–82.
1930   Ancora dei pretesi errori di Colombo nella determinazione delle latitudini. *Bollettino della Società Geografica Italiana* 67:497–515.
1933   Incertezze e contrasti delle fonti tradizionali sulle osservazioni attribuite a C. Colombo intorno ai fenomeni della declinazione magnetica. *Bollettino della Società Geografica Italiana* 70: 595–641.

MAHN-LOT, MARIANNE
1982   *Bartolomé de las Casas et le droit des Indiens*. Paris: Payot.
1988   *Portrait historique de Christophe Colomb*. Paris: Editions du Seuil.

MAJOR, R. H.
1871   The landfall of Columbus. *Journal of the Royal Geographical Society* 41:193–210.

MALKIN, IRAD, AND ARIE FICHMAN
1987   Homer, *Odyssey* III.153–85: A maritime commentary. *Mediterranean Historical Review* 2:250–58.

MALLA, KAMAL P.
1985   Epigraphy and society in ancient Nepal: A critique of Regmi 1983. *Contributions to Nepalese Studies* 13:57–94.

MANRIQUE, ANTONIO MARÍA
1890   *Guanahaní: Investigaciones histórico-geográficas sobre el derrotero de Cristóbal Colón por las Bahamas y costa de Cuba*. Arrecife: Imp. de Lanzarote.

MANZANO, JUAN
1964   *Cristóbal Colón: Siete años decisivos de su vida*. Madrid: Cultura Hispánica.

MARÍN MARTÍNEZ, TOMÁS
1970   *Memoria de las obras y libros de Hernando Colón del bachiller Juan Pérez*. Madrid: Cátedra de Paleografía y Diplomática.

MARKHAM, ALBERT H.
1917   *The life of Sir Clements R. Markham*. London: J. Murray.

MARKHAM, CLEMENTS R.
1889   Sul punto d'approdo di Cristoforo Colombo. *Bollettino della Società Geografica Italiana* 26:101–24.

1892   *Life of Christopher Columbus.* London: George Philip and Son.

MARTENS, LORNA
1985   *The diary novel.* Cambridge: Cambridge University Press.

MARTÍN POSTIGO, MARÍA DE LA SOTERRAÑA
1959   *La cancillería Castellana de los Reyes Católicos.* Valladolid: Universidad de Valladolid.

MARTÍNEZ, MANUEL MARÍA
1959   Las Casas historiador. II: La "Historia de las Indias." *Ciencia Tomista* 80:77–103.

MARTÍNEZ HIDALGO Y TERÁN, JOSÉ MARIÁ
1985   Las naves de los cuatros viajes de Colón al Nuevo Mondo. In *Scritti in onore del Prof. Paolo Emilio Taviani,* 3:201–29. Genoa: Edizioni Culturali Internazionali.

MARTINI, DARIO G.
1986   *Cristoforo Colombo tra ragione e fantasia.* Genoa: Edizioni Culturali Internazionali.

MATHEW, GERVASE
1963   The East African coast until the coming of the Portuguese. In *History of East Africa,* edited by Roland Oliver and Gervase Mathew, 1:94–127. Oxford: Clarendon Press.
1975   The dating and significance of the *Periplus of the Erythrean Sea.* In *East Africa and the Orient,* edited by Neville Chittick and Robert Rotberg, 147–63. New York: Africana.

MATTINA, ANTHONY
1987   North American Indian mythography: Editing texts for the printed page. In *Recovering the word: Essays on Native American literature,* edited by Brian Swann and Arnold Krupat, 129–48. Berkeley: University of California Press.

MAUNDER, RICHARD
1988   *Mozart's Requiem: On preparing a new edition.* London: Oxford University Press.

MAURY, MATTHEW H.
1871   An examination of the claims of Columbus. *Harper's New Monthly Magazine* 42:425–35, 527–35.

METZGER, B. M.
1968   *The text of the New Testament.* London: Oxford University Press.

MEZCIEMS, JENNY
1982   Utopia and "the thing which is not": More, Swift, and other lying idealists. *University of Toronto Quarterly* 52:48–54.

MILANI, VIRGIL I.
1973   *The written language of Columbus.* Buffalo: State University of New York.

MILHOU, ALAIN
1983   *Colón y su mentalidad mesiánica en el ambiente franciscanista español.* Valladolid: Casa-Museo de Colón.

MILLER, HUNTER
1935   A point of punctuation. *American Journal of International Law* 29:118–23.

MITCHELL, STEVEN W., AND WILLIAM F. KEEGAN
1987   Reconstruction of the coastline of the Bahama Islands in 1492. *American Archeology* 6/2:88–96.

MOBERG, OVE
1989   The battle of Helgeå. *Scandinavian Journal of History* 14:1–19.

MOLANDER, ARNE B.
1981   Columbus landed here—or did he? *Americas* 33 (October): 3–7.
1985   A new approach to the Columbus landfall. In *IWC,* 113–49.
1987   Egg Island is the landfall of Columbus: A literal interpretation of his journal. In *CW,* 141–71.

MONTLÉZUN, BARON DE
1828   Du premier voyage de Christophe Colomb au Nouveau-Monde. *Nouvelles Annales des Voyages* 2/10:299–349.

MONTOJO, PATRICIO
1892   *Las primeras tierras descubriertas por Colón: Ensayo crítico.* Madrid: Sucesores de Rivadeneyra.

MOORE, JOHN R.
1941   The geography of *Gulliver's Travels. Journal of English and Germanic Philology* 40:214–28.

MORALES PADRÓN, FRANCISCO
1955   Descubrimiento y toma de posesión. *Anuario de Estudios Americanos* 12:321–80.

MORALES Y PEDROSO, LUIS
1923   *Lugar donde Colón desembarcó por primera vez en Cuba.* Havana: Burgay.

MORCKEN, ROALD
1989   Old Norse nautical distance tables in the Mediterranean Sea. *Mariner's Mirror* 75:53–77.

MORGAN, J. R.
1985   Lucian's *True Histories* and the *Wonders beyond Thule* of Antonius Diogenes. *Classical Quarterly,* n.s. 35:475–90.

MORISON, SAMUEL ELIOT

1939a   *The second voyage of Columbus from Cadiz to Hispaniola and the discovery of the Lesser Antilles*. Oxford: Clarendon Press.

1939b   Texts and translations of the journal of Columbus's first voyage. *Hispanic American Historical Review* 19:235–61.

1939–41   The route of Columbus along the north coast of Haiti, and the site of Navidad. *Transactions of the American Philosophical Society*, n.s. 21:239–85.

1942   *Admiral of the Ocean Sea: A life of Christopher Columbus*. 2 vols. Boston: Little, Brown and Company.

1955   *Christopher Columbus, mariner*. Boston: Little, Brown, and Company.

1974   *The European discovery of America: The southern voyages, 1492–1616*. New York: Oxford University Press.

MORISON, SAMUEL ELIOT, AND MAURICIO OBREGÓN

1964   *The Caribbean as Columbus saw it*. Boston: Little, Brown, and Company.

MORÓN, FERMÍN GONZALO

1842–46   Don Martín Fernández de Navarrete. In *Galería de Españoles célebres contemporáneos*, edited by Nicomedes Pastor Díaz and Francisco de Cárdenas, vol. 3. Madrid: Ignacio Boix.

MOULTON, GARY E., ED.

1983   *The atlas of the Lewis and Clark Expedition*. Lincoln: University of Nebraska Press.

MOULTON, GARY E., AND THOMAS W. DUNLAY, EDS.

1983–87   *The journals of the Lewis and Clark Expedition*. 3 vols. Lincoln: University of Nebraska Press.

MULTHAUF, ROBERT P.

1966   *The origins of chemistry*. London: Oldbourne.

MUÑOZ, JUAN BAUTISTA

1793   *Historia del Nuevo-Mundo*. Madrid: Ibarra.

MURDOCK, J. B.

1884   The cruise of Columbus in the Bahamas. *Proceedings of the U.S. Naval Institute* 10:449–86.

1931   Joseph Ballard Murdock. In *National cyclopaedia of American biography*, 24:268–69.

NAESS, ARNE

1968   *Scepticism*. London: Routledge and Kegan Paul.

NAGY, MOSES M.

1988   Christopher Columbus in the eighteenth and early nineteenth century French theatre. *Claudel Studies* 15/2:4–13.

NAVARRETE, MARTÍN FERNÁNDEZ DE
1954–55 *Obras*. Edited by Carlos Seco Serraño. 3 vols. Madrid: Ediciones Atlas.

NEBRIJA, ANTONIO DE
1516/1973 *Vocabulario de romance en Latín*. Edited by Gerald J. MacDonald. Philadelphia: Temple University Press.

NEUMANN, GERHARD
1988 Script, work, and published form: Franz Kafka's incomplete text. *Studies in Bibliography* 41:77–99.

NEWMAN, JANE O.
1985 The word made print: Luther's 1522 *New Testament* in an age of mechanical reproduction. *Representations* 11 (Summer): 95–133.

NIN, ANAÏS
1968 *The novel of the future*. New York: Macmillan.

NUNN, GEORGE E.
1924 *The geographical conceptions of Columbus*. New York: American Geographical Society.

OBER, FREDERICK A.
1893 *In the wake of Columbus*. Boston: D. Lothrop Co.

OBREGÓN, MAURICIO
1987a Columbus' first landfall: San Salvador. In *CW*, 185–95.
1987b Obregon leaves Judge theory adrift in sea of imprecision. *Encounter '92* (July): 6–7.

O'HANLON, JOHN, HANS WALTER GABLER, THOMAS F. STALEY, AND JOHN KIDD
1988 Continuing scandal of "Ulysses": An exchange. *New York Review of Books* 14 (29 September): 80–83.

OLSCHKI, LEONARDO
1941 What Columbus saw on landing in the West Indies. *Proceedings of the American Philosophical Society* 84:633–59.
1960 *Marco Polo's Asia: An introduction to his "Description of the World" called "Il Milione."* Berkeley: University of California Press.

ORGEL, STEPHEN
1988 The authentic Shakespeare. *Representations* 21 (Winter): 1–25.

ORTH, RALPH H.
1984 An edition of Emerson's poetry notebooks. *Documentary Editing* 6 (March): 8–11.

ORWELL, GEORGE
1949 *Nineteen eighty-four*. New York: Harcourt, Brace and Co.

O'SCANLAN, TIMOTEO
1831   *Diccionario marítimo Español.* Madrid: Imprenta Real.

OVIEDO Y VALDÉS, GONZALO FERNÁNDEZ DE
1851–55   *Historia general y natural de las Indias, islas y Tierra-Firme del mar océano.* Edited by José Amador de los Ríos. 4 vols. Madrid: Imprenta de la Real Academia de Historia.

OWEN, RICHARD
1838   *A nautical memoir descriptive of the surveys made in H. M. ships "Blossom" and "Thunder" from 1829 to 1837.* Dublin: A. Thom.

PARISH, HELEN RAND, AND HAROLD E. WEIDMAN
1976   The correct birthdate of Bartolomé de las Casas. *Hispanic American Historical Review* 56:385–403.

PARKER, JOHN
1981   Original sources and weighty authorities: Some thoughts on revisionism and the historiography of discovery. *Terrae Incognitae* 13:31–34.
1985   The Columbus landfall problem: A historical perspective. In *IWC,* 1–28.

PARRY, J. H.
1974   *The discovery of the sea.* London: Weidenfeld and Nicolson.

PEARSALL, RONALD
1976   *The alchemists.* London: Weidenfeld and Nicolson.

PECK, DOUGLAS T.
1989   Reconstruction and analysis of the 1492 Columbus log from a sailor-navigator viewpoint. *Encounter '92* (March): 6–7.

PEPYS, SAMUEL
1970–76   *The diary of Samuel Pepys.* Edited by Robert Latham and William Matthews. 11 vols. Berkeley: University of California Press.

PERAGALLO, PROSPERO
1884   *L'autenticità delle Historie di Fernando Colombo e le critiche del Signor Enrico Harrisse.* Genoa: Instituto Sordo-Muti.

PEREZ, ALEJANDRO RAYMUNDO
1987   *The Columbus landfall in America and the hidden clues in his journal.* Washington: Abbe Publishers Association.

PÉREZ DE TUDELA Y BUESO, JUAN
1983   *Mirabilis in Altis: Estudio crítico sobre el origen y significado del proyecto descubridor de Cristóbal Colón.* Madrid: Instituto Gonzalo Fernández de Oviedo.

PÉREZ EMBID, FLORENTINO
1948   *Los descubrimientos en el Atlántico y la rivalidad Castellano-*

Portuguesa hasta el Tratado de Tordesillas. Seville: Escuela de Estudios Hispano-Americanos.

PÉREZ FERNÁNDEZ, ISACIO

1981   *Inventario documentado de los escritos de Fray Bartolomé de las Casas.* Bayamón: Centro de Estudios de los Dominicos del Caribe.

1984   *Cronología documentada de los viajes, estancias y actuaciones de Fray Bartolomé de las Casas.* Bayamón, Puerto Rico: Centro de Estudios de los Dominicos del Caribe.

PESCADOR DEL HOYO, MARÍA DEL CARMEN

1955   Comó fué de verdad la toma de Granada a la luz de un documento inédito. *Al-Andalus* 20:283–344.

PETER, KARL H.

1972   *Wie Columbus navigierte.* Herford, West Germany: Koehlers.

PIEDRA, JOSÉ

1989   The game of critical arrival. *Diacritics* 19:34–61.

PINA, RUI DE

1950   *Cronica de el-rei D. João II.* Edited by Alberto Martins de Carvalho. Coimbra: Atlántida.

PINTO, JOÃO ROCHA

1989   *A viagem: Memória e espaço; A literatura Portuguesa de viagens, Os primitivos relatos de viagem ao Indico, 1497–1550.* Lisbon: Sá da Costa.

PLEITOS

1892–94   De los pleitos de Colón. In *Colección de documentos inéditos.* 2d ser., vols. 7, 8. Madrid: Sucesores de Rivadeneyra.

PLEITOS COLOMBINOS

1989   Vol. 4: *Probanzas del fiscal (1512–1515).* Edited by Antonio Muro Orejón. Seville: Escuela de Estudios Hispano-Americanos.

PLUTSCHOW, HERBERT E.

1982   Japanese travel diaries of the Middle Ages. *Oriens Extremus* 29: 1–136.

POLO, MARCO

1928   *Il Milione.* Edited by Luigi Foscolo Benedetto. Florence: L. Olschki.

PONTILLO, JAMES J.

1975   Nautical terms in sixteenth-century American Spanish. Ph.D. diss., State University of New York–Buffalo.

POWER, ROBERT H.

1985   The discovery of Columbus's island passage to Cuba, October 12–27, 1492. In *IWC,* 151–72.

POWLES, LOUIS D.
1888   *The land of the pink pearl.* London: Low, Marston, Searle, and Rivington.

PROCTOR, DENNIS
1971   *Hannibal's march in history.* Oxford: Clarendon.

PRÜFER, CURT MAX
1988   *Rewriting history: The original and revised World War II diaries of Curt Prüfer, Nazi diplomat.* Edited by Donald M. McKale. Translated by Judith M. Melton. Kent, O.: Kent State University Press.

PUYSÉGUR, ANTOINE-HYACINTHE-ANNE DE CHASTENET, COMTE DE
1787   *Détail sur la navigation aux côtes de Saint-Domingue et dans ses débouquermens.* Paris: Imprimerie royale.

RAMOS GÓMEZ, LUIS J.
1989   Los Lucayos, ¿guías naúticos de Colón en el primer viaje? (La navegación entre Guanahaní y Samoet). *Revista de Indias* 49:11–25.

RAMOS PÉREZ, DEMETRIO
1977   La carta de Colón dando cuenta del descubrimiento en relación con las Islas Canarias y las gestión de la bula de donación. In *I Coloquio de Historia Canario-Americano (1976),* edited by Francisco Morales Padrón, 11–41. Gran Canaria: Ediciones del Excelentísimo Cabildo Insular.

1982   *El descubrimiento "humano" de América: Las suposiciones colombinas sobre los Caribes y su importancia como guía conductora.* Granada: Diputación Provincial.

1983a   *La carta de Colón sobre el descubrimiento.* Granada: Excma. Diputación Provincial.

1983b   *Las elites andaluzas ante el descubrimiento Colombino: La acogida en el retorno y la crítica sobre lo descubierto.* Granada: Excma. Diputación Provincial.

1986   *La primera noticia de América* [*Cuadernos Colombinos* 14]. Valladolid: Seminario Americanista de la Universidad de Valladolid.

RAMSEY, R. VANCE
1986   Paleography and scribes of shared training. *Studies in the Age of Chaucer* 8:107–44.

RANQUE, GEORGES
1972   *La pierre philosophale.* Paris: Laffont.

RAPOPORT-ALBERT, ADA
1988   Hagiography with footnotes: Edifying tales and the writing of history in Hasidism. In *Essays in Jewish history,* edited by Ada

Rapoport-Albert, 119–59. Middletown, Conn.: Wesleyan University Press.

READ, JOHN
1966   *Prelude to chemistry.* Cambridge, Mass.: MIT Press.

REAL ACADEMIA DE LA HISTORIA
1892   *Bibliografía Colombina: Enumeración de libros y documentos concernientes a Cristóbal Colón y sus viajes.* Madrid: Fortanet.

REDWAY, JACQUES W.
1894   The first landfall of Columbus. *National Geographic* 6 (December): 179–92.

REGAZZONI, SUSANNA
1987   La historia de Cristóbal Colón en el siglo decimononico: Biografías o novelas? *Rassegna Iberistica* 29 (September): 15–23.

REICHERT, FOLKER
1988   Columbus und Marco Polo: Asien in Amerika. *Zeitschrift für historische Forschung* 15:1–63.

REID, T.B.W.
1984   The right to emend. In *Medieval French textual studies in memory of T.B.W. Reid,* edited by Ian Short, 1–32. London: Anglo-Norman Text Society.

RESENDE, GARCIA DE
1902   *Chrónica de el-rei D. João II.* Edited by Gabriel Pereira. 3 vols. Lisbon: Escriptorio.

RICHARDSON, PHILIP L., AND ROGER A. GOLDSMITH
1987   The Columbus landfall: Voyage track corrected for winds and currents. *Oceanus* 30 (Fall): 2–10.

RIGG, J. LINTON
1973   *Bahama Islands: A boatman's guide to the land and the water.* 4th ed. New York: Scribners.

RILEY, CARROLL L., AND JONI L. MANSON
1983   The Cíbola-Tiguex route: Continuity and change in the Southwest. *New Mexico Historical Review* 58:347–67.

ROBBINS, FRANK E., ED.
1966   *Epistola de insulis nuper inventis.* Ann Arbor, Mich.: University Microfilms.

ROBERTS, MICHAEL
1985   *Biblical epic and rhetorical paraphrase in late antiquity.* Liverpool: Francis Cairns.

ROBERTSON, WILLIAM
1778   *The history of America.* 2d ed. 2 vols. London: W. Strahan.

ROBINSON, CHRISTOPHER
1979   *Lucian and his influence in Europe.* Chapel Hill: University of North Carolina Press.

ROBSON, JAMES
1955–56   Ibn Ishaq's use of the isnad. *Bulletin of the John Rylands Library* 38:449–65.

ROGERS, ROBERT F., AND DIRK A. BALLENDORF
1989   Magellan's landfall in the Mariana Islands. *Journal of Pacific History* 24:193–208.

ROGERS, WOODES
1712   *A cruising voyage around the world.* . . . London: Bell and Lintot.

ROMERA CASTILLO, JOSÉ
1989   Rasgos kinésicos en el "Diario" de Cristóbal Colón. In *Literatura Hispánica, Reyes Católicos y Descubrimiento*, edited by Manuel Criado de Val, 115–24. Barcelona: PPU.

ROMILLY, JACQUELINE DE
1988   Plutarch and Thucydides, or the free use of quotations. *Phoenix* 42:22–34.

ROSELLY DE LORGUES, ANTOINE-FÉLIX
1880   *Christophe Colomb.* Paris: Palmé.

ROTHSTEIN, EDWARD
1990   Jolly Roger and the musical past. *New Republic,* (5 March), 29–34.

ROUKEMA, E.
1959   Columbus landed on Watlings Island. *American Neptune* 19: 79–113.

RUÍZ DE TELLO, MARÍA DEL CARMEN
1974   Acerca de los conocimientos náuticos del Padre Las Casas. In *Estudios sobre Fray Bartolomé de las Casas*, 191–225. Seville: Universidad de Sevilla.

RUMEU DE ARMAS, ANTONIO
1944   Colón en Barcelona. *Anuario de Estudios Americanos* 1:437–524.
1968   Descripción geográfica de la Isla de Guanahaní. *Anuario de Estudios Atlánticos* 14:305–61.
1970   La expedición científica a las islas Bahamas. *Anuario de Estudios Atlánticos* 16:579–96.
1973a   *Alfonso de Ulloa, introductor de la cultura española en Italia.* Madrid: Gredos.
1973b   *Hernando Colón: Historiador del descubrimiento de América.* Madrid: Instituto de Cultura Hispánica.

1976   El "diario de a bordo" de Cristóbal Colón: El problema de la paternidad del extracto. *Revista de Indias* 36:7–17.

RUTLAND, ROBERT A.

1976   Recycling early national history through the papers of the Founding Fathers. *American Quarterly* 28:249–61.

SADLER, H. E.

1981   *Turks Islands landfall*. Grand Turk: Sadler.

SADOUL, JACQUES

1972   *Alchemists and gold*. London: Spearman.

SAHAGÚN, BERNARDINO DE

1950–69   *General history of the things of New Spain*. Edited by Arthur J. O. Anderson and Charles E. Dibble. 13 vols. Santa Fe: School of American Research.

SAINT-LU, ANDRÉ

1981   La marque de las Casas dans le "journal de la découverte" de Christophe Colomb. *Langues Néo-Latines* 239:123–34.

SALMON, MERRILEE H.

1982   *Philosophy and archaeology*. New York: Academic Press.

SALONE CARTEI, ANNA MARIA

1979   Saggio bibliografico su Cristoforo Colombo nel dramma e melodramma Italiano (1600–1910). In *Atti del III Convegno Internazionale di Studi Colombiani*, 583–98. Genoa: Civico Istituto Colombiano.

SAMS, ERIC

1989   Shakespeare, or Bottom? The myth of "memorial reconstruction." *Encounter* 72 (January): 41–45.

SANTIAGO, MIGUEL

1955   Colón en Canarias. *Anuario de Estudios Atlánticos* 1:337–96.

SANZ, CARLOS

1956   *La carta de Colón anunciando el descubrimiento del Nuevo Mundo, 15 febrero–14 marzo 1493*. Madrid: Maestre.

1958   *Henry Harrisse (1829–1910): Príncipe de los Americanistas; Su vida, su obra*. Madrid: Victoriano Suárez.

SCAMMELL, G. V.

1981   *The world encompassed: The first European maritime empires, c. 800–1650*. Berkeley: University of California Press.

SCHACHNER, NATHAN

1951   *Thomas Jefferson: A biography*. 2 vols. New York: Appleton-Century-Crofts.

SCHÄFER, JÜRGEN
1970   The orthography of proper names in modern-spelling editions of
           Shakespeare. *Studies in Bibliography* 23 : 1– 19.
SCHOLAR, NANCY
1984   *Anaïs Nin.* Boston: Twayne.
SCHULTZ, CONSTANCE B.
1988   "From generation unto generation": Transitions in modern
           documentary historical editing. *Reviews in American History* 16 :
           337– 50.
SCHWAB, RICHARD N.
1988   New clues about Gutenberg in the Huntington 42-line Bible:
           What the margins reveal. *Huntington Library Quarterly* 51 :
           177– 209.
SCOTT, PATRICK G., AND WILLIAM B. THESING
1989   Conversations with Victorian writers: Some editorial questions.
           Documentary Editing 11 (June): 37– 42.
SEALEY, NEIL E.
1987   New developments on the Columbus landfall issue. *Journal of the
           Bahamas Historical Society* 9 (October): 5– 13.
SEARS, WILLIAM H., AND SHAUN O. SULLIVAN
1978   Bahamas prehistory. *American Antiquity* 43 : 3– 25.
SEIBERT, JAKOB
1986   Die alpenüberquerung Hannibals. *Antike Welt* 17/4 : 44– 54.
SERRANO Y SANZ, MANUEL
1905   *Autobiografías y memorias.* Madrid: Bailly/Bailliere.
SEVERIN, TIMOTHY
1987   *The Ulysses voyage: Sea search for the Odyssey.* London: Hutch-
           inson.
SHAKESPEARE, WILLIAM
1986   *William Shakespeare: The complete works.* Edited by Stanley
           Wells and Gary Taylor. Oxford: Oxford University Press.
SHANKS, MICHAEL, AND CHRISTOPHER TILLEY
1987   *Re-constructing archaeology.* Cambridge: Cambridge University
           Press.
SHATTUCK, GEORGE B., ED.
1905   *The Bahama Islands.* New York: Macmillan.
SHAW, PETER
1976– 77   The American heritage and its guardians. *American Scholar* 45 :
           733– 51.

SHELDON, RICHARD N.

1979   Editing a historical manuscript: Jared Sparks, Douglas Southall Freeman, and the battle of Brandywine. *William and Mary Quarterly* 36:255–63.

SHERBO, ARTHUR

1979   Swift and travel literature. *Modern Language Studies* 9:114–27.

SMITH, G. HUBERT

1980   *The explorations of the La Vérendryes in the Northern Plains, 1738–1743.* Edited by W. Raymond Wood. Lincoln: University of Nebraska Press.

SMITH, LARRY

1988   From 1988 discovery fly-out, sand from Columbus' landfall beach goes to Spain. *Encounter '92* (October): 1–2.

SMITH, MARVIN T.

1976   The route of de Soto through Tennessee, Georgia, and Alabama: The evidence from material culture. *Early Georgia* 4:27–48.

SNODGRASS, ANTHONY M.

1989   *An archaeology of Greece.* Berkeley: University of California Press.

SPÄTH, EBERHARD

1987   Das private und das Üffentliche Tagebuch. Zum Verhältnis von Fiktion und Journalismus im englischen Roman. *Poetica* 19:32–55.

STEFFEN, JUAN

1892   La polémica sobre la autenticidad de la biografía mas antigua de Colón. *Anales de la Universidad de Chile,* special issue, 119–50.

STEWART, GLENN

1931   San Salvador Island to Cuba: A cruise in the track of Columbus. *Geographical Review* 21:124–30.

STEWART, PHILIP

1969   *Imitation and illusion in the French memoir-novel, 1700–1750.* New Haven, Conn.: Yale University Press.

STRABO, GNAEUS POMPEIUS

1917–33 *The geography of Strabo.* Edited and translated by Horace L. Jones. 8 vols. London: William Heinemann.

STRUIK, D. J.

1968   The prohibition of the use of Arabic numerals in Florence. *Archives internationales d'histoire des sciences* 84/85:291–94.

SUKENICK, LYNN

1976   The *diaries* of Anaïs Nin. *Shenandoah* 27 (Spring): 96–103.

SWETZ, FRANK J.

1987   *Capitalism and arithmetic.* La Salle, Ill.: Open Court Publish-
            ing Co.

SZÁSZDI, ADAM

1985   El descubrimiento de Puerto Rico en 1492 por Martín Alonso Pin-
            zón. *Revista de Historia* [Puerto Rico] 1/2 : 9–45.

TANSELLE, G. THOMAS

1978   The editing of historical documents. *Studies in Bibliography* 31 :
            1–56.

1979   External fact as editorial problem. *Studies in Bibliography* 32 :
            1–47.

1986   Historicism and critical editing. *Studies in Bibliography* 39 : 1–46.

1989   *A rationale of textual criticism.* Philadelphia: University of Penn-
            sylvania Press.

TARRANT, R. J.

1987   Toward a typology of interpolation in Latin poetry. *Transactions
            of the American Philological Society* 117 : 281–98.

TAVIANI, PAOLO EMILIO

1984   *I viaggi di Colombo.* 2 vols. Novara: Istituto Geografico De
            Agostini.

1985   Non fu certo un santo, ma grande fu la sua fide. *Jesus* [journal;
            Milan].

1987a   Columbus the man: A psychologically modern man of the Middle
            Ages. In *CW,* 1–12.

1987b   Why we are favorable for the Watling–San Salvador landfall. In
            CW, 197–227.

TAYLOR, GARY

1986   Inventing Shakespeare. *Shakespeare-Jahrbuch* [Bochum, W. Ger.],
            26–44.

TAYLOR, P.A.M.

1977   Samuel Eliot Morison, historian. *Journal of American Studies*
            11 : 13–26.

TAYLOR, ROBERT J.

1981   Editorial practices: An historian's view. *Newsletter of the Associ-
            ation for Documentary Editing* 3 (February): 4–8.

TERLINGEN, JOHANNES H.

1943   *Los Italianismos en Español desde la formación del idioma hasta
            principios del siglo XVII.* Amsterdam: N. V. NoordHollandsche
            Uitgevers Maatschappij.

TERWIEL, B. J.

1989   Kaempfer and Thai history: The documents behind the printed texts. *Journal of the Royal Asiatic Society*, pp. 64–80.

TEUTE, FREDRIKA J.

1980   Views in review: A historiography. *American Archivist* 43 : 43–56.

THACHER, JOHN BOYD

1903–4   *Christopher Columbus: His life, his work, his remains*. 3 vols. New York: G. P. Putnam's Sons.

TINSLEY, BARBARA S.

1987   Pope Joan polemic in early modern France: The use and disabuse of myth. *Sixteenth Century Journal* 18 : 381–97.

TIÓ, AURELIO

1961   *Nuevas fuentes para la historia de Puerto Rico*. San Germán: Universidad Interamericana de Puerto Rico.

1966   *Dr. Diego Alvarez Chanca: Estudio biográfico*. San Juan: Instituto de Cultura Puertorriqueña.

1978   Notas sobre el descubrimiento: La luz en las tinieblas. *Boletín de la Academia Puertorriqueña de la Historia* 5 : 13–40.

TOLSTOY, NIKOLAI

1982   The diary of nobody at all: Penguin, the BBC, and a spurious documentary. *Encounter* 58 (August): 35–39.

TODOROV, TZVETAN

1984   *The conquest of America: The question of the other*. New York: Harper and Row.

TOV, EMANUEL

1988   Hebrew biblical manuscripts from the Judaean desert: Their contribution to textual criticism. *Journal of Jewish Studies* 39 : 6–37.

TOWNSEND, DABNEY

1988   The problem of paraphrase. *Metaphor and Symbolic Activity* 3 : 37–54.

TYLER, S. LYMAN

1988   *Two worlds: The Indian encounter with the European, 1492–1509*. Salt Lake City: University of Utah Press.

TYNDALL, JOHN

1898   *Fragments of science*. 2 vols. New York: Appleton.

UNITED STATES NAVY. DEPARTMENT OF DEFENSE. DEFENSE MAPPING AGENCY. HYDROGRAPHIC/TOPOGRAPHIC CENTER.

1985   *Distances between ports*. 5th ed. Washington, D.C.: Government Printing Office.

URKOWITZ, STEVEN

1986a   Reconsidering the relationship of quarto and folio texts of *Richard III*. *English Literary Renaissance* 16:442–66.

1986b   "Well-sayd olde mole": Burying three *Hamlets* in modern editions. In *Shakespeare Study Today*, edited by Georgianna Ziegler, 37–70. New York: AMS Press.

1988   "If I mistake in those foundations which I build upon": Peter Alexander's textual analysis of *Henry VI* Parts 2 and 3. *English Literary Renaissance* 18:230–56.

VALENTINI, PHILLIP J. J.

1892   The landfall of Columbus at San Salvador. *Proceedings of the American Antiquarian Society*, n.s. 8:152–68.

VANDER LINDEN, H.

1916   Alexander VI and the demarcation of the maritime and colonial domains of Spain and Portugal, 1493–1494. *American Historical Review* 22:1–20.

VANSINA, JAN

1979–80   Bantu in the crystal ball. *History in Africa* 6:287–333; 7: 293–325.

VAQUERO, MARÍA

1987   Las Antillas en la *Historia General* de Gonzalo Fernández de Oviedo. *Revista de Filología Española* 67:1–18.

VARNHAGEN, ADOLPHO DE

1864   *La verdadera Guanahaní de Colón*. Santiago: Imprenta Nacional.

VÁZQUEZ, J. A.

1971   Las Casas' opinions in Columbus' diary. *Topic* 21 (Spring): 45–56.

VELDINK, CONNIE

1989   The honey-bee language controversy. *Interdisciplinary Science Reviews* 14:166–75.

VERHOOG, PIETER

1947   *Guanahaní again*. Amsterdam: C. de Boer.

1954   Columbus landed on Caicos. *Proceedings of the U.S. Naval Institute* 80:1101–11.

1985   Columbus landed on Caicos. In *IWC*, 29–34.

VIDAL GORMAZ, FRANCISCO

1892   Las primeras tierras que vió Colón al descubrir el Nuevo Mundo. *Anales de la Universidad de Chile*, special issue, 207–38.

VIGNAUD, HENRY

1909   L'ancienne et la nouvelle campagne pour la canonisation de Christophe Colomb. *Journal de la Société des Américanistes* 6:17–44.

1911   *Histoire critique de la grande enterprise de Christophe Colomb.*
            2 vols. Paris: H. Welter.

VINAVER, EUGÈNE

1939   Principles of textual emendation. In *Studies in French language
            and literature presented to Professor Mildred K. Pope,* 351–69.
            Manchester: University of Manchester Press.

WAGNER, HENRY R.

1945   Three studies on the same subject. *Hispanic American Historical
            Review* 25:155–211.

WAGNER, HENRY R., AND HELEN RAND PARISH.

1967   *The life and writings of Bartolomé de las Casas.* Albuquerque:
            University of New Mexico Press.

WALBANK, FRANK W.

1956   Some reflections on Hannibal's Pass. *Journal of Roman Studies*
            46:37–45.

WALTERS, RAYMOND, JR.

1957   The James Gallatin diary: A fraud? *American Historical Review*
            62:878–85.

WARREN, MICHAEL J.

1985   Textual problems, editorial assertions in editions of Shakespeare.
            In *Textual criticism and literary interpretation,* edited by Jerome J.
            McGann, 23–37. Chicago: University of Chicago Press.

WASHBURN, WILCOMB E.

1979   Samuel Eliot Morison, historian. *William and Mary Quarterly*
            36:325–52.

WASHINGTON, GEORGE

1838–39   *Writings of George Washington: Being his correspondence, ad-
            dresses, messages, and other papers, official and private, selected
            and published from the original manuscripts; with a life of the au-
            thor, notes and illustrations.* Edited by Jared Sparks. 12 vols. Bos-
            ton: F. Andrews.

WATTS, PAULINE MOFFITT

1985   Prophecy and discovery: On the spiritual origins of Christopher
            Columbus's "Enterprise of the Indies." *American Historical Re-
            view* 90:73–102.

WEBER, DAVID J.

1988   *Myth and the history of the Hispanic Southwest.* Albuquerque:
            University of New Mexico Press.

WEINSTEIN, RICHARD A.

1985   Some new thoughts on the de Soto expedition through western
            Mississippi. *Mississippi Archaeology* 20 (December): 2–24.

WELLES, GIDEON

1960   *Diary of Gideon Welles, Secretary of the Navy under Lincoln and Johnson.* Edited by Howard K. Beale. 3 vols. New York: W. W. Norton.

WELLS, STANLEY

1988   Revision in Shakespeare's plays. In *Editing and editors: A retrospect,* edited by Richard Landon, 67–97. New York: AMS Press.

WHITMAN, WALT

1874   Prayer of Columbus. *Harper's New Monthly Magazine* 48 (March): 524–25.

WILLIAMS, LINDSEY W.

1986   *Boldly onward.* Charlotte Harbor, Fla.: Precision Publishing Company.

WILSON, DOUGLAS EMORY

1985   Joyce's masterpiece rescued from its textual corruption. *Documentary editing* 7/3 : 1–5.

WILSON, S. R.

1977–78   The form of discovery: The Columbus Letter announcing the finding of America. *Revista Canadiense de Estudios Hispánicos* 2 : 154–68.

WINDEATT, B. A.

1979   The scribes as Chaucer's early critics. *Studies in the Age of Chaucer* 1 : 119–41.

WINSLOW, JOHN H.

1988   Was the landfall of Columbus at Great Harbour Cay? *Nassau Guardian,* 7 November, 17A–18A.

n.d.   Columbus's San Salvador as one of the northern Berry Islands. Unpublished paper in possession of the author.

WINSOR, JUSTIN

1892   *Christopher Columbus and how he received and imparted the spirit of discovery.* Boston: Houghton, Mifflin.

WINTER, JOHN

1987   San Salvador in 1492: Its geography and ecology. In *CW,* 313–20.

WINTHROP, ROBERT C.

1882–83   Obituary of Gustavus Fox. *Proceedings of the Massachusetts Historical Society* 20 : 353–55.

WOLPER, RUTH G. DURLACHER

1964   *A new theory identifying the locale of Columbus's light, landfall, and landing.* Smithsonian Miscellaneous Collections, vol. 148, no. 1. Washington, D.C.: Smithsonian Institution.

YACHTSMAN'S GUIDE
1987   *Yachtsman's Guide to the Bahamas.* Edited by Meredith H.
            Fields. Miami: Tropic Isle Publishers.
YOUNG, FILSON
1906   *Christopher Columbus and the New World of his discovery.* 2 vols.
            Philadelphia: J. B. Lippincott.
YOUNG, JAMES E.
1986–87   Interpreting literary testimony: A preface to rereading Holocaust
            diaries and journals. *New Literary History* 18:403–23.
1988   *Writing and rewriting the Holocaust: Narrative and the conse-
            quences of interpretation.* Bloomington: Indiana University Press.
ZAMORA, MARGARITA
1989   "Todas son palabras formales del Almirante": Las Casas y el diario
            de Colón. *Hispanic Review* 57:25–41.
ZETZEL, JAMES E. G.
1981   *Latin textual criticism in antiquity.* New York: Arno Press.

INDEX

44–48, 49, 109–10; use of by Fuson, 26–27; and *Historia*, 4, 33–34, 35, 38–39, 59; history of, 31, 32–34; Italian and Spanish editions, 34n, 35, 38; and log, 38–39; Morison on, 40, 42; and 7 Oct. entry, 29; and 11 Oct. entry, 178; and 15 Oct. entry, 252; reliability of, 32n; and Rumeu de Armas, 37–38
"Hize," 88–89, 94
Holographs: of diario, 67, 68, 69, 75, 78, 81, 84–85, 93; of *Historia*, 36n, 76. *See also* Manuscripts
"Hombre," 88–89, 93
Humboldt, Alexander von, 205, 262
Hysteron proteron, as rhetorical device, 166

Iguanas, 60n, 281, 282n
Indians: and claiming ceremonies, 108, 269; and Columbus, 41, 58–59, 60, 148, 184, 186–87, 243–44, 269; of Cuba, 90; diario descriptions of, 188–89, 190; Ferdinand's interest in, 39; and gold, 72, 184, 236, 237n; and Guanahaní, 8, 55–56, 61, 110–12, 181, 188–90, 230, 231,234, 282n; on Hispaniola, 41; in *Historia*, 55, 58–59, 202, 271; and lagoon, 216n; and Las Casas, 3, 7, 22, 24, 25, 34, 57, 58; in light account, 56, 172, 174, 176; in marginalia, 83; and naming of islands, 244, 246, 247, 270; on Santa María de la Concepción, 62; Spanish treatment of, 19, 44; trading with, 61, 62, 189, 190, 221n, 234; and water, 217, 218, 219
Inter Caetera Bull of 1456, 114n
Irving, Washington: and Columbus biography, 17n; and "de las isla,"

79; disputed by Gibb, 211; and distance to landfall, 178n; and Guanahaní, 205; and visibility of islands, 241; and lagoon, 211, 212; and light account, 175, 176; and 15 Oct. entry, 256; and Slidell, 141; and water, 216
Isabela (island), 51, 133, 140, 207, 269, 279n
Isabella. *See* Ferdinand and Isabella
"Isla," 72, 193, 198
Islands: descriptions of, 57, 188–91, 247; around Guanahaní, 197, 237; as "isleta," 198; naming of, 244, 246, 247, 269; numbers of, 62, 237, 262; and sightlines, 145–148; size of and distance to, 154, 233, 242; unnamed, 124, 262–64, 270; visibility of, 240–41, 254, 271n. *See also names of individual islands*
"Isla," 193, 198
"Isleo," 198, 199
"Isleta," 192, 197, 198
Italianisms, 181n
Italics in modern editions of the diario, 18, 69, 73
Italianisms in the diario, 181n
Izquierdo, Pedro, 174n

Jane, Cecil: on "acordó," 28; and "cabo," 272n; and changes to diario, 69, 92n, 96; criticism of, 67n; and "de las isla," 78; and "hago," 237; and "laguna," 209; and letters, 50, 52n; and "muchas aguas," 208; and 15 Oct. entry, 252n, 268, 271n
January (1493): 5th, 88, 192n; 11th, 71, 90; 18th, 90; 21st, 138n; 22d–31st, 136; 25th, 137n; 29th, 139
Jefferson, Thomas, 119
João II, 52, 112, 113, 114, 202

and Letter to Santangel, 52n; and numbers in diario, 85, 86, 132; and "otra parte," 228–29; and "pusiéronse a la corda," 145n; and Santa María de la Concepción, 262

Navidad, 107n, 169

New Providence Island, 160, 186, 259, 263

Niña: and banners, 108; and birds, 28; and recorded distances, 128, 129, 130, 131; return voyage of, 45, 47, 48, 50, 52, 116, 117, 137; and *Santa María,* 43n

Niza, Marcos de, 162n

"No," 82, 84

"Nombre," 88–89, 93

"Nornordeste" (14 Oct.), 227–28

"Nota" in diario margins, 84

November (1492): 1st, 73, 77, 83; 2d, 132, 133, 134n; 6th, 88; 12th, 74; 13th, 145n; 15th, 75n, 88; 18th and 20th, 88; 22d, 72; 24th, 88; 25th, 84; 27th, 40–41, 88

"No" in diario margins, 82, 84

Numbers and numerals: 61, 62, 69, 71–72, 85–86, 99–100

Ober, Frederick A., 142, 146, 147n, 164, 194n, 282n

Obregón, Mauricio, 149, 177, 182, 184, 222n, 238, 259n, 277

October (1492): 1st and 2d, 129, 130; 3rd–11th, 129, 130; 7th, 27, 88–89; 10th, 165, 173; 11th, 77n, 106–8, 168, 174, 177, 178, 183; 11th/12th, 27, 72, 110–11, 150, 175, 188–89; 11th–16th, 6, 55; 12th, 77n, 108, 144, 167–68, 180, 183, 214, 281; 12th–Nov. 2, 75, 134, 183; 13th, 72, 111–12, 167, 174, 184, 188–90, 193, 236; 16th, 77, 88–89, 97, 250, 270, 271; 17th, 83, 150, 214n; 19th,

88–89, 133, 21st, 88–89, 282n; 24th, 133, 242; 27th, 133; 29th, 82, 88–89; 30th, 77, 88–89, 133; 31st, 76, 77, 88–89

October 14th: direction of course on, 240; distances on, 242, 254; and Graham's Harbour, 148; and Guanahaní, 145, 183, 184, 220–35; and "isla," 193; islands seen, 62, 206, 242; itinerary of, 63n; and landfall debate, 220; problems with entry of, 74, 88–89, 236; text of diario for, 290–91; and water supply, 218–19

October 15th: diario compared to *Historia* for, 59, 63; distances estimated on, 143, 242, 251; islands seen on, 79, 195n, 242; and landfall debate, 220; problems with entry of, 88–89, 250, 255, 260; textual analysis of, entry for, 264–72; visibility on, 147

Odyssey, 159, 286n

Omissions: by Columbus, 139; in diario, 18, 26, 67, 80, 81, 92, 104, 197; by editors, 14; in *Historia,* 54, 58–59, 61n

Oral texts, 15–16

Oral traditions, 26, 31, 48, 175n, 202

Oviedo y Valdés, Gonzalo Fernández de, 34, 55, 56, 107, 169n, 173–75, 181, 183

Paleography, 69n, 87, 91

Palos, 50n, 125, 126

Papacy, 1, 52, 114, 115

Papal bulls, 112, 113, 114n

Paraphrasing and paraphrases: compared to quotations, 74–75; in 25 Dec. entry, 44, 49; and diario, x, 3, 4, 6, 7, 20, 22, 23, 24–25, 105; errors in tense in, 73, 95; in 14 Feb.

and Ferdinand, 241n; and Guana-
haní, 196, 200, 206; and lagoon,
212n, 214n; and "laguna," 215; and
light account, 166, 168n, 169n,
170n
Todorov, Tzvetan, 188n
Tortuga, 72, 100
Translations: of diario, ix, 18, 25–30,
65, 66, 67; documentary, 26; of
Historie, 31, 38; Keen's compared to
Morison's, 42, 44n; literary vs. his-
torical, 29; of 15 Oct. account,
143–44
Treaty of Alcáçovas of 1479, 53, 112–13
Treaty of Tordesillas (1494), 103, 104
Triana, Rodrigo de, 165, 167–68,
172n, 174, 175, 177n, 181, 182
Trinidad, 169n
"Tuob," 90–91, 93

Ulloa, Antonio de, 31, 33, 35
Ur, 162n

Valentini, Phillip J. J.: on descriptions
of islands, 206; and distance to
landfall, 178n; and Guanahaní, 196,
205, 222n; and lagoon, 216n; on
NNE route, 224; and peninsula,
234n
Varela, Consuelo: on cask letter, 47n;
and changes to diario, 82, 89, 91,
93, 94, 95, 98; and "de la isla," 78;
on diario account of light, 166; and
distances, 85; and errors in dates,
76; and footnotes, 80; and Historia,
21n; and Historie, 36–37n, 38n,
45n; and marginalia, 82, 84; and
misspelling, 87; on shape of Guanahaní, 201n; and "sudueste," 236n
Varnhagen, Adolpho de, 81, 238,
239

Verhoog, Pieter, 141, 196, 199, 232n,
238, 239, 246n, 259
Vignaud, Henry, 102n, 103, 104
Villa, Pedro de, 116, 118
Villages on Guanahaní, 190, 221, 279
Visibility in Bahamas, 147, 148, 254,
271n
Voyages: of discovery and piracy, 120;
imaginary, 159, 163, 164; of Sinuhe,
162n
Voyages of Columbus: first, ix–x,
163–64 (see also Niña, return voyage of; and names of individual
texts); second, 36, 103, 202; third,
169n; fourth, 36

Wagner, Henry R., 2, 19n, 21n
Washington, George, 13
Water, 209n, 218, 219; fresh, 57, 93–
94, 211, 212, 216, 217, 219, 280n;
salt, 211, 216, 217
Watlings Island: archaeological study
of, 275–76, 277, 278; and Cronau,
198; and Ferdinand's testimony,
225; and Gould, 239; and Guanahaní, 112, 171, 195, 203, 204, 219,
248; harbor on, 232; and lagoon,
208, 210, 213–15; as landfall, 181–
84; and light, 170, 176, 177, 178,
179; and McElroy, 154; map of,
161, 183, 185; and Molander, 281;
and Ober, 282n; and peninsula,
234; and reef, 152; and rowing, 221,
223; and Rum Cay, 240, 242, 246,
251, 253, 255, 257, 259; and sightlines, 147, 148; and southwesterly
course from, 237; stones on, 151;
topography of, 194–95, 201, 205,
206; water on, 209, 217, 218
Welles, Gideon, 119n
West Plana Cay, 201n, 238

Winslow, John H., 114n, 151, 176n, 248n, 253n, 263n

Winsor, Justin, 29n

Wolper, Ruth G. Durlacher: and Graham's Harbour, 149; and Guanahaní, 194; and hills, 247n; and light, 177; and Rum Cay, 264n; and sightlines, 147, 148; and Watlings Island, 184, 194n, 204

Yachtsman's Guide, 194n, 205, 207, 210n

Yáñez Pinzón, Vicente, 175

About the Author

DAVID HENIGE received a doctorate in African history from the University of Wisconsin-Madison in 1973. He taught African history at the Centre of West African Studies at the University of Birmingham in 1973–74 and since 1974 has been African Studies bibliographer at the Memorial Library of the University of Wisconsin-Madison. His academic interests are in oral tradition, chronology, textual criticism and editing, and historical method. He is the author of *Oral Historiography*, and his recent articles include "If Pigs Could Fly: Timucuan Population and Native American Historical Demography," *Journal of Interdisciplinary History* 16 (1985–86): 701–20; "In Quest of Error's Sly Imprimatur: The Concept of 'Authorial Intent' in Modern Textual Criticism," *History in Africa* 14 (1987): 87–112; and "Samuel Eliot Morison as Translator and Interpreter of Columbus' *Diario de a Bordo*," *Terrae Incognitae* 20 (1988): 69–88.